Neurological Malingering

Neurological Malingering

Edited by
Alan R. Hirsch

CRC Press
Taylor & Francis Group
Boca Raton London New York

CRC Press is an imprint of the
Taylor & Francis Group, an **informa** business

CRC Press
Taylor & Francis Group
6000 Broken Sound Parkway NW, Suite 300
Boca Raton, FL 33487-2742

Printed on acid-free paper

International Standard Book Number-13: 978-1-4987-4246-7 (Hardback)

Library of Congress Cataloging-in-Publication Data

Names: Hirsch, Alan R. editor.
Title: Neurological malingering / [edited by] Alan R. Hirsch.
Description: Boca Raton : Taylor & Francis, 2018. | Includes bibliographical references and index.
Identifiers: LCCN 2018001399 | ISBN 9781498742467 (hardback : alk. paper)
Subjects: | MESH: Malingering | Nervous System Diseases | Diagnostic Techniques, Neurological
Classification: LCC RC346 | NLM W 783 | DDC 616.8--dc23
LC record available at https://lccn.loc.gov/2018001399

Visit the Taylor & Francis Web site at
http://www.taylorandfrancis.com

and the CRC Press Web site at
http://www.crcpress.com

Contents

Foreword

Sherlock Holmes had his fingerprints, neurologists have EMGs, nerve conduction velocities, and PET scans. Being a neurologist in many ways is like being a detective. In search not of Professor Moriarty, but rather, of Charcot's triad of neurologic diseases: (1) is there neurologic disease; (2) if so, where is it localized; and (3) what is the pathological process occurring? With malingering, the detective work is focused on (1) is there the presence of true neurological disease? Understanding this one step further, what is the motivation of such behavior? In this book, these questions are explored from a myriad of perspectives—historical, diagnostic, legal, and even from the perspective of the physicians' countertransference and feelings towards the malingering patient.

I would like to thank the many who selflessly gave of their time and effort to allow this book to come to fruition. First and foremost is Denise Fahey, without whose relentless assistance in editing, organizing, and commitment this work would have remained an unrealized idea. Also, kudos to Randy Brehm of CRC Press for her continued support, understanding, and encouragement. Thanks to all the authors for their efforts and time devoted to this project.

Lastly, a special thank you to my family, who patiently put up with me during the endless hours spent on this project.

Alan R. Hirsch, MD

Introduction

As a practicing neurologist on a quotidian, or at least a hebdomadal basis, patients with disorders are presented which defy diagnosis and whose complaints challenge physiological explanation. Occasionally, these ultimately turn out to be common diseases manifesting with unusual presentations, such as stroke-induced Capgras syndrome (with misinterpretation of familiar faces as strangers) or multiple sclerosis manifesting with paroxysmal unilateral phantosmias, with hallucinated odors confined to one nostril. The struggle the clinician faces, is delineating when such bizarre presentations are in fact a rarely seen symptom of a common disease, a truly rare disease, a functional disorder, or a conscious attempt to appear ill for secondary gain.

As a medical student, we learn of Waddell's sign, paradoxical inhibition of unaffected unilateral rapid alternating movements when tested bilaterally, astasia-abasia, but of few other signs indicating malingering. It is the aim of this book to help further the diagnostic ability to determine, detect, and diagnose malingering.

Beyond the how-to make the diagnosis, the impact of making such an emotionally-laden diagnosis affects both the patient and the physician. Observing the rule "primum non nocere" (first do no harm), one is reticent to make the diagnosis of malingering. The diagnosis of malingering in medicine is the equivalent to Nathaniel Hawthorne's scarlet 'A' branded onto the medical records rather than embroidered on the bodice. This diagnosis of malingering acts to destroy the physician–patient relationship. Based on trust, this relationship assumes that the patients will attempt to be truthful in their presentation with the physician. In the physician–patient relationship the goals are, if not identical, at least parallel to work together to treat disease and alleviate suffering. With malingering, the goals have diverged—the aim of the malingerer is to fool the physician. The ramification of the diagnosis impacts negatively on myriad aspects of not only the patient–physician dyad, but also the patient's life. With this diagnosis, the patient is likely to be rejected in claims for workmen's compensation, disability, or monetary reward in litigation. In the era of electronic medical records, the diagnosis is likely to follow the patient as he or she approaches other physicians for care. This may lead treaters to be skeptical of the patient's complaints, with a bias against the patient even at the start of their relationship, possibly rejecting them altogether as a patient. One would anticipate that the diagnosis would similarly negatively affect a patient's ability to obtain health insurance and, if the medical records became public, seek a higher-level job, as well as dim their chances of successfully being elected to public office. Hence, it is much more important to correctly diagnose malingering, since a false-positive diagnosis could ruin the patient's life. Beyond the cost to society, a false-negative diagnosis of no malingering when malingering is actually present may subject the patient to inappropriate and dangerous diagnostic testing and treatment. It can also add cost to society or businesses. Thus, the importance of correctly diagnosing malingering in those who malinger cannot be overemphasized.

With so much riding on the correct diagnosis, one would anticipate that there is a large amount of literature available as a resource in the diagnosis of this condition. Such an assumption would be false. While there is literature available, most of it is anecdotal and not scientifically validated to differentiate true disease as opposed to malingering. For instance, most studies reporting the use of neuropsychological testing rely on a lack of effort or inconsistency of effort to explain the test results, suggesting the diagnosis of malingering. However, lack of effort does not necessarily mean malingering. Low effort could be due to a plethora of origins ranging from fatigue, having auditory or visual hallucinations, or having anger, hostility, or frustration with the examiner. An examiner's predisposed bias may inadvertently affect his or her results—if the examiner prejudges the patient to be malingering, he or she may be unconsciously punishing the patient, making the patient angry and less likely to cooperate. This may be manifest as uneven response performance, suggestive of malingering. When the patient notices the examiner's hostility, he or she will be less motivated on requested tasks. This may lead to test scores indicating absence of cooperation, invalidating test results, which is then interpreted as malingering. The negative countertransference from the physician to the patient becomes a self-fulfilling prophecy.

This book aims to correct some of the deficiencies in the assessment and treatment of malingering.

Emphasizing the ubiquitous cross-cultural and cross-civilization nature of malingering, Chapter 1 delves into the historical perspective of malingering, demonstrating that it is not a contemporary problem, but has afflicted mankind throughout the ages.

The importance of obtaining a history in the diagnosis of malingering goes beyond the traditional concept of history, but rather, using the mechanics of performing the history as part of the objective evidence of malingering. Thus, the history in this instance is actually part of the signs of malingering—it could even be considered as a part of the physical examination. By using both verbal and nonverbal cues, further evidence can be obtained to solidify the diagnosis of malingering. These concepts are reviewed in Chapter 2.

Chapter 3 summarizes many of the commonly described tests indicative of malingering. While some of these have been scientifically validated as firmly demonstrating malingering, others are based on clinical anecdotes, clinical practice, and tradition.

Chapters 4, 5, 6, and 7 address the most common clinical complaint that one would see with malingering, which deals with the phenomena of low back pain. Because low back pain is so common in our society, and often occurs associated with work injuries or motor vehicle accidents, it is often associated with litigation. Thus, the diagnosis of malingering becomes a virtually ubiquitous issue. Some of the common diagnostic testing for this is addressed as well as the validity of signs, including Waddell's tests and electrophysiological testing for this group of patients.

A wide variety of other areas of malingering are addressed as well. Toxicological malingering, where litigation frequently occurs, is commonly seen yet rarely formally addressed as is discussed in Chapter 8. Similarly, malingering attention deficit–hyperactivity disorder while in pursuit of amphetamines is seen by clinicians on a daily basis yet is rarely, if ever, addressed. This is illustrated in Chapter 9. Also frequently observed is malingering for opioids, and as such, contribution of malingering to the opioid epidemic as the result of the prescribing habits of physicians is also addressed in Chapter 10. Chemosensory malingering, although rarely noted, is becoming more frequent as patients become aware that chemosensory loss is a compensable injury and as more attorneys become aware of the involvement of chemosensory dysfunction with head trauma. This is the topic of Chapter 11.

Another chapter addressing an area not frequently considered is malingering of the elderly, both in terms to maximize placement or for other secondary gains. This will become an increasing problem to this demographic segment as our population increases in age. This endemic of geriatric malingering is uncovered in Chapter 12.

The next section of this book, Chapters 13, 14, and 15, deals with legal issues both in the forensic approach to the detection of malingering, for those who are awaiting civil and criminal trial, as well as malingering and secondary gain from an attorney's perspective.

Lastly, physicians' responses to neurologic malingering is addressed in Chapter 16. The idea that countertransference occurs, which causes physicians to negatively view and negatively respond to malingerers, has virtually been unaddressed in literature, and it can clearly impact upon the physician–patient dyad.

In these chapters, many of the issues currently facing physicians in the diagnostic and management of neurologic malingering are expressed. However, it is clear that much more research needs to be devoted to help further define and clarify this disorder. Once the diagnosis is made, it is essential to maximally manage the patient to minimize the harm to the patients and reduce the effects of malingering not only on society, but on the patient's life as well. While methods to approach this are revealed, further formal study is warranted.

Editor

Alan R. Hirsch, MD, FACP, a board certified neurologist and psychiatrist specializing in the treatment of smell and taste loss, is the neurological director of the Smell & Taste Treatment and Research Foundation in Chicago. He is a senior attending in the Department of Medicine at Mercy Hospital and Medical Center. Dr. Hirsch is certified by the American Board of Neurology and Psychiatry in Neurology, Psychiatry, Pain Medicine, Geriatric Psychiatry, Addiction Psychiatry, and Brain Injury Medicine, and by the United Council for Neurologic Subspecialties – Behavioral Neurology and Neuropsychiatry.

Dr. Hirsch conducts in-depth studies of the chemosensory system and its relation to all aspects of life. Some examples include studies observing the effects of aromas on behavior, emotions, mood, and interactions between individuals.

An inventor and investigative researcher in the areas of smell and taste, Dr. Hirsch frequently lectures across the country and has extensively published many of his studies' findings. He has served as an expert on smell and taste for *CNN, Good Morning America, Dateline, 20/20, The Oprah Winfrey Show, CBS Early Show*, and *Extra*. Dr. Hirsch's expertise has also been utilized by many national and local governmental agencies such as the Illinois State's Attorney Office, the Environmental Protection Agency, and the Attorney General of the United States.

Additionally, Dr. Hirsch is a member of numerous professional organizations, including the American Academy of Neurology, American College of Physicians, and the American Medical Association. He has served on the Editorial Advisory Board of *The International Journal of Aromatherapy*, as associate editor of *Neurology Healthcare USA*, on the Advisory Board of the National Academy of Sports Medicine, on the Medical Advisory Board of the Chronic Fatigue Syndrome Society of Illinois, and on the Editorial Advisory Board of the *Professional Journal of Sports Fitness/CPT News*. He has also served as an ad hoc reviewer for peer-reviewed publications such as *Journal of Neurology, Neurosurgery, and Psychiatry, Physiology & Behavior, Laryngoscope*, and *Journal of the Neurological Sciences*, to name a few.

Dr. Hirsch earned both his BA and MD degrees from the University of Michigan in Ann Arbor and completed his residencies in both neurology and psychiatry at Rush University Medical Center in Chicago.

Also a prolific author, Dr. Hirsch has written several books: *Dr. Hirsch's Guide to Scentsational Weight Loss, Scentsational Sex, What Flavor Is Your Personality?, Life's a Smelling Success, What Your Doctor May Not Tell You About Sinusitis, What's Your Food Sign?, How to Tell if Your Teenager Is Lying,* and *Nutrition and Sensation.*

Contributors

Mariam Agha, HBSc
Caribbean Medical University
Des Plaines, Illinois

Ather M. Ali, MD
Monroe Clinic
Monroe, Wisconsin

Richard Paul Bonfiglio, MD
Physical Medicine and Rehabilitation
Murrysville, Pennsylvania

Jasmine M. Campbell, BA
Caribbean Medical University
School of Medicine
Willemstad-Curacao, Netherlands Antilles

Gregory DeClue, PhD, ABPP
Forensic Psychologist in Independent Practice
Sarasota, Florida

Anton N. Dietzen, DC, MD
Marianjoy Rehabilitation Hospital
Northwestern Medicine
Wheaton, Illinois

Henry Phillip Gruss, JD
Henry Phillip Gruss, Ltd.
Chicago, Illinois

Jason J. Gruss, MD
Advanced Rehabilitation Care
Schwab Rehabilitation Hospital
Chicago, Illinois

Valerie Gruss, PhD, APN, CNP-BC
University of Illinois at Chicago—College of Nursing
Chicago, Illinois

Kamran Hanif, MD
Caribbean Medical University
School of Medicine
Willemstad-Curacao, Netherlands Antilles

Jose L. Henao, MD
Brandon Regional Hospital
Brandon, Florida

Alan R. Hirsch, MD
Smell & Taste Treatment and Research Foundation
Chicago, Illinois

Marissa A. Hirsch, BS
St. George's University School of Medicine
Grenada, West Indies

Khurram A. Janjua, MD
Atlantic University School of Medicine
Gros Islet, St. Lucia

Pouyan Kheirkhah, MD
Department of Neurosurgery
University of Illinois at Chicago
Chicago, Illinois

Jerrold B. Leikin, MD
NorthShore University Health Systems—OMEGA
Chicago, Illinois

and

Division of Emergency Medicine
Department of Medicine
University of Chicago Pritzker School of Medicine
Glenview, Illinois

Jasir T. Nayati, AAS, CNMT
St. James School of Medicine
Park Ridge, Illinois

Angela Rekhi, BSc, MD
Aureus University School of Medicine
Oranjestad, Aruba

Roberto P. Segura, MD
Chicago Peripheral Nerve Center
Chicago, Illinois

Carl M. Wahlstrom, Jr., MD
Department of Psychiatry
Rush University Medical Center
Chicago, Illinois

Anum Wani, HBSc
Caribbean Medical University
Des Plaines, Illinois

Chevelle Winchester, BS
American University of Barbados
Bridgetown, Barbados

1 Malingering
A Historical Perspective

Pouyan Kheirkhah, MD

CONTENTS

The *Merriam-Webster Dictionary* defines malingering as, "to pretend to be sick or injured in order to avoid doing work" (Merriam-Webster, 2016).

On the other hand, it means intentionally fabricating or exaggerating the symptoms of mental or physical disorders for secondary gain including financial compensation, avoiding school, work, or military service, as well as obtaining drugs, getting lighter criminal sentences, or simply to attract attention or sympathy (American Psychiatric Association, 2000).

While one may assume malingering is a uniquely human activity, zoologists have theorized that malingering was present among certain kinds of primates even before the existence of humanity (Byrne and Stokes, 2003). Malingering clearly has existed prior to the current state of the American tort and litigation system. The history of malingering goes all the way back to the book of Samuel in which King David faked his insanity to Achish, King of Gath (Ackroyd, 1971a). Odysseus also had to pretend that he was mad in order to avoid fighting in the Trojan war (Smith and Trzakoma, 2007). Malingering has been reported and documented as early as ancient Roman times by the physician Aelius Galenus (Galen). He stated that one of his patients faked a colic pain in order to escape from a public meeting. Another case was that of a man complaining of a knee pain just to avoid going on a long trip with his master (Lund, 1941).

The current use of painful procedures to help define malingering, such as electromyography (EMG) (see Chapter 7) is not new. Physicians were often involved in detecting malingerers and may have used noxious remedies to test slaves who did not wish to work, or citizens and soldiers trying to escape political and military duties (Magner, 1992).

In the "Profane History," Solon, the Greek lawmaker, feigned a mania in order to motivate the Athenians, thus saving the island of Salamis from the grasp of Megarenses (Gavin, 1843). The earliest documented malingerer was Rachel, wife of Jacob the patriarch. Rachel stole Laban's idols and hid them by sitting on them and then pretended she was menstruating- as an excuse to not stand up when Laban reached her tent to retrieve them (Genesis 31: 35).

In history, there is a plethora of examples of pretending to be diseased or injured. From Cardinal Montalto pretending to be sick, to Pope Sixtus V, to Lucius Junius Brutus who had to feign being mentally slow and limited in order to avoid mistrust from his uncle, King Tarquins (Martial and Bohn, 1890). Amnon, son of David, King of Israel, pretended to be sick so when David came to visit him he said, "Let my sister Tamar come, I pray thee, and make me a couple of cakes in my sight, that I may eat at her hand" (Ackroyd, 1971b).

Charles, Duke of Bourbon, feigned sickness so he could stay behind because he wanted to desert the Emperor. Sir Henry "Hotspur," Percy's father, feigned sickness to avoid the battle of Shrewsbury. Robert Devereux, the Second Earl of Essex, and Queen Elizabeth's favorite, faked a serious sickness so as to acquire her empathy (Hume, Hughes, and Smollett, 1854a). Sir Walter Raleigh pretended to be sick and mad in order to prolong his examination and facilitate his escape (Hume, Hughes, and Smollett, 1854b). Gustavus Adolphus IV, King of Sweden, malingered a musket ball wound to his leg (Gustaf IV, 1812). In 1588, Portuguese soldiers pretended to be sick; some even made themselves bleed to avoid fighting the British Army (Adelon, 1812). During the French Long Wars, it was typical for young soldiers to malinger diseases to escape fighting. Fodéré wrote, "They brought feigning to such a perfection that sometimes it was hard to detect feigned from real diseases" (Fodéré, 1813).

Sometimes the illness or defect that someone fakes, to some extent, becomes real. For example, Michel de Montaigne wrote about a Roman who faked blindness by putting a plaster over his eye and pretending to be blind. After removing the plaster, horrified, he discovered he had truly become blind. Another person malingered having gout by wrapping his legs to make them appear swollen. Later, it became apparent that the man was truly suffering from gout (Cotton, 1905).

Pope Julius III faked a sickness to avoid holding the Church Council by incarcerating himself inside his house and changing his dietary habits. Soon, he discovered that he was becoming truly sick from malingering and died as a result of the effects of malingering (Robinson and Sebag-Montefiore, 1871).

Throughout history, one can encounter odd examples of malingering. From Dionysius the Elder, tyrant of Syracuse, who feigned difficulty in distinguishing objects (Mahon, 1834), to Louis XIV of France, who malingered having an anal fistula and became truly sick as a result of an unsuccessful surgery to treat his fictional disease—his wound taking 2 months to heal (Adelon, 1828). Throughout history, faking a disease to escape military service would result in being discharged without honor and deprived of privileges otherwise entitled. However, the punishments were sometimes even more severe. They varied from corporal punishment to life in prison, or even death (Isfordink, 1825).

In Europe, a few months after the introduction of the use of ether in surgeries a French surgeon, Jean Baptiste Lucien Baudens, used etherization to distinguish malingering from real disease among two soldiers claiming skeletal problems (Anon, 1847). In August 1847, Spencer Wells, a British surgeon, used ether on 106 cases among which one was a known malingerer (Wells, 1847). Other military surgeons used similar methods to find malingerers (Ballingall, 1852). In the United States, malingering was common during the Civil War between 1861 and 1865, primarily because of a $300 incentive for new volunteers to sign up for the Union military. Thus, soldiers tended to fake a disease in order to be discharged, just to volunteer again elsewhere and get the additional bounty (Deutsch, 1944). Doctors like William Keen, George Morehouse, and Silas Weir Mitchell used anesthesia to distinguish malingering from real disease in cases of joint contractures, spinal deformities, aphonia, deafness, blindness, paralysis, epilepsy, and urethral stricture (Keen, Weir Mitchell, and Morehouse, 1864). Introduction of progressive social legislation in Germany, between 1880 and 1890, alongside the Workmen's Compensation Act in 1908 and the National Insurance Act of 1911 in England allowed malingerers more freedom to escape from duties. These legalizations provided the opportunity for financial rewards to the malingerers (Palmer, 2003). Therefore, many believe that malingering started when humankind gathered to form communities. Each community member had different and various responsibilities and some used malingering to avoid them. Suetonius was a Roman Knight who amputated his sons' fingers so as to exempt them from military service, but Emperor Augustus punished Suetonius and sent his sons to service anyway—fingerless (Suetonius and Forrester, 2009). More contemporary examples are beggars and vagabonds faking an illness or disability for money. There are many other examples in the political, military, and industrial fields of how malingerers tried to escape their duties and responsibilities by feigning a disease.

By the end of the nineteenth century and the beginning of the twentieth, malingering tended to shift from the political arena to the medical field (Palmer, 2003). Between 1880 and 1900, new changes in laws allowed malingerers to take economic advantage, and physicians, especially in developed countries like Germany, began to worry about the outcome of this crisis. For example, almost one-third of the functional neurological cases, which German neurologists encountered were classified as malingering. Over the next 20 years, the number of diagnosed cases of malingering decreased dramatically as doctors overcame their worries of patients abusing the new changes in law. Nevertheless, many of doctors blamed the new system and held it responsible for the rapid increase in malingering. Since the approval of the Workers' Compensation Act in 1906, the rate of claims and nonfatal accidents have increased dramatically (Collie, 1917). Throughout the years physician had to play detective to uncover malingerers. This required the physician to use a mixture of detective work and clinical examinations. Their frustration in this regard was summarized by, "I am not doctor but detective" (Bourke, 1996a).

Pilowski discussed the term malingerophobia among doctors. It is not the fear of malingering, but rather, the fear of missing a malingerer (Yelin, 1986). So it has become an uneasy game for doctors and malingerers; they both know that if they lose there will be consequences, although more so for the malingerer than the physician. In making correct diagnoses, doctors will be considered astute and professional and will gain fame and fortune, as opposed to malingerers who need to show that they are truthful and of good character in order to win the game (Eghigian, 2000). The first World War brought about a new wave of malingerers to avoid military service; malingering was abused on a much larger scale compared to previous conflicts like the U.S. Civil War (Wessely, 2003). Some soldiers even mutilated their own bodies in order to escape their duties (Bourke, 1996b). Self-mutilation varied from intentionally exposing their body parts to enemy gunfire to even shooting themselves. Fortunately, medical technology during that time helped doctors in the detection of malingering. Physicians used different chemical analyses to detect abscesses induced by turpentine, uncover adding egg albumin to urine, or faking jaundice by ingesting picric acid (Cooter, Harrison, and Sturdy, 1998). X-rays were also used to detect any underlying pathology in the soldiers (Garrison, 1921).

In World War II, both Axis and Allied powers spread propaganda leaflets or brochures to encourage soldiers on opposing sides to escape from the war using different methods of malingering. The propaganda extensively described the horrors of war and the risk of being killed in action, and reminded soldiers that they had family waiting for them, which they might not be able to see again. The proposed malingered diseases ranged from fake skin inflammation using iodine potassium, stomach ulcers, heart disease, malaria, abuse of laxatives to fake severe diarrhea, pretending to have a temporary limb paralysis, and many more (Friedman, n.d.).

By the end of the 1970s, physicians were found to be poor at distinguishing between brain dysfunction and malingering (Morgan and Sweet, 2008). Ever since the 1980s, malingering has received much attention amongst clinical neuropsychologists and it has been suggested that neuropsychologists actually might not be able to accurately detect it (Faust, Hart, Guilmette, and Arkes, 1988).

The pervasive historical and cross-cultural ubiquitous existence of malingerers vaticinates its continued presence in today's advanced contemporary societies for the foreseeable future.

REFERENCES

Ackroyd, P.R. 1971a. Saul and David. *The First Book of Samuel*, 172. Cambridge: Cambridge University Press.

Ackroyd, P.R. 1971b. Absalom's religion. *The Second Book of Samuel*, 118. Cambridge: Cambridge University Press.

Adelon, N.P. 1812. *Dictionnaire des Sciences Médicales*, 194. Paris: C.L.F. Panckoucke.

Adelon, N.P. 1828. *Dictionnaire des Sciences Médicales, Vol. 1.* Paris: C.L.F. Panckoucke.

American Psychiatric Association. 2000. *Diagnostic and Statistical Manual of Mental Disorders: 4th Edition: DSM-IV-TR*, p. 739. Washington, DC: American Psychiatric Association.

Anon. 1847. Des inhalations d'éther comme moyen de reconnaître les maladies simulées. *Gaz Méd Paris* 3:2:209.

Ballingall, G. 1852. *Outlines of Military Surgery 4th Ed.*, 586. Edinburgh: Archibald Constable and Company.

Bourke, J. 1996a. Malingering. In *Dismembering the Male: Men's Bodies, Britain, and the Great War*, 89. Chicago: University of Chicago Press.

Bourke, J. 1996b. Malingering. In *Dismembering the Male: Men's Bodies, Britain, and the Great War*, 86. Chicago: University of Chicago Press.

Byrne, R.W., and E.J. Stokes. 2003. Can monkeys malinger? In *Malingering & Illness Deception*, eds. P.W. Halligan, C. Bass, and D.A. Oakley, 52–65. New York: Oxford University Press.

Collie, J. 1917. Malingering and feigned sickness. *Forensics* 14. http://digitalcommons.hsc.unt.edu/cgi/viewcontent.cgi?article=1013&context=forensics

Cooter, R., M. Harrison, and S. Sturdy. 1998. *War, medicine and modernity*, 127. Stroud: Sutton.

Cotton, C. 1905. *The Essays of Michel de Montaigne* (trans), Vol. 2, Chapter 25, 412. London: George Bell and Sons.

Deutsch, A. 1944. Military psychiatry: The Civil War 1861–1865. In *One Hundred Years of American Psychiatry*, eds. J.K. Hau, G. Zilboorg, and H.A. Bunker, 367–384. New York: Columbia University Press.

Eghigian, G. 2000. *Making Security Social: Disability, Insurance, and the Birth of the Social Entitlement State in Germany*, 245–246. Ann Arbor: University of Michigan Press.

Faust, D., K.J. Hart, T.J. Guilmette, and H.R. Arkes. 1988. Neuropsychologists' capacity to detect adolescent malingerers. *Professional psychology: Research and Practice* 19:5: 508–515.

Fodéré, F.E. 1813. *Traité de médecine légale et d'hygiène publique ou de police de santé: adapté aux codes de l'Empire français et aux connaissances actuelles, à l'usage des gens de l'Art, de ceux du Barreau, des jurés et des administrateurs de la santé publique, civile, militaire et de marine, 2ème edition*, 2:452. Paris: Mame.

Friedman, H.A. (n.d.). *Malingering psyop.* http://www.psywarrior.com/malingering.html, 12/26/2016.

Garrison, F.H. 1921. *An Introduction to the History of Medicine, with Medical Chronology, Suggestions for Study and Bibliographic Data*, 409. Philadelphia: W.B. Saunders Company.

Gavin, H. 1843. *On Feigned and Factitious Diseases, Chiefly of Soldiers and Seamen*, 123. London: A and J Churchill.

Gustaf IV, A. 1812. *A Historical Sketch of the Last Years of the Reign of Gustavus the 4th Adolphus, Late King of Sweden*, 57. London: John Cawthorn.

Hume, D., T.S. Hughes, and T.G. Smollett. 1854a. *History of England, by Hume and Smollett; with a continuation by T.S. Hughes*, 63. London: George Bell (Oxford University Collections).

Hume, D., T.S. Hughes, and T.G. Smollett. 1854b. *History of England, by Hume and Smollett; with a continuation by T.S. Hughes*, 402. London: George Bell (Oxford University Collections).

Isfordink, J.N. 1825. *Militärische Gesundheits-Polizei, mit besonderer Beziehung auf die k. k. österreichische armee, Vol. 2*. Wien: J.G. Heubner.

Keen, W., S. Weir Mitchell, and G. Morehouse. 1864. On malingering, especially in regard to simulation of diseases of the nervous system. *American Journal of the Medical Sciences* 48:367–394.

Lund, F.B. 1941. Galen on malingering, centaurs, diabetes and other subjects more or less related. *Proceedings of the Chaka Club X*, 52–55.

Magner, L.N. 1992. Greco-Roman medicine. *A History of Medicine*, 94. New York: CRC Press.

Mahon, P.A. 1834. *Médecine Légale, et Police Médicale*, 1:325. Paris: G. Baillière.

Martial, and H.G. Bohn. 1890. *The Epigrams of Martial*. London: G. Bell & Sons.

Merriam-Webster, s.v. "malinger," accessed 12/1/2016, https://www.merriam-webster.com/dictionary/malinger.

Morgan, J.E., and J.J. Sweet. 2008. *Neuropsychology of Malingering Casebook*, XIV. New York: Psychology Press.

Palmer, I.P. 2003. Malingering, shirking, and self-inflicted injuries in the military. In *Malingering and Illness Deception*, eds. P.W. Halligan, C. Bass, and D.A Oakley, 42–53. New York: Oxford University Press.

Robinson, J.C., and C. Sebag-Montefiore. 1871. Notice of works of art, having relation to the Emperor Charles V, in *The Collection of Robert Napier, Esq., of West Shandon*. London: Chiswick Press.

Smith, R.S., and S.M. Trzaskoma. 2007. *Apollodorus' Library and Hyginus' Fabulae*, 77. Indianapolis: Hackett Publishing.

Suetonius and T. Forester 2009. Augustus. *The Twelve Caesars*, trans. A.M. Thomson. Aukland: The Floating Press.

The Book of Genesis, 31: 35.

Wells, T.S. 1847. Remarks on the results of the inhalation of ether in 106 cases. *London Medical Gazette* 5:547–549.

Wessely, S. 2003. Malingering: Historical perspectives. In *Malingering and Illness Deception*, eds. P.W. Halligan, C. Bass, and D.A. Oakley, 31–41. New York: Oxford University Press.

Yelin, E. 1986. The myth of malingering: Why individuals withdraw from work in the presence of illness. *Milbank Quarterly* 64:4:622–649.

2 Historical Indications of Malingering

Marissa A. Hirsch, BS

CONTENTS

Dr. Russell DeJong, former chairman of neurology at the University of Michigan is the antithesis of Dr. Gregory House from the TV series, House, who attempts to avoid talking with patients at any cost, often repeating "the patient only tells lies." While rounding in the neurology ward, it has been told that he would unambiguously proclaim that more than 90% of the diagnosis of a patient is based on the history. After that, he would look at an otherwise nonplus diagnostic enigma and through several well-placed questions, reveal a heretofore-unconsidered diagnosis. Such is the importance of the history in neurology, including in the diagnosis of malingering.

In medical school, we are lectured about Lesch–Nyhan syndrome, a genetic disorder afflicting one in 380,000 live births, situs inversus, with a prevalence of one in 10,000, and Moyamoya disease, affecting one in 1,160,000, but we are given no lectures on the diagnosis or detection methods to help determine malingering. This diagnosis was barely uttered—except in reference to Hoover's sign, the flip sign, and camptocormia postures during the assessment of low back pain and weakness (see Chapter 3).

Thus, the diagnosis of malingering was relegated to nonreal diseases, along with pseudoneurologic syndromes (i.e., hysterical blindness, hysterical aphasia, and pseudoseizures)- and the functional illnesses which fall in the psychiatrists' realm, including Munchausen's syndrome and the somatoform disorders—malingering was considered an inconsequential diagnosis deemed not worthy of wasting a neurologist's time.

But accuracy of the diagnosis of malingering is essential in the everyday practice of neurology—from the determination of disability and maximum medical improvement to the assessment of true pain in those seeking narcotics (see Chapter 4), or simulation in those complaining of attention and concentration problems in an attempt to obtain amphetamines.

No one knows to what extent neurologists are accurate in determining mendacity. The specialty, which one would anticipate should demonstrate the greatest ability, is psychiatry since the focus of attention during each visit delves into behaviors, emotions, and motivations. Psychiatrists traditionally spend longer with the patient on visits than other specialties and thus are privy to more information and direct observation of the behavioral styles of their patients. Given psychiatrists' experience and training in dealing with conduct disorders and sociopathy one would hypothesize they are experts in the diagnosis of malingering. Hence, it would be logical to suggest that psychiatrists would have the most accurate acumen in diagnosing malingering, far more than other physicians. However, assigning such expertise to psychiatrists would be just plain wrong.

A psychiatric assessment is just about as good as flipping a coin in the detection of malingering, with an accuracy rate of 57% (Eckman and O'Sullivan, 1991). The estimated incidence of malingering in nonforensic patients is 7.4% (Cunnien, 1988), but the actual frequency of this diagnosis is far less than 1% among practicing psychiatrists (Kapp, 1999). They correctly identify malingering only one in seven times—suggesting that practicing psychiatrists' diagnostic acumen of malingering is actually far worse than flipping a coin.

Not only are psychiatrists' poor at differentiating mendacity from truthfulness but they are also falsely self-confident in their abilities. They are unaware of their incapacity, demonstrating an inverse correlation between their ability to determine the truth and the belief in their own accuracy. Lees-Haley vaticinates: "Mental health professionals who claim they cannot be fooled may have been fooled already" (Lees-Haley, 1985).

If psychiatrists are so poor at this, it is illogical to expect neurologists or other specialists to be any better. In a study of pediatricians, for instance, the error rate for detection of malingering was 100% (Faust, 1995).

Assessment for malingering as a component of the history can help in uncovering this diagnosis. While performing the history, one not only obtains the information directly requested, but one also looks for inconsistencies in presentation, dichotomies between complaints of disability and history of functional ability, and motivational factors (lawsuits, money, economic hardship) for malingering.

The history itself can also serve as an informal examination. The examiner gets a sense or feeling of the patient's true functional abilities. How is it that the patient has severe cognitive problems but still can provide a cogent history? This has even been defined as an informal mental status examination, which correlates with formalized mental status examinations (Mungas, 1991). But even beyond this the examiner—despite trying to maintain a Rogerian unconditional positive regard—may experience the feeling that he or she is being deceived or lied to (Sullivan, 1970). Such an impression is often a gut reaction based on the physician's past experience (and a gestalt judgment inferred from pattern matching of what he or she hears and sees during the history) of evaluating malingering patients—and how well these match. However, such an informal experiential approach doesn't comport with evidence-based medicine. Such subjective assessment is influenced by how much the examiner likes the patient—if he or she is liked, the more likely the patient is believed. The malingerer intuitively realizes this and adjusts his/her behavior to induce the examiner to like them more. For instance, leaning forward towards the examiner during the history in order to psychologically include them as a friend or insider to enhance the perception of their friendliness. In our egalitarian society, reciprocity dominates. If he or she is showing a friendly disposition towards me, I should similarly demonstrate friendship towards him or her in the form of believing their lies. Since we are more apt to like those who are similar to ourselves, in American society where physicians are predominantly white, one would anticipate that those of minority cultures would more likely be diagnosed as malingerers, independently of the validity of the diagnosis. If an examiner is aware of his or her emotions and biases, he or she is less likely to misdiagnose malingering.

Another way to gain accuracy in assessing malingering is through a more thorough examination for the presence of lying on the history. To do this the history is evaluated in a formal way, as if part of the examination, with quantitative evaluation of specific criteria in parallel to a 0–4+ rating scale of deep tendon reflexes or with a 0–5 scale of muscle strength (Paternostro-Sluga et al., 2008). This same formal approach has been applied to the history to assess the clinical parameters of mendacity or lying.

Hirsch and Wolf evaluated 20 books and 64 peer reviewed articles about mendacity and distilled 23 verbal and nonverbal clues which are discriminators for truthfulness (Hirsch and Wolf, 2001); examples of verbal lying would be:

- *Qualifiers/modifiers.* More frequent use of: "not necessarily," "but," "however," "ordinarily," "almost," "most of the time," "generally," "essentially," "basically," "sometimes," "usually," "hardly ever," "possibly," "actually," "rarely," "specifically," and "some." (Walters, 1996b; Kraut, 1978; Resnick, 1984; Hall and Pritchard, 1996; Sannito and McGovern, 1985b; DePaulo, 1992; Ford, 1996)
- *Expanded contractions.* Emphasize the "not" to declare, for example, that they were "not" involved; use of the expanded form of a verb more frequently than the contraction, for example, "did not" versus "didn't," "could not" versus "couldn't," and "would not" versus "wouldn't." (Lieberman, 1998)
- *Denials of lying.* Denies lying and emphasizes the truthfulness of his answers, i.e., "I have absolutely no reason to lie," "Frankly," "obviously," "to be one-hundred percent honest," "to tell you the truth," "I am being straightforward," "believe me," "honestly," "to the best of my knowledge," and "as far as I know." (Walters, 1996b; Kraut, 1978; Hall and Pritchard, 1996; DePaulo, 1992)
- *Speech errors.* Changes of thought in mid-sentence, grammatical errors, including tense, person, and pronoun, and Freudian slips. (Walters, 1996a; Kraut, 1978; Sannito and McGovern, 1985a; DePaulo, 1992; Ekman, 1985a; Depaulo, Stone, and Lassiter, 1985)
- *Pause fillers.* Nonliterate sounds used to fill in time during a period of hesitations, i.e., "uh," "er," "um," and "ah." (Walters, 1996a; Kraut, 1978; Sannito and McGovern, 1985b; Fiedler and Walka, 1993)
- *Stuttering.* The slurring of speech, stammering, and stuttering. (Walters, 1996a; Kraut, 1978; Hall and Pritchard, 1996; DePaulo, 1992; DePaulo, Stone, and Lassiter, 1985)
- *Throat clearing.* Throat clearing and various other sounds such as moaning, groaning, or grunting. (Kraut, 1978)

Nonverbal (kinesthetic) signs of lying would be:

- *Less finger pointing.* Avoiding pointing or raising a single finger to illustrate a point, possibly out of fear that the truth will escape through the fingers. (Walters, 1996e; DePaulo, Stone, and Lassiter, 1985)
- *Liar's lean/postural shifts.* Coincident with lying, leaning forward, resting elbows on knees or a table, constantly changing posture or position in a chair. (Walters, 1996f; Kraut, 1978; Dimitrius and Mazzarelia, 1998)
- *Lip licking.* Increased frequency of bringing the tongue to the external lips. (Walters, 1996c; Kraut, 1978; Dimitrius, and Mazzarelia, 1998)
- *Lip puckering/tightening lips.* Tightening the mouth as though to prevent the lie from escaping. (Walters, 1996c; Kraut, 1978; Sannito and McGovern, 1985c; Ekman, 1985a; Dimitrius and Mazzarelia, 1998)
- *Drinking/swallowing.* Increased drinking and swallowing. (Walters, 1996c; Hall and Pritchard, 1996; Ekman, 1985a)
- *Smiling/laughing.* Increased smiling and insincere smiles or laughing inappropriately. (Ekman and O'Sullivan, 1991; Walters, 1996c; Kraut, 1978; Sannito and McGovern, 1985d; DePaulo, 1992; Ekman, 1985a; Fiedler and Walka, 1993)
- *Fewer hand gestures.* Liars use fewer hand gestures and when used, are not sweeping. (Ekman, 1985a; Knapp, 1978; Ekman, 1972)
- *Hand-to-face grooming (excluding nose).* Increased touching of the face, ears, or hair. (Ekman and O'Sullivan, 1991; Kraut, 1978; Fiedler and Walka, 1993)
- *Sighs/deep breaths.* Increased audible or visible sighs or deep breaths. (Walters, 1996a; Ford, 1996)
- *Hand and shoulder shrugs.* Flipping the hands with the palms up in open fashion and shrugging the shoulders as if uncertain. (Ekman and O'Sullivan, 1991; Walters, 1996e; Ford, 1996)
- *Handling objects.* To prevent the lie from escaping through the hand, occupying the hands with objects such as eyeglasses, pen, and papers. (Sannito and McGovern, 1985e)
- *Averting gaze.* Looking away, to the side, or down, after having made eye contact. (Walters, 1996g; Kraut, 1978; Sannito and McGovern, 1985a; Ekman, 1985a; Dimitrius and Mazzarelia, 1998)
- *Less blinking.* Infrequent blinking. (Ekman, 1985a)
- *Crossing arms.* Folding or crossing the arms as if making a barrier against the one being lied to. (Walters, 1996h; Hall and Pritchard, 1996; Sannito and McGovern, 1985b; Dimitrius and Mazzarelia, 1998)
- *Closing hands/interlocking fingers.* Either hand is closed like a fist, with no fingers shown, or the two hands have their fingers interlocked. (Ekman and O'Sullivan, 1991; Walters, 1996i; Sannito and McGovern, 1985f; Dimitrius and Mazzarelia, 1998)
- *Touching nose.* Scratching, rubbing, or touching the nose. (Walters, 1996d; Sannito and McGovern, 1985g; Fiedler and Walka, 1993; Dimitrius and Mazzarelia, 1998)

Why do these signs appear? In a normal nonmalingering individual, the moral violation and ambivalence about lying culminates in guilt. This emotion generated from the mismatch between internalized self-expectation and behavior triggers an internal or unconscious conflict that the subject expresses in speech or actions. Just as the sociopath is so comfortable lying that the lie detector—a test of sympathetic nervous system activation—doesn't register, the sociopathic malingerer will not show sympathetic activation, which is the basis for several of the above signs including throat clearing, lip licking, drinking, and swallowing. They will still manifest many of the other signs, especially those designed to lure the examiner into a friendly (not objective) relationship with the malingerer. These includes smiling, laughing, and the liar's lean.

2.1 NOTES ON INTERPRETATION OF VERBAL AND NONVERBAL SIGNS OF MALINGERING

Certain caveats need to be applied in interpretation of these vaticinations of mendacity. The premise is that even if the patient is lying it does not make the prevaricator a malingerer. Lying occurs for all sorts of reasons, usually out of social embarrassment or narcissistic pride. The patient may be too anxious to admit his or her hidden problems or agenda, and thus lies about what is truly bothering him or her. Alternatively, we all like to save face. If revealing one true history would subject him or her to narcissistic insult, a convenient lie may be substituted for such a hurtful truth. These lies are easily understandable and don't define a malingerer. Alternatively, altruistic lying to get medication for a sick relative rather than for personal gain, while prevaricating, is not a self-motivated malingerer. These signs are not necessarily useful when applied to such a pattern of altruistic lying—their validity in such circumstance is unknown.

The more signs appear with greater frequency, the more reliable the assessment becomes. Thus, compulsive nasal hair trichotillomania with recurrent touching of the nose, in pursuit of the object of obsessional interest, does not a liar make. Limbic system discharge, as occurs with temporal lobe epilepsy, may lead to rhinorrhea, nasal discharge, and nasal touching (Hirsch, 1999).

Anxiety alone may produce many of these signs (Resnick, 1984). Stress increases articulatory errors and mid-sentence changes (Ekman, 1985b; Walters, 1996a; Walters, 1996b; Sannito and McGovern, 1985a; Sannito and McGovern, 1985b).

Labeled the Othello error in deference to Shakespeare's recognition of the confusion between anxiety and lying, Desdemona's somatic manifestation of fear is misinterpreted by Othello as evidence of a liar's guilt. In order to avoid such a trap, one should interview the patient with anxiety-provoking questions unrelated to about malingering issues, which the patient will be anxious about but that are unlikely to cause him or her to lie (Walters, 1996a). For instance, for someone with a suspicion of malingering of memory loss, it would be asking about sexual function. Such a high anxiety topic is likely to generate a baseline response of anxiety-induced signs of lying (a truthful control response). One could then compare the frequency of these signs to the lying condition. The greater number of such indicators in the latter compared to the control conditions suggests that lying, rather than anxiety, is the source of the mendacity signs.

Another possible false negative finding in these signs is built into the definition of malingering—a malingerer must be *intentionally* lying to fool the examiner. As such, someone who is psychotic, delusional, or cognitively impaired so as not to know the truth from a lie may confabulate a story and not be aware it is false and thus, not demonstrate any of these findings. For example, the alcoholic suffering from Wernicke–Korsakoff's syndrome may be unaware of the falsity of his/her history and not demonstrate any signs of lying—such an example would not be malingering because no intentional prevarication is present. The more malingerers believe the lie, the less signs they manifest. Hence, someone with delusional disorder without insight, fully invested in their delusions, won't display these objective signs of lying. With self-deception, "liars are undetectable" (Ekman, 1985c).

While ignorance or confusion as to the truth may invalidate this test, more concerning is that two other factors may also serve to minimize these signs' efficacy. Penultimate amongst these is the practice effect (Ekman, 1985d). In our current medical environment, in academic institutions, a patient admitted to the hospital is likely to have a plethora of history and physical examinations. For instance, it was related to me that at the Hospital of the University of Michigan Medical School, every patient is interviewed and receives a full history and physical examination starting with the third-year medical student, the fourth-year medical student, the intern, the second-year resident, the third-year resident, the chief resident, and finally, the attending—a total of seven histories and physicals. Such a barrage of repetitive questions and examinations would serve to reinforce the abilities of a malingerer, who would show more confidence and lie better as his knowledge and experience in the medical establishment grows. Thus, the experienced malingerer would be all the harder to diagnose than the novice liar. Through the practice effect, the malingerer's presentation would improve over time and be most convincing when examined by the most experienced (attending) and most likely to reveal his true intentions to the one who is least experienced and, therefore, least likely to recognize the indications of malingering. Therefore, the system at the University of Michigan—and most academic medical centers—functions to enhance the malingerer's ability to malinger more effectively. The malingerer also learns to manipulate the display of emotion. This may be viewed as a malingerer's variant of the Stanislavsky technique of actors. Through this approach, when attempting to portray an emotion in a realistic manner, the thespian will imagine a strong past emotional experience, i.e., a kitten or puppy dying during his or her childhood. By evoking these emotional memories, the emotion is reexperienced and displayed in their portrayal (Liberman, 1998). Similarly, the skilled malingerer can harken back to past experiences of pain, weakness, confusion, or whatever he or she is trying to prevaricate, and enhance their emotional and ratiocinate presentation—in essence, perfecting their guileful private performance piece for the unsuspecting physician. Winning a metaphorical Academy Award for the malingerer may have the same, or even greater, economic effect as it does for actors in Hollywood, allowing for a life of sustained comfort and relief from social hardship.

However, the paramount reason for which malingerers are effective in their prevarification is in the pathological underpinning to malingering—that of a moral lacunae to lying and deception (Ekman, 1985d). Just as in antisocial personality disorder, lying is not held as being inherently wrong but rather a means to an end, no different than any other technique to manipulate others to obtain something. It is used as a technique—like politeness or friendliness—viewed as a valid and morally acceptable approach to obtaining a goal.

Why do the lying signs in the previous two lists appear? In a normal nonmalingering individual the moral violation and ambivalence about lying culminates in guilt. This emotion, generated from the mismatch between internalized self-expectation and action, triggers internal or unconscious conflicts which the subject experiences in speech or actions.

The objective signs of lying can be further investigated based on their physiological and psychological mechanisms. Freud suggested that pressure to reveal the truth hides behind the lie. This latent impulse would thus seek ways to express itself, releasing the underlying tension. Like an itch needing to be scratched, a sneeze awaiting exsufflation, or the orgasmic phase of sexual arousal, the urge to divulge the truth is energized by the relief such revelation provides. Thus, a powerful force to confess the truth confronts the prevaricating malingerer. Even if he or she can consciously prevent the truth from being expressed in the interview it will escape. "He that has eyes to see and ears to hear may convince himself that no mortal can keep a secret. If his lips are silent, he chatters with his fingertips, betrayal oozes out of him at every pore" (Freud, 1903).

Thus, the erstwhile liar unconsciously tries to keep the truth from escaping by covering their orifices—puckering and tightening the lips, or in a primitive manner holding their breath with sighing and deep breathing. In another variation of this, closing the glottis also prevents air (truth) from projecting outward. Hence, the glottis is forcefully closed for prolonged periods requiring drinking, swallowing, throat clearing, stuttering, and pause fillers—all mechanisms developed to hold in the lie.

Since lying may escape through nonverbal expression, these also must be inhibited. In a liar's version of metoposcopy, or judging a person based on the appearance of his or her face, placing the hand over the face restricts the ability of others from interpreting the true facial expression, as does grimacing or posturing with insincere smiles. This connection is validated based on evidence of facial muscle patterns being functionally and neuroanatomically linked to limbic lobe function (Buck, 1999). Thus, it requires cognitive effort to override such predetermined facial expressions, and truthful affect may reveal itself—with incongruities of content of speech and affect. While verbal content may be controlled, facial expression tends to manifest the true affect. Thus, a sidelong smile may express an incongruence of speech and affect.

In nonverbal expression through body language and hand posture, the prevaricator also assumes the lie may be revealed. Therefore, he actively prevents the expressions of such nonverbal cues. Finger pointing and hand gestures are avoided, aided in this by holding objects, making fists, interlocking fingers, and even crossing the arms.

The belief prevails ubiquitously in our cultural zeitgeist—movies, television programs, and gambling lore—that the truth will be revealed through the eyes of the liar. "He cannot look into my eyes" is a common cinematic phrase during police interrogations. However, my experience is that malingerers learn to overcome this and in and of its own is an unreliable sign of truthfulness.

The physiological origins for signs of lying derive from autonomic nervous system discharges resulting from amygdaloid activation due to fear of being discovered in the lie. Increase in sympathetic (fight or flight) firing causes inhibition of salivation, and thus, a dryness of the mouth and throat, resulting in thirst and drinking, swallowing, and throat clearing (Walters, 1996c). This elevated sympathetic tone also increases blood pressure and thus blood flow, especially to the erectile tissues of the body including in the nose (Walters, 1996d; Lillie, 1923; Anggard and Edwall, 1974). As these tissues within the nose expand, mass cells degranulate and release histamine. This histamine induces small nerve fiber discharge, inducing a sensation of pain, irritation, or itch. The behavioral response to this is to scratch or touch the proboscis. Such touching of the nose in response to lying has been named the Pinocchio phenomena (Hirsch and Wolf, 2001).

Lying requires more concentration or cognitive demand than telling the truth (Elliott, 1979). Thus, the liar demonstrates signs of diverted attention and concentration. One example of this is decreased blink frequency—with a greater degree of concentration, the less frequent the blink (in those not on dopamine agonists, antagonists, or agents which dry the corneal membranes) (Irwin, 2011). In response to diverted attention the liar slows down—using pause fillers, throat clearing, or even stuttering, and uses expansion of words not only to emphasize the lie but also to buy time for thinking (Dimitrius and Mazzarella, 1998; Knapp, 1978). Being more distracted by the lie, the prevaricator is thus inclined to speak erroneously and make Freudian slips (Ford, 1996).

Hence, the malingerer tries to avoid lying by not being fully dishonest through more frequent utilization of qualifiers and modifiers—"generally," "most of the time," "etcetera," and the body language of the shoulder shrug. Moreover, the malingerer tries to emphasize that their lie is not a lie through the use of expanded contractions, using "did not" instead of "didn't," denial of lying ("honestly"), and the liar's lean.

This technique was applied to a political celebrity known for having lied. President Clinton's Grand Jury Testimony of August 17, 1998, was examined for the presence of the 23 clinically practical signs of dissimulation. A segment of his testimony that was false was compared with a control portion during the same testimony (internal control). A fund-raising speech to a sympathetic crowd served as a second control (external control). The periods and differences, were analyzed for statistical significance (Hirsch and Wolff, 2001). During the mendacious speech, the subject markedly increased the frequency of 20 out of 23 (87%) signs compared with their frequency during the fund-raising control speech ($p < 0.0005$). (See Table 2.1.)

TABLE 2.1
Frequency of Signs Indicative of Deception in the Mendacious Speech Versus the External Control

	Times per Minute		
	External Control	Mendacious Speech	% Change
	Verbal Signs		
Qualifiers and modifiers	1.4	2.26	+61
Expanded contractions	0.2	0.39	+95
Denials of lying	0.0	1.34	>100
Speech errors	0.4	1.65	+313
Pause fillers	1.0	1.78	+78
Stuttering	0.4	1.39	+248
Throat clearing	0.0	0.74	>100
	Nonverbal Signs		
Less finger pointing	1.6	0.52	−52
Lean or postural shift	0.0	0.87	>100
Lip licking	1.4	1.4	no change
Lip tightening	0.4	0.43	−7.5
Drinking and swallowing	0.2	0.91	+355
Smiling	0.8	0.52	−35[a]
Fewer hand gestures	7.8	3.4	−56
Hand to face	0.2	0.70	+250
Sighs	0.0	0.22	>100
Shrugs	0.0	0.22	>100
Handling objects	0.0	0.57	>100
Averting gaze	1.2	3.83	+219
Less blinking	11.8	43.4	+268[a]
Crossing arms	0.0	0.04	>100
Closing hands	0.6	1.9	+217
Touching nose	0.0	0.26	>100

[a] The changed frequency of the sign is not in the direction suggestive of deception.

His behavior showed an increase in the frequency of 19 (83%) signs compared with their frequency during the control period of the same testimony ($p < 0.003$). (See Table 2.2.)

Tables 2.1 and 2.2 demonstrate that with practice and without requiring special equipment, written forms, or extensive time, these parameters can be readily performed and lying can be objectively detected as part of the physical examination component of the history.

TABLE 2.2
Frequency of Signs Indicative of Deception in the Mendacious Speech Versus the Internal Control

	Times per Minute		
	External Control	Mendacious Speech	% Change
	Verbal Signs		
Qualifiers and modifiers	0.45	2.26	+402
Expanded contractions	0.18	0.39	+117
Denials of lying	0.82	1.34	+63
Speech errors	0.09	1.65	+1733
Pause fillers	0.55	1.78	+224
Stuttering	0.09	1.39	+1444
Throat clearing	0.18	0.74	+311
	Nonverbal Signs		
Less finger pointing	0.00	0.52	>100[a]
Lean or postural shift	0.18	0.87	+383
Lip licking	0.91	1.4	+54
Lip tightening	0.55	0.43	−22[a]
Drinking and swallowing	0.64	0.91	+42
Smiling	0.27	0.52	+93
Fewer hand gestures	0.36	3.4	+844[a]
Hand to face	0.09	0.70	+678
Sighs	0.36	0.22	−39[a]
Shrugs	0.18	0.22	+22
Handling objects	0.27	0.57	+111
Averting gaze	2.91	3.83	+32
Less blinking	50.5	43.4	−14
Crossing arms	0.0	0.04	>100
Closing hands	0.64	1.9	+197
Touching nose	0.0	0.26	>100

[a] The changed frequency of the sign is not in the direction suggestive of deception.

REFERENCES

Anggard, A., and L. Edwall. 1974. Effects of sympathetic nerve stimulation on the tracer disappearance rate and local blood content in the nasal mucosa of the cat. *Acta Otolaryngol* 77:131–139.

Buck, R. 1999. *Communication of Emotion*. New York: Guilford Press.

Cunnien, A.J. 1988. Psychiatric and medical syndromes associated with deception. In *Clinical Assessment of Malingering and Deception*, ed. R. Rogers, 13–33. New York: Guilford Press.

DePaulo, B. 1992. Nonverbal behavior and self-presentation. *Psychological Bulletin* 111:203–243.

DePaulo, B., J. Stone, and G. Lassiter. 1985. Deceiving and detecting deceit. In *Self and Social Life*, ed. B. Schlenker, 323–370. New York: McGraw-Hill.

Dimitrius, J.E., and M. Mazzarella. 1998. *Reading People*. New York: Random House Publishers.

Ekman, P. 1985a. *Clues to Deceit in the Marketplace, Politics, and Marriage*. New York: W.W. Norton.

Ekman, P. 1985b. *Clues to Deceit in the Marketplace, Politics, and Marriage*, 286. New York: W.W. Norton.

Ekman, P. 1985c. *Clues to Deceit in the Marketplace, Politics, and Marriage*, 1140. New York: W.W. Norton.

Ekman, P. 1985d. *Clues to Deceit in the Marketplace, Politics, and Marriage*, 292. New York: W.W. Norton.

Ekman, P., and M. O'Sullivan. 1991. Who can catch a liar? *American Psychologist* 46:913–920.

Elliott, G.C. 1979. Some effects of deception and level of self-monitoring on planning and reacting to a self-presentation. *Journal of Personality and Social Psychology* 37: 1282–1292.

Faust, D. 1995. The detection of deception. *Neurology Clinics* 13:23–265.

Fiedler, K., and I. Walka. 1993. Training lie detectors to use nonverbal cues instead of global heuristics. *Human Communications Research* 20:199–223.

Ford, C.V. 1996. *Lies! Lies!! Lies!!! Psychology of Deceit*. Washington, D.C.: American Psychiatric Press.

Freud, S. 1903. Fragment of an analysis of a case of hysteria. In *Collected Papers, Volume 3*, 1959, trans. A. and J. Strachey, 24. New York: Basic Books.

Hall, H.Y., and D.A. Pritchard. 1996. *Detecting Malingering and Deception*. Port St. Lucie: St. Lucie Press.

Hirsch, A.R., and C.J. Wolf. 2001. Practical methods for detecting mendacity: A case study. *Journal of the American Academy of Psychiatry and the Law* 29:438–444.

Hirsch, A.R. 1999. Postictal nose wiping: the lateralized sign in temporal lobe complex seizures. *Neurology* 52:8:1721.

Irwin, D.E. 2011. Where does attention go when you blink? *Attention, Perception & Psychophysics* 73:5:1374–1384.

Kapp, A. 1999. Advanced Management, Inc.: Personal communication.

Knapp, M. 1978. *Nonverbal Communication in Human Interactions, 2nd ed.* New York: Holt Rinehart Winston.

Kraut, R.E. 1978. Verbal and nonverbal cues in the perception of lying. *Journal of Personality and Social Psychology* 36:380–391.

Lees-Haley, P.R. 1985. Psychological malingerers. *Trial* 21:68–69.

Lieberman, D.J. 1998. *Never be Lied to Again*. New York: St. Martin's Press.

Lillie, H.I. 1923. Some practical considerations of the physiology of the upper respiratory tract. *Journal of the Iowa Medial Society* 13:403–408.

Mungas, D. 1991. In-office mental status testing: A practical guide. *Geriatrics* 46:54–66.

Paternostro-Sluga, T., M. Grim-Stieger, M. Posch et al. 2008. Reliability and validity of the Medical Research Council (MRC) Scale and a modified scale for testing muscle strength in patients with radial palsy. *Journal of Rehabilitation Medicine* 40:8:665–671.

Resnick, P.J. 1984. Detection of malingered mental illness. *Behavioral Sciences and the Law*, 2:21–38.

Sannito, T., and P.J. McGovern. 1985a. *Courtroom Psychology for Trial Lawyers*, 142. New York: John Wiley & Sons.

Sannito, T., and P.J. McGovern. 1985b. *Courtroom Psychology for Trial Lawyers*, 151. New York: John Wiley & Sons.

Sannito, T., and P.J. McGovern. 1985c. *Courtroom Psychology for Trial Lawyers*, 120. New York: John Wiley & Sons.

Sannito, T., and P.J. McGovern. 1985d. *Courtroom Psychology for Trial Lawyers*, 126. New York: John Wiley & Sons.
Sannito, T., and P.J. McGovern. 1985e. *Courtroom Psychology for Trial Lawyers*, 143. New York: John Wiley & Sons.
Sannito, T., and P.J. McGovern. 1985f. *Courtroom Psychology for Trial Lawyers*, 139. New York: John Wiley & Sons.
Sannito, T., and P.J. McGovern. 1985g. *Courtroom Psychology for Trial Lawyers*, 117–118. New York: John Wiley & Sons.
Sullivan, J.S. 1970. *Psychiatric Interview*. New York: W.W. Norton.
Walters, S.B. 1996a. *Principles of Kinesic Interview and Interrogation*, 20. Boca Raton: CRC Press.
Walters, S.B. 1996b. *Principles of Kinesic Interview and Interrogation*, 32–33. Boca Raton: CRC Press.
Walters, S.B. 1996c. *Principles of Kinesic Interview and Interrogation*, 82–84. Boca Raton: CRC Press.
Walters, S.B. 1996d. *Principles of Kinesic Interview and Interrogation*, 79. Boca Raton: CRC Press.
Walters, S.B. 1996e. *Principles of Kinesic Interview and Interrogation*, 105. Boca Raton: CRC Press.
Walters, S.B. 1996f. *Principles of Kinesic Interview and Interrogation*, 121–122. Boca Raton: CRC Press.
Walters, S.B. 1996g. *Principles of Kinesic Interview and Interrogation*, 91. Boca Raton: CRC Press.
Walters, S.B. 1996h. *Principles of Kinesic Interview and Interrogation*, 101–102. Boca Raton: CRC Press.
Walters, S.B. 1996i. *Principles of Kinesic Interview and Interrogation*, 103–111. Boca Raton: CRC Press.

3 Neurological Examination of Malingering

Jose L. Henao, MD, Khurram A. Janjua, MD, and Alan R. Hirsch, MD

CONTENTS

The role of the neurologic examination in detection of malingering can be divided into four different areas. (1) A normal examination with discordant findings, (2) abnormal examination findings which rule out malingering or suggest a co-occurring condition, (3) functional neurologic findings on examination, for instance, slowness, stop medicine sign, or slowness in the mental status examination, and (4) objective findings and presence of objective findings which can and cannot be malingered.

Like a cherry, delicately gracing the top of a hot fudge sundae, the neurologic examination completes the history—for without the diagnosis, the examination is like an isolated maraschino cherry: a condiment in search of whipped cream context. With a sufficient history, the examination fluidly conforms, like hot fudge melting the vanilla ice cream, to the presumptive diagnosis.

If one could only perform a history or examination it would fall to the wayside. Despite *f*MRI and PET scans, the neurological examination is not yet antediluvian, assigned to the relic heap of neurology with the likes of Galvanic stimulation or phrenology. The examination does have utility in perfecting the diagnosis of malingering and warrants performance. Four general constructs appear regarding the neurologic examination and the diagnosis of malingering: (1) discordance between the neurologic examination—anticipated examination findings based on history or functional disability—and actual findings. The history may include chronic bilateral lower extremity paralysis functionally preventing the malingerer from working. In such a scenario, one would not expect to observe normal muscle bulk, tone, or strength, or reflexes in both lower extremities. If due to an upper motor neuron lesion, the atrophy and weakness would be reduced, but the spasm, tonicity, and reflexes would be greater than if due to lower motor neuron lesions. Thus, flaccid atrophic paralysis suggests weakness due to lower motor neuron lesions or peripheral nerves whereas weakness with hyperreflexia as well as spasm, clonus, and atavistic reflexes suggest upper motor neuron lesions.

However, presence of one or the other form of weakness should be present with the complaints of chronic bilateral lower extremity paralysis. Thus, normal bulk, tone, and reflexes with absent strength would be inconsistent with these diseases.

The one exception would be normal reflexes due to an upper motor neuron lesion with hyperreflexia with a concurrent lower motor neuron lesion with hyporeflexia—these abnormalities superimpose upon each other in an additive manner to create apparently normal 2+ reflexes, with spasm and atonicity mixing to create normal tone. In these situations, bulk would still be reduced and over time one would predominate over the other (usually presenting with lower motor neuron signs).

Similar discrepancies can be observed in other realms of the nervous system; for instance, complaints of total blindness with examination findings of visual acuity of no light perception, but normal pupil reflexes, funduscopic examination, optokinetic nystagmus, and extraocular movements. While it remains possible that this represents Balint's syndrome or "top of the basilar" syndrome, one would vaticinate abnormalities on saccadic eye movements and pursuit of optokinetic nystagmus and upper cranial neuropathies in the "top of the basilar" syndrome.

Alternatively, complaints of being insensate with absent pinprick, light touch, vibration, proprioception, temperature, graphesthesia, stereognosis, and Romberg on sensory examination with normal reflexes, trigeminal function, and motor function, is inconsistent with anatomic distribution. A bilateral cortical parietal lobe infarction which eliminates stereognosis and graphesthesia would leave the first order thalamic sensory system intact. Bilateral thalamic infarctions or tumors would involve not only the body- but the face as well. Spinal cord dysfunction, as would be seen with tabes dorsalis, B_{12} deficiency, or combined system disease would affect the posterior columns but not the anterior pathways. Small fiber sensory neuropathy, as with leprosy or amyloidosis, tends to spare the long fibers of vibration and also affects trigeminal sensation of the face and tongue. While total sensory neuropathy can be seen with systemic dysfunction, such as Riley Day or multiple system atrophy, autonomic abnormalities and extrapyramidal disorders are almost always accompanying features.

Likewise, complaints of traumatic brain injury, executive dysfunction, abulia, and amotivational syndrome implicating abnormalities in the frontal lobe would be unusual without findings of other frontal lobe dysfunction such as elevated an olfactory threshold or reduced identification and frontal lobe release signs (including bilateral atavistic reflexes: grasp, jaw jerk, snout, Myerson's, Palmomental, Hoffman's, and Babinski). Concurrent abnormalities in the mental status examination may include preservation in attention or continuous performance testing, bradyphrenia, and lack of effort with reduction in number on semantic fluency or animal fluency tests, as well as evidence of pseudobulbar affect with elevation on the Center for Neurologic Studies Lability Scale. Furthermore, the go-no-go test may also demonstrate errors suggesting lack of attention.

As a general rule, absence of associated findings as opposed to presence of unexpected findings is seen in those with malingering. However, exceptions to the rule revolve around those with an underlying neurologic condition. Malingering is easier to detect if the findings are unrelated to the complaints; for instance, complaints of generalized sensory loss with preexisting epilepsy (while not on medications which induce polyneuropathy).

What remains the most challenging in detecting malingering is malingering exaggeration of symptoms with an actual underlying illness present. The physical examination findings are frequently consistent with the primary disease and when the complaints involve a subjective perspective it becomes nearly impossible to rule in malingering; for instance, causalgic pain and reflex sympathetic dystrophy or phantom limb phenomena associated with amputation. Assessment to validate exaggeration of such complaints requires ancillary testing along with follow-up with analysis of behavioral inconsistencies—for instance, are the complaints of 10/10 pain actually functionally disabling to the patient or is he or she able to perform all the activities of daily life without difficulty? If yes, is he or she still unable to attempt the simplest work conditions?

Such a dilemma is particularly relevant in those patients with headache or chronic pain, where objective evidence is lacking, seeking progressively greater doses of narcotics to help control their intractable pain. In such instances, pain standardized assessment devices such as the Hendler, Forest, and COWS, are particularly enlightening.

An abnormal neurologic examination may aid not only in the diagnosis of malingering but also in ruling it out with findings suggestive of unsuspected neurologic disease. For instance, an individual whose history suggests malingering of pain and weakness, to gain unemployment compensation or reward in litigation, may actively display upper motor neuron or lower motor neuron findings with weakness and hypo or hyperreflexia, respectively; evidence of true underlying neurologic illness.

3.1 FUNCTIONAL NEUROLOGIC FINDINGS ON EXAMINATION

There is a gaggle of neurologic signs which point to nonorganic origin of the patient's condition. This does not necessarily suggest malingering. A positive sign may reflect lack of motivation or understanding, pain, fatigue, depression (with lack of motivation or drive), or pain with guarding which prevent full effort on movement. Reviewing these signs, in a system-wide fashion, may be the best way to delve into their potential utility in the diagnosis and management of malingering.

3.1.1 Physical Examination

Every patient has a history which portrays a picture to the clinician, giving a starting point for the physical examination. A full neurological examination starts when the patient walks into the clinic or hospital setting—noticing the gait and how they hold their posture while sitting is critical in identifying different types of organic versus nonorganic pathologies. The general appearance gives many details for any astute clinician to notice. If patients have the ability to fully dress themselves without help, then some of the neurological examination has been tested, based on the sequence it takes to self-dress. Coordination and executive functions (planning, attention, and abstract reasoning) are used the most during dressing. Being able to put shoes on after putting on their pants or shorts shows that the patient can understand the order of operations (abstract thinking) compared to a patient with true dementia who may be wearing different shoes or have missing socks. In the case of a true parkinsonism patient with bradykinesia featuring slow tremulous fine motor movements, one usually notices the absence of ability to tie shoes or fasten fine buttons on shirt and shorts. If a patient has driven to the clinic or hospital then the patient must be alert and oriented to time, perception, and place by showing he or she has the capacity to follow road rules and process them in a proper sequence to arrive at the wanted destination at the expected time and date. This is in contrast to organic dementia that leads to disorientation with loss of place (Scott and Barrett, 2007) and directional difficulties.

Observation of patients that present with pain is one of the most powerful methods used to distinguish organic as opposed to nonorganic pathologies; low back pain complaints baffle physicians every day. Focusing on how patients sit on a chair allows the experienced physician to determine which side of the lower back is actually in pain (Dankaerts, O'Sullivan, Burnett, and Straker, 2006). Patients with abnormal postures should lead the physician to ask about occupation or history of trauma to see if any attempts at secondary gain might be occurring. If the patient has the ability to stand and sit on a chair without assistance, the physician can then notice balance and stability of the lower back. Hesitation to follow a command, which wouldn't lead to any certain pain, like standing from a sitting a position with exaggerated pain can be a sign of malingering in patients. This is because in the true pathology of the disease standing from a sitting position hardly changes the space of the lumbar spine, which would only lead to minor, if any, discomfort. Gathering a vast history from a patient that is vague about his or her symptoms, but who prefers to focus on nonspecific lower back pain should give some insight of secondary gain.

When confronted with patients who might be looking for secondary gain, the examiner may notice that they may seem somewhat anxious during the initial history taking and that they are actively leading the physician to diagnoses of injury or pain which may be vague and not clearly described. Noticing their speech throughout the history can give subtle clues to notice any sympathy or empathy. Some patients who do not have empathy tend to be looking for secondary gain. Mood is a common physical characteristic that is generally missed during the overall general examination. Mood indicates the patient's feelings at the time of the visit. Some patients may have a flat affect and lead the physician to focus on just one issue instead of the overall picture. Patients with an agitated mood will speak of vague symptoms, which might not follow the history. This part of the physical examination involves active listening to first rule out organic pathologies (Saberi et al., 2013). Facial expression, when being asked about history of pain, can be subtle, and some clinicians in their inchoate stages of training would miss these. Hirsch (1987) describes the "Stop Medicine Sign," where patients that are in pain, state, "... I stopped taking my medicine so I can show you how I look when I'm off my medication." Fearful that otherwise they will appear to be healthy such a presentation should warrant greater investigation because patients in true pain would actively avoid taking themselves off medication. Patients attempting to attain secondary gains, like pain medication, would attempt to fake a high amount of pain. Instead of worrying about the underlying condition they will exhibit the exaggerated pain sign (Fishbain, Cutler, H. Rosomoff, and R. Rosomoff, 1999). This sign focuses on patients worrying more about the pain than the other diagnoses which might cause the pain. There are limited studies on different facial grimaces and the understanding of malingering. Different types of facial expression may give a clue that there is the incentive of secondary gain.

Be wary of the patient wearing dark or rose-colored glasses. The presence of such spectacles may indicate photophobia in a migraineur or light-induced triggers in those with unstable epilepsy; however, the presence of the "rose-colored glasses sign," as explained by Joel Saper, MD, director of the Michigan Headache Institute, as an indication of Axis-II-DSMV Cluster B diagnosis, usually borderline personality disorders, with underlying anger. Although not being treated for malingering, this group of patients who initially idealize and then devalue those they meet are particularly difficult to manage, often parting ways with the physician when bitter, angry, or hostile.

3.1.2 Mental Status Examination

Cognitive impairment is associated with a plethora of etiologies. One common cause of cognitive impairment is traumatic brain injury (TBI), precipitating litigations from minor TBI at the work place. A test which helps separate psychogenic fugue states from true organic disorders involves orientation. Under normal conditions, oriented x3—person, place, and time—exists. In true organic disease, orientation to time is lost first, followed by loss of place, and last loss of person. In psychogenic states of fugue or amnesia, loss will occur in reverse order—loss of knowledge of whom they are, followed by disorientation of place with preservation of orientation to time. So, for instance Gilligan of *Gilligan's Island*, the television show of the 1960's portrays the protagonist who is hit in the head with a coconut falling from a tree. He then loses knowledge of who he is and what he is doing on the island, while still preserving understanding of where he is. This episode ends with another coconut falling onto his head, which restores his orientation to normal rather than exacerbating his traumatic brain injury and worsening his symptoms—not a recommended treatment approach. In real life patients are occasionally found having wandered off who are now living a different life with an entirely new name and family in a new location. While not necessarily malingering, such behavior suggests a nonorganic basis for their behavior.

Measuring memory is a grueling task, but being able to measure effort during a simple examination can help point toward malingering or lack of effort. One common erroneous belief about brain injury, prevalent in laypersons, is that there are resulting memory sequelae (Aubrey, Dobbs, and Rule, 1989) and that testing the memory would be the best approach to detect malingering during the mental status examination. Exaggeration of cognitive impairment in patients will produce lower than normal tests results in the malingerer compared to patients with true cognitive impairment. Inconsistent tests can point toward malingering. If a patient performs well on memory tests but poorly on tests of attention and concentration, it may be an indication of malingering (Hartlage, 1998).

The Rey 15 Item Test is a visual recall task in which 15 items are presented for ten seconds in a three by five array. Once the items are removed, patients are asked to recall and reproduce the items immediately. Patients with TBI will perform either normally or below normal, but will not score below nine items recalled. Less than this points to a lack of effort since patients with true cognitive impairment and severe TBI have the ability to score, above nine on average, (Bryant, Duff, Fisher, and McCaffrey, 2004). Hence, poor performance suggests malingering when less than nine items are reproduced correctly (Spreen and Strauss, 1998).

The Amsterdam Short-Term Memory Test (ASTM) also takes advantage of the fact that patients with true brain injury perform well on simple recognition tests (Schagen, Schmand, deSterke, and Lindebloom, 1997). This exam consists of 30 items. In each item, the patient is presented with five printed words from the same semantic category (cat, dog, parrot, guinea pigs, and rabbit). They are asked to read them out loud, to remember them, and are then given a simple addition or subtraction task to solve mentally. Finally, they are given five more words from the same semantic category and asked to identify the three words that were in the original five words. The maximum score for this examination is 90 (30 items with three words correct). Patients with a score below 86 are considered to be feigning. Contrary to belief this test does not require effortful retrieval from memory, but rather, recognition. As a result, patients with true moderate head injury perform well on this test, having on average scores of 87–90. This examination can recognize up to 90% of naïve malingerers, but is affected by coaching. Patients that are coached can reduce the sensitivity of this examination to 75% (Jelicic, Merckelbach, Candel, and Geraerts, 2007).

Reliable Digit Span is an examination of attention span and immediate recall with little effort of memory. Digit span forward is normal at seven; in everyday life the ability to transiently recall seven digits is a common everyday functional requirement as telephone numbers have seven digits. Normal patients should have the ability to immediately recall seven digits forwards and five digits backwards. During the digit span test, the examiner speaks out loud seven random nonconsecutive digits and asks the patient to repeat the digits in the same order forwards. If they do not repeat the seven digits forward correctly, then the examiner drops down to six digits forward and so on until they repeat the digits correctly. Once forward digit testing is performed backward testing should begin, and instead of starting with five numbers, the clinician starts with two. The examiner asks the patient to repeat the digits backwards and, if correct, the clinician presents three numbers and again asks the patient to repeat the sequence backwards. This process is repeated until the patient reaches the maximum of five digits backwards or until they cannot repeat a certain number of digits lower than five. Once the Digit Span test is finished and recorded, both the number of digits forwards and backwards is totaled. For example, seven digits forwards and five digits backwards equals 12. This is the Reliable Digit Span (RDS). It has been reported that for anyone with a Reliable Digit Span score of less than seven the diagnosis of malingering should be considered (Greve et al., 2007). In studies, patients with severe TBI and dementia demonstrated RDS averages of greater than seven. Meaning that even with a major cognitive deficit patients have the ability to immediately recall at least four digits forwards and three digits backwards. In patients with cerebrovascular accidents and true dementia it may be worthwhile to reduce the cutoff from less than seven to less than six to provide greater sensitivity and specificity. This is a performance examination, so coaching can reduce the sensitivity of this simple test.

The structured inventory of the malingered symptomology (SIMS) is a personal questionnaire which is given to patients before the physical exam. This self-admitting questionnaire provides 75 yes or no items which are bizarre and atypical symptoms and complaints. Total scores range from zero to 75 positive responses. The cutoff of 14 is regarded to be indicative of malingering since these self-endorsement complaints are not typical of normal complaints of cognitive dysfunction. An example of some of the bizarre symptoms are, "I cannot remember whether or not that I have been married," or "I forget my name." Atypical item examples would be, "When I can't remember something, hints do not help" (Smith and Burger, 1997). Sensitivity of this examination among naïve malingers is 90% and even with coaching this simple questionnaire can still detect up to 90% of malingering patients (Jelicic, Merckelbach, Candel, and Geraerts, 2007).

Memory loss can be a by-product of TBI and organic disorders; however, studies suggest that immediate recognition and recall are the same in the normal population as in those who suffer from TBI and organic disease. The common fallacy is that patients with TBI perform terribly at these examinations, but studies show the contrary—that patients would perform in the normal range during examination. Coaching from attorneys is a true problem in the legal world, allowing for litigation to proceed to the courtroom. Additional cognitive testing may also be performed to help rule out a malingering diagnosis (Youngjohn, 1995).

3.1.3 Cranial Nerve Examination

3.1.3.1 Olfactory CN I

See Chapter 11.

3.1.3.2 Optic Nerve (CN II)

Malingerers usually complain of defective vision, which may be divided into three classes: (1) total blindness in one eye, (2) partial blindness in one eye, and (3) total or partial blindness in both eyes (Singhal, 1972). During the examination, the physician should note any hesitation to be examined or argumentativeness, which can point to patients malingering about their vision loss. Visual loss is one of the toughest complaints to interpret in nonspecialized clinics or hospitals which do not have access to computer simulations for visual acuity. Pupillary constriction is based on the cranial nerve II and cranial nerve III being intact and functional. It is possible for patients to have an intact cranial nerve II and cranial nerve III and still have cortical blindness. Pupillary diameter is not under somatic control, but rather under sympathetic and parasympathetic control. Therefore, some patients may use medications that can cause either mydriasis or miosis. The important feature of this is that even with medication the pupils will still accommodate with light, so one would be able to differentiate between organic or inorganic disease. With cranial nerve III palsy, the pupil is enlarged and deviated inferiorly and temporally—without being able to react to light.

The prism base test (Singhal, 1972) can also be used to help detect malingering if the patient states that they are blind in one eye. This can be tested by placing a prism in front of the affected eye and observing how the patient performs ambulating up and down stairs. A patient with true organic disease will not have any issue going up and down the stairs, but patients malingering will notice difficulty going up the stairs. This is because the prism causes diplopia. Thus, malingering patients will stumble up and down the stairs while holding on to the handrails. Informing the patient that the prism will help them navigate the stairs after the initial trial of ascending and descending the stairs without the prism can help detect malingering. Comparing the data gathered with and without the prism may help increase specificity and sensitivity of this test (Singhal, 1972).

One specific reflex that physicians should focus on when evaluating a patient with possible malingering is the menace reflex (Singhal, 1972). In this test, patients naturally blink when faced with a specific threat to the eye. Patients who have true organic vision loss would not be able to see the threat and there would be no blinking in the affected eye. Even malingering patients who have trained themselves to stop blinking when tested by a physician will still have an increased heart rate. Thus, the use of a pulse oximeter to distinguish true organic disease from nonorganic disease may result in higher sensitivity and specificity. To test this reflex, the patient should be in a comfortable position while the physician is out of sight, and object should suddenly be waved in front of the patient's eyes to provoke a reflex. When testing false visual field defects in malingering patients, one needs to focus on using the menace reflex from different angles. One specific aspect is to distract the patient from the test being conducted. This is because of the patient's awareness of the hand in the affected visual field can lead to the patient anticipating movements and reducing the reflexes' sensitivity.

Visual fields are normally cone shaped, providing clinicians with the understanding that the field expands as the distance from the patient increases. In true disease, the correct response would be an increase in the visual field as the physician moves objects further away from the patient. Thus, the unenlightened malingerer complains of visual field defect with lack of such dispersion known as tubular vision or tunnel vision. Myopia and hypermyopia distort the object but do not affect the visual field based on distance. Patients do not understand the concepts of visual fields unless they have researched them and have become knowledgeable in the realm of visual pathways. Patients who complain of visual field defects and do not trip or run into walls when being examined should suggest to the examiner another type of etiology instead of true visual field defects. Patients with visual field complaints should be tested for a range of distances (e.g., testing with an object right next to the patient and then four to five feet away from them). True organic disease would present a wider visual field when the clinician moves away. In functional visual field loss the patient would not distinguish between distances and have the same visual field loss close and afar (Dooley and Gordon, 2011).

3.1.3.3 Oculomotor (CN III), Trochlear Nerve (CN IV), Abducens Nerve (CN VI)

The main focus of CN III, CN IV, and CN VI assessments are extraocular movements. For patients who complain of ocular motility disorders clinicians should be aware of those pretending to have ptosis. This can be revealed with the Depressed Eyebrows Sign (Incesu and Sobaci, 2011) (Figure 3.1). The nerve that supplies the orbicularis oculi is the facial nerve (CN VII). In addition, observing the patient while performing the physical examination on different parts of the body can reveal the oscillating ptosis characteristic of inorganic illness (in organic illness it does not change with position or observations). Organic illnesses, like myasthenia

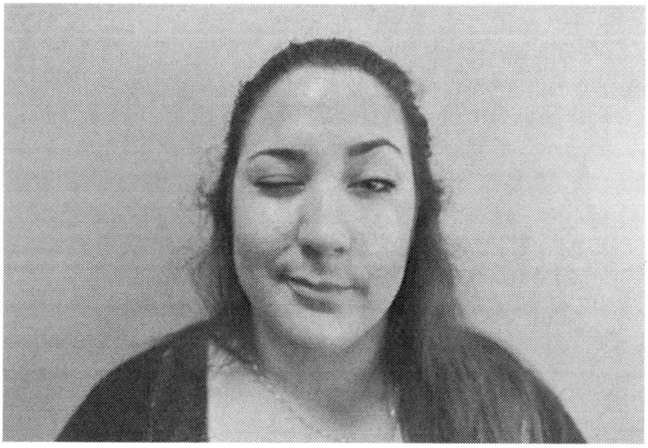

FIGURE 3.1 Patient demonstrating closed levator palpebrae, as well as an activated orbicularis oculi (Depressed Eyebrow Sign). Pseudoptosis patients also experience photophobia with eye closure. True ptosis does not incorporate the orbicularis oculi.

gravis and oculomotor nerve palsy ptosis, may be prominent and not encompass the eyebrow or other facial muscles, which are innervated by the facial nerve. One caveat is that with fatigue ptosis will worsen thus creating fatigue with blinking of the affected eye which helps to differentiate between true and false ptosis.

Another technique to unmask malingering is the cover–uncover test for misalignment or strabismus. In true organic disease there would be a positive deviation during the examination. That is in contrast to an inorganic disorder where the examination is normal. With a history of complaints of gaze-dependent diplopia. In inorganic illness, the patient would exaggerate the issue without problems with vertigo. Patients that are malingering can manipulate the test by knowing what the physician is looking for during the examination. The greenhorn doctor would accept that the patient has strabismus. But, in real organic illness, misalignment would affect only one eye and not change the movement of both eyes during the cover–uncover test. In patients showing the same type of deviation in both eyes, the physician should be aware of possible malingering (Alder, 1962). Because of true dipoplia during ambulation, the patient will frequently stumble. Binocular misalignment can lead to vertigo and problems when ascending and descending stairs. A normal head tilt can be observed in patients with true binocular misalignment to compensate for the angle of the tropia.

Saccade testing within neurology tends to be specific for early manifestations of neurological disease. Focusing on different types of nystagmus allows the physician to correlate different pathologies throughout diverse levels of the cortex, cerebellum, and basal ganglia. The optokinetic nystagmus strip may elucidate the patients' true extraocular movements—despite attempts of suppression, as well as demonstrate that the visual fields are intact. The test shows that in true organic disease patients have small erratic searching with slow eye movements in the direction of the tape, and fast movements in the opposite direction. Malingering patients can easily jump to the presented fixation point in one directional large saccade pointing towards inorganic signs (Zinkernagel, Pellanda, Kunz, and Mojon, 2009). Sensitivity of this test is 87% and specificity is 100%. Combined with other positive tests for malingered visual complaints, the accuracy of a diagnosis of malingered increases. However, the validity of the above test is reduced in children. When subjected to optokinetic nystagmus testing, children without nystagmus may demonstrate inattention or the purposeful avoidance of near fixation giving the clinician the wrong perception that the patient is not fully trying during the test (Dooley and Gordon, 2011). This might cause the physicians to render a false positive diagnosis of malingering.

3.1.3.4 Trigeminal Nerve (CN V)

There are three distinct parts of CN V—ophthalmic (V1), maxillary (V2), mandibular (V3), and bilaterally, which cross the midline in a heterogeneous fashion. Thus, patients do not complain of midline splitting in true disease with the exception of thalamic strokes which affect the ventroposterior medial nucleus of the contralateral thalamus. Thalamic strokes would present with sensory midline splitting as well as residual muscle weakness, leading to other physical examination findings consistent with this condition. Patients who specifically state that only one part of their face feels a pinprick while demarcating a line down the middle (midline splitting) should arouse a clinician's suspicion of nonorganic disease. Requiring patients to undergo forced "yes or no" choice testing of sensory perception can further delineate underlying malingering. Initial testing should begin with patients having their eyes open followed by retesting with their eyes closed. With their eyes closed, the physician touches different areas of the face with a standard thread requesting patients to say "yes or no" if they feel the touch. It should make the physician suspicious if the patient states "no" to areas that are affected after touching them without telling them where the needle thread was placed. Touch followed by a "no" in an area of report of loss implies the patient felt touch in order to respond "no." Increasing the speed of placement of the thread will force the patient to say "yes" or "no" and may yield different results than the initial evaluation during which the patients had their eyes open. Patients with true disease would not have any problems distinguishing sensory loss with eyes open or closed, but they would not state "no" when the affected side is touched since they are not actually sensing stimuli in that area (Daum, Hubschmid, and Aybek, 2014). The difference between evaluations with eyes open or closed points towards psychological disturbance or malingering as an etiology of the facial sensory loss. Children with functional facial sensory loss will also present the same scenario and would also report "no" for stimuli within the "affected" area (Dooley and Gordon, 2011).

3.1.3.5 Facial Nerve (CN VII)

Facial expression is innervated by the facial nerve (CN VII). CN VII innervates muscles of facial expression and branches a nerve to the stapedius muscle for audition. Functional facial paralysis tends to occur with tonic muscular contraction resembling dystonia. In true acute paralysis of CN VII the muscle will first be flaccid, whereas in false paralysis the muscle contracts. Contraction of the muscle can point to overactive nerve signals but not to paralysis. Patients may demonstrate the isolated lower lip dystonia, where lower lip pulling downward is prevalent (Figure 3.2a), but which normalizes with volitional smile suggesting malingering (Figure 3.2b). Involvement of the lower face, seen in upper motor neuron dysfunction, also appears to be a characteristic of psychogenic facial movement disorder (Fabbrini, Defazio, Colosimo, Thompson, and Berardeli, 2009). The "Smirk Sign," as Tarsy coins it, is exhibited by the patient with lower lip deviating downward, at the angle of the mouth combined with ipsilateral platysma co-contraction (Tarsy, Dengenhardt, and Zadiloff, 2006). This sign, when present, suggests malingering. In true hemifacial spasm (HFS) there is the "Babinski sign" which is characterized by ipsilateral eyebrow rising during eye closure due to simultaneous contraction of the orbicularis oculi and the internal part of the frontalis (Babinski, 1900). This sign has a 100% specificity to true HFS. This sign is not exhibited in psychogenic HFS. Asymmetric spasm of the orbicularis oculi has the eyebrow rising contralateral to the closing eye, as seen in nonorganic illness (Fasano et al., 2012). Another hallmark of true HFS is sleep spasm (seen in 80% of patients), which wakes the patient up from sleep. False HFS patients do not complain of sleep spasms, which indicates malingering. Conditions such as spontaneous improvement during sleep, fixed or paroxysmal unilateral contraction, reduction or abolition of facial spasm with distraction, and a coinciding normal neurological examination should help delineate malingering.

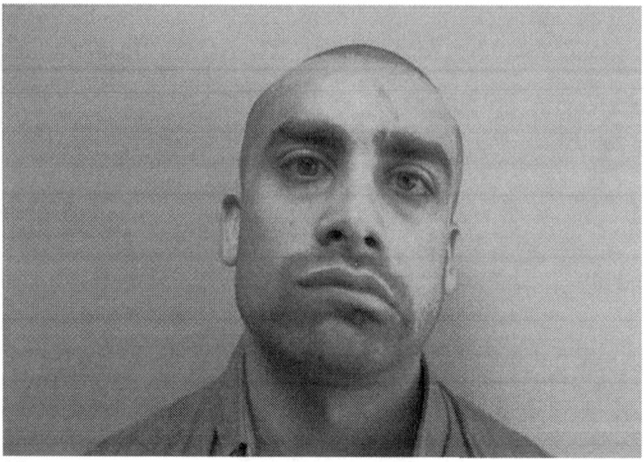

(a)

(b)

FIGURE 3.2 (a) Patient demonstrating a deviated contracted lip that is pulling downward in weakness or a dystonic state. Smirk Sign: The lip pulling with the co-contraction of the ipsilateral platysma. (b) Patient demonstrating volitional smiling. All muscles are intact, loss of lip pulling without deviation.

In Bell's palsy, a symptom is hyperacusis because the nerve innervates the stapedius muscle. This muscle tenses to help prevent the stapes movement in the middle ear, reducing noise. If there is true facial nerve paralysis, a patient will experience sensitivity to loud noise. Patients with acute facial paralysis without hearing sensitivity should raise suspicions of malingering.

3.1.3.6 Vestibular-Cochlear Nerve (CN VIII)

Cranial nerve VIII focuses on hearing components. It has two divisions—the cochlear and the vestibular component. The cochlear works as the initial nerve for sound conduction, while the vestibular component works for balance (Scadding and Losseff, 2011). The question becomes how to differentiate between organic hearing losses and functional hearing losses at the bedside? Without the audiogram, there is no true test to detect hearing loss with accurate precision, but there are certain quick examination techniques that will help distinguish true hearing loss from functional hearing loss.

In the initial assessment of hearing loss, patients should be unobtrusively observed without their knowledge. For instance, in the waiting room a doctor can increase the television intensity and observe the patient's reaction. Malingering patients will still have the ability to detect a loud noise causing twitching of the pinna and contraction of the palpebral muscle during exposure. In true hearing loss, a patient's voice intensity increases. Thus, if patients complaining of hearing loss have a normal voice intensity then malingering should be suspected. A simple lip-reading test can help to detect patients that are feigning. Monosyllabic, homophonous words should be presented with a gradual reduction in intensity level until only visual stimuli are received. Homophonous words look alike (like mud, but, bun) but sound different and cannot be perceived correctly only by lip-reading—they require actual hearing. Correct responses depend upon audition. Patients who are feigning deafness will continue to respond correctly even at lower volumes. This is in contrast to organic illness in which patients reach a point where they cannot hear the words, and pronounce homophonous words in the same way, or are not able to comprehend the words spoken (Falconer, 1966).

Patients are usually unaware of the physiology of conduction versus sensorial hearing loss, making it possible to exploit this when testing for organic versus nonorganic hearing loss. Erhardt's test helps with detection of unilateral hearing loss (McDermott and Feldman, 2007). It is based on the phenomenon that occlusion of an ear at the tragus will only cause an attenuation of 30 dB. However, normal speech is 70 dB. In this case, occlusion would drop it to 40 dB, clearly in the range of hearing. Patients are asked to close their eyes—while being told their good ear is being occluded—and words are spoken into the affected ear. If there is failure to repeat the words, or the patient states that they "cannot hear the spoken words" then the diagnosis of malingering should be entertained. In unilateral hearing loss, deafness is not bilateral. The unaffected ear should be able to conduct the words and allow the patient with true organic disease to repeat them.

Lombard's test is based on the fact that people will raise their voice when speaking in a noisy environment. This test consists of asking the patient to read a book out loud while the examiner speaks into the ear in which the patient complains of a hearing loss to see if the patient raises their voice or not. If they do, then they perceive the physician's voice, which is suggestive of the lack of true hearing loss. Also, another positive indication in this test is if the patient stops reading out loud because of the increased noise is distracting him or her from reading. If there is no change in voice intensity and the patient consistently keeps reading, then organic hearing loss is possible. The Doerfler–Stewart test uses music instead of random noise or voice as in the Lombard test. To demonstrate, with false hearing loss, the patient will raise their voice in the presence of a noisy environment (McDermott and Feldman, 2007).

The Hummel double conversation test focuses on the fact that patients have difficulty multitasking. This is shown when trying to talk to people, or hearing different stimuli, while simultaneously trying to understand them. This is performed by asking the patient two different questions simultaneously in both ears to see if the patient can record one question or is confused. Patients with true organic disease will have the ability to hear the question in the unaffected ear and not be confused at all. Patients with normal hearing would be confused since they do not have the ability to concentrate on one ear only when being asked simultaneously another question in the opposite ear. Two-tube test of Teuber is a modification of the Hummel double conversation test. Instead of talking into the patient's ears, two examiners use tubes attached to the ears to ask two questions simultaneously, each to a different ear. In true organic disease only one question will be heard and responded to. In malingering unilateral hearing loss, confusion and lack of ability to respond will be observed (Thiagarajan and Arjunan, 2012).

The swinging story test focuses on patients that complain about unilateral hearing deafness. In this test patients are read a story by two examiners positioned at each ear. The examiners then alternately read parts of the story, thus the story must be heard by both ears to be fully understood. With true organic disease patients would not be able to fill in the gaps caused by the affected ear. Patients who are malingering would be able to repeat the story with all the gaps filled in, revealing their ability to hear from the affected ear (Thiagarajan and Arjunan, 2012).

Tuning fork tests, especially Rhine's and Weber's, can be utilized to detect conductive and sensorial hearing loss. Normal individuals will exhibit air conduction greater than bone conduction, known as Ingrassia's Phenomenon. Normal patients, during the Weber's test will not lateralize to any area during bone conduction. Instead, it will remain midline since bone conduction transmits through the inner skull bilaterally. A 512 Hz tuning fork is usually best for testing. Unilateral malingering tends to be easier to identify compared to bilateral malingering hearing loss, since the tuning fork can still be detected through conduction throughout the whole skull base.

The Judd–Persaud test focuses on the principle that bone conduction can be felt throughout the whole skull base. To perform this examination the examiner places a vibrating tuning fork on the unaffected mastoid and queries if the patient can hear it. If they acknowledge that they can hear it then the same tuning fork is placed on the mastoid of the affected side and the patient is asked again. Patients with true disease will be able to hear the conduction through the bone across the skull with the opposite unaffected ear. Patients feigning hearing loss will state that they hear the sound when the tuning fork is placed in the unaffected ear but not when placed near the affected ear. This will not be observed in true unilateral deafness (Judd and Persaud, 2016). If the patient truly has complete unilateral hearing loss, the unaffected cochlea would receive the sound efficiently when the tuning fork is placed on the contralateral (affected ear) mastoid bone. In patients with nonorganic disease, the affected cochlea will receive the sound and give the patient the ability to say "I cannot hear the sound." Examination of this technique was performed on 28 cases and found no inaccuracies in the diagnostic pathway compared to other standard tests (Judd and Persaud, 2016). These cases were also examined using a computerized audiometric Stenger test and the same results were obtained.

The Teal test is another bedside technique which uses physician knowledge to confuse malingering patients about complaints of conductive hearing loss. This test is employed for patients who state they can only hear bone conduction. First, the examiner begins by placing the vibrating tuning fork on the affected ear's mastoid bone. The patient would acknowledge they can hear the noise. Then the patient is either blindfolded or asked to close his or her eyes while repeating the examination. In the second part of the examination two tuning forks are used, but only one vibrates. The nonvibrating tuning fork is placed on the mastoid bone of the affected ear while the other is placed over the external auditory canal. True conductive hearing loss patients would accept the fact that they are not able to hear the noise, since the vibrating fork is not on the bone and only projects through air conduction. Feigning patients will state that they can hear the noise, thus revealing their ability to perceive air conduction since the nonvibrating tuning fork is placed on the affected mastoid (Sethi, Pearson, and Bajaj, 2017).

The Chimani–Moos test applies the same concepts as Weber's tuning fork test. When the tuning fork is placed on the vertex of the head the patient has the ability to hear the noise (conduction) in the good ear, which causes lateralization. Normal patients would be able to hear conduction even if the clinician's fingers occludes both ears. So, in the second part of the examination the good ear is occluded. The examination is repeated and the patient is asked where they hear the noise. The malingering patients will state they cannot hear the noise since their good ear is occluded; however, the occlusion effect causes patients with an occluded ear to hear bone conduction with increased intensity due to the reduction of ambient noise. So, this effect can provide clues about patients malingering hearing loss (Sethi, Pearson, and Bajaj, 2017).

3.1.3.7 Spinal Accessory Nerve (CN XI)

This nerve innervates the sternocleidomastoid (SCM) muscle bilaterally and the upper portion of the trapezius muscle during head rotation and shoulder shrugs. Patients complaining they have problems rotating their head, should have their sternocleidomastoid trapezius muscles examined. There are certain diseases which can lead to dystonia. For instance, torticollis is associated with neuroleptics. Sternocleidomastoid testing focuses on the fact that CN XI bilaterally innervates the SCM, so the lesion has to affect both nuclei to cause paralysis of the SCM. When testing, the patient should be asked to resist against the examiner's hand when rotating their head to that side. A positive sign is when the patient states "There is weakness of rotation to the ipsilateral side" (Diukova, 1999). If a patient has weakness to one side of the SCM, then he should also present trapezius weakness as in the case of a single nuclei lesion to CN XI. In true disease, patients display difficulty turning their head to the contralateral side. In false disease, patients display difficulty to the ipsilateral side, as the SCM works to rotate the head contralaterally.

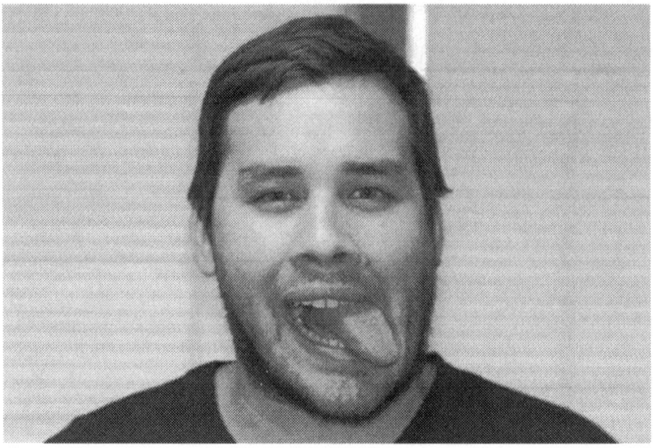

FIGURE 3.3 Patient demonstrating excessive deviation of the tongue, compared to normal hypoglossal dysfunction with minor deviation.

3.1.3.8 Hypoglossal Nerve (CN XII)

CN XII innervates the tongue muscles, allowing for mastication and speech throughout normal activities. CN XII lesions to CN XII would lead to deviation of the tongue towards the lesion with fasciculation. Patients with chronic lesions would have prominent muscle atrophy of the tongue with minor deviation compared to patients that have functional paresis of the tongue. Babinski noticed that patients with functional paresis of the tongue had strong deviations towards or away from the lesion (Okun and Koehler, 2004). A patient's tongue will protrude in an excessively deviated manner, emphasizing unilateral weakness (Figure 3.3). The physician should be aware of the timing of this paresis. In acute paresis of the tongue the patient should present some fasciculation too. The tongue should not change in terms of weakness when being observed compared to when not being observed and lingual dysarthria will be variably present. In 1986, wrong way deviation was documented with inability to cross the midline. This can be seen in anterior medullary lesions, but the presentations should be with fasciculation corresponding to body weakness. This type of deviation should point towards an anterior medullary lesion, but in its absence it can also point to malingering (Keane, 1986). With upper motor neuron lesions during strokes, especially in the brain stem, other physical weaknesses should be observed. Patients that do not have the physical signs of brain stem lesion, typical of a stroke, and only present signs of tongue deviation which doesn't cross the midline, should raise suspicions of malingering. Speech is another function of the tongue and so it is imperative for the examiner to notice any changes in speech, especially lingual dysarthria.

3.1.3.9 Motor Examination

Historically, the motor examination has been the most studied out of all the neurological examinations for signs of feigning or malingering. This is to determine whether patients are trying to find compensation after motor vehicle accidents or TBIs. When examining the motor system physicians will concurrently check the strength, bulk, and tone of the muscle while checking the actions of the nerves that are innervating specific muscle strands. Clinically, every muscle should be examined with precision, but in the clinic or hospital there are certain muscle groups that are examined the most. Starting systematically, the list below indicates muscles that can be examined as a quick screen while looking at the nerves that innervate them.

- Sternocleidomastoid, platysma, strap muscles
- Trapezius, levator scapulae
- Deltoid
- Biceps, brachialis
- Triceps
- Pectoralis major, subscapularis
- Infraspinatus, teres minor
- Extensor carpi radialis, extensor carpi ulnaris
- Intrinsic of the hand
- Abductor pollicis brevis
- Iliopsosa
- Gluteus medius
- Adductor group
- Gluteus maximus
- Quadriceps femoris
- Gastrocnemius, soleus
- Anterior tibialis

Patients with a history of prolonged muscle weakness may exhibit atrophy of the weakened area. Some pathological illnesses demonstrate specific types of motor findings such as frontal lobe lesions, which produce paratonia (Gegenhalten). Gegenhalten is described as the resistance to movement in all directions and is speed-dependent on passive movement. If the examiner increases speed on passive movement the patient's resistance increases. When a patient's focus is removed from the physician's movement the resistance will decrease.

3.1.3.10 Sternocleidomastoid, Platysma, and Strap Muscles

The facial nucleus and upper cervical nerves innervate platysma and strap muscles, so patients who complain of right- or left-sided neck weakness after a traumatic event at work should have these nerves examined. Platysma is defined by asymmetry of contraction with wide opening of the mouth when flexing the chin towards the chest against the examiner's pressure (Daum, Hubschmid, and Aybek, 2014) (Figure 3.4). This sign is critically important for the astute physician since there has been no documentation of a patient with this disease who did not demonstrate this sign, so this simple bedside test should provide a fundamental understanding of the patient's history. This simple maneuver should be incorporated in all physical examinations to help provide important information about the patient's credibility.

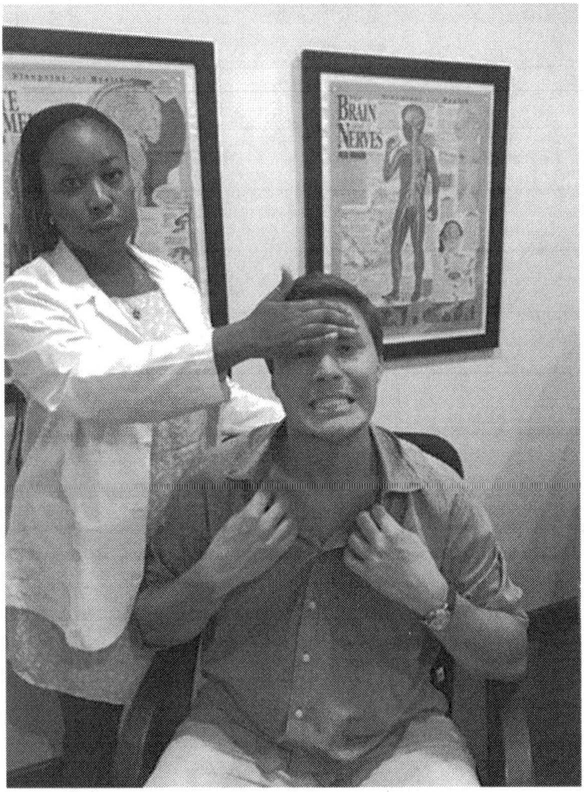

FIGURE 3.4 While the patient opens their mouth wide, an examiner places force on the forehead, allowing for the contraction of the platysma muscles (Platysma Sign). A negative sign is exhibited when both platysmas are activated equally. A loss of platysma contraction is seen in high cervical spinal cord lesions.

3.1.3.11 Deltoids/Trapezius

When patients are in a coma, or even complaining of arm weakness, there are certain examinations that can test the patient's candor. The drop arm test is a classic test which allows the physician to see if the patient has true organic paralysis compared to functional paralysis. In this test, the arm is positioned above the face or head of the patient, and then dropped by the examiner to see if the patient consciously moves the arm away from the face or head. This demonstrates that the patient has the strength and is aware that there is a threat coming towards the head or face. Physicians can also apply this to the deltoid. In patients with true disease the deltoid is paralyzed and does not have the ability to withstand abduction, which leads to the arm landing on the patient's face or head. Patients with true paralysis would not have the ability to move their arm or contract any of the muscles to help move the arm away from its natural falling path. This examination maneuver should be performed with patients that have been pretested and are suspected of malingering since this can potentially be harmful to patients with true paralysis and facial pathology. Patients can also be tested by abducting the arm as high as it can go and letting it drop to see if the arm drops straight down to the body or if the patient attempts to control its speed of drop. This maneuver is not sensitive, but when it is positive there should be high suspicion of malingering. The drop arm test can be applied to different parts of the body. For example, a drop leg test, in which the patient's leg is raised above the other leg and released to see it drops straight down or if it is moved away by contracting apparently falsely paralyzed muscles.

3.1.3.12 Intrinsics of the Hand

A patient may present arm weakness by holding up the weak arm with the nonaffected arm. During the examination, the doctor should focus on the intricate anatomy of the arm that presents in a plethora of presentations in organic diseases. It is imperative that both hands be examined to have a comparison while giving the physician and the patient the certainty that the examination is thorough. Hand paralysis can originate from diverse pathologies which span the neuromuscular system. One specific examination, which is helpful, is the abductor finger sign (Tinazzi et al., 2008). When exhibiting this reflex, the patient is told to close his or her eyes and abduct their unaffected hand with maximal effort, against resistance by the examiner for over two minutes (Figure 3.5a). The synergistic movement of the affected hand is noted (Figure 3.5b). If cocontraction is present, then the patient does not have paralysis of the affected hand. Since there has to be an intact neuromuscular tract to produce this sign, it should point to possible secondary gain. The sensitivity and specificity of this simple examination is 100% since there has never been a case where patients with the true organic disease can do this (Tinazzi et al., 2008).

The honest palm sign is a simple bedside maneuver to help with the examination of upper extremity weakness. This novel technique grades the patient's effort as full or incomplete. In the honest palm sign, the patient is asked to squeeze the examiner's index and middle finger as tightly as possible and to resist from pulling out of the grip as much as possible." This test allows the examiner to notice any fingernail imprint on the hands of the patient to see if the maximal effort for grasp was put forth (Black, 2014). If the patient has no fingernail imprints, he is not putting enough effort into the exam. It should be noted that some patients have very short fingernails and would show fingerprints instead of fingernail prints. Patients with flaccid paralysis or bilateral arm weakness would not have the ability to squeeze, but other signs would be positive for true disease, such as loss of tone or fasciculations.

3.1.3.13 Extensor Carpi Radialis

Patients with a history of falling and catching themselves with their outstretched hands during work will come to the clinic or hospital seeking secondary gains. A routine physician examination can prevent frivolous imaging studies that will come up negative, and allow the doctor to lead the patient to better psychological care. Radial nerve palsy complaints are common within neurological and primary care centers throughout the community. But how does one distinguish between true versus nonorganic disease? True disease is seen in patients that present with weakness in the wrist dorsiflexion (wrist drop) with fingers extended. Also, patients with true radial neuropathy would report sensory loss in the distribution of the radial nerve. Be leery of

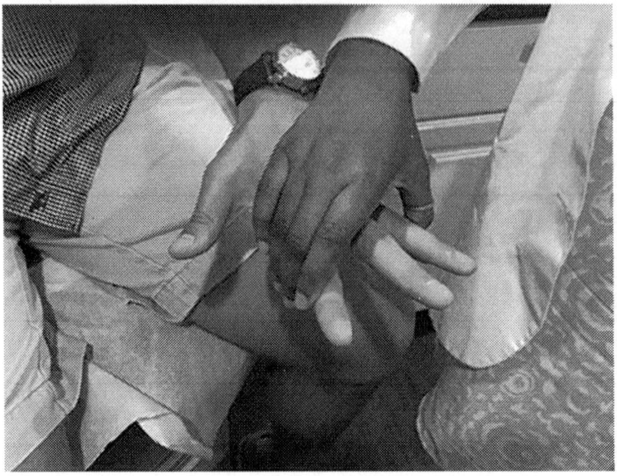

(a)

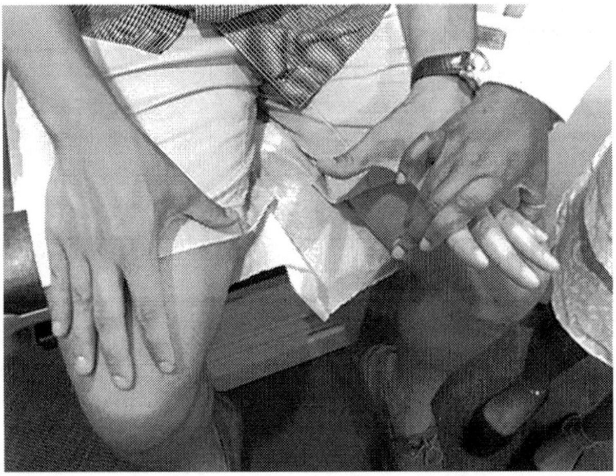

(b)

FIGURE 3.5 (a) Examiner tests the intrinsic muscles of the unaffected hand for 2 minutes with full strength being applied by the patient. (b) Affected side demonstrates the synergistic movement indicating intact intrinsic muscles of the affected side (Positive Abductor Finger Sign).

the patient who complains of radial nerve palsy without sensory loss in the dorsum of the hand with fifth digit spared. The supine catch test can also help with the differential diagnosis of malingering. In this test, patients with radial nerve palsy are instructed to supinate both affected and nonaffected hands and are asked to maintain that position. In true organic disease the affected hand will not drop and will maintain a palmar flexion (supine catch sign) due to an unopposed pull of the flexor compartment of the forearm (Sethi, Sethi, and Torgovnick, 2010) (Figure 3.6a). In false nerve damage the hand would drop straight down without the supine catch sign, suggesting malingering (Figure 3.6b). Patients will focus on the weakness

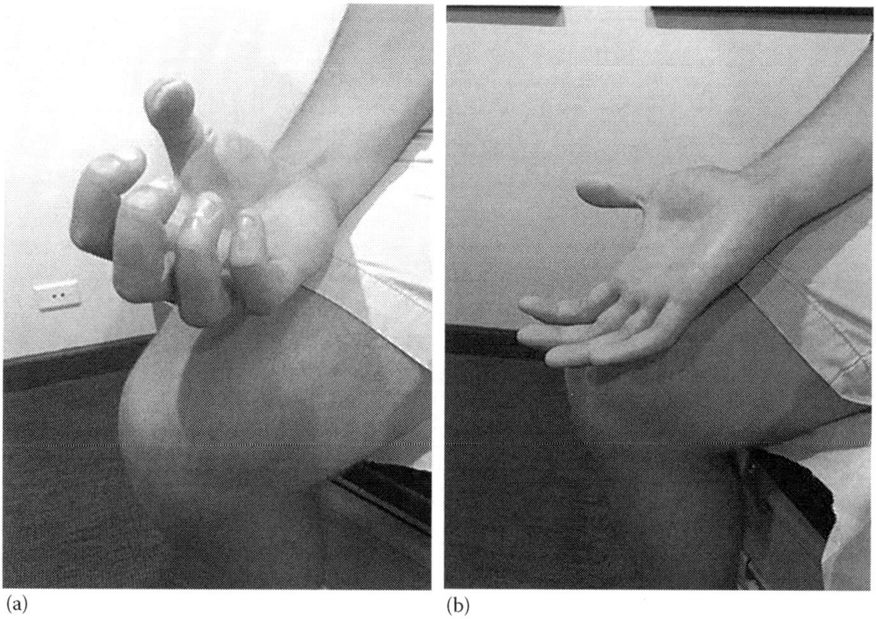

FIGURE 3.6 (a) Patient demonstrating claw hand with wrist drop, when the hand is placed in a supine position, exhibiting true disease. Supine Catch Sign: Where the hand stays in the supine position as they are catching something. (b) Shows a patient that is complaining of wrist drop. During supination of the arm and hand, the patient demonstrates dropping of the wrist instead of it being in the claw deformity—as in true disease. This is a negative supine catch sign, demonstrating wrist weakness, not nerve palsy.

instead of the actual physiology of the muscles, which will maintain different positions of the wrist.

3.1.3.14 Biceps Brachialis, Triceps

For every action there is an opposite and equal reaction. Newton's third law of motion can be applied to the human body as well. We all take advantage of this law, since the body relies on balance to stay erect or in a certain position against gravity. An examination, which takes advantage of positional cocontraction to keep the body in balance, is the elbow flex-ex sign test. An oppositional study was done with the Hoover sign test (Hoover, 1908) of the lower limb applied to the upper limbs. The elbow flex-ex sign test is elicited by having the patient resist external pull at the wrist during flexion of the unaffected arm, while holding the other wrist to see if the affected triceps extends to oppose the flexion (Tremolizzo et al., 2014). In true organic disease, there is no contralateral flexion or extension resistance in the affected side. In nonorganic illness, as in malingering, one notices a subtle resistance with hesitation to relaxation. Lombardi et al., reported a 100% sensitivity and specificity in this test for malingering (Lombardi et al., 2014).

When suspecting arm weakness biceps and triceps reflexes should be tested at the same time to notice if there is areflexia, hyporeflexia, or hyperreflexia in order to help delineate true disease. The C5 and C6 roots innervate the biceps and brachioradialis reflexes. If a patient states there is paralysis, then the examiner should test the reflex to find areflexia for lower motor neuron lesions and hyperreflexia for upper motor neuron damage. C7 and C8 innervates the triceps reflex, making it possible to see if the etiology affects just the upper trunk of the brachial plexus or both upper and lower trunks.

3.1.3.15 Gluteus Medius

Abductor signs have been one of the prominent signs to aid physicians with a differential diagnosis of patients with lower paresis (Figure 3.7a and 3.7b). Patients with true disease try hard to abduct their affected limb and produce a synkinetic abduction of the unaffected limb confirming that there is true paresis. Asking the patient to abduct their affected leg against resistance will allow the examiner to overcome the leg medially, while the unaffected leg abducts. Patients with nonorganic disease would have no resistance at all on the unaffected sides because they will not be putting efforts on the affected side (Figure 3.7c). Hoover described this phenomenon when it comes to lower limb weakness, which can be applied at other parts of the body that have both agonist and antagonist muscles (Sonoo, 2014). When looking at this phenomenon, Sonoo focused on the overall abduction of the test. He noted a positive sign if the patient was asked to fully abduct his or her the legs against resistance and the affected leg didn't move past the midline. This signified that the patient had the ability to maintain the abductor muscles of the leg contracted. If the paretic leg moved in during full abduction it was considered to be a negative test. Sonoo demonstrated that this sign signified up to 100% sensitivity and specificity when looking at patients who were not truly paralyzed (Sonoo, 2014). This muscle should also be assessed when looking for weakness during the gait, to produce the classic Trendelenburg's sign which shows weakness of the superior gluteal nerve innervating both the gluteus medius and maximus. This discrepancy suggests malingering.

3.1.3.16 Quadricep Femoris

As the biceps and triceps act as antagonist muscles in the upper extremities, patients should be examined for contralateral contraction while trying to maintain balance while either extending or flexing at the knee. Asking the patient to extend their lower leg during resistance will allow the physician to note the physiological flexion of the unaffected leg for balance. Reflex testing should also be consistent with paresis of the leg based on the history as reduced with lower motor neuron damage, and increased with upper motor neuron lesions. Reflexes should also not be changed based upon position of the patient. Standing, sitting, and lying supine, reflexes should be consistent with each other. Patients should also not exhibit different types of movements when standing compared to lying flat on the bed. True paralysis will not be affected by position of the patient, therefore discrepancies should make the doctor suspicious of possible malingering.

3.1.3.17 Abdominalis Muscles

Patients trying to mimic different types of spinal cord injuries should be tested to elicit specific signs of malingering. Organic disease would lead to diminished reflexes below the level of spinal cord damage. If below T9, the patient would exhibit abdominal

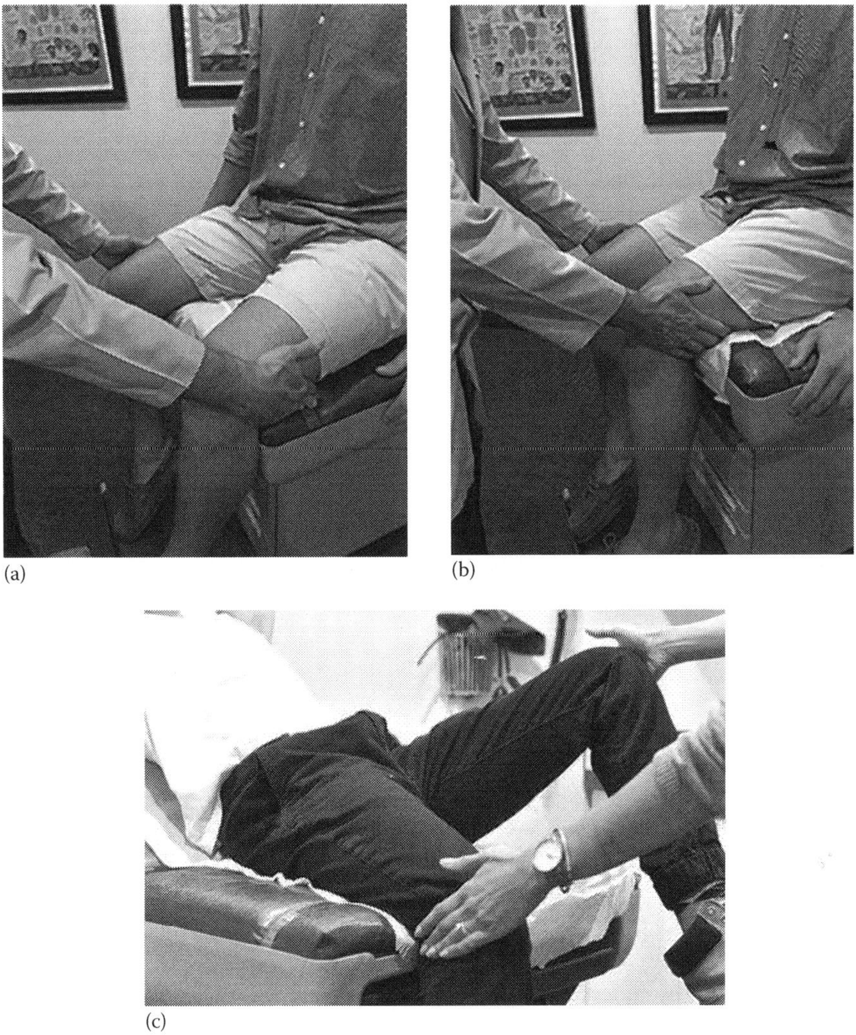

FIGURE 3.7 (a–b) Testing the abductors of the legs: Have the examiner put force on the outside of both legs while moving them inwards resisting abduction. While the patient is attempting to abduct his legs, the examiner looks for weakness or paresis. Full abduction of one side will be accompanied with abduction of the opposite leg. (c) Patient demonstrates contraction and abduction of the left leg and hip, but no contraction of the right leg or hip. Lack of force on the left side without normal contraction (Abductor Sign). Some patients may demonstrate hyper-adduction of the nonorganic paretic leg.

muscle weakness. Charles Edward Beevor has described this (Desai, 2012). Beevor's sign is tested with the patient in the recumbent position. Patient are asked to raise their heads or sit up while the physician focuses on the umbilicus. A positive sign would be the umbilicus moving in the cephalic direction more than one centimeter, or moving rostrally more than one centimeter for the inverted Beevor's sign; both are positive tests for true disease (Leon-Sarmiento, Baona, and Bayona-Prieto, 2007). Positive signs will provide reassurance to the physician that this is not malingering since the sensitivity of this sign is 95% and specificity is 93% (Leon-Sarmiento et al. 2007). If patients do not exhibit this positive finding it suggests possible secondary gain. In a patient without true disease, the umbilicus will stay stationary because both parts of the abdomen muscles are working against each other to stabilize the umbilicus in the same position. Organic diseases such as amyotrophic lateral sclerosis and facioscapulohumeral muscular dystrophy, demonstrate Beevor's sign. This physical finding is often missed since physicians routinely test their patients in the seated position.

3.1.3.18 Pronator Drift Test

Diseases affecting different locations in the nervous system will induce variations in drift. In the pronator drift test physicians ask the patient to extend out their arms supine with their fingers widely spread as if holding a pizza box (Figure 3.8a). The patient should be tested in this manner with their eyes open for more than ten seconds and with their eyes closed more than 20 seconds. Patients with true disease may have drift with pronation, as seen in upper motor neuron lesions Also, inward and outward drift, as exhibited in cerebellum lesions or with position sense loss (posterior column and parietal lobe lesion) as exhibited with the arm moving cephalically above the

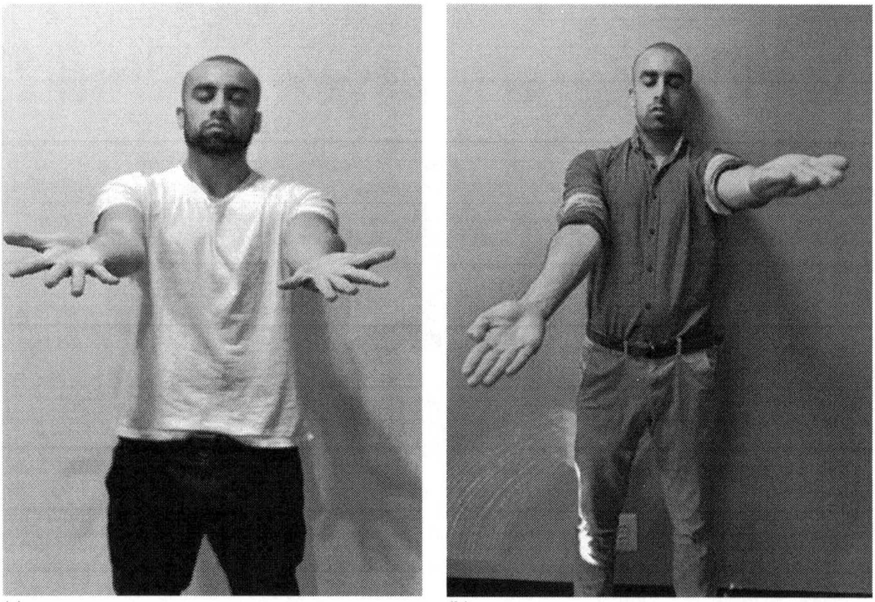

(a) (b)

FIGURE 3.8 (a) Patient demonstrating the initial steps in the examination of a drift: Arms supinated around shoulder level, fingers spread apart, and eyes closed for over 30 seconds. (b) Patient demonstrates a right arm drift without pronation, possibly indicating either a shoulder weakness or malingering. This type of drift focuses on shoulder weakness and is not seen while the patient's eyes are open.

head. Patients that demonstrate straight down drift without pronation would arouse suspicion of malingering (Figure 3.8b). This sign is called drift without pronation. Patients with shoulder weakness would have the inability to raise their arms, therefore, with a negative physical sign of the shoulder, a drift without pronation sign is not seen in organic disease (Carone and Bush, 2013a).

3.1.3.19 Musculoskeletal Pain of the Lower Back

Bending forward increases the space between the top and lower vertebrae, especially in the lumbar region. This reduces nerve compression pain in true disease. The standard Schober's test may also be performed. This test is conducted by placing one mark approximately five centimeters below the posterior superior iliac spine (PSIS) and another mark about ten centimeters above the PSIS. The patient is then asked to touch his or her toes. This maneuver increases the distance between the two marks and the increment increase is measured and documented (Schober, 1937). Patients with true diseases, like ankylosing spondylitis, will have little resistance to forward bending until they meet the angle where they reach pain. Patients that have secondary gain motives will resist the examiner's hand when guided to bend forward, instead of passively bending forward until they feel pain. This specific sign is called the positive resistive forward bend test. The increment increase during the Schober's test will show an increased spacing in patients with true organic disease before resistance or pain, compared to nonorganic disease where there is early-resistance prior to reaching increasing increments. This can also be applied to the patient who complains of hip weakness and resists before a fully bending forward. This shows that they are incorporating their hip flexors to help with resistance against the physician's hand. This positive resistive forward bend test demonstrates 82% sensitivity and 61% specificity in patients with malingering (Kumar et al., 2012).

The straight leg raising test is used when patients are complaining of lower back pain with radiation. This examination is performed in the supine position where the patient's leg is raised in the full extension position until production of pain or until the leg raised reaches 90 degrees. Also, patients should not have a discrepancy between pain produced during the maneuver being performed in the supine position compared to pain felt during the sitting straight leg raising test or the Lasegue test. In the Lasegue test, patients sit with their legs dangling and then extend them at the knee until straight or until pain is produced. When straight, there is an equivalent compression at 90 degrees. If the straight leg test is painful at less than 90 degrees and the Lasegue test is negative without pain, this suggests false complaints. When flexing the hip the patient sometimes will resist the physician in a manner to show that they are unable to raise their leg because of their weakness. When the patient is in the supine position, the examiner raises the affected leg to see if there is any pain elicited. If the patient creates resistance against the examiner's hand it denotes a positive resistive straight leg test. A positive resistive straight leg raising test demonstrates that the patient is trying to show reduction in raising the affected leg. Patients in true pain would allow the examiner to raise the leg without resistance until they are at 90 degrees or until pain is elicited. Patients with malingering pain will demonstrate less resistance than required to elicit pain. The clinician should be aware of facial grimaces while performing this examination to see if there are any signs of exaggerating pain. The positive resistive straight leg test demonstrates a 74% sensitivity with a high 94% specificity for malingering patients

(Kumar et al., 2012). This should be conducted along with other physical examination maneuvers that can increase the sensitivity and specificity for malingering.

The heel compression test gives the examiner a method to deceive the patient without actually causing any harm in order to elicit nonorganic pain. Patients with low back pain will exhibit that anything which affects the legs will exacerbate low back pain. This is because they believe it is part of the lower back. Patients that exhibit exaggeration of their symptoms may also have this specific examination finding. Patients are told that putting compression on their heel may elicit low back pain, and if it does this sign is positive (Kumar et al., 2012). In true disease, the heel compression test would only elicit pain if there was a pathology occurring in the heel itself, without radiating to the lower back. This test does not affect the spinal column and should not produce any pain in the lower back. This positive sign points to patients exaggerating. This maneuver demonstrates an 87% sensitivity and 79% specificity for malingering of lower back pain.

Waddell's signs have been historically used to distinguish psychological back pain compared to true back pain. Classic nonorganic Waddell's signs include tenderness, simulation, distraction, regional weakness, and overreaction (Fishbain et al., 2003). Tenderness is noted when the patient is gently touched superficially; this leads to pain over the entire area of touch and not to one specific point. Waddell's signs are also elicited with deep palpation leading to tenderness, which is not localized to the area of palpation, but spreads to the back. Simulation is considered positive when the clinician puts pressure on the skull of a standing person and this leads to lower back pain. This should not produce any change to the spinal column of the lower back and therefore not lead to increased pain—leading to a red flag for the patient. Also, rotating the position of the patient by rotating both shoulder and pelvis at the same time should not lead to lower back pain in true disease since the rotation is equal in both shoulder and pelvis. Distraction is another of the Waddell's signs. This is elicited when certain maneuvers, which are not affected by position, are tested in different positions leading to a pain difference. For example, the straight leg test can be performed both in the sitting position and in the supine position. This should not reveal a discrepancy. Regional weakness is another sign which can give clinicians clues as to what is going on within the muscle. The patient may "give way," demonstrating false weakness; instead of having true weakness which does not have any strength. Here the patient would first have strength then suddenly none. This is important because if it is associated with overreaction it can point to nonorganic pathology.

3.1.3.20 Lower Extremity Weakness

Patients that present with the inability to stand on their own—but drove themselves to the office—should be evaluated for secondary gain. The Hoover sign examines the effort of the patient when moving with lower extremity weakness. This is based on the fact that muscles work as levers and pulleys focusing on the push and pull of the lower extremities. In this test, the examiner places his or her hand under the heel of the nonparetic leg and pushes downward on the paretic leg shin while asking the patient to try and lift the affected leg. In normal circumstances, as patients are lifting one of their legs against gravity or pressure the natural tendency is for the other leg to counteract the movement by pushing down and creating a good balance.

When patients lift their legs they are incorporating their hip flexors and quadriceps femoris and—to counteract that movement—the gluteus maximus and iliopsoas muscles contract in the opposite leg. Therefore, both the gluteus maximus and the iliopsoas muscles would be contracting and forcing the unaffected limb to push downward against the examiner's hand. This downward force on the examiner's hand suggests that the patient is providing maximum effort. On the other hand, malingerers will not demonstrate full effort. The good leg does not push opposite of the impaired leg's movement.

The Babinski trunk-thigh test is another examination which allows the clinician to see how much effort a patient is putting forth when asked to perform a task with the lower extremities. In this test, patients with lower extremity weaknesses are instructed to lie in the supine position with their arms crossed over their chest, and asked to sit up. In true organic disease, the weak leg is flexed at the hip with the heel being brought up from the bed and the shoulders make a forward bending motion (Okun and Koehler, 2004) (Figure 3.9a). Patients that exhibit no effort in performing this task will lie flat and show no asymmetry between both sides of the body (Figure 3.9b). There should no discrepancy between a patient's physical examination at the bedside and what the physician witnesses when the patient does not think he or she is being observed. This examination has a high specificity when it is positive, giving the physician clues that this is a nonorganic process.

The Barré test also helps provide insight in nonorganic diseases of the lower extremity weakness. In the supine position, the patient's legs are flexed at a 90-degree angle. The examiner discloses to the patient that this takes little or no effort to maintain this position. In true disease, the affected leg would drop suddenly after the examiner's support is removed with a downward extension movement of the quadriceps. This is a positive Barré test (Figure 3.10a and 3.10b). Patients with functional disease will not exhibit this sign at all and keep their legs in the 90-degree flexed angle, or just show a drop of the legs without the extension (Figure 3.10c). Barré tested this maneuver and found it to be positive in 33/36 organic pyramidal weaknesses and negative in 7/7 functional pareses (Barré, 1919).

3.1.3.21 Sensory Examination

Numbness is one of the classic types of subjective complaints physicians face in clinics. A thalamic stroke in the ventroposterior lateral nucleus (VPL) can lead to midline splitting of the body, but ventroposterior medial nucleus (VPM) will lead to midline splitting of the face, with residual physical findings. A sensory examination consists of fine touch, pinprick, temperature, and vibration and can be tested separately during an examination. The ability to sense proprioception allows humans to walk with self-recognition of arms and legs. Patients with true posterior column disease would show areflexia with loss of vibration. Patients complaining of feeling that they have no idea where their body is in space—despite a normal neurological examination—is suggestive of malingering.

With dermatome patterns crossing throughout the body, cutaneous nerves should not display sensory loss which splits the body in the midline. Loss of sensation should be in a dermatomal pattern instead of involving the entire limb, or side of body which does not cross midline. The genital region cutaneous nerves cross over in a manner that physiologically does not lead to midline splitting in this region, even after a thalamic stroke (Stone, Zeman, and Sharpe, 2002). Midline splitting of sensory deficits is a well-demarcated line which splits the body in half without any apparent dermatome pattern, as one would expect in organic disease. An organic explanation of this type of midline splitting is lacunar infarction or tumor in the VPM for the face and VPL for the body (Daum, Hubschmid, and Aybek, 2014). Patients who complain of the loss of sensation in either the left or right part of the

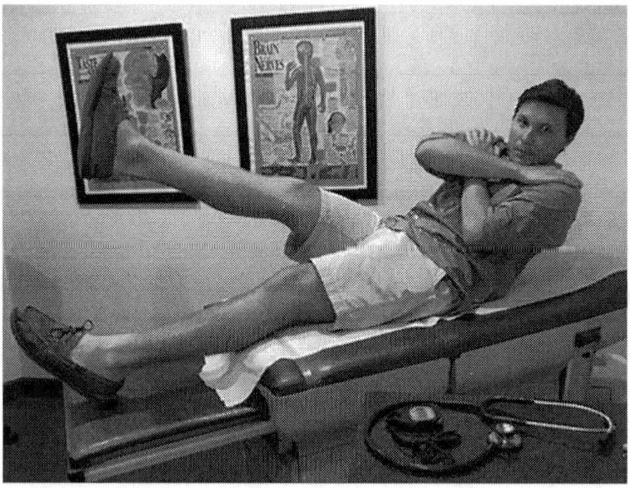

(a)

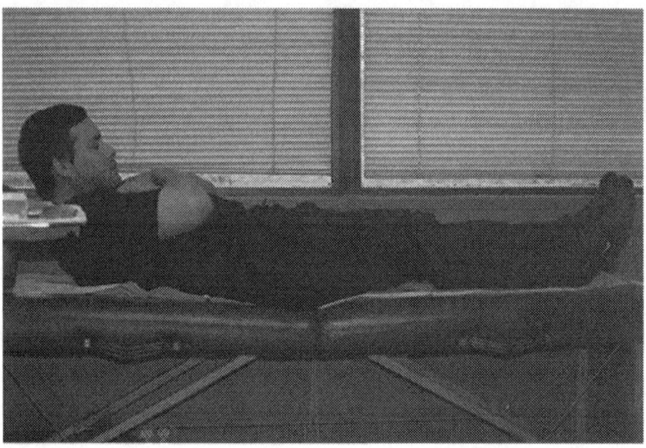

(b)

FIGURE 3.9 (a) Babinski trunk-thigh test: Patient is asked to lie flat, cross his hands across his chest, and attempt to raise himself. In true organic disease, the patient would demonstrate an attempt to raise himself with uneven shoulders and legs. The asymmetry demonstrates that the patient is using full force during this examination. (b) Patient demonstrates lack of effort in attempting to raise himself. The shoulders are uneven, and lower half shows no contraction even in the abdominal region. This type of result in the Babinski trunk-thigh test shows lack of asymmetry and points towards malingering.

body can be examined with a monofilament test. Testing the patient with a monofilament should be done with the patient's eyes closed so he or she does not have the ability to see what area is being tested. Asking the whether they feel the touch with a simple yes or no answer will make it difficult for the patient with functional loss to respond without hesitation. Midline splitting has been reported in one controlled study, looking specifically at sensory deficits, as having 20% sensitivity and 93% specificity. This means that if found it is highly suggestive of malingering.

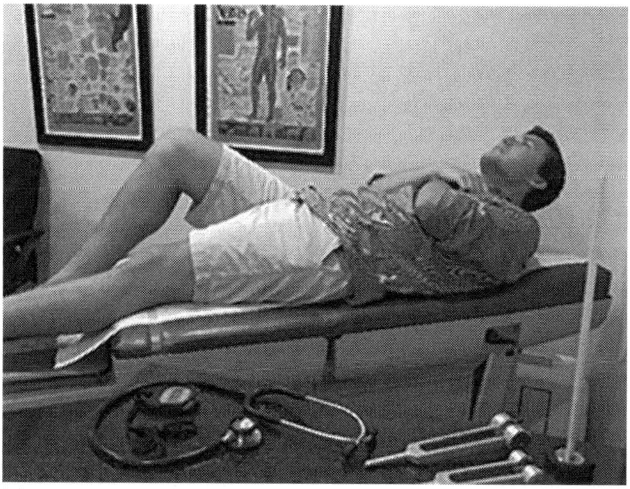

(a)

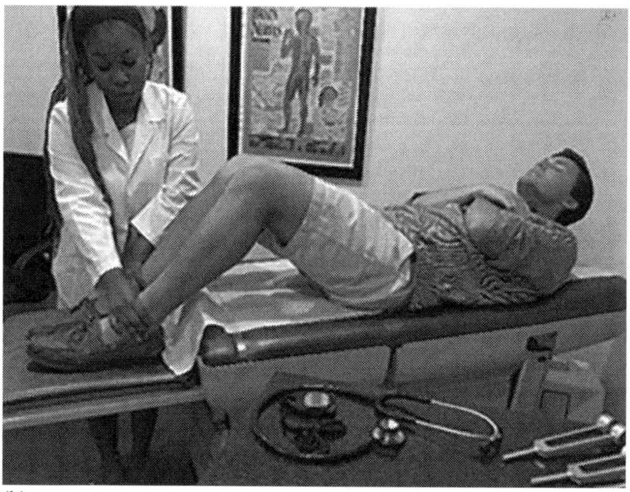

(b)

FIGURE 3.10 (a–b) Barré test for lower leg paresis: The examiner places the patient's knees flexed at a 90-degree angle while telling the patient that it takes little to no effort to maintain that position. In true organic disease, the paretic leg will drop and the quadriceps will contract attempting to maintain the position (positive Barré test). *(Continued)*

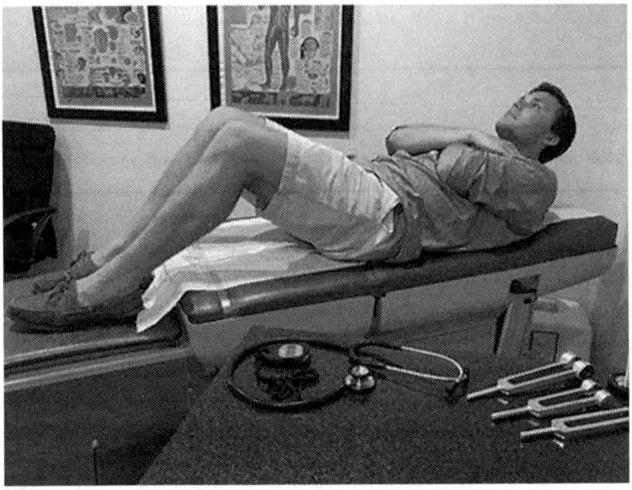

(c)

FIGURE 3.10 (CONTINUED) (c) The patient keeps the legs in a flexed position without any effort demonstrating nonorganic paresis (negative Barré test). Some patient's may exhibit a drop of the legs without any quadriceps contractions indicating a lack of effort.

Pacinian corpuscles cells transverse throughout the body, especially on the joints and bones, making it possible for a person to know the specific location of their limbs in space. Vibration and position sense are transmitted through the posterior column of the spinal cord. Organic vibratory loss can induce gait disturbances since they are unable to judge the location of their limbs in place, as in long-term vitamin B12 deficiency. Vibration should be felt equally bilaterally if placed within a midline bone which is being tested because Pacinian corpuscles traverse the bone (Gilman, 2002). Since vibration is sensed mainly through bone conduction, presentation of vibration through the midline bone should be felt bilaterally. Thus, splitting of vibration in the midline points toward patients with functional sensory loss. By simply placing a tuning fork to the forehead or sternum of the patient, the Pacinian corpuscles activate widely throughout the periosteum of the forehead or sternum leading to bilateral vibratory sensation. Placing the tuning fork lateral to the middle of the forehead or sternum should not be detected unilaterally, but rather bilaterally. Thus, splitting of the sternum or forehead—feeling it on one side and not on the other—is a sign of functional vibration loss (Daum, Hubschmid, and Aybek, 2014). This examination finding is 95% sensitive and 14% specific for malingers.

Nonanatomical sensory loss (Daum, Hubschmid, and Aybek, 2014) focuses on patients demarcating sensory loss from either the anterior or posterior aspect of the patient. Dermatomes wrap around the body in a specific pattern giving the examiner a strong tool to screen for malingering patients who demonstrate loss from this specific pattern. Other aspects of nonanatomical sensory loss can be in areas which are innervated by the same nerve, but where the patient's description suggests innervations of multiple nerves. For instance, this the case when patients complain of anterior deltoid anesthesia but not posterior. These sensory discrepancies are 69.6%

sensitive and 100% specific, as demonstrated among 20 functional paraplegic subjects compared with 23 organic controls in a study by Daum, Hubschmid, and Aybek (2014). Inconsistent sensory loss can be evaluated with patients complaining of sensation loss in the upper extremity, but with normal postural, signs, leading to a discrepancy on physiology of human sensation.

The Bowlus-Currier test focuses on mixing the fingers and testing different fingers while the eyes are closed, so as not to see which finger is actually being touched (Figure 3.11). This maneuver starts with the clinician asking the patients to extend both hands while having both thumbs facing the ground, and then asking them to clasp their hands together while maintaining both thumbs aiming at the ground. The clinician then instructs the patient to internally rotate their arms while bringing them to the chest. In this position the hands are mixed and, while their eyes are closed the examiner randomly touches the patient in affected areas, and asks the patient to say yes or no if they feel the touch or not. This will be difficult in patients that do not

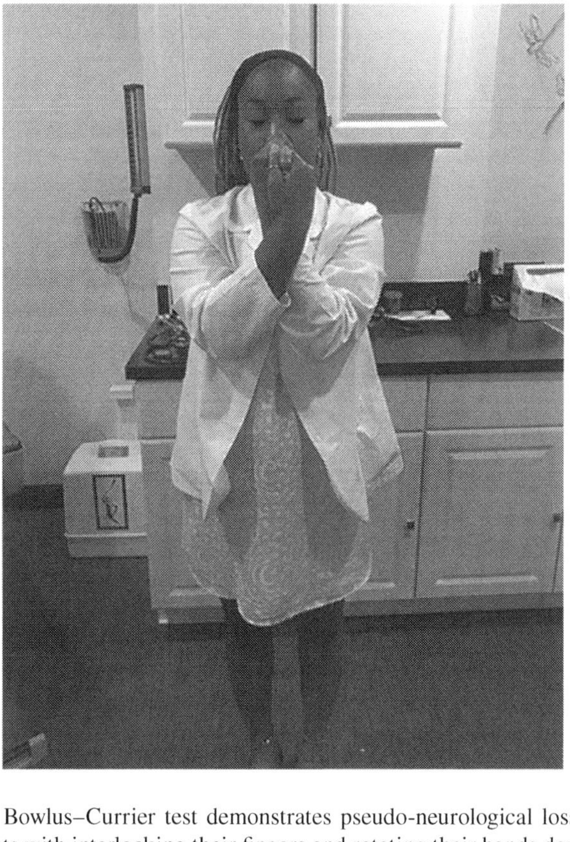

FIGURE 3.11 Bowlus–Currier test demonstrates pseudo-neurological loss of sensory by confusing patients with interlocking their fingers and rotating their hands downward, inward and up in front of the chest. With the patient's eyes closed, the examiner randomly touches affected areas with unaffected parts of the hands to distinguish true vs. nonorganic causes of sensory loss.

have true organic disease. If the patients states they feel touch on an area that is supposedly numb, it should raise red flags for malingering (Bowlus and Currier, 1963).

The yes/no test is a simple bedside test which can provide evidence to distinguish between organic and nonorganic etiologies. First, test the patient with their eyes open as a control. Touch the patient in the anesthetic area and ask if he or she feels it or not, forcing him or her to answer. Then ask the patient to close his or her eyes and repeat the sequence while recording the yes or no answer. If there is no consistency between the two, malingering should be suspected.

The Romberg test, originally used for investigation of tabes dorsalis, confirms the integrity of the posterior column. During this examination patients are asked to stand with their feet together and their arms by their sides with their eyes closed. This is not a test of cerebellar function, so one would not expect titubation or hips jerking during the exam. Classic "hip jerking sign" during Romberg testing can point towards malingering since the posterior column gathers positions of joints. The whole body will sway instead of just the hips. Granted, there can be false positive in patients with vestibular apparatus lesions. After syphilis (tabes dorsalis) and vitamin B12 deficiency have been ruled out, there should be no hip jerking—only body swaying during Romberg testing.

3.1.3.22 Cerebellum

The finger-to-nose test is used to detect dysmetria. In this test patients are asked to touch their nose with the tip of their index finger, followed by reaching out to touch the examiner's finger. When repeating this process the examiner will place his or her finger at different locations for the patient to touch. In true ataxia, patients will produce a side-to-side oscillating tremors which is not smooth and increases with amplitude distally, but eventually they will touch the examiner's index finger. Malingerers dissimulate, as if unable to touch their finger to their own nose (Figure 3.12a). They may circle around the nose with wandering movements which would eventually lead them to touching the very tip of their nose (Figure 3.12b). Making exaggerated movements while being able to touch the tip of the nose is difficult compared to the normal performance of the finger-to-nose to test. Some patients may constantly tap one part of the face to demonstrate that they cannot touch their nose (Figure 3.12c). These positive findings can invoke suspicion for malingering (Campbell, DeJong, and Haerer, 2005).

The cerebellum also helps with normal gait function, so examining the gait helps delineate cerebellar malingering as well.

3.1.3.23 Gait Examination

Noticing the patients' gait when they first come to the clinic or hospital will allow the clinician to determine a baseline for how the patients walks when they are unobserved. There should be no discrepancy between observed and unobserved gait balance. If there is a discrepancy, the clinician should focus on other types of examinations which can help point to malingering. The huffing and puffing signs involves efforts which consist of grimacing, huffing, grunting, crying, and breath holding during ambulation (Laub et al., 2015). These signs were evaluated in patients with functional gait disorder and no associated pain during ambulation. The huffing and puffing signs were revealed in functional gait disorder. These types of signs have a

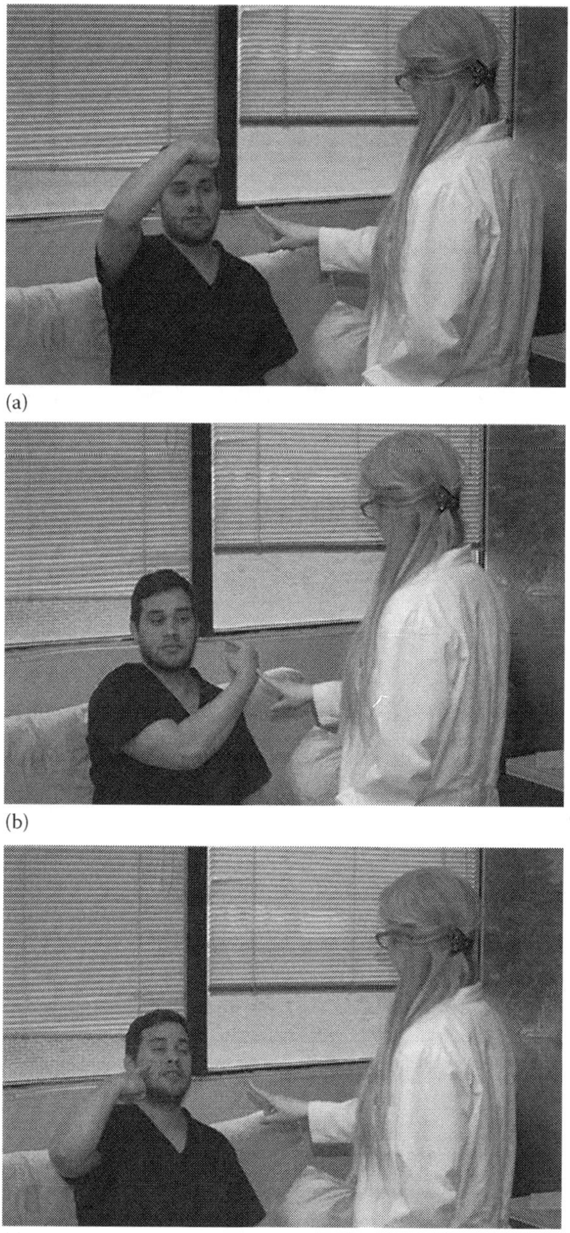

(a)

(b)

(c)

FIGURE 3.12 (a) Patient demonstrating an erratic approach to the finger-to-nose test. The patient in this figure exhibits the inability to touch his nose, emphasizing ataxia with inability to follow command. (b) Patient demonstrating erratic movement on the way back to touching his nose. This circling around the nose and touching of others parts but the nose is associated with malingering patients. (c) Patient directly places his finger on the side of the cheek demonstrating to the examiner that he cannot touch his nose. This is not exhibited in any type of true ataxia.

low sensitivity (17–57%) but have a greater specificity (89–100%) for nonorganic gait disorder.

A classic sign which will help physicians investigate malingering is astasia-abasia. This appears as an almost drunken gait with near falls, but no actual falls to the ground (Carone and Bush, 2013b) (Figure 3.13a). This type of display takes more acrobatic maneuvering than regular walking. This sign should be a red flag for non-organic gait disorder. People with true disease would not be able to control the way they walk or be able to stop themselves from falling to the ground. Patients with cerebellar disease tend to fall towards the side of the lesion during tandem walking, compared to patients with false disease who fall in all directions (Figure 3.13c). Patients are unable to walk forwards but can walk backwards or run without difficulty indicate malingering patients (Campbell, 2016).

Malingering gait imbalance appears erratic with uneconomic postures, which would not be part of certain types of pathologies or injuries. Forced or exaggerated efforts and constantly pointing out to the physician about their gait imbalance should give a physician a clue to look for psychogenic aspects of their imbalance (Benbir, Hanagasi, Ertan, Hanagasi, and Ertan, 2013). Constant knee buckling after normal knee examination, especially when it is forced in front of the physician, can be a sign of malingering. True disease does not have constant knee buckling with variation. Greater persistence of knee buckling, while being observed, may be intentional instead of a symptom of true disease. Broad-based gait points towards cerebellar ataxia, but instead of near falling or knee buckling, they will show true swaying with titubation and other vermial and hemispheric cerebellum findings.

With abnormal acrobatic movements like in astasia-abasia, patients can also exhibit the pseudo-ataxia gait. These patients, when observed, demonstrate an odd gait in which their legs cross each other while maintaining balance with short side steps (Stone, Zeman, and Sharpe, 2005) (Figure 3.13b). They seem as if they are "walking on ice," acting as though they are slipping everywhere without actual falls. These two positive findings should point toward malingering (Stone, Zeman, and Sharpe, 2005).

Patients with true weakness would have a circumduction gait to provide relief from the foot dragging. Nonorganic patients keep their leg dragging behind them on the ground as if their feet weigh a thousand pounds. This sign, called dragging monoplegic gait, is considered to be a functional weakness in patients without organic causes (Tremolizzo et al., 2014). Even patients with spastic paralysis will exhibit the circumduction at the hip to assist the leg from dragging on the ground. Patients with true common peroneal lesion leading to foot drop will exhibit higher steppage gait or circumduction, but not dragging. Upper motor neuron damage can induce spasticity, and lower motor neuron can induce flaccid leg with atrophy.

Major gait and history discrepancies should be evaluated when the patient is walking normally and sitting down. Incongruent ambulation can point towards malingering. Incorporating the swivel chair test can help determine malingering. This examination begins with the patient walking 20 to 30 feet forwards and backwards. Then, the clinician asks the patient to sit on a swivel chair and propel him- or herself forwards and backwards. In true disease, patients would not be able to ambulate themselves linearly in the chair, which is congruent with normal ambulation.

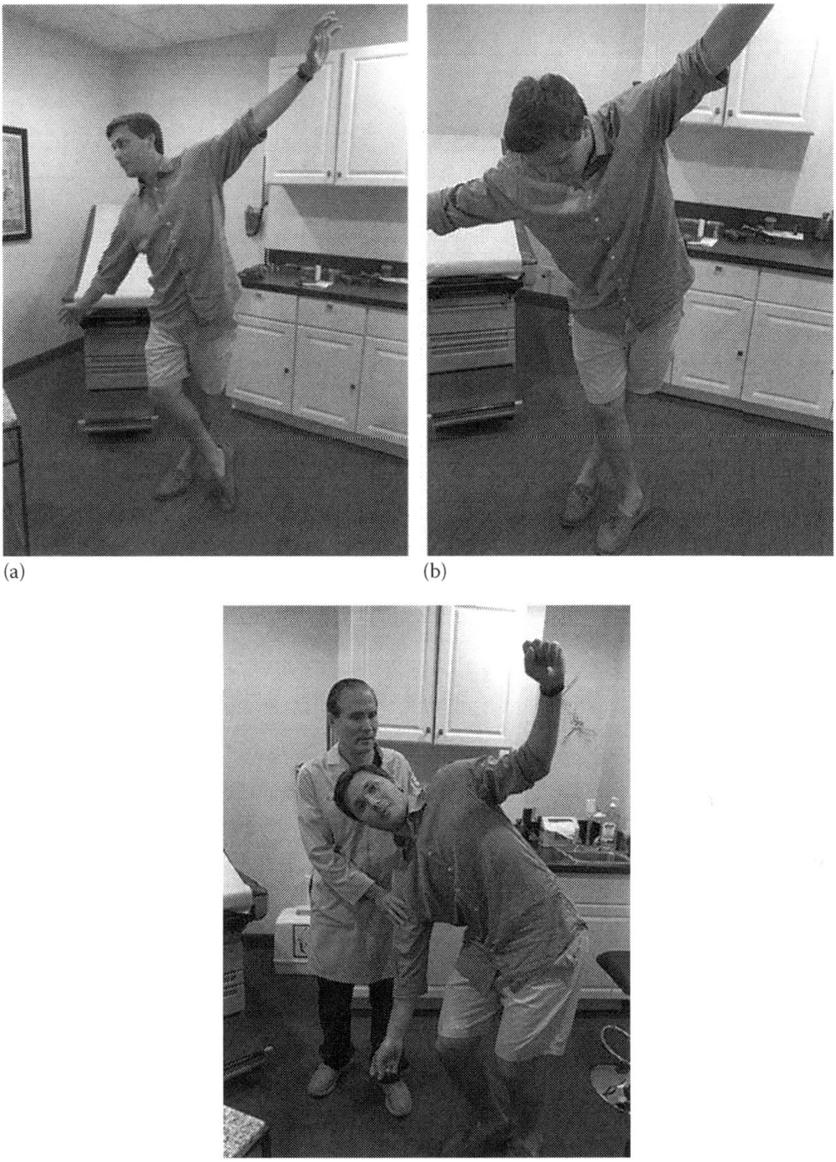

(a) (b) (c)

FIGURE 3.13 (a) Patient demonstrates normal ambulation while crossing their legs, which can be seen in patients who have uneconomical postures with no falls. Patient exhibits more near falls when being observed by the examiner. (b) Patient demonstrates legs crossed while appearing to fall without falling. Uneconomical postures with crossed legs and wide-open arms are staged to exaggerate falling. (c) Patient demonstrating falling towards the examiner, who is predicting which way the patient will fall during the gait exam. The examiner holds the patient, giving security to them about noticing the exaggerated unequal balance (Uneconomical Posture).

Patients with nonorganic ambulation will propel themselves linearly in the swivel test without any effort at all (Okun, Rodriguez, Foote, and Fernandez, 2007). Okun reported that eight out of nine patients with functional gait disturbance exhibited normal propulsion on the chair. One caveat is that in Parkinsonism, there also is a positive swivel chair test in organic gait disorders.

Odd presentations of foot positions during examination can help find the etiology of the abnormal gait. Psychogenic toe sign, at first glance, appears to be a striatal-like toe. This sign is characterized by an increased resistance to manipulation by the extended first toe, which can be forcibly flexed only at the point of pain (Skolol and Espay, 2016). This sign should be distinguished from the first toe dorsiflexion seen in focal dystonia associated with neurodegenerative diseases. The difference is the ability of the examiner to displace the toe with ease and no associated pain. Psychogenic toe sign can be associated with other signs during the examination. Fixed plantar flexion inversion or eversion can manifest it is rapidly unilaterally or bilaterally with pain during movement. Some of these signs were reported in times of war to avoid being drafted (Skolol and Espay, 2016).

There are some common features among all functional movement disorders. Patients usually have a rapid onset of weakness without neurological evidence of stroke or trauma. Variability is another specific sign which is common with psychogenic disorders. Patients' symptoms vary throughout the day and may be apparent throughout the examination. Sometimes these symptoms may worsen during times of stress, bringing a new onset of symptoms during times of litigation. Improvement with distraction is the classic sign of functional movement disorders. Asking the patient to perform a task can help reduce the movement. But it can also have the opposite effect. With more attention focused on the affected area symptoms can get worse (Stone, Carson, and Sharpe, 2005).

Understanding the different types of gait movements can provide a plethora of information on different organ system dysfunctions, which can provide clues to physicians. Unfortunately, during this age of electronic medicine physicians rely less on the physical examination, but on scans that are supposed to provide better analysis. Malingering patients have the upper hand when it comes to masking their candor because the patient–physician relationship is widening instead of narrowing in this new era of medicine. Instead of noticing and observing the gait of patients from the beginning, we are stuck to the computer, typing. Medicine does not start with scans—a detailed history and physical examination can provide the patients' diagnoses without having to rely on them.

REFERENCES

Adler, F.H. 1962. *Textbook of Ophthalmology, 7th ed.* London: W.B. Saunders Co.

Aubrey, J.B., A.R. Dobbs, and B.G. Rule. 1989. Laypersons' knowledge about the sequelae of minor head injury and whiplash. *Journal of Neurology, Neurosurgery, and Psychiatry* 52:7:842–846.

Babinski J. 1900. Diagnostic différentiel de l'hémiplégie organique et de l'hémiplégie hystérique. *Gazette des Hôpitaux de Paris* 73:533–537.

Barré, J. 1919. La manoeuvre de la jambe: Nouveau signe objectif des paralysies ou paresis dues aux perturbations du faisceau pyramidal. *La Presse Medicale* 79:793–795.

Benbir, G., F. Hanagasi, S. Ertan, H.A. Hanagasi, and T. Ertan. 2013. Pure gait disturbance displayed by malingerers: Case report of two patients. *Clinical Neurology and Neurosurgery* 115:7:1177–1179.

Black, D. 2014. Detecting malingering: The honest palm sign. *Neurology* 82:10:P7.030.

Bowlus, W.E., and R.D. Currier. 1963. A test for hysterical hemianalgesia. *New England Journal of Medicine* 269:1253–1254.

Bryant, S.E., K. Duff, J. Fisher, and R.J. McCaffrey. 2004. Performance profiles and cut-off scores on the Memory Assessment Scales. *Archives of Clinical Neuropsychology* 19:489–496.

Campbell, W.W., R.N. DeJong, and A.F. Haerer. 2005. *DeJong's the neurologic examination.* Philadelphia: Lippincott Williams & Wilkins.

Campbell, W.W. 2016. *Clinical Signs in Neurology: A Compendium.* Philadelphia: Wolter Kluwer.

Carone, D.A., and S.S. Bush. 2013a. *Mild Traumatic Brain Injury: Symptom Validity Assessment and Malingering.* New York: Springer Publishing.

Carone, D.A., and S.S. Bush. 2013b. *Mild Traumatic Brain Injury: Symptom Validity Assessment and Malingering*, 211. New York: Springer Publishing.

Dankaerts, W., P. O'Sullivan, A. Burnett, and L. Straker. 2006. Differences in sitting postures are associated with nonspecific chronic low back pain disorders when patients are subclassified. *Spine* 31:6:698–704.

Daum, C., and S. Aybek. 2013. Validity of the "drift without pronation" sign in conversion disorder. *BMC Neurology* 13:31.

Daum, C., M. Hubschmid, and S. Aybek. 2014. The value of 'positive' clinical signs for weakness, sensory and gait disorders in conversion disorder: A systematic and narrative review. *Journal of Neurology, Neurosurgery and Psychiatry* 85:2:180–190.

Desai, J.D. 2012. Beevor's sign. *Annals of Indian Academy of Neurology* 15:2:94–95.

Diukova, G.M. 1999. Weakness of the sternocleidomastoid muscle: A diagnostic test in hysterical paralysis. *Zhurral Nevrologii i Psikhiatrii Imeni S Korsakova* 99:1:56–59.

Dooley, J.M., and K.E. Gordon. 2011. Spurious neurological signs and symptoms in children. *Paediatrics & Child Health* 16:7:e51–e53.

Fabbrini, G., G. Defazio, C. Colosimo, P.D. Thompson, and A. Berardeli A. 2009. Cranial movement disorders: Clinical features, pathophysiology, differential diagnosis and treatment. *Nature Clinical Practice Neurology* 5:93–105.

Falconer, G.A. 1966. A "lipreading test" for nonorganic deafness. *Journal of Speech and Hearing Disorders* 31:3:241–247.

Fasano, A., A. Valadas, K.P. Bhatia et al. 2012. Psychogenic facial movement disorders: Clinical features and associated conditions. *Movement Disorders* 27:12:1544–1551.

Fishbain, D.A., R. Cutler, H.L. Rosomoff, and R.S. Rosomoff. 1999. Chronic pain disability exaggeration/malingering and submaximal effort research. *Clinical Journal of Pain* 15:4:244–274.

Fishbain, D.A., B. Cole, R.B. Cutler et al. 2003. A structured evidence-based review on the meaning of nonorganic physical signs: Waddell signs. *Pain Medicine* 4:2:141–181.

Gilman, S. 2002. Joint position sense and vibration sense: Anatomical organisation and assessment. *Journal of Neurology, Neurosurgery & Psychiatry* 73:5:473–477.

Greve K.W., S. Springer, K.J. Bianchini et al. 2007. Malingering in toxic exposure. *Assessment* 14:1:12–21.

Hartlage, L.C. 1998. Clinical detection of malingering. In *Detection of Malingering During Head Injury Litigation; Critical Issues in Neuropsychology*, ed. C.R. Reynolds, 239–260. New York: Plenum Press.

Hirsch, A.R. 1987. The stopped medicine sign. *Headache* 27:2:109.

Hoover, C.F. 1908. A new sign for the detection of malingering and functional paresis of the lower extremities. *JAMA* 51:746–747.

Incesu, A.I., and G. Sobacı. 2011. Malingering or simulation in ophthalmology-visual acuity. *International Journal of Ophthalmology* 4:5:558–566.

Jelicic, M., H. Merckelbach, I. Candel, and E. Gerarerts. 2007. Detection of feigned cognitive dysfunction using special malinger tests: A simulation study. *International Journal of Neuroscience* 117:8:1185–1192.

Judd, O., and R. Persaud. 2016. The Judd–Persaud Test: A simple office-based tuning fork test for unilateral feigned hearing loss. *Annals of Otolaryngology and Rhinology* 3:5:1105.

Keane, J.R. 1986. Wrong-way deviation of the tongue with hysterical hemiparesis. *Neurology* 36:1406–1407.

Kumar, N., S.I. Wijerathne, W.W.J. Lim et al. 2012. Resistive straight leg raise test, resistive forward bend test and heel compression test: Novel techniques in identifying secondary gain motives in low back pain cases. *European Spine Journal* 21:11:2280–2286.

Laub, H.N., A.K. Dwivedi, F.J. Revilla et al. 2015. Diagnostic performance of the "huffing and puffing" sign in functional (psychogenic) movement disorders. *Movement Disorders Clinical Practice* 2:1:29–32.

Leon-Sarmiento, F., E. Bayona, and J. Bayona-Prieto. 2007. A sudden Beevor's sign. *Clinical Medicine & Research* 5:2:121–122.

Lombardi, T.L., E. Barton, J. Wang et al. 2014. The elbow flex-ex: A new sign to detect unilateral upper extremity nonorganic paresis. *Journal of Neurology, Neurosurgery and Psychiatry* 85:165–167.

McDermott, B.E., and M.D. Feldman. 2007. Malingering in the medical setting. *Psychiatric Clinics of North America* 30:4:645–662.

Okun, M.S., and P.J. Koehler. 2004. Babinski's clinical differentiation of organic paralysis from hysterical paralysis. *Archives of Neurology* 61:778–783.

Okun, M.S., R.L. Rodriguez, K.D. Foote, and H.H. Fernandez. 2007. The "chair test" to aid in the diagnosis of psychogenic gait disorders. *Neurologist* 13:87–91.

Saberi, S.M., A. Sheikhazadi, M. Ghorbani et al. 2013. Feigned symptoms among defendants claiming psychiatric problems: Survey of 45 malingerers. *Iranian Journal of Psychiatry*, 8:1:14–19.

Scadding, J.W., and N. Losseff. 2011. *Clinical neurology, 4th ed.* London: Hodder Arnold.

Schagen, S., B. Schmand, S. deSterke, and J. Lindeboom. 1997. Amsterdam short term memory test: A new procedure for the detection of feigned memory deficits. *Journal of Clinical and Experimental Neuropsychology* 19:1:43–51.

Schober, P. 1937. The lumbar vertebral column and backache. *Munchener Medizinische Wochenschrift* 84:336–338.

Scott, K.R., and A.M. Barrett. 2007. Dementia syndromes: Evaluation and treatment. *Expert Review of Neurotherapeutics* 7:4:407–422.

Sethi, N.K., Sethi, P.K., and Torgovnick, J. 2010. Supine catch sign—A simple clinical test to differentiate between true and false (pseudo) radial nerve palsy. *Clinical Neurology and Neurosurgery* 112:5:441–442.

Sethi, N., A. Pearson, and Y. Bajaj. 2017. *Key clinical topics in otolaryngology.* London: JP Medical.

Singhal, N.C. 1972. Hysterical blindness versus malingering. *Indian Journal of Ophthalmology* 20:4:173–178.

Smith, G.P., and G.K. Burger. 1997. Detection of malingering: Validation of the structured inventory of malingered symptomatology. *Journal of the American Academy of Psychiatry and the Law* 25:183–189.

Sokol, L.L., and A. J. Espy. 2016. Clinical signs in functional (psychogenic) gait disorders: A brief survey. *Journal of Clinical Movement Disorders* 3:1–4.

Sonoo, M. 2014. Importance of clinical tests to detect nonorganic paresis. *Journal of Neurology, Neurosurgery and Psychiatry* 85:2:129.

Spreen, O., and E. Strauss. 1998. *A Compendium of Neuropsychological Tests: Administration, Norms, and Commentary*. New York: Oxford University Press.

Stone J., A. Zeman, and M. Sharpe. 2002. Functional weakness and sensory disturbance. *Journal of Neurology, Neurosurgery and Psychiatry* 73:3:241–245.

Stone, J., A. Carson, and M. Sharpe. 2005. Functional symptoms and signs in neurology: Assessment and diagnosis. *Journal of Neurology, Neurosurgery and Psychiatry* 76:1:i2–i12.

Tarsy, D., A. Dengenhardt, and C. Zadikoff. 2006. Psychogenic facial spasm (smirk) presenting as hemifacial spasm. In *Psychogenic Movement Disorders*, eds. M. Hallett, S. Fahn, J. Jankovic, A.E. Lang, C.R. Cloninger, and S.C. Yudofsky, 341–343. Philadelphia: Lippincott Williams & Williams.

Thiagarajan, B., and L. Arjunan. 2012. Tests for malingering. *WebmedCentral ENT Scholar* 3:4: WMC003265. http://www.webmedcentral.com/article_view?3265

Tinazzi, M., S. Simonetto, L. Franco et al. 2008. Abduction finger sign: A new sign to detect unilateral functional paralysis of the upper limb. *Movement Disorders* 23:2415–2419.

Tremolizzo, L., E. Susani, M.A. Riva et al. 2014. Positive signs of functional weakness. *Journal of the Neurological Sciences* 340:1–2:13–18.

Youngjohn, J.R. 1995. Confirmed attorney coaching prior to neuropsychological evaluation. *Assessment* 2:279–283.

Zinkernagel, M.S., N. Pellanda, A. Kunz, and D.S. Mojon. 2009. Saccade testing to distinguish between nonorganic and organic visual field restriction. *British Journal of Ophthalmology* 93:9:1247–1250.

4 The Challenge of Detecting Malingering among Persons with Lower Back Pain

Richard Paul Bonfiglio, MD

CONTENTS

Providing medical care for individuals with chronic back pain for nearly 40 years has taught me an important lesson, "be humble." Since the primary symptom, pain, cannot be compared, quantified, or even verified with current technology, clinicians are dependent on their patients accurately describing their pain and associated symptoms, contributing and relieving factors, and resulting functional limitations.

A patient's ability to accurately report symptoms and participate in a comprehensive examination may be affected by cognitive impairments from a brain injury or psychological impairments due to an underlying psychiatric condition. Compensation considerations may also influence a patient to demonstrate findings to bolster and insure continued financial and social benefits from a demonstrated disability. A patient may intentionally or unintentionally affect findings on history taking and examination which may mask malingering.

Although radiographic testing (including spine X-rays, spine CT and MRI scans, discograms, and CT myelograms) may demonstrate pathology (including disc space and foraminal narrowing, degenerative disc and facet osteoarthritic changes, and even nerve root and spinal cord impingement), pain remains radiolucent.

The extent of radiological abnormalities does not necessarily correlate with the extent of symptoms including the severity of pain experienced. I have seen diagnostic testing of individuals who are pain free, for whom the testing is done for another reason, who have profound abnormalities, which would be consistent with their pain, if they actually had pain. Alternatively, I have had patients with completely normal diagnostic studies who report having intolerable disabling pain.

Electrodiagnostic testing may indicate abnormalities within a nerve root distribution. Although these findings may be consistent with a radiculopathy or other neuropathic process, they cannot confirm that a person is experiencing debilitating chronic back pain. There are persons having abnormalities like diffusely distributed sharp waves who have no recognized underlying pathology. A limited electrodiagnostic test for such individuals could easily inappropriately result in the diagnosis of a radiculopathy.

It has been proposed that diagnostic blocks can help determine whether or not someone is malingering (Bogduk, 2004). Unfortunately, even the use of such blocks is not foolproof. An astute malingering patient would likely report a positive, but transient response from the block and continue to report otherwise intractable pain. Additionally, diagnostic blocks do not impact all chronic back pain generators. Thus, a negative test does not rule out an organic and legitimate cause of pain.

Diagnosing malingering in patients reporting back pain is further complicated by the tendency of most patients with chronic back pain to experience the pain more intensely than individuals experiencing acute pain and to exaggerate and dramatize their symptoms. A patient recognizing the necessity of demonstrating a disabling condition to maintain disability payments, like workers' compensation, may be inclined to embellish the clinical history and examination findings. The background of symptom magnification in a chronic back pain patient makes it more difficult to recognize the rare patient without true underlying pathology.

Thus, identifying malingering, that is, the feigning of disability for avoidance of responsibilities for material gain or to obtain prescriptions for controlled substances, especially opiate pain medications, in a person claiming to have lower back pain, is usually a complex and arduous process (Enslin and Taylor, 2013). Because of the diagnostic limitations of radiographic and electrodiagnostic testing, clinicians must carefully consider all available information to rule out an organic etiology for chronic back pain.

A clinician should consider that any patient could be a malingerer. However, knowing typical clinical patterns of symptomatology, physical examination findings, and diagnostic testing results allows for the accurate diagnosis of clinical conditions including lumbar radiculopathy, fibromyalgia, complex regional pain syndrome, and spinal stenosis. A patient with an atypical or inconsistent presentation should be especially scrutinized for the potential of being a malingerer.

4.1 HISTORY TAKING

Identifying malingerers begins with a thorough and precise clinical history. Clues to malingering include discrepancies in the medical history, evidence of secondary gain, and untruthfulness in other parts of the intake information. A patient with a work history of frequent job changes and poor work performance assessments is more likely to be a malingerer. Likewise, a patient with a history of complete lack of responsiveness to appropriate treatment measures is also suspect.

As an example of the need for precision, obtaining a thorough pain history is essential to evaluating a potential malingerer. The nature and character of the pain should be determined. In English-speaking patients, pain is generally described as one of the following: aching, burning, throbbing, electrical, pressure-like, or sharp. Pain is never constant, since constant pain implies unvarying. Pain always varies, but can be continuous with fluctuating intensity or intermittent with periods of complete resolution. Identifying contributing and relieving factors is important. Determining the radiation of the pain and associated symptoms is also helpful. The only way to "measure" pain is by having the patient rate it from zero to ten. For me, a rating of ten is the most severe pain that the patient has previously experienced over a lifetime. Other clinicians describe it as the most severe that a patient can imagine, but I believe that previously experienced pain is easier for a patient to use as a guide than one's imagination.

Comparing the patient's medical records to the current clinical history can be used to identify discrepancies. This may be heightened with the use of a pain scale and pain drawing. A focus on the functional implications of the pain may also be helpful. If a patient reports impairment in lifting, carrying, upper limb use, and endurance, there should be corresponding physical examination findings to verify the functional impairments. A malingering patient will often be unable to provide the precise historical information that a patient with a legitimate injury will report. Additionally, surveillance films may provide evidence which contradicts the patient's reported functional limitations.

4.2 PHYSICAL EXAMINATION

The physical examination of patients with chronic spine pain requires a thorough and precise evaluation including components to check for malingering. A person who malingers will often present with hypervigilance and hyperresponsiveness; fidgeting is often displayed. Excessive pain behavior may also be exhibited. Observation during history taking provides data regarding the patient's ability to maintain positions. Pain behavior including facial grimacing and vocalizations may be evident. The wearing of a lumbosacral support outside of clothing may indicate that the patient is attempting to enhance the appearance of impairment. Ambulatory aids including a cane or walking stick may also be used for the same purpose. Ambulation without any ambulatory aid may reveal a more normal gait pattern.

All examination findings for a patient with chronic lower back pain has a subjective component. The sensory evaluation including pinprick, light touch, hot versus cold, and even vibratory sensation is completely dependent on the patient accurately describing his or her experience. Manual muscle testing also requires the active participation and full effort of the patient. Subtle weakness can be easily missed, especially when the patient is naturally much stronger than the examiner. Apparent give-way weakness can be due to pain inhibition, anticipated discomfort, a learned response, or malingering. Although checking muscle stretch reflexes is more objective, a well-studied patient can reduce a reflex by volitionally contracting the antagonist muscles. I learned early in my career that patients can be coached by friends, family members, or coworkers to recognize the symptoms and signs of a radiculopathy. The advent of the Internet has made the discovery of these markers that much easier.

Gait analysis is especially helpful in detecting malingering. A thorough analysis of cadence, stride length, stability including initiation and turns, and consistency provides information regarding bilateral lower limb and lower back motor and joint functioning. This analysis should be consistent with the patient's clinical history and diagnostic testing. A patient presenting with a limp should be carefully evaluated to determine if it is a legitimate condition. A consistent limp will cause reduced weight bearing on the symptomatic limb leading to muscle atrophy. Obtaining precise thigh and calf circumference measurements should detect asymmetries for an individual who has a consistent limp with the symptomatic side being smaller than the contralateral limb. A consistent limp should also cause reduced callus formation on the plantar aspect of the foot on the symptomatic limb. Even shoe wear can be affected with less wear being evident on the symptomatic limb. Another check of limping is having the patient walk backwards. A patient with a pain generator will limp forward and backward with a consistent pattern. A malingerer will often limp backwards with an antalgic pattern favoring the contralateral limb. Comparing the duration of vibratory sensation on the medial malleoli of the ankles can help determine the validity of reported sensory loss.

In 1980, Gordon Waddell proposed five types of physical examination signs which he considered indicative of exaggeration or a psychological basis for pain (Jensen, 1994). Dr. Waddell did not propose these signs as evidence of malingering, but other authors have. These signs include diffuse tenderness extending beyond recognized neurological patterns, simulation tests producing pain without movement of the affected joints like axial loading, and distraction testing like straight leg raising done with the patient's attention being diverted. Dr. Waddell also included regional disturbances like weakness and sensory changes in an area not consistent with neurophysiology, and overreaction with excessive pain behavior to testing. Abnormality in three of these five areas was considered abnormal and consistent with symptom magnification. I believe that Dr. Waddell was right that these signs are indicative of symptom magnification but not necessarily evidence of malingering.

4.3 DIAGNOSTIC TESTING

Diagnostic testing consistent with a patient's history, examination, and the clinical impression of the evaluating physician should be enhanced by radiological and electrodiagnostic testing. However, pain is radiolucent. There are many individuals who are asymptomatic who have evidence of radiological spine abnormalities. Just because plain X-rays show degenerative changes, or spine MRI's reveal disc disease or nerve root compression, this does not confirm that these abnormalities are actually symptomatic (Jung and Reidenberg, 2007).

Additionally, the relationship of a diagnostic abnormality to a particular episode of trauma is often complex. Patients rarely have diagnostic testing done before being injured. Therefore, it is difficult to determine after injury whether diagnostic findings are the result of a particular episode of trauma. The abnormalities may result from earlier trauma or the aging process. As I frequently tell patients, "We are all fighting two losing battles, time and gravity."

4.4 CASE EXAMPLES

Early in my career, I provided medical care to a 31-year-old who reported back pain of three months duration which had developed when he lifted a 25-pound piece of equipment at work. He had been employed as a machine operator. His job was generally repetitive without significant lifting, carrying, bending, climbing, or getting into awkward positions. He did have to smooth the edges of various products passing along the assembly line. I prescribed a comprehensive rehabilitation program which included a physical therapy regimen with various modalities and back extension and conditioning exercises. He also had an occupational therapy program including instruction in proper body mechanics for lifting. We also provided a work hardening regimen which included using his normal machine from work that his company had lent to our outpatient clinic.

The patient admitted to making progress in therapy with reduced back pain and overall improvement in his physical condition. However, he maintained that he could not return to his job since he could not stand for eight hours on the concrete floor of his place of employment. This was before the Americans with Disability Act (ADA) and his employer believed that it would be a safety risk to modify his normal work station with a piece of carpeting or other softer surface on which he could stand. His supervisor also believed that the company had already been accommodating by providing his machine for use in the work hardening program.

Prior to being asked to provide a deposition regarding my care of this patient, I was provided with written documentation that he had gone skydiving more than 150 times while on workers' compensation. Additionally, he had won a national skydiving competition by getting closest to a target. I had the privilege of watching surveillance videotape of one of his dives. At my next appointment with this patient, I inquired about his skydiving. His opinion was that what he did on his own time had nothing to do with his work capability. My understanding of physiology and pathology differed and I provided the opinion in my deposition that he had sufficiently recovered to return to his regular job duties without restrictions.

A recent courtroom question caught me by surprise. I was testifying on behalf of a plaintiff who had suffered a traumatic, right, above-knee amputation. He was further functionally limited by severe stump and phantom pain and lower back discomfort. I had determined with my evaluation of him and review of his medical records that in addition to his amputation he had an L_5 lumbar radiculopathy on the same side as his amputation. After delineating my opinions about his ongoing medical problems and impairments including his inability to return to work as a railroad trackman, I was flummoxed by the cross-examination. The defense attorney asked if I believed that his amputation caused a permanent disability.

Upon further reflection, I considered the possibility that the defense attorney had attended a legal conference where there was a discussion about the long term consequences of disabling conditions and the notion that with rehabilitation and appropriate prostheses, although the impairment persisted, disability could be minimized. If the amputee's gait pattern was near normal with a prosthesis and the person was independent with daily activities and work, the disability could be minimized despite the significant ongoing impairment. The *AMA Guides to the Evaluation of Permanent Impairment, Sixth Edition*, defines impairment as "a significant deviation, loss, or loss of use of any body structure or function in an individual with a health condition, disorder, or disease" (American Medical Association, 2009). A disability is defined as "an umbrella term of activity limitations and/or participation restrictions in an individual with a health condition, disorder, or disease" (American Medical Association, 2009). Thus, a person could theoretically have a significant impairment, like an impairment that is permanent, but have function restored with medical treatment including rehabilitation and prosthetic provision with reduction in disability. However, I still testified that this individual had significant impairments and disability due to his work injury which caused the amputation and lumbar radiculopathy.

4.5 CONCLUSION

Pain is a personal experience and cannot be compared, quantified, or validated. Diagnostic testing can demonstrate pathology, but does not necessarily provide correlation with symptomatology or pathophysiology. Patients with chronic lower back pain frequently display excessive pain behavior. These factors make it more difficult to identify patients presenting with lower back pain who are malingering. Proving malingering requires careful analysis of a patient's medical records, clinical presentation, diagnostic testing, and physical examination.

REFERENCES

American Medical Association. 2009. *Guides to the Evaluation of Permanent Impairment. 6th ed.*, eds. R.D. Rondinelli, E. Genovese, R.T. Katz, T.G. Mayer, K.L. Mueller, M.I. Ranavaya, and C.R. Brigham. Chicago: American Medical Association.

Bogduk, N. 2004. Diagnostic blocks: A truth serum for malingering. *The Clinical Journal of Pain* 20:6:409–414.

Enslin, N., and A. Taylor. 2013. Distinguishing neurological from non-organic conditions. *CME* 31:3:80–84.

Jensen, M.C., M.N. Brant-Zawadzki, N. Obuchowski et al. 1994. Magnetic resonance imaging of the lumbar spine in people without back pain. *The New England Journal of Medicine* 331:2:69–73.

Jung, B., and M.M. Reidenberg. 2007. Physicians being deceived. *Pain Medicine* 8:5:433–437.

5 Malingering
A Physical Medicine Perspective

Jasmine M. Campbell, BA, Chevelle Winchester, BS, Angela Rekhi, BSc, MD, Khurram A. Janjua, MD, Anton N. Dietzen, DC, MD, and Alan R. Hirsch, MD

CONTENTS

5.1 INTRODUCTION

Lower back pain or lower back disability has been endemic since World War II (Deyo and Tsui-Wu, 1987), but back pain has been acknowledged as early as 1500 B.C. when first described in the surgical text papyrus bought by Edwin Smith. Lower back pain is not only a common medical condition but also an exasperating and diagnostically intangible ailment. It is pertinent to note that although pain and disability are related they are not the same. Seventy to 85% of patients who seek medical care for lower back pain cost society billions of dollars annually (Dagenais, Caro, and Haldeman, 2008). Of the conditions encountered in medicine, few present with the biopsychosocial challenges of malingering, an exaggerated or feigned illness; and back pain tends to be a common condition for malingerers. Medical education on the identification and management of malingering is limited, if provided at all. This experience is often gained through experience. Physicians are generally poorly trained on the subject of malingering and when it is suspected they rarely comprehend how to approach it with the patient. Although there are many different orthopedic assessments used to detect patients feigning back pain, their accuracy is unknown; thus, diagnosis of malingering becomes mostly subjective.

Before a meaningful discussion of malingering can be had, the diagnosis must be differentiated from similarly presenting conditions. An in-depth review of these disorders is beyond the scope of this chapter; however, we will briefly discuss the key differences between malingering and similarly presenting issues including somatic symptom disorder, conversion disorder, factitious disorder, and anxiety disorder. Essential to a diagnosis of malingering is secondary gain (value) which can include medications (frequently narcotics), disability status, financial gain, employment factors, avoidance of school, occupational, military duty, legal duty, including incarceration. The feigning patient is psychiatrically healthy and deception is deliberate through fabrication or exaggeration of symptoms, which typically resolve after the patient's objective is complete. These patients will often be unwilling to undergo painful or strenuous tests or procedures.

In contrast, somatic symptom disorder presents in a psychologically unwell patient who unconsciously feigns symptoms with no physical cause; complaints are often multiple, vague, and span multiple organ systems. Conversion disorder may be thought of as an extreme of somatic symptom disorder in which a stressor often precipitates a significant sensory or neurological symptom, which cannot be explained by a neurological disease or another medical condition. Factitious disorders are similar to malingering in that patients are pursuing a goal, particularly attention or sympathy from doctors, friends, or family rather than financial secondary gain. Patients having psychiatric involvement and behavior is deliberate. However, unlike malingering, these individuals are often willing to undergo painful/dangerous tests or treatments. Lastly, illness anxiety disorder can be observed in patients who are psychologically unwell, where they genuinely believe they may be affected by a condition but seek no intrinsic or extrinsic gain. Malingerers, compared to the aforementioned disorders, consciously seek extrinsic gain.

5.2 BACK PAIN

The Neanderthal man was one of the earliest human remains that showed degenerative changes in the spine (Stauss and Cave, 1957). Studies today have revealed that there is an inconsequential relationship between degeneration and symptoms. More often than not, back pain has been classified and treated as a disease when it is merely a symptom which stems from a prior condition. There are four anatomical classifications of back pain: neck/cervical, middle back/thoracic, lower back pain/lumbar, and coccydynia/sacral. This pain arises from various areas of the body, such as the nerves, muscles, joints, and bones. The extent of back pain is reviewed as acute (12 weeks), subacute (6–12 weeks), and chronic (persists beyond 12 weeks). Back pain is not specific to any one group of persons, but there are a few characteristics which may increase an individual's risk, such as being between 30 to 40 years old, in poor physical condition overweight, having a poor diet. Also, other factors are heredity predisposition, genetics (ankylosing spondylitis), job type, smoking, and race (black women are two to three times more likely than white women to have slipped their disc in the lower spine) (Wang, Kaplar, Deng, and Leung, 2017).

Back pain symptoms range from the simple backache, which most people have at some time in their lifetime, to serious spinal diseases and lower back disabilities. Since the time of Hippocrates deformities and fractures have been well documented (Allan and Waddell, 1989). Lower back pain has been described with such diseases; however, most speculate that it was just a simple backache and have received little medical attention. The question then becomes, when is it a simple backache and when is it regarded as a medical problem? The nineteenth century laid the foundation for the current approach to back pain. A physician, Brown, in 1828 wrote a paper in the Glasgow Royal Infirmary on spinal irritation and documented for the first time that the nervous system and vertebral column could be the source of back pain (Allan and Waddell, 1989). Papers continued to follow thereafter; however, the exact pathology was never shown for back pain and eventually the diagnosis disappeared. Nevertheless, today the thought of vertebral and nervous system irritation remains, and a thorough history, evaluation, and diagnosis is required.

While back pain may have several causes, a large percentage of patients are diagnosed with nonspecific acute back pain with no proof of any major structural disease. Statistics regarding the incidence and prevalence of lower back pain, both worldwide and in the United States, are staggering. Lower back pain is the number one cause of disability worldwide. At any given time, millions of Americans suffer from low back pain over the course of a year; just about half of all Americans have experienced it (Freburger et al., 2009). With regards to work, lower back pain is the most common medical reason individuals use as an excuse to avoid work and is the second most common reason for visits to the doctor following upper respiratory infections (Atlas and Deyo, 2001). The economic burden caused by lower back pain in the United States is estimated to be between 100 and 200 billion dollars per year (Freburger et al., 2009). Of the money spent on lower back pain, the majority of direct costs are incurred by physical therapy and inpatient services, at 17% each, respectively. The largest overall expenses associated with lower back pain were indirect costs due to missed work. Incredibly, 5% of lower back injuries account for 75% of these costs.

There are several ways to estimate the incidence and prevalence of malingering including patient reports, expert medical reports, covert surveillance, and surveys of the general population. However, patient reports would likely tend to underestimate actual rates of malingering due to concerns for retribution. In patients with both chronic pain and financial incentive, the prevalence of malingering is estimated to range from 20–50% (Greve, Ord, Bianchini, and Curtis, 2009).

5.3 DIAGNOSTIC TESTING

As in many areas of malingering, objective diagnostic testing proving causation and supporting symptomatology is all but impossible. Several diagnostic techniques are commonly used in the workup of lower back pain including X-ray, magnetic resonance imaging (MRI), myelography, computed tomography (CT), nerve conduction velocity (NCV) testing, electromyography testing, diskography, as well as laboratory testing for markers of inflammation and underlying arthritis. Psychological evaluation, for example, the Minnesota Multiphasic Personality Inventory and specialist consultation are also used in the diagnosis of back pain (Dagenais, Caro, and Haldeman, 2008).

A thorough history and physical examination are usually sufficient to distinguish the majority of patients in which a specific therapy is required. While diagnostic radiology is of little use in the initial evaluation for most spinal disorders, standard radiographs are frequently required by insurance companies before more sophisticated testing can be done. Radiographs provide little data on back pain but are important for ruling out significant and serious pathologies.

MRI is the most frequently used diagnostic test to determine suspected lumbar nerve root compression in characterizing lower back pain. With most of the medical costs of lower back pain coming from the use of diagnostic testing, the optimal choice among the varied diagnostic tests still remains a controversial issue. MRI studies have demonstrated that over 50% of asymptomatic adults have disc bulges while over one-quarter have a protrusion, and 1% have an extrusion (Jensen, Brant-Zawadzki, Obuchowski, Modic, Malasian, and Ross, 1994).

These statistics call into question the diagnostic accuracy of MRI in identifying the relationship between tissue injury and lumbago. If over half of the patients who are asymptomatic have abnormalities in MRI can this be relied upon to diagnose malingering? One would suggest it does not meet scientific validity as a stand-alone test for diagnosis of true symptomatic disease.

5.4 HISTORY REGARDING WARNING SIGNS

Notably, the history in the malingering patient may be either consistent or inconsistent. In the case of patients who have rehearsed their history, the physician may note that the patient's story sounds practiced. On the other hand, some patient histories, especially when taken on multiple accounts, may reveal inconsistencies in events related to the injury or the order in which it occurred. In either case, the physician should note that the pattern of injury does not match the insult described in the history. Additionally, the physician may notice that the patient tends to speak ill of their workplace, superiors, or coworkers while some patients may attempt to mislead the physician into documenting the events in a way that supports a work injury claim. Those patients that present with both chronic pain and financial incentives are more likely to malinger or show an exaggeration of an injury. Therefore, it is best that patients are asked about prior injuries with special attention being paid to the history of their chronic pain. Chronic pain affects the brain and may in turn impair logical reasoning (Freburger et al., 2009).

Physical examination findings to look for in a malingerer center on consistency of effort and compliance. In fact, many of the 'tests' of malingering are actually examining the patient's willingness to follow the physician's instructions. Many of the requirements given by caseworkers are testing these same principles including patient attendance record and timeliness of arrival for appointments. Functional capacity evaluations, similarly, allow the clinician to spend more time with the patients in order to recognize inconsistencies in effort and patient compliance. It is important to note that both these characteristics can be falsely noted as positive in patients with pain behaviors, avoiding provocation. Avoidance of pain is a basic human trait and it has been demonstrated that humans will go to great lengths to avoid it. The majority of the factors at play in the identification of malingering concern discrepancies between complaints and physical, neurological, gait and posture examination and the patient's subjective complaints and presentation of illness. There are several orthopedic tests and signs used to diagnose malingering; However, whether or not these tests present 100% true findings of malingering is still up for debate. Difficulty arises when the physician is left to determine how much of the symptoms are directly due to tissue damage in the spine or a subconscious amplification of a minor problem which may be perceived as severe pain causing chronic disability.

There are specific signs seen during physical exams, which can be used to pinpoint patients with nonorganic components to their issues, such as exaggerated pain reactions in their facial expression, shaking, and falling to the floor. Other findings may include widespread superficial tenderness which is not correlated with anatomical distribution; findings of a limited Straight Leg Test in a patient who can sit forward with legs extended; and disturbances of sensory loss or limb weakness without findings of nerve root damage. Having a single positive result doesn't rule-in a malingered patient; however, multiple positive results should warrant further evaluations. The issue then becomes how to identify patients who purposely exaggerate their symptoms from those that genuinely experience pain (see Chapter 6). Waddell's signs have gained in popularity and are frequently used to support a diagnosis of malingering. Waddell's nonorganic physical signs were proposed as a simple clinical screen to identify patients who may require a more detailed assessment of psychological factors. The five parts to this test are:

1. Tenderness unrelated to anatomic structures (e.g., tenderness to light pinch of skin over a wide area).
   a. Superficial: The suspected malingerer would show positive signs if back pain is experienced by delicately pinching the skin above the lumbar spine.
   b. Nonanatomic: The suspected malingerer would show positive signs if there are any significant nonanatomic distributions of the area of tenderness.
2. Tests to simulate spine loading or rotation without actually producing the simulated effect.
   a. Axial loading: The suspected malingerer would show positive signs with the production of lower back pain when an axial compression is applied on the head.
   b. Rotation: The practitioner will squat in front or behind the patient while holding the patient's forearms on their trochanteric region. The practitioner will suggest that the movement may cause pain. The practitioner will then rotate the pelvis of the patient. The suspected malingerer would show positive signs that the movement causes pain (Figure 5.1).
   c. Distraction: Careful monitoring of the same signs or tests through a series of different situations.

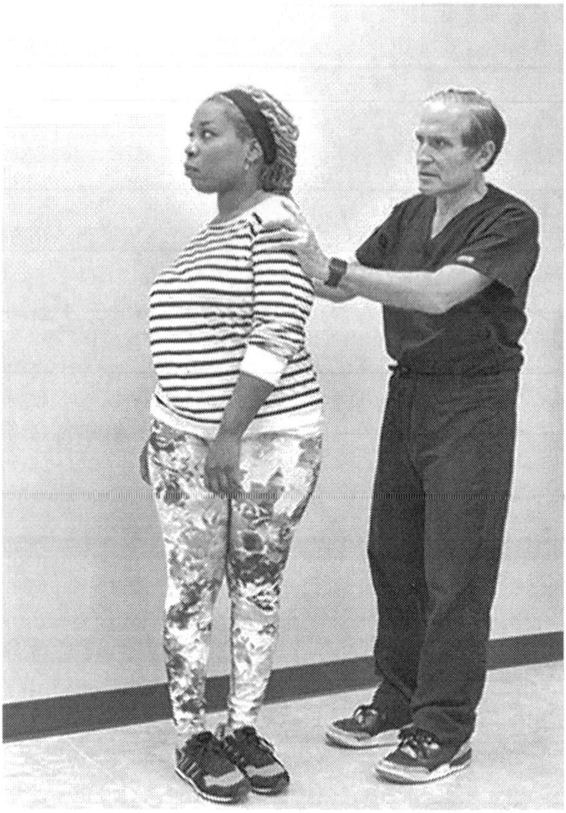

FIGURE 5.1 Rotation.

3. Straight leg raising in the sitting position.
   a. The physician would examine the lower back of the patient while they sit upright with their legs in an extended position. The suspected malingerer would show a positive sign if, when asked to raise the straightened leg, there is restriction. The patient is still able to sit erect with their knees extended.
4. Neurologic deficits without a physiologic or anatomic explanation (e.g., "cogwheel" release of muscle tone on strength testing, or "stocking" as opposed to dermatomal sensory deficits).
5. Overreaction during the examination, including disproportionate verbalization, facial expression, muscle tension or tremor, collapsing, and sweating.

5.5 ADDITIONAL BEHAVIORAL SIGNS AND TESTING

There are other behavioral signs described in literature. Physicians may perform these simulation tests in physical examination of patients with low back pain and suspected malingering. The simulation tests are as follows:

Burns' bench test: The patient is asked to kneel on a pad without any arm support while flexing the hips and knees as much as possible so as to position oneself as if they are sitting on their calves. An attempt is made to flex forward by the patient and touch the floor with their fingertips. The suspected malingerer shows a positive sign when they are unable to flex or touch the floor (Figure 5.2).

McBride's test: While leaning againts a wall and standing on both feet, the patient is asked to raise and flex the affected leg at the hip and knee while bringing the knee towards the chest with their hands. This removes the stretch on the sciatic nerve. The suspected malingerer would show a positive sign if they are unable to carry out this maneuver or express pain (Figure 5.3).

Kummel's neck movement: While standing erect, the physician asks the patient to move their neck in two different directions. When asked to move the cervical spine the physician would place a hand on the patient's chest preventing motion of the thoracic or lumbar spine. The suspected malingerer would show a positive sign by informing the physician of back pain while moving the neck in two different directions.

Kummel's shoulder movement: The patient is asked to move each shoulder in turn while standing erect. The physician prevents movements of the lumbar spine by placing their hand on the patient's trunk at nontender areas. The suspected malingerer would show a positive sign by limiting the movement and informing the physician of pain caused by the movement of the shoulders (Figure 5.4).

Heel tap test: The patient is asked to sit on a couch with knees and hips flexed to 90 degrees. The physician suggests to the patient that this particular test may cause them some lower back pain. The physician, with the base of their hand, taps the patient's heel. The suspected malingerer will show a positive sign by letting the physician know that there is sudden lower back pain (Figure 5.5).

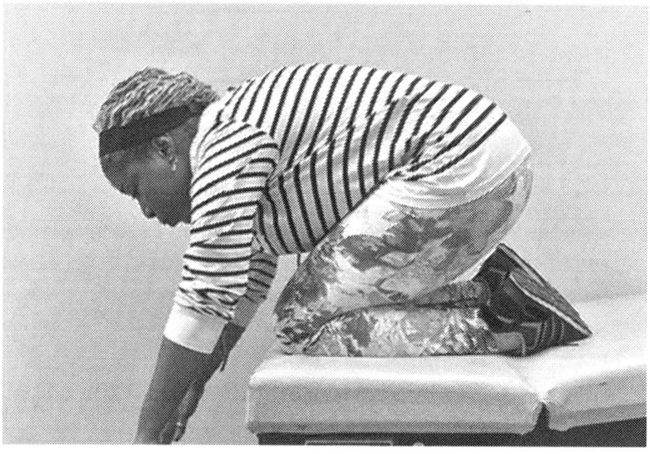

FIGURE 5.2 Burns' bench test.

FIGURE 5.3 McBride's test.

Plantar flexion of the ankle: The patient's foot is plantar flexed and the physician asks if they are feeling any leg pain. The suspected malingerer shows a positive sign by letting the physician know there is increased pain with plantar flexion.

Hoover test: The physician will place both hands on the seat below the patient's heels, while the patient is lying in a supine position. The patient is then asked to raise each straightened leg. For normal patients with no chronic back pain, when real effort is placed, a counter pressure is felt on their contralateral heel. The patient would then push their heel into the practitioner's palm. The suspected malingerer would show a positive sign if there is an absence of counter pressure.

O'Donoghue's maneuver: Passive range of motion will be considerably more when compared to the active range of motion of patients with an actual

FIGURE 5.4 Kummel's shoulder movement.

disease. The suspected malingerer will show a positive sign when active range of motion is more than passive range of motion.

Mankopf's test: For a normal individuals a noxious stimulus will have an autonomic effect by increasing their pulse rate. Therefore, if the physician palpates the painful lumbar spine, there should be an increase in pulse rate when the practitioner palpates the painful lumbar spine. The suspected malingerer would have a positive sign if there is no increase in pulse on the pulse oximeter.

Pallesthesia: This tests the absence of the ability to discern vibration. It is performed on a wide range of areas through the bone and a great overlap of dermatomes. If there is damage to a nerve root, then there will be no difference in the perception of that sensation of vibration. The suspected malingerer will show a positive sign if there is an altered vibration sensation, not followed by other signs of general neurological disorder.

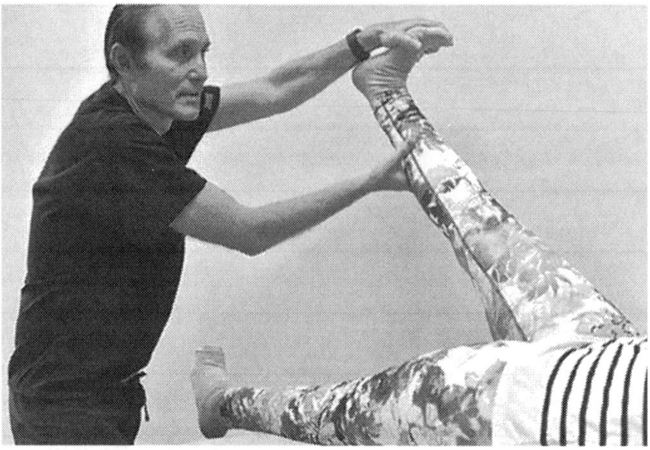

FIGURE 5.5 Heel tap test.

5.6 PHARMACOTHERAPY: OPIOIDS

With their abuse labeled an epidemic/crisis, opioids are the leading cause of drug overdose in America. It was reported that 33,091 deaths in 2015 were caused by opioids and since 1999, overdoses have quadrupled (Rudd, Noah-Aleshire, Zibbell, and Gladden, 2016). The rates of death from overdose of prescription opioids has dramatically increased between 1999 and 2010. This far exceeds the combined death toll from cocaine and heroin overdoses. In 2010 alone, prescription opioids were involved in 16,651 overdose deaths, whereas heroin was implicated in 3036 deaths (Volkow, Frieden, Hyde, and Cha, 2014).

The abuse of opioids in individuals with lower back pain is quickly becoming a great concern. The problem presents when persons malingering back pain are prescribed opioids. Obtaining drugs for resale is another external incentive for malingering. This is documented as the criminological model of malingering. For some, malingering to preserve delivery of narcotics could be due to a prior opioid addiction. What must be asked is how often chronic nonmalignant pain patients who are exposed to chronic opioid analgesic therapy actually develop an addiction. Fortunately it is documented that these numbers seem to be very low. Seventy-nine references subjected to 12 quality criteria, as well as 67 reports, scored a quality rating greater than 65%. Of chronic nonmalignant pain patients, only 0.59% of those who were exposed to chronic opioids later developed abuse (Fishbain, Cole, Lewis, Rosomoff, and Rosomoff, 2008).

The question now is what can be done to bring these figures down even further. Clinicians must be more observant of drug-seeking behaviors such as irrational, persistent demands for immediate action, atypical knowledge of certain controlled substances involving requests for specific agents, nonadherence or hastened dismissal of nonopioid alternatives, lack of concern of the diagnosis, strange mood disturbances, frequent misplaced prescriptions, exaggeration of medical problems, continuous visits for exactly the same complaint, and adoption of unmeasurable grievances like headaches.

5.7 SUGGESTIONS

Numerous studies have shown that with many back injuries and disabilities, gradual return to work or daily activities are often a highly effective part of the recovery process. Frequently, patients with lower back pain are under the presumption that they should only return to work once they are symptom free; however, this has proven not to be the case. Patients may be less motivated to return to work, especially since they continue to receive an income while remaining off work. Most patients also worry that their injuries may get worse by returning to work. Such cases may benefit from additional help from a case manager who can provide extra guidance and information regarding "return to work duties." In cases with malingering patients, case managers may be encouraged to hire private investigators to determine whether or not employees are lying about the functional limitations of lower back pain or injuries.

Physical ailments go beyond the scope of just the injury. While assessing patients with back pain the biopsychosocial model should be taken into consideration as opposed to simply assessing for an organic etiology. Incorporating the biopsychosocial model entails thorough history taking and physical examinations. Recognition that ailments have a dynamic relationship with mental, physical, and social components allows for better assessment and treatment of back pain. A study by van der Giezen (2000) found that psychosocial aspects of health and work in conjunction with economic aspects significantly affected return to work in patients with lower back pain (van der Giezen, Bouter, and Nijhuis, 2000). This indicates the importance of assessments of health behavior, job satisfaction, and economic incentives for return to work in such patients.

REFERENCES

Allan, D.B., and G. Waddell. 1989. An historical perspective on low back pain and disability, *Acta Orthopaedica Scandinavica* 60:234:1–23.

Atlas, S.J., and R.A. Deyo. 2001. Evaluating and managing acute low back pain in the primary care setting. *Journal of General Internal Medicine* 16:2:120–131.

Dagenais, S., J. Caro, and S. Haldeman. 2008. A systematic review of low back pain cost of illness studies in the United States and internationally. *The Spine Journal* 8:1:8–20.

Deyo, R.A., and Y.J. Tsui-Wu. 1987. Descriptive epidemiology of low back pain and its related medical care in the United States. *Spine* 12:3:264–268.

Fishbain, D.A., B. Cole, J. Lewis, H.L. Rosomoff, and R.S. Rosomoff. 2008. What percentage of chronic nonmalignant pain patients exposed to chronic opioid analgesic therapy develop abuse/addiction and/or aberrant drug-related behaviors? A structured evidence–based review. *Pain Medicine* 9:4:444–459.

Freburger, J.K., G.M. Holmes, R.P. Agans et al. 2009. The rising prevalence of chronic low back pain. *Archives of Internal Medicine* 169:3:251–258.

Greve, K.W., J.S. Ord, K.J. Bianchini, and K.L. Curtis. 2009. Prevalence of malingering in patients with chronic pain referred for psychologic evaluation in a medico-legal context. *Archives of Physical Medicine and Rehabilitation* 90:7:1117–1126.

Jensen, M.C., M.N. Brant-Zawadzki, N. Obuchowski, M.T. Modic, D. Malasian, and J.S. Ross. 1994. Magnetic resonance imaging of the lumbar spine in people without back pain. *New England Journal of Medicine* 331:2:69–73.

Rudd, R.A., J.D. Noah Aleshire, J.E. Zibbell, and R.M. Gladden. 2016. Increases in drug and opoid overdose deaths—United States 2000–2014. *Morbidity and Mortality Report (MMWR), CDC Centers for Disease Control and Prevention* 64:50:1378–1382.

Stauss, W.L., and A.J.E. Cave. 1957. Pathology and the posture of Neandertal man. *Quarterly Review of Biology* 32:348–363

van der Giezen, A.M., L.M. Bouter, and F.J. Nijhuis. 2000. Prediction of return-to-work of low back pain patients sick listed for 3–4 months. *Pain* 87:3:285–294.

Volkow, N.D., T.R. Frieden, P.S. Hyde, and S.S. Cha. 2014. Medication-assisted therapies—Tackling the opioid-overdose epidemic. *New England Journal of Medicine* 370:2063–2066.

Wang, Y.X., Z. Kaplar, M. Deng, and J.C. Leung. 2017. Lumbar degenerative spondylolisthesis epidemiology: A systematic review with a focus on gender-specific and age-specific prevalence. *Journal of Orthopaedic Translation* 11:39–52.

6 Validity of Waddell's Sign

Jasir T. Nayati, AAS, CNMT and Ather M. Ali, MD

CONTENTS

6.1 INTRODUCTION

Among a population at risk of over 1.48 billion persons per year, with a 1.39 per 1000 persons per year incidence rate, there are an estimated 2.06 million episodes of lower back pain in the United States (Waterman, Belmont, and Schoenfeld, 2012). Lower back pain accounted for 3.15% of all emergency visits in 2012 (Waterman, Belmont, and Schoenfeld, 2012). In 1998, there was a one-year prevalence of 15% among the 30- to 40-year-old population, with an incidence approaching 70% among the 40 year-old (Leboeuf-Yde and Kyvik, 1998).

Lower back pain is the leading cause of chronic pain and it has become very difficult to treat, as clinicians contemplate whether or not physical exercise, medical, or surgical treatment are the best options. Often times, the treatment management is ineffective in providing relief, so much so that severe "temporary" measures are taken to alleviate the pain. Thus, the administration of opiate medications has become a very common practice amongst both medical and surgical physicians for temporary pain relief. In some ways, this has intensified the opiate epidemic in the United States. In 2012, 259 million prescriptions were written for opioid medication, with a prescribing rate of 81.3 prescriptions per 100 persons (CDC Centers for Disease Control and Prevention, 2017). However, the overall national opioid prescribing rate declined over four years, such that in 2016 it had decreased to 66.5 prescriptions per 100 persons (over 214 million total opioid prescriptions), the lowest it had been in over 10 years (CDC Centers for Disease Control and Prevention, 2017). From 2010 to 2015, the amount of opioids prescribed in the United States decreased from 782 to 640 morphine milligram equivalents (MME) per person. This means that every American is medicated 24 hours a day, 7 days a week, for 3 weeks; moreover, 640 MME per person equals approximately 5 milligrams of hydrocodone every four hours, for every living person in the United States from babies to centenarians (Guy et al., 2017).

While dropping over the last couple years, the amounts of opioids prescribed in 2015 remained approximately three times as high as in 1999; yet, it varied substantially across different counties in the United States (Guy et al., 2017). It was found that counties which have higher opioid prescribing rates shared similar characteristics, such as a larger percentage of non-Hispanic whites, lower educational attainment, more dentists and physicians per capita, a higher prevalence of diagnosed diabetes mellitus, arthritis, disability, higher suicide rates, higher rates of unemployment, and higher rates of uninsured and Medicaid enrollment (Guy et al., 2017). Together, these factors explain 32% of the variation in the amounts of opioids prescribed at the county-level. In a study conducted by Cicero et al. (2014), retrospective data from self-administered surveys was gathered on past drug use patterns among patients entering substance abuse treatment programs across the country. It was reported that 94% of the surveyed individuals treated for opioid addiction chose to use heroin because prescription opioids were "far more expensive and harder to obtain" (Cicero, Ellis, Surratt, and Kurtz, 2014). With the association of the modern health insurance reform, this debilitating epidemic has caused individuals who are not insured to resort to other means of purchasing opiates. This in turn has resulted in an increase in prison population, illegal drug trafficking, and additional health ailments stemming from the use of illegal substances.

A national survey was conducted by the Center for Behavioral Health Statistics and Quality in 2015 (Bose, Hedden, Lipari, Park-Lee, Porter, and Pembert, 2016), which presented numbers and statistics regarding the prevalence of use and dependence of pain relievers and related dependence disorders. The survey indicated that 20.8 million Americans, ages 12 years or older, had a substance use disorder. Substance use disorder is defined as recurrent use of either alcohol, medications, or illicit drugs causing clinical and functional impairment (American Psychiatric Association, 2013). Out of these 20.8 million Americans, 3.8 million did not use pain relievers as prescribed and two million have a pain reliever use disorder. In the same survey, it was found that approximately 1.1 million Americans from ages 12 to 25 were misusing pain relievers, and among those, 549,000 individuals had an addiction to prescription pain relievers. Most importantly, 591,000 Americans were diagnosed as having a heroin use disorder in 2015, with 329,000 actively using the drug. In the same year, an estimated 161,000 Americans between the ages 12 to 25 suffered from heroin use disorder, in which 93,000 continued to use heroin actively.

This has caused physicians to fall under extreme scrutiny and to be the center of blame as physicians prescribe these medications. Many physicians have lost their licenses due to enhanced regulatory enforcement secondary to this epidemic, and are at a disadvantage of not knowing whether or not their patients are truly suffering from pain or just presenting with pain in order to seek pain-relieving prescriptions. This has brought forth a challenge for today's medical professionals in the sense that they must distinguish whether their patients are truly in pain or succumbing to a severe opiate dependence disorder.

When a patients present themselves to a new physician, either after leaving their previous medical provider or as a new consult to evaluate back pain, the history of the patient's illnesses are recorded and past medical records are obtained from the previous physician. This process is in place to ensure that whomever is working with the patient is updated on the patient's past history. Information shared includes, but is not limited to, history of medical and psychiatric diagnoses, medications, surgeries, family, laboratory results, diagnostic imaging, and electrophysiological results. The patient's past medical history is of critical importance, and it is necessary to adequately address the patient's needs in order to better strategize medical management. However, the drawback to this comes in the form of "observer bias." This is when a physician discusses the patient's condition and shares a diagnosis which may influence another physician's decision-making (Hróbjartsson et al., 2014). Thus, the new physician may want to rule out a previous diagnosis (i.e., polysubstance abuse disorder) if the patient is drug-seeking, and may end up overlooking whether or not the pain the individual is suffering, is from an organic cause. Other psychiatric diagnoses, such as malingering with secondary gain, may play a significant role regarding the diagnoses.

When a patient presents to a physician for chronic pain his or her behavior can affect the overall experience with the physician. For instance, if you imagine yourself in agonizing pain trying to seek help from your physician, what will your overall attitude be? What about the contents of your thoughts? Your mood? Will you be angry? Impatient? Will you be hysterical because of the pain? More often than not, patients who truly are in chronic pain will not present themselves in the best behavior. This, in turn may cause the physician, whom the patient is seeking help from, to be more irritable or frustrated and thus impacts their decision on how to better help treat the ailment. As Newton's third law of motion states, for every action, there is an equal and opposite reaction. Both physicians and patients need to find themselves on the better half of the spectrum, which will allow for ideal treatment and management. However, this consideration should be the responsibility of physicians, as they must always conduct themselves professionally and find ways to not be influenced by previous diagnoses or patient's behavior and perform the proper examinations to rule out the patient's root cause of pain, as opposed to just temporary treatment. Within this construct, Waddell's signs have been developed.

6.2 BIOGRAPHY

Dr. Gordon Waddell (1943–2007) was a Scottish surgeon who specialized in orthopedic surgery. Throughout his years he spent a great deal of time focusing on the common man and woman dealing with back pain, so much so that he published many articles (over 100) and books (over ten) discussing orthopedic and rheumatological pain. Through his literary work, he had a clear message; physicians need to stop overmedicalizing back pain. In order to do so, he suggested detailed histories, thorough physical examinations, and the use of noninvasive imaging procedures. This allowed clinicians to safely distinguish simple back pain and those suffering with extremely debilitating back pain. Dr. Waddell further suggested that back pain-related issues should first be treated by primary care physicians, with minimal intervention. If the condition is urgent or requires more attention, specialists may be sought out. If there is no resolution of the back pain as expected, even after noninvasive procedures are performed, social and psychological factors should be taken into consideration. For these types of patients therapy should be targeted towards keeping them as active as possible and getting them back to daily activities and work as soon as possible even if the pain persists (Shakelle, 1999).

In 1979, Dr. Waddell was awarded the Volvo Award in Clinical Science for research he conducted with his colleagues. In 2003, he was honored by the Queen of England with the title "Commander of the British Empire" for his work with social policy and disability assessment (research). Waddell et al., helped pioneer a noninvasive method in ascertaining whether there is a nonorganic or psychological element to the etiology of a patient's chronic lower back pain (Waddell, McCulloch, Kummel, and Venner, 1980). He grouped five physical signs together to assess lower back pain and the possibility of associated malingering, which a practitioner can perform without the use of diagnostic imaging. It consisted of five tests: tenderness, simulation, distraction, regional disturbance, and an overreaction test. These are collectively known as "Waddell's Signs."

6.3 BACKGROUND

Waddell's Signs were first introduced in the March/April 1980 issue of *Spine*, in "Nonorganic Physical Signs in Low-Back Pain." Dr. Waddell and his colleagues discussed how they performed a prospective study in which they evaluated the results of 350 patients suffering from chronic lower back pain. It was established that not only are the nonorganic signs distinct from physical pathology, but also that they correlate with other psychological data. By separating physical from nonorganic etiology, clinicians are better able to clarify the assessment of purely physical pathologic conditions. Waddell et al. (1980) also suggested that the nonorganic signs can be used as a simple clinical screening tool to help identify patients who require more detailed psychological assessment, i.e., poor surgical candidates (Waddell, McCulloch, Kummel, and Venner, 1980). Eventually, physicians who initially looked at the study results came to a general consensus not based on calculating statistical significance and concluded that a finding of three or more of the five types of tests is clinically significant for nonmechanical, pain-focused behavior (Waddell, McCulloch, Kummel, and Venner, 1980).

In order to understand pain-focused behavior one must understand the full scope of pain. Pain is a symptom, not a sign, and therefore, can be a result of multidimensional interactions. According to the Gate Control Theory of Pain (Melzack and Wall, 1965) and its later derivatives (Melzack and Casey, 1968) the perception of pain is dependent upon a system of intricate neuronal interactions in the nervous system in which impulses are generated at the site of tissue injury and are then sent to the brain. It is modified, via neurophysiological mechanisms, at the dorsal horns of the spinal cord by both the ascending pathways and descending pathways in which pain-suppressing systems are activated by numerous external and psychological factors. The Gate Control Theory of Pain integrated peripheral stimuli and cortical variables which account for mood states affecting pain perception; Waddell took this into consideration and perceived pain within a wider model. He integrated the biopsychosocial model and formulated the biopsychosocial model of pain and disability

(Waddell, 1998). The "biopsychosocial" approach coalesces physical, psychological, and social factors which influence the experience of a certain ailment. Originally conceived by the American psychiatrist George Engel in the 1970s, Waddell and Mansel Aylward adapted the biopsychosocial model to form the theoretical basis for the current government of the United Kingdom's thinking on disability (Shakespeare, Watson, and Alghaib, 2016). In Waddell's biopsychosocial model of low back pain and disability, with pain being the center of the model, pain is assessed while considering and incorporating the patient's attitude, beliefs, psychological distress, illness and behavior, and social environment.

6.4 WADDELL'S SIGNS

Given that the Gate Control Theory of Pain has generated a wide range of research (Melzack and Wall, 1996), Waddell encouraged careful investigation with regards to the nature of chronic low back pain and pain-associated disability. In 1980, Waddell's article titled, "Nonorganic Physical Signs in Low-Back Pain" introduced a new method to distinguish physical lower back pain from nonorganic lower back pain. The eight physical findings from five categories as well as the techniques and the methodologies of each of Waddell's signs, are as follows (Waddell, McCulloch, Kummel, and Venner, 1980):

1. *Tenderness Tests.* When pain or tenderness in the lower back is being experienced, and if truly organic in nature, it will be localized to a particular skeletal or neuromuscular structure. This test is done by dividing this test into *superficial* and *nonanatomic* tenderness exams. If nonorganic, the pain and tenderness will be diffused.

   The *Superficial Tenderness* examination involves lightly pinching the skin over the lumbar area. If the skin is tender to a light pinch over a wide area, the test is deemed positive for a nonorganic cause. However, one must take nerve distribution (dermatomes) into consideration. While conducting this test, in cases of nerve impingement or irritation, a band-like pain in the posterior primary ramus distribution may present (Gunn and Milbrandt, 1978). In such a case, the cause can be considered organic and malingering can be ruled out.

   The *Nonanatomic Tenderness* examination is performed by a deep palpation to a localized area. If the pain is not localized to one portion of the back and extends to the upper back or very low back (i.e., thoracic, sacrum, or pelvic region) it may suggests malingering.
2. *Simulation Test.* This test is based on movement-induced pain and will give the patient the perception that a particular examination will result in pain when in fact it will not. During a formal examination, a particular movement will result in a localized tender area reported by the patient. That same movement which elicited pain will be simulated, but not actually be performed. This is done by the clinician by exerting force on a body part or moving the body in such a way that it anatomically should not elicit much pain. If the patient reports pain during simulation nonorganic influence is suggested.

This examination is also subdivided into two exams, the *axial loading* and *rotational* examinations.

The *Axial Loading* examination is performed by the clinician lightly exerting force straight down on the patient's skull while they are in a standing position. This should not result in lower back pain. If pain is reported, it is deemed a positive, indicating malingering. However, the patient may report pain in the cervical region. This is common, and it may be consistent with organic disease as opposed to malingering.

The *Rotational* examination is performed when the clinician turns the patient's shoulders and pelvis in the same plane, with the entire body, and without twisting of the back. Since the lumbar spine is not twisted this test should not elicit lower back pain. If pain is reported by the patient, then this test suggests malingering.

3. *Distraction Tests*. This test is done by indirect observation, observing the unaware patient while they are in the examiner's presence. To put this simply, the clinician is retesting a painful physical examination sign while the patient is distracted and not aware that the test is being performed again. However, the distraction must not be painful, must not draw emotions or be of emotional content, and must not be surprising or of shockvalue. During this examination, parts of the body other than the particular part being overtly tested should be observed. The clinician should observe the patient as they walk around the exam room, while the patient is giving the history, and while performing the *straight leg raising* test, and other components of the physical examination. Any finding that is consistently present is likely to be physically based. Findings that are present only on formal examination and then disappear at other times, especially when distracted, may have a nonorganic component.

   The *Straight Leg Raising* test is the most useful distraction test to perform. It should be done while the patient is supine and when the patient is seated upright. While supine, the clinician should raise the patient's leg up to about 90 degrees towards the ceiling. If the patient reports pain, then one can say that there is a true organic cause (i.e., spinal injury) for their lower back pain. Repeat the process with the opposite leg, and if there is more pain on the opposite side it is then indicative of a pathologic cause. However, it should be retested when the patient is sitting in an upright position, as when testing plantar flexion. If straight leg raise testing is improved in either a supine or seated position, it is deemed as a nonorganic finding.

4. *Regional Disturbance Tests*. Also known as "exaggerated body pain test," it involves a widespread region of neighboring parts, such as the leg below the knee, the entire leg, or a quarter or half of the body. The accepted feature is the divergence from accepted neuroanatomy. In other words, if nonorganic etiology is at play the patient will exhibit pain in areas where no pain should exist based upon dermatome (nerve) distribution. Similar to the preceding tests, this is subdivided into two examinations as well: *weakness* and *sensory*.

The *Weakness* examination is demonstrated on formal testing by a partial "giving way" of many muscle groups which cannot be explained on a localized neurologic basis. In other words, a clinician needs to be looking for weakness in the body which is not connected to the nerve root that is allegedly damaged. For instance, a patient will present or have a confirmed nerve root injury in the lumbar region. However, instead of the muscles that are innervated by the nerve root that is damaged, the patient will exhibit severe weakness of all the leg muscles. A sudden uneven weakness in a patient who demonstrate normal strength on muscle testing, supports malingering.

The *Sensory* examination involves the clinician looking for sensory disturbances, which include diminished sensation to light touch, pinprick, and other modalities that fit a "stocking" rather than a dermatomal pattern. "Giving way" and sensory changes commonly affect the same area, and there may be associated nonanatomic regional tenderness. For instance, if the patient has suffered from back injury, sensory loss should be present in areas that correlate with its nerve innervation. However, if the patient exhibits sensory loss elsewhere, a nonorganic caveat should be considered. An exception to this caveat would be in those with peripheral neuropathy, a stock-glove distribution of sensory loss will often be present, which is not a sign of malingering.

5. *Overreaction Test.* Overreaction during examination may take the form of disproportionate verbalization, facial expression, muscle tension and tremor, collapsing, or sweating. The response to procedures such as venipuncture or myelography provides additional information. However, judgments should, be made with caution while minimizing the examiner's own emotional reaction; there are considerable cultural variations and it is very easy to introduce observer bias or to provoke this type of response unconsciously. The overreaction test is the single most important nonorganic physical sign. Unfortunately, this sign is also the most subjective given that it is influenced by the subjective impressions of the observer. Be aware of false positives of this test, especially in those with blood or needle phobia.

6.5 SCORING

With regard to scoring Waddell states that any individual sign counts as a positive sign for each particular test. A finding of three or more within the five test categories, clinically indicates nonorganic back pain. Isolated positive signs should be ignored (Waddell, McCulloch, Kummel, and Venner, 1980). It is important to note that predictive values will greatly improve when there are more than three positive signs.

6.6 DISCUSSION

Since being introduced in 1980, Waddell's Signs test is still practiced to this day by many clinicians. Although the primary use of these tests has shifted from Waddell's original idea (identifying patients who will likely be poor surgical candidates) it has become a screening tool for physicians to rule out malingering/secondary gain, hysteria, psychological distress, magnified presentation, abnormal illness behavior, abnormal pain behavior, and somatic amplification. Currently, there is significant confusion as to what the findings truly mean and how well they correlate with the diagnosis of malingering. There is very limited data on the reliability or validity of Waddell's Signs tests. There has been growing evidence that Waddell's Signs do not help distinguish nonorganic from organic pathology. In fact, there also has been growing evidence that Waddell's Signs do not help predict whether or not a patient is showing signs of malingering and secondary gain (Fishbain, Cutler, Rosomoff, and Rosomoff, 2004).

In order to distinguish nonorganic from organic back pain a clinician must know what he or she is looking for. Organic back pain simply means back pain resulting from a physical source or due to physiological change. This can include such things as muscle strain or spasms, spondylosis, traumatic or compression fractures, spinal stenosis, kyphosis, scoliosis, spondylolisthesis, bone malignancy or metastases, Paget's disease, osteochondrosis, spondylitis, infection, or referred pain from retroperitoneal irritation (i.e., pancreatitis, pelvic inflammatory disease, or abdominal aortic aneurysms). Nonorganic findings of back pain most commonly present as pain at the tip of the tailbone, diffuse leg pain or numbness in a global distribution, acute give-way weakness of the lower limbs, absence of even brief periods of relative pain relief, failure or intolerance of numerous treatments, and numerous urgent care visits or hospitalizations for back pain (Waddell, Bircher, Finlayson, and Main, 1984).

Throughout the years, with the advancement of technology and various diagnostic imaging modalities, it has become easier to localize the cause of back pain. Imaging studies include radiographs, computed tomography, magnetic resonance imaging (MRI), electromyography, nerve conduction studies, and many more. Although these diagnostic imaging modalities are available to assess back pain, it is estimated that only 15% of all lower back pain has an identifiable anatomic explanation, while the other 85% is identified as nonspecific (White and Gordon, 1982). Carragee et al. (2006) performed a five-year prospective observational study in which 200 subjects presenting with a first-time episodes of lower back pain and 51 subjects (25%) were evaluated with lumbar MRI for clinically severe lower back pain episodes. Baseline characteristics were evaluated along with physical examinations, plain radiographs, and MRIs. Follow-up lumbar MRIs were taken within six to 12 weeks after initial onset of the new lower back pain episode and were compared with baseline images. Among the study population group 43 subjects (84%) who had primary lower back pain had an unchanged MRI compared to baseline (Carragee, Alamin, Cheng, Franklin, van den Haak, and Hurwitz, 2006). Thus, it was concluded that follow-up MRIs, within 12 weeks of clinically severe acute-lower back pain, will have a very low probability of revealing any new structural changes. Carragee et al. (2006), showed that follow-up MRIs do not demonstrate change despite serious incidents of new lower back pain compared to baseline and new findings are most commonly due to age-related changes—i.e., disc signal loss (10%), progressive facet arthrosis (10%), or increased end plate changes. With MRIs having the most sensitivity and specificity compared to other diagnostic imaging when evaluating for lower back pain, recent data is showing a very low percentage in localizing the etiology.

This may bring about question whether performing the Waddell's Signs tests and following up with diagnostic imaging helps improve the positive predictive value of nonorganic causes for lower back pain. In one study (Cox, Blizzard, Carlson, Hiratzka, and Yoo, 2017), MRIs were performed on patients who were separated into two groups: those who were Waddell's Signs positive and those who were Waddell's Signs negative. Cox et al. (2007) wanted to evaluate whether or not an organic etiology was present in either group. What they found was that patients who were Waddell's Signs negative had significantly more pathologic findings (100% of the study group), in comparison to those who were Waddell's Signs positive (70% of the study group). Even though the study group of patients who were Waddell's Signs negative had significantly more organic pathology associated with their lower back pain, there was still a significant number of patients who were Waddell's Signs positive that had comparable organic spinal pathology with equivalent severity. Thus, Waddell's Signs can mislead a clinician to diagnose a patient with nonorganic pathology if further workup is not done.

When associating Waddell Signs with malingering, Fishbain et al. (2003) conducted a study in which they did a computer and manual literature search on Waddell's Signs and malingering for secondary gain. After looking at 64 studies they found there was little evidence indicating an association between Waddell's Signs and malingering for secondary gain. They concluded that Waddell's Signs do not correlate with psychological distress and malingering, do not discriminate organic from nonorganic back pain, and that Waddell's signs are associated with poor treatment outcome with greater pain levels; yet, Waddell's signs are not associated with secondary gain. Contrarily, in 2017, Wygant et al. (2017), found significantly increased odds of exhibiting somatic amplification when Waddell's Signs test scoring is greater than two or three (Wygant, Arbisi, Bianchini, and Umlauf, 2017). Somatic amplification is when symptoms experienced by the patient are out of proportion to the physical exam, and, in response the patient may feel intense, noxious, and disturbed (Barsky, Goodson, Lane, and Cleary, 1988).

The validity of Waddell's Signs has been questioned and criticized in demonstrating nonorganic pain and malingering for secondary gain. The maneuvers performed in Waddell's Signs tests are based on the reaction of the patient and how the initial findings are interpreted by the clinician performing the exam. These interpretations can lead to an observer bias, resulting in subjective findings. Waddell's Signs can also be present in other medical conditions, such as fibromyalgia or complex regional pain syndrome, in which psychological factors are known to trigger pain (Littlejohn, 2015). Some examples of psychological factors include stress (from psychosocial events) and pain-anticipation, which are thought to initiate a cascade of events leading to elevated levels of substance P in C-fiber bodies within the dorsal root ganglia. This will further exacerbate the patient's perception of pain (Eccleston, 2001). In addition, since Waddell's Signs are subjective findings, given that the assessment is based upon the clinicians performing and scoring these tests, it is of critical importance to follow-up patient suffering from lower back pain with diagnostic imaging (i.e., MRI) to rule out nonorganic causes.

Often times, Waddell's Signs have been used in court cases to determine whether or not individuals are suffering from organic lower back pain or malingering and secondary gain. There has been a myriad of cases in which patients filed lawsuits against companies and state governments in order to receive workers' compensation, disability insurance, or so their medical expenses taken care of. However, it is the responsibility of the court system to judge whether or not someone is truly in need or exaggerating information for financial gain. For instance, in the case of *Etter v. Colvin*, the plaintiff was denied Social Security disability insurance benefits even though the plaintiff listed severe spinal stenosis with severe dural sac compression as her disabling condition (*Etter v. Colvin*, 2016). The administrative law judge found the plaintiff to be not entirely credible, and noted that the *regional disturbance test* (exaggeration test) found the plaintiff's response to palpation exaggerated. The administrative law judge referred to and described the Waddell's Signs test as, "a standard test for symptom magnification or malingering." However, cases have ruled in favor of the plaintiff as well, despite showing malingering for secondary gain according to the Waddell's Signs. In a 2008 case, *Whitley v. Hartford Life & Accident Insurance Company*, the plaintiff was a former employee (truck driver) who was no longer able to work due to his lower back pain (*Whitley v. Hartford Life & Accident Insurance Company*, 2008). He filed a lawsuit against his insurance company for terminating his long-term disability benefits and presented evidence which showed that he was suffering from degenerative disc disease and a bulging disc in his lumbar spine. Even though Waddell's Signs test was performed and the plaintiff scored a seven out of 16 on the Waddell's questionnaire (associated with the 2001 functional capacity evaluation) the court ruled in favor of the plaintiff.

6.7 CONCLUSION

Waddell's Signs test has become a common practice amongst clinicians and helps determine whether or not a patient is better suited for surgical treatment for lower back pain. However, it should not be the standard for differentiating organic from nonorganic causes of lower back pain. These physical examination maneuvers, like many others, have been universally indoctrinated and applied. This should be of great concern and physicians need to question whether or not certain physical examinations being performed hold any scientific credentials, especially when examining chronic pain. Thus, as Waddell proposed, the biopsychosocial model for pain should be taken into careful consideration given that positive signs of malingering are present, even when there is an organic etiology to pain. Therefore, Waddell's Signs test should not be regarded as a psychological screener (Apeldoorn, Ostelo, Fritz, van der Ploeg, van Tulder, and de Vet, 2012); moreover, it may not help the current opioid epidemic in the United States.

REFERENCES

American Psychiatric Association. 2013. *Diagnostic and Statistical Manual of Mental Disorders*, 5th ed., 61. Washington, D.C.: American Psychiatric Association.

Apeldoorn, A.T., R.W. Ostelo, J.M. Fritz, T. van der Ploeg, M.W. van Tulder, and H.C. de Vet. 2012. The cross-sectional construct validity of the Waddell score. *Clinical Journal of Pain* 28:4:309–317.

Barsky, A.J., J.D. Goodson, R.S. Lane, and P.D. Cleary. 1988. The amplification of somatic symptoms. *Psychosomatic Medicine* 50:5:510–519.

Bose, J., S.L. Hedden, R.N. Lipari, E. Park-Lee, J.D. Porter, and M.R. Pembert. 2016. Key substance use and mental health indicators in the United States: Results from the 2015 National Survey on Drug Use and Health. *Substance Abuse and Mental Health Services Administration* 16:H-51:2–25.

Carragee, E., T. Alamin, I. Cheng, T. Franklin, E. van den Haak, and E. Hurwitz. 2006. Are first-time episodes of serious LBP associated with new MRI findings? *The Spine Journal* 6:6:624–635.

CDC Centers for Disease Control and Prevention. 2017. Opioid overdose. U.S. prescribing rate maps. https://www.cdc.gov/drugoverdose/maps/rxrate-maps.html (accessed 10/7/2017).

Cicero, T.J., M.S. Ellis, H.L. Surratt, and S.P. Kurtz. 2014. The changing face of heroin use in the United States: A retrospective analysis of the past 50 years. *JAMA Psychiatry* 71:7:821–826.

Cox, J.S., S. Blizzard, H. Carlson, J. Hiratzka, and J.U. Yoo. 2017. Lumbar magnetic resonance imaging findings in patients with and without Waddell signs. *The Spine Journal* 17:7:990–994.

Eccleston, C. 2001. Role of psychology in pain management. *British Journal of Anaesthesology* 87:1:144–52.

Etter v. Colvin, No. 1:16-cv-00406-JMS-MJD. S.D. Ind. 9/23/2016.

Fishbain, D.A., B. Cole, R.B. Cutler, J. Lewis, H.L. Rosomoff, and R.S. Rosomoff. 2003. A structured evidence-based review on the meaning of nonorganic physical signs: Waddell signs. *Pain Medicine* 4:2:141–181.

Fishbain, D.A., R.B. Cutler, H.L. Rosomoff, and R.S. Rosomoff. 2004. Is there a relationship between nonorganic physical findings (Waddell signs) and secondary gain/malingering? *Clinical Journal of Pain* 20:6:399.

Gunn, C.C., and W.E. Milbrandt. 1978. Early and subtle signs in low-back sprain. *Spine* 3:3:267–281.

Guy, Jr., G.P., K. Zhang, M.K. Bohm et al. 2017. Vital signs: Changes in opioid prescribing in the United States, 2006–2015. *MMWR Morbidity and Mortality Weekly Report* 66:697–704.

Hróbjartsson, A., A.S. Thomsen, F. Emanuelsson et al. 2014. Observer bias in randomized clinical trials with time-to-event outcomes: Systematic review of trials with both blinded and nonblinded outcome assessors. *International Journal of Epidemiology* 43:3:937–948.

Leboeuf-Yde, C., and K. Kyvik. 1998. At what age does lower back pain become a common problem? *Spine* 23:2:228–234.

Littlejohn, G. 2015. Neurogenic neuroinflammation in fibromyalgia and complex regional pain syndrome. *Nature Reviews Rheumatology* 11:639–648.

Melzack, R., and K.L. Casey. 1968. Sensory, motivational, and central control determinants of pain. A new conceptual model. In *The Skin Senses, Proceedings of the First International Symposium on the Skin Senses Held at The Florida State University in Tallahassee, Florida*, ed. D.R. Kenshalo, chapter 20, 423–429. Springfield: Charles C. Thomas.

Melzack, R., and P.D. Wall. 1965. Pain mechanisms: A new theory. *Science* 150:971–979.

Melzack, R., and P.D. Wall. 1996. *The Challenge of Pain, 2nd ed.* London: Penguin UK.

Shakespeare, T., N. Watson, and O.A. Alghaib. 2016. Blaming the victim, all over again: Waddell and Aylward's biopsychosocial (BPS) model of disability. *Critical Social Policy* 37:1:22–41.

Shekelle, P.G. 1999. Book review: The back pain revolution. *New England Journal of Medicine* 341:545–546.

Waddell, G. 1998. *The Back Pain Revolution*. Edinburgh: Churchill Livingstone.

Waddell, G., H.A. McCulloch, E. Kummel, and R.M. Venner. 1980. Nonorganic physical signs in low-back pain. *Spine* 5:2:117–125.

Waddell, G., M. Bircher, D. Finlayson, and C.J. Main. 1984. Symptoms and signs: Physical disease or illness behavior? *British Medical Journal (Clinical Research Edition)* 289:6447:739–741.

Waterman, B.R., P.J. Belmont, and A.J. Schoenfeld. 2012. Low back pain in the United States: Incidence and risk factors for presentation in the emergency setting. *The Spine Journal* 12:1:63–70.

White, A.A., and S.L. Gordon. 1982. Synopsis: Workshop on idiopathic low-back pain. *Spine* 7:141–149.

Whitley v. Hartford Life & Accident Insurance Company, No. 06-2189. 4th Cir. 1/28/2008.

Wygant, D.B., P.A. Arbisi, K.J. Bianchini, and R.L. Umlauf. 2017. Waddell nonorganic signs: New evidence suggests somatic amplification among outpatient chronic pain patients. *The Spine Journal* 17:4:505–510.

7 The Electrodiagnostic Evaluation of Malingering

Roberto P. Segura, MD

CONTENTS

This chapter will evaluate the usefulness of the electrodiagnostic examination for the detection of malingering behavior.

7.1 DEFINITION

The electrodiagnostic examination is a proven procedure to diagnose disorders of the neuromuscular system which is comprised of the spinal nerve roots, plexi, peripheral nerves, neuromuscular junction, and muscles. It is divided into two parts: (1) nerve conduction studies, and (2) needle electromyography.

The nerve conduction studies are entirely objective and do not require active participation by the subject. During this procedure, the nerves are stimulated at different current intensities with a handheld stimulator. Responses are measured by small surface electrodes taped on the skin over the respective muscles. Two parameters are measured: the conduction time between simulating and recording site, and the amplitude and configuration of the responses. Basically, these parameters indicate the status of myelin and axonal components of the nerves respectively.

The needle electromyography component demonstrates the status of the muscle both at rest and under voluntary contraction. Analysis at rest does not require the subject's participation. On the other hand, full subject participation is required to assess the status of muscle fiber function. In this case, the degree of voluntary activation of muscle fibers can be affected by discomfort or pain intolerance, and very importantly, a purposeful lack of effort due to a specific gain, as in malingering. Therefore, weakness from true disease or poor effort can be distinguished.

In my experience, an exaggerated response to nerve stimulation, or lack of it, can also suggest different states of psychopathology. Poor voluntary effort can also be detected by careful muscle testing performed by a trained clinician although a definite corroboration can only be obtained by detailed electromyographic testing.

7.2 DEFINITION OF MALINGERING BEHAVIOR

The DSM-IV-TR (American Psychiatric Association, 2000) defines malingering as the "intentional production of false or grossly exaggerated physical or psychological symptoms motivated by external incentives such as avoiding military duty, avoiding work, obtaining financial compensation, evading criminal prosecution, or obtaining drugs." Malingering can be conceptualized as a behavior (not as a diagnosis or illness) which can be manifest in any individual whether or not there is an illness, and, if there is an illness, whether or not the malingered symptoms relate to the illness from which the individual is "genuinely" suffering. This suggests that malingering can coexist with any illness. Some authors have even gone so far as to suggest it can coexist with hysteria (Gorman, 1982) and with factitious disorder (Cramer, Gershberg, and Stern, 1971). As a corollary, the difficulty with this point of view is that it appears to imply that an individual can malinger hysteria or a factitious disorder. A better understanding of the subject can be gained by looking at the inter-relationships between deceit, gain, personality disorder, hysteria, and factitious disorders (Turner, 1997).

In essence, there are two components to the definition of malingering. First, the symptoms must be invented or exaggerated. Second, that this is done deliberately for the purposes of gain.

7.3 CLINICAL CORRELATES

Subjects usually present with the chief complaint of pain, muscle weakness, or both. It is possible that pain can be present in the absence of neuromuscular disorders as in soft tissue or arthritic pathologies. However, if true weakness is secondary to chronic pain, clinical evidence of muscle wasting or autonomic skin changes can be observed ("frozen shoulder"). Assessments of sincerity of effort and faked weakness have been studied using maximal handgrip strength and pinch strength tests (Smith, Nelson, S. Sadoff, and A. Sadoff, 1989; Tredgett and Davis, 2000; Schapmire et al., 2002; DeSmet and Londers, 2003; Ghori and Chung, 2007).

Other methods include finger tapping test scores (Arnold et al., 2005), tactile discrimination (Greve et al., 2005), as well as psychometric approaches (Sullivan and Richter, 2002; Bianchini et al., 2014; Kucyi, Scheinman, and Defrin, 2015).

Pain perception studies have utilized the Pain Patient Profile (P3) to assess for malingering or exaggerating complaints of pain (McGuire, Harvey, and Shores, 2001) and detecting deception by analysis of facial expressions of pain (Hill and Craig, 2004).

7.4 ELECTRODIAGNOSTIC STUDIES

Very sparse literature is available pertaining to detailed studies in malingering behavior (Solzi and Lotem, 1990; Wilbourn, 1995).

In cases of true neurogenic lesions, nerve conduction studies will easily detect loss of nerve fibers due to underlying disease or mechanical nerve entrapments. In cases of malingering or hysteria, the motor or sensory nerve amplitudes are normal in apparently weak or paralyzed muscles or anesthetic skin regions, respectively.

In dissimulation, on needle EMG examination, insertional activity is normal, no spontaneous activity is seen and the motor unit potential configuration is not altered. The only component of the electrodiagnostic exam, which is affected in cases of hysteria or malingering, is the firing pattern of the motor unit potentials: either there is no activation at all, or they fire in decreased numbers at a slow rate or in poorly synchronized groups in a tremorous fashion. In cases of simulated weakness, the two most important findings are normal motor amplitudes recorded from the "weak" muscles on nerve conduction studies, and normal insertional activity and absence of spontaneous activity demonstrated on needle examination of "weak" muscles.

When assessing for nontrue weakness, it is important to record from as many involved muscles as possible, rather than performing the standard motor nerve conduction studies. Also, with unilateral symptoms, it is important to do comparative studies with the noninvolved side. Eliciting normal nerve conduction amplitudes while recording from several muscles from a paretic limb is particularly important with malingering because these cases usually culminate in lawsuits or workmen's compensation proceedings. The more objective data accumulated demonstrating a lack of neurogenic involvement, the better.

Overall, the needle exam is of somewhat lesser value than the motor nerve conduction studies because the motor unit firing pattern is not that reliable since it is under voluntary control. Nevertheless, if the motor unit potentials in a paretic muscle fire in decreased numbers at only a slow-to-moderate rate, then the weakness is not due to motor unit abnormality, then some other firing problem coexists with the abnormality. Also, the presence of normal insertional activity and absence of spontaneous activity in a weak muscle provides important supportive evidence that the muscle fibers composing it are both viable and innervated.

During the needle examination, the nonorganic nature of the reputed weakness sometimes can be convincingly demonstrated. Some malingerers, for example, soon learn that the volume of sound generated by the activation of their muscles is proportional to the degree of effort they are making. They then begin to base the strength of their contractions on the feedback they are receiving via the electromyographic sounds, being careful to ensure that their efforts are very submaximal. If the volume controls on the electromyographic machines are turned down and the malingerers are urged to contract the assessed muscles more vigorously, and thereby "produce some muscle noise," they often will—unwittingly—begin to make progressively greater efforts while attempting to do so. Sometimes they will achieve a full motor unit potential firing pattern visible on the electromyographic screen which promptly disappears when the volume controls are abruptly returned to normal and they can once again hear their motor unit potential activity. Similarly, both hysterics and malingerers sometimes demonstrate negative activation. Rather than voluntarily activating the muscle being assessed when requested, hysterics and malingerers relax it and instead activate its antagonist. This is readily demonstrated simply by asking them to activate the antagonist muscle while leaving the needle-recording electrode in place. Suddenly, voluntary motor unit potentials appear in a muscle that was completely paralyzed a moment before (Wilbourn, 1995). In cases of poor voluntary effort secondary to pain or malingering, an erratic recruitment pattern of motor unit potentials will be observed, exemplified by either no visible motor unit activity or markedly irregular firing patterns of otherwise normal looking motor unit potentials.

7.5 CONCLUSION

Electrodiagnostic studies coupled with a detailed neurological examination can be a useful tool to determine the existence of malingering behavior or other psychophysiological disturbances.

REFERENCES

American Psychiatric Association. 2000. *Diagnostic and Statistical Manual of Mental Disorders, 4th edition. DMS-IV-TR®*. Washington, D.C.: American Psychiatric Association.

Arnold, G., K.B. Boone, P. Lu et al. 2005. Sensitivity and specificity of finger tapping test scores for the detection of suspect effort. *The Clinical Neuropsychologist* 19:1:105–120.

Bianchini, K.J., L.E. Aguerrevere, B.J. Guise et al. 2014. Accuracy of the modified somatic perception questionnaire and pain disability index in the detection of malingered pain-related disability in chronic pain. *The Clinical Neuropsychologist* 28:8:1376–1394.

Cramer, B., M. Gershberg, and M. Stern. 1971. Munchausen syndrome: Its relationship to malingering, hysteria, and the physician-patient relationship. *Archives of General Psychiatry* 24:6:573–578.

DeSmet, L., and J. Londers. 2003. Repeated grip strength at one month interval and detection of voluntary submaximal effort. *Acta Orthopaedica Belgica* 69:2:142.

Ghori, A.K., and K.C. Chung. 2007. A decision-analysis model to diagnose feigned hand weakness. *The Journal of Hand Surgery* 32:10:1638–1643.

Gorman, W.F. 1982. Defining malingering. *Journal of Forensic Sciences* 27:2:401–407.

Greve, K.W., J.M. Love, M.T. Heinly et al. 2005. Detection of feigned tactile of sensory loss using a forced-choice test of tactile discrimination and other measures of tactile sensation. *Journal of Occupational and Environmental Medicine* 47:718–727.

Hill, M.L., and K.D. Craig. 2004. Detecting deception in facial expressions of pain: Accuracy and training. *Clinical Journal of Pain* 20:6:415–422.

Kucyi, A., A. Scheinman, and R. Defrin. 2015. Distinguishing feigned from sincere performance in psychophysical pain testing. *The Journal of Pain* 16:10:1044–1053.

McGuire, B.E., A.G. Harvey, and E.A. Shores. 2001. Simulated malingering in pain patients: A study with the pain patient profile. *The British Journal of Clinical Psychology* 40:1:71–79.

Schapmire, D., J.D. James, R. Townsend et al. 2002. Simultaneous bilateral testing: Validation of a new protocol to detect insincere effort during grip and pinch strength testing. *Journal of Hand Therapy* 15:3:242–250.

Smith, G.A., R.C. Nelson, S.J. Sadoff, and A.M. Sadoff. 1989. Assessing sincerity of effort in maximal grip strength tests. *American Journal of Physical Medicine & Rehabilitation* 68:2:73–80.

Solzi, P., and M. Lotem. 1990. Malingering detected by electromyography (EMG). *Clinical Neurophysiology* 75:S142.

Sullivan, K., and C. Richer. 2002. Malingering on subjective complaint tasks: An exploration of the deterrent effects of warning. *Psychiatry Research* 17:7:691–708.

Tredgett, M., and T. Davis. 2000. Rapid repeat testing of grip strength for detection of faked hand weakness. *The Journal of Hand Surgery (Edinburg, Scotland)* 25:4:372–375.

Turner, M. 1997. Malingering. *The British Journal of Psychiatry* 171:409–411.

Wilbourn, A.J. 1995. The electrodiagnostic examination with hysteria-conversion reaction and malingering. *Neurologic Clinics* 13:385–404.

8 Toxicologic Malingering

Jerrold B. Leikin, MD

CONTENTS

Presumed toxic exposures have a connotation that can be alarming to any individual; thus, an inferred or assumed toxic trigger leading to myriad, vague symptoms, or complaints is frequently encountered in the outpatient clinic setting. Often, the workup is inconclusive, thus cementing the toxicant association to the individual—even if it is biologically implausible. Individuals are convinced that there is an ongoing exposure which requires a search for a single confirmatory explanation (Senecal and Chalut, 2000; Leikin, Mycyk, Bryant, Cumpston, and Hurwitz, 2004).

For a toxicological cause to be considered, several factors should be present (see factors to consider associating with a toxic etiology list below). Probably, the most important association is a temporal relationship; for example, the peaked therapeutic effect of a drug may be temporally associated with its peak adverse effect (Leikin, Mycyk, Bryant, Cumpston, and Hurwitz, 2004). In general, intravenous administration of a drug will elicit an adverse effect in a much shorter time period than oral or transdermal drug administration. Dose–effect relationship (as originally articulated by the Renaissance Italian alchemist Paracelsus [1493–1541]), is a principal pillar of medical toxicology. It is the dose that makes the poison; for example, while five tablets of aspirin can result in mild adverse effects (such as gastrointestinal irritation), fifty tablets of aspirin can be lethal and result in metabolic acidosis, seizures, and coma development. Thus, dose estimation (if available) relating to exposure is an important consideration. A plausible, documentable, and reproducible biologic relationship to toxicant exposure must exist. Known target organ response to toxicant exposure must be present in some manner to determine a plausible relationship. If an adverse event occurs following a toxicant exposure with no dose–effect relationship established, an allergic or hypersensitivity (immunologic) response could be considered. In these cases, symptoms such as cough, rhinitis, sinusitis, throat/eye irritation, or rash may predominate depending on the mode of exposure (i.e., body interface). The rash can take form as either an irritant-based contact dermatitis or an urticarial-based contact dermatitis.

A second pillar of medical toxicology is toxidrome recognition: the spectrum of symptom complexes relatable to a specific toxic exposure (Mofenson and Greensher, 1970; Nice, Leikin, Maturen, Madsen, Zell, and Hryhorczuk, 1988). For example, organophosphate insecticide exposure usually presents with a cholinergic response (salivation, lacrimation, urination, defecation, wheezing, and pinpoint pupils).

Most gases are mucosal irritants—thus, eye/throat irritation, along with coughing or wheezing, are prominent symptoms. Ammonia and chlorine gases are common examples of mucosal irritant gases with otherwise few symptoms. Very few gases/toxicants will cause neurological-based problems without mucosal irritation (cyanide, carbon monoxide, and lead are the primary examples). Factors to consider associating with a toxic etiology are listed below:

- Temporal relationship
- Dose–effect relationship (dose–estimation)
- Bioavailability
- Plausible anatomical or physiological response to toxicant
- Toxidrome recognition

In our experience, individuals with nonspecific chronic symptoms, which they attribute to obscure toxic (usually environmental) etiologies with a negative comprehensive laboratory workup, account for approximately 8% of our total medical toxicology clinic population. Examples of these presumed correlations include elemental mercury exposure from dental amalgams, household mold exposure, silicone breast implants, and pediatric neurological complications from vaccine components (Kales and Goldman, 2002; Bellen, 2001; Hardin, Kelman, and Saxon, 2003). In all of these cases, toxicological-based sequela have been disproven (although mold exposure can result in hypersensitivity). In the cases of environmental exposures, an air/water/soil evaluation by a certified industrial hygienist could be considered in order to properly determine if such an exposure exists and can be documented. Medical-based laboratory investigations can be limiting. In general, hair testing or provoked urine metal mobilization tests (by use of chelators) do not provide diagnostic value in correlating metals to symptoms (Seidel, Kreuter, Smith, McNeel, and Gilliss, 2001; Steindel and Howanit, 2001; Ruha, 2013; American College of Medical Toxicology, 2010). These individuals often do not accept the opinion that there is no toxicologic causation to their symptoms; approximately 30% have sought alternative medical therapy to deal with these issues. Rarely do individuals agree to psychotherapy as part of their treatment regimen (Leikin, Mycyk, Bryant, Cumpston, and Hurwitz, 2004).

Certainly, these individuals may appear to possess some characteristics of idiopathic environmental illness or IEI (formerly known as multiple chemical sensitivity or MCS), whereupon a presumed toxic trigger or exposure is the source of a variety of symptoms or complaints which do not follow the symptom complex relatable to the toxicant (or toxidrome) (Bomschein et al., 2008; Black, Okiishi, and Schlosser, 2000; Black, 2000; McKay, Holland, and Nelson, 1999; Bianchini et al., 2003; Zilker, 2002). Neurocognitive dysfunction is a common presenting complaint; fatigue alone (without any documentable medical cause such as anemia) usually cannot be ascribed solely to a toxic exposure. Individuals usually report issues with impaired concentration, memory, irritability, and problems with impulse control (Bianchini et al., 2003; Zilker, 2002; Ben-Avi, Rabin, Melamed, Kreiner, and Ribak, 1998; Williamson, 2007; Robertson, 2002; Van Hout, Hageman, and van Valen, 2014). These individuals usually do not have a previous psychiatric or substance abuse history; however, it does appear that symptom projection, somatization, depression/anxiety, panic disorder, and post-traumatic stress disorder (to the type of exposure) may be involved in development of these symptoms (which can be quite disabling).

Questionnaires can be furnished to assist in biological validity of complaints. Such areas of focus could include demographic characteristics, symptom development (primarily neurological), mood states, or hazard exposures. These self-reported measures can be important to validate toxicant exposures as a source for symptom development, but it must be emphasized that questionnaires are an adjunct (to physical examination/clinical acumen) to the overall investigative process (Ben-Avi, Rabin, Melamed, Kreiner, and Ribak, 1998; Williamson, 2007; Robertson, 2002; Van Hout, Hageman, and van Valen, 2014).

Extensive neuropsychological testing may be indicated; although, even then it may be difficult to identify malingering. Reliable Digit Span (RDS) and the WAIS-III Digit Span (DS) Scale scores may aid in such determinations (Greve et al., 2007).

8.1 CONCLUSION

A significant number of patients present to outpatient clinics with chronic nonspecific symptoms and are convinced that they were poisoned through a self-limited but implausible manner. These scenarios do not involve any dose–effect relationship and clinical investigation is usually negative. Even though these complaints do not follow any physiologic, anatomic, or toxicologic principles, the patients usually do not accept that there is no clinical evidence of any poisoning and often pursue alternative routes for diagnostic toxic linkage. Specific toxin identification or toxicology-based treatment for these patients is unlikely to occur (Leikin, Mycyk, Bryant, Cumpston, and Hurwitz, 2004).

REFERENCES

American College of Medical Toxicology. 2010. American College of Medical Toxicology position statement on post-chelators challenge urinary metal testing. *Journal of Medical Toxicology* 6:1:74–75.

Bellen, L. 2001. Haunted by mold. *New York Times Magazine*. Section 6, 8/12/2001, 28–34.

Ben-Avi, I., S. Rabin, S. Melamed, H. Kreiner, and J. Ribak. 1998. Malingering assessment in behavioral toxicology: What, why, and how. *American Journal of Industrial Medicine* 34:4:325–330.

Bianchini, K.J., R.J. Houston, K.W. Greve et al. 2003. Malingered neurocognitive dysfunction in neurotoxic exposure: An application of the slick criteria. *Journal of Occupational and Environmental Medicine* 45:10:1087–1099.

Black, D.W. 2000. The relationship of mental disorders and idiopathic environmental intolerance. *Occupational Medicine* 15:3:557–570.

Black, D.W., C. Okiishi, and S. Schlosser. 2000. A nine-year follow-up of people diagnosed with multiple chemical sensitivities. *Psychosomatics* 41:3:253–261.

Bornschein, S., C. Hausteiner, and C. Pohl et al. 2008. Pest controllers: A high-risk group for Multiple Chemical Sensitivity (MCS)? *Clinical Toxicology* 46:3:193–200.

Greve, K.W., S. Springer, K.J. Bianchini, F.W. Black, M.T. Heinly, J.M. Love et al. 2007. Malingering in toxic exposure: Classification accuracy of reliable digit span and WAIS-III Digit Span scaled scores. *Assessment* 14:1:12–21.

Hardin, B.D., B.J. Kelman, and A. Saxon. 2003. Adverse human health effects associated with molds in the indoor environment. *Journal of Occupational and Environmental Medicine* 45:470–478.

Kales, S.N., and R.H. Goldman. 2002. Mercury exposure: Current concepts, controversies, and a clinic's experience. *Journal of Occupational and Environmental Medicine* 44:2:143–154.

Leikin, J.B., M.B. Mycyk, S. Bryant, K. Cumpston, and S. Hurwitz. 2004. Characteristics of patients with no underlying toxicologic syndrome evaluated in a toxicology clinic. *Clinical Toxicology* 42:643–468.

McKay, Jr., C.A., M.G. Holland, and L.S. Nelson. 2003. A call to arms for medical toxicologists: The dose, not the detection, makes the poison. *International Journal of Medical Toxicology* 6:1:1–6.

Mofenson, H.C., and J. Greensher. 1970. The non-toxic ingestion. *Pediatric Clinics of North America* 17:583–590.

Nice, A., J.B. Leikin, A. Maturen, L.J. Madsen-Konczyk, M. Zell, and D.O. Hryhorczuk. 1988. Toxidrome recognition to improve efficiency of emergency urine drug screens. *Annals Emergency Medicine* 17:7:676–680.

Roberston, W.D. 2002. Global "toxicolization"—Pre and post September 11th! *Veterinary and Human Toxicology* 44:5:311–312.

Ruha, A.M. 2013. Recommendations for provoked challenge urine testing. *Journal of Medical Toxicology* 9:4:318–325.

Seidel S., R. Kreutzer, D. Smith, S. McNeel, and D. Gilliss. 2001. Assessment of commercial laboratories performing hair mineral analysis. *JAMA* 285:1:67–72.

Senecal, P.E., and D. Chalut. 2000. Patients "intoxicated" by multielement urine, hair or stool results: A toxicology clinic experience. (Abstract). *Journal of Toxicology – Clinical Toxicology* 38:525.

Steindel, S.J., and P.J. Howanitz. 2001. The uncertainty of hair analysis for trace metals. *JAMA* 285:1:83–85.

Van Hout, M., G. Hageman, and E. van Valen. 2014. Pitfalls in clinical assessment of neurotoxic diseases: Negative effects of repeated diagnostic evaluation, illustrated by a clinical case. *Neurotoxicology* 45:247–252.

Williamson, A. 2007. Using self-report measures in neurobehavioral toxicology: Can they be trusted? *Neurotoxicology* 28:2:227–234.

Zilker, T. 2002. Assessment of risks from environmental exposure: Practical implications in clinical toxicology. *Journal of Toxicology: Clinical Toxicology* 40:3:296–297.

9 Pretending to Not Concentrate

Malingering Attention Deficit Hyperactivity Disorder

Angela Rekhi, BSc, MD, Jasmine M. Campbell, BA, and Alan R. Hirsch, MD

CONTENTS

9.1 INTRODUCTION

Attention deficit hyperactivity disorder (ADHD) prior to the 1970s was considered a childhood disorder, which ultimately was outgrown with age. Cases have been described as early as 1775 in Melchior Adam Weikard's textbook publication, *Der Philosophische Arzt*, in the chapter *Mangel der Aufmerkksamkeit, Attentio Volubilis* (Barkley and Peters, 2012). In writing this, he broke the popular belief that disorders of emotion and behavior were caused by astrological phenomena and medieval hypotheses, but instead were largely of medical and physiological origin. Before the *Diagnostic and Statistical Manual of Mental Disorders* (DSM) even acknowledged ADHD as being prevalent in adulthood, Weikard described inattentiveness in adults and children due to distractibility from anything, including their own imagination, lacking perseverance and persistence, overactivity, and impulsivity (American Psychiatric Association, 2013). He also believed that these individuals "will be shallow everywhere, mostly reckless, imprudent and most inconstant in execution" (Barkley and Peters, 2012).

Although the majority of ADHD cases are of genetic origin, external factors which cause low birth weight, prematurity, or impaired central nervous system (CNS) development in-utero increase the risk of acquiring ADHD (Stergiakouli and Thapar, 2010). By the twentieth century, ADHD became a subject of focus and was fundamentally viewed as a behavioral disorder of childhood characterized by a persistent pattern of distractibility and hyperactivity. The DSM has been defining ADHD as a childhood disorder since 1968 (American Psychiatric Association, 1968), but by 1994 it was acknowledged as being prevalent in both childhood and adulthood (American Psychiatric Association, 1994). Malingering, the conscious fabrication or exaggeration of physical or psychological symptoms in pursuit of a recognizable goal (American Psychiatric Association, 1994), can be a potential risk factor for misdiagnosing adult ADHD. Falsifications of physical symptoms and exaggerations on self-assessments are used as tools for malingering and obtaining a diagnosis of ADHD. Recent studies have begun to recognize the prevalence of individuals malingering ADHD for incentives, including obtaining disability, prescriptions for stimulant medications for enhanced performance, or for recreational use (Perugi and Vannucchi, 2015). It is also a valuable commodity in the pharmaceutical black market (Moncrieff and Timimi, 2010).

9.2 EVOLUTION OF DSM

ADHD was first defined in DSM-II for health professionals in 1968 as Hyperkinetic Reaction of Childhood (American Psychiatric Association, 1968). As indicated by the name, the disorder was primarily seen as a set of symptoms of excessive motor activity, and not of inattention. Prior to the publication of the DSM-II, clinicians broadly used terms such as minimal brain damage, minimal brain dysfunction, minimal brain disorder, and learning and behavioral disabilities to classify the symptoms of what eventually became known as Hyperkinetic Reaction of Childhood in 1968. Over time, as research and public awareness of this condition grew, the disorder name and description has evolved. In 1980, the DSM-III introduced the term Attention Deficit Disorder (ADD), describing the condition as encompassing symptoms of attention, hyperactivity, and impulsivity (American Psychiatric Association, 1980). Furthermore, it differentiated ADHD into two subtypes—ADD with hyperactivity and ADD without hyperactivity. Although not known, it has been questioned whether the two subtypes are forms of a single disorder or distinct disorders (American Psychiatric Association, 1980). There is also a residual subtype where individuals who were once diagnosed with ADHD outgrew the hyperactivity component of the condition but still show signs of having the disorder (American Psychiatric Association, 1980). A revision to the DSM-III in 1987 eliminated the term ADD and introduced ADHD, the name we use today.

The DSM-IV was the first of the diagnostic manuals to recognize that ADHD can continue into adulthood (American Psychiatric Association, 1994). Increasing media coverage, educational books, and public awareness led to an influx of adults seeking evaluation, diagnosis, and treatment for this condition. ADHD is a disorder of inattention and/or hyperactivity–impulsivity; however, some symptoms that may cause impairment are not present prior to the age of 7. To be validated, the impairments must be present in two or more settings, such as in home and at school. Inattention may be perceived in an academic, occupational, or social setting. For example, in a school setting the child often appears as if their mind is elsewhere and that they are not attentive to instructions by their teacher, whereas at home, it may be that they are unable to complete chores, homework, or follow through on parental requests. Hyperactivity can be seen as excessive fidgeting, squirming or restlessness in one's seat, or even not remaining seated when instructed to do so. Excessive gross motor movement can be seen as wriggling of feet and legs, continuous tapping, seated rocking, or shifting of position or posture when presented with perceived boring tasks. In younger children, this excessiveness is presented as running and climbing during inappropriate situations like quiet playtime. In teenagers, this type of motor hyperactivity declines; however, they are still more restless than their peers. In adulthood, the restlessness is less observable as compared to adolescents and young children and is more so reported as a subjective restlessness.

As of 2018, the current DSM-V still defines ADHD as the persistent pattern of inattention and/or hyperactivity–impulsivity, which impedes functioning or development, and is characterized by three different presentations: inattention, hyperactivity–impulsivity, or combined inattention and hyperactivity–impulsivity (American Psychiatric Association, 2013). As seen in the DSM-IV, the DSM-V outlines the need to have six or more symptoms, or at least five in the case of adolescents and adults (17 and older in age), in either of two characteristics of inattention or hyperactivity–impulsivity. These symptoms must be present for at least six months, be inconsistent with age appropriate behavior, and must affect social and daily living. The possible nine inattention criteria to choose from include: (1) the inability to pay close attention to details causing inaccuracy in schoolwork, work, or other activities; (2) inability to stay focused while completing tasks or during activities; (3) easy distractibility, even in the absence of obvious distraction; (4) inability to follow instructions and complete homework or tasks at work; (5) inability to remain organized while completing tasks or during activities, resulting in failure to meet deadlines; (6) hesitation to commit to tasks requiring continued mental effort; (7) often misplacing or losing things required for completing tasks or work; (8) easily sidetracked (including by uncorrelated thoughts); and (9) often absent-minded.

According to the DSM-V Manual, there are nine features of the hyperactivity–impulsivity spectrum of which at least six must be present to fulfill the diagnosis of ADHD. Adolescents and adults (17 and older in age) only require a minimum of five of the following nine to meet the diagnosis: (1) frequent restless movements; (2) inability to remain seated especially when required to do so; (3) often pacing back and forth or climbing while in inappropriate settings (Note: with adolescents or adults, this may only be perceived as restlessness); (4) inability to participate in activities or tasks quietly; (5) overly energized and unable to sit still for long periods of time; (6) excessive talkativeness; (7) is often interruptive during conversations; (8) lacking patience; and (9) intrusive, either verbally and/or physically, during conversations or activities.

In addition to the criteria for inattention and/or hyperactivity–impulsivity being met, the DSM-V requires that several symptoms in two categories must appear prior to the age of 12, whereas the DSM-IV requires several symptoms to have presented prior to the age of 7. The change in age cutoff was implemented as significant research since 1994 indicated no clinical difference in regard to course, severity, prognosis, and treatment between children who present with symptoms prior to age 7 in comparison to children who present symptoms at a later age (Epstein and Loren, 2013).

Research studies, as well as clinical studies, supported the notion that impairments caused by symptoms of ADHD may only be noticed once academic and social life demands increase (Epstein and Loren, 2013). The DSM-V also indicates the need for symptoms to be present in two or more environments. It must be evident that the signs interfere with and reduce the quality of functioning in academic, occupational, or social life. Last, the aforementioned symptoms must not occur exclusively during episodes of schizophrenia or any other psychotic disorder, and must not be explained by any other mental disorder such as anxiety disorder, dissociative disorder, mood disorder, personality disorder, substance intoxication, or withdrawal. Unlike past manuals, both DSM-IV and DSM-V had modifiers which were added to specify severity of the disorder (i.e., mild, moderate, or severe) (American Psychiatric Association, 2013). Another modifier was added to specify whether an individual is in "partial remission." This is indicated when partial criteria for ADHD has been met for the past six months with full criteria being fulfilled previously, and that the symptoms still result in impairments in social, academic, or occupational functioning.

9.3 DIAGNOSIS

Past history of ADHD is helpful in the diagnosis in childhood. Generally, ADHD symptoms may have been present in early childhood and presence of these past behaviors is helpful in the confirmation of the diagnosis. Children as young as four years of age can be diagnosed with ADHD. According to the 2010–2011 National Survey of Children's Health, 194,000 preschoolers from age 2 to 5, have been given the diagnosis of ADHD (Danielson, Visser, Gleason, Peacock, Claussen, and Blumberg, 2017). Although some outgrow the symptoms, preschool-age children who show symptoms of ADHD are much more likely to also meet the criteria in adolescence. Of the 11% diagnosed with ADHD in childhood, more than 75% continue into adulthood. As per the DSM-V criteria, multiple symptoms, such as excessive motor movement in toddler years, are required to be present prior to the age of 12 (American Psychiatric Association, 2013). Having said this, ADHD symptoms such as impulsivity, inattentiveness, and active behavior are difficult to differentiate as these are ubiquitous in children under four years of age. Although the current American Academy of Pediatrics (AAP) guidelines have made it possible to diagnose and manage ADHD in children from ages 4 to 18 (expanding the criteria from the previous guidelines from 2000 and 2001, where it covered children only from ages 6 to 12), it is generally still recommended not to diagnose ADHD prior to the age of 12. Clinical assessments of ADHD must be both comprehensive and multidimensional. Children with hyperactivity and impulsivity who do not meet the full ADHD diagnostic criteria, are eligible and strongly recommended for interventions such as cognitive behavioral therapy. In making the full ADHD diagnosis, it is required for children to present with six or more symptoms in the inattentiveness and/or hyperactivity–impulsivity criteria.

Objective assessment from multiple arenas is also essential. This entails making careful observations of the child's in-home behavior by parents or caretakers. Teachers should also make vigilant observations in the classroom setting. Both guardians and teachers should have regular meetings in which the child's behavior and progression is discussed, as well as additional involvement of their pediatrician. Guardians and teachers are often guided to utilize any of the assessment tools below as recommended by the American Academy of Child and Adolescent Psychiatry:

1. ADD-H: Comprehensive Teacher Rating Scale
2. Barkley Home Situations Questionnaire
3. Barkley School Situations Questionnaire
4. Conners Parent and Teacher Rating Scales
5. Parent-completed Child Behavior Checklist
6. Teacher Report Form of the Child Behavior Checklist
7. Vanderbilt Parent Rating Scale
8. Vanderbilt Teacher Rating Scale

As academic and social demands increase in adolescence, the disability of ADHD becomes more apparent. ADHD symptoms in adolescence may become more definitive as manifestations of academic underachievement, substance abuse, and difficulty sustaining relationships. A substantial number, 10% to 25%, of adolescents with ADHD develop drug dependence or abuse legal or illegal substances, with this risk being greatest among those who have coinciding conduct disorder or delinquency. Diagnosing adolescent ADHD requires that symptoms were present prior to the age of 12 (American Psychiatric Association, 2013); however, recall of past symptoms and how far back they began becomes an issue. The DSM-V lists the current criteria used for diagnosing ADHD and is essentially described for younger children, all of which may not be applicable for diagnosing adolescents and adults. Procuring assessments and reports from guardians and teachers becomes arduous and unreliable as adolescents have several different teachers for shorter bouts of time and interact less with their parents. Also, symptoms of hyperactivity are subtler in teens than younger children. As with younger children, the presence of other disorders must first be considered and ruled out. There are fewer adolescent assessment scales as there are for younger children, and much of diagnosing is history-based.

Malingering of ADHD is predominantly an issue of adult ADHD. Thus, the correct diagnosis of ADHD is much more significance. The lifetime prevalence of adult ADHD is 8.1% in the U.S. adult population; however, it should be noted that older adults within the age range of 45–60+ do not report symptoms of ADHD to a clinician (Kessler, Chiu, Demler, and Walters, 2005). Adults with ADHD tend to be undereducated and underemployed relative to their intellectual ability and family's educational background. They also change their jobs more often than others, likely out of boredom, as a result of interpersonal problems in the workplace, or possibly that the concentration impairment with ADHD is interfering with adequate performance on the job. ADHD also has implications on social aspects of adult life, whereby there is difficulty maintaining friendships and dating relationships and sufferers are more susceptible to marital discord and divorce. As with children and adolescents, diagnosing adults with ADHD is most accurately made with information from multiple sources. These sources include behavior rating scales, detailed histories of past and current functioning, symptom checklists (i.e., Adult ADHD Self-Report Scale [ASRS-vI.I] Symptom Checklist), and information from significant others or family members who know them well. Adult diagnosis of ADHD also requires thorough history of childhood behavioral and academic issues. (See Figure 9.1.)

Some of the most common problems which may warrant seeking an evaluation for ADHD are:

- Constant stress and worry due to the inability to accomplish goals and meet responsibilities;
- Constant intense feelings of frustration, guilt or blame;

Patient name		Today's date				
Please answer the questions below, rating yourself on each of the criteria shown using the scale on the right side of the page. As you answer each question, place an X in the box which best describes how you have felt and conducted yourself over the past 6 months. Please give this completed checklist to your healthcare professional to discuss during today's appointment.	Never	Rarely	Sometimes	Often	Very often
1. How often do you have trouble wrapping up the final details of a project, once the challenging parts have been done?					
2. How often do you have difficulty getting things in order when you have to do a task which requires organization?					
3. How often do you have problems remembering appointments or obligations?					
4. When you have a task which requires a lot of thought, how often do you avoid or delay getting started?					
5. How often do you fidget or squirm with your hands or feet when you have to sit down for a long time?					
6. How often do you feel overly active and compelled to do things, like you were driven by a motor?					
					Part A
7. How often do you make careless mistakes when you have to work on a boring or difficult project?					
8. How often do you have difficulty keeping your attention when you are doing boring or repetitive work?					
9. How often do you have difficulty concentrating on what people say to you, even when they are speaking to you directly?					
10. How often do you misplace or have difficulty finding things at home or at work?					
11. How often are you distracted by activity or noise around you?					
12. How often do you leave your seat in meetings or other situations in which you are expected to remain seated?					
13. How often do you feel restless or fidgety?					
14. How often do you have difficulty unwinding and relaxing when you have time to yourself?					
15. How often do you find yourself talking too much when you are in social situations?					
16. When you're in a conversation, how often do you find yourself finishing the sentences of the people you are talking to, before they can finish them themselves?					
17. How often do you have difficulty waiting your turn in situations when turn taking is required?					
18. How often do you interrupt others when they are busy?					
					Part B

FIGURE 9.1 Adult ADHD self-report scale (ASRS-v1.1) symptom checklist.

- Forgetting to complete important tasks or meet deadlines;
- History of poor achievement in academic and/or occupational life;
- Inconsistent performance at work or losing/quitting jobs frequently;
- Poor management of day-to-day responsibilities, such as household chores, paying bills, etc.
- Relationship issues as a result of poor organization and failure to complete tasks.

9.3.1 Differential Diagnoses

In assessing ADHD, it is imperative to rule out other medical conditions which may present with similar symptoms. Examples include:

- Brain injury
- Learning or language problems
- Mood disorders such as depression or anxiety
- Other psychiatric disorders
- Seizure disorders
- Sleep disorders
- Substance abuse
- Thyroid problems
- Tourette syndrome
- Vision or hearing problems

Five to ten percent of those with ADHD may develop more serious mental disorders, such as manic-depression or bipolar disorder (Kessler et al., 2006). A proportion of those with ADHD are at greater risk for developing other disorders, such as bipolar disorder (5%–10%), depression (25%), antisocial disorder and conduct disorder (25%–45%), learning disabilities (25%–40%), and oppositional defiant disorder (50%) (Barkley, 2017).

At the time of diagnosis, those with ADHD are also found to have coexisting conditions. At least one other coexisting condition can be found in two-thirds of individuals with ADHD. These other conditions can commonly be overlooked as symptoms such as constant motion and fidgeting, interrupting and blurting out, difficulty sitting still, and need for constant reminders can be found to be more disruptive. Just as undiagnosed ADHD can be detrimental to daily living and functioning, taking into consideration the possibility of a coexisting condition is imperative to assessment and treatment in ADHD.

9.4 MALINGERING

Unlike children, diagnosing adult ADHD has an additional component of malingering which adds a layer of difficulty in diagnosing the condition. Symptoms of ADHD are easy to feign because one is able to effortlessly reproduce a fake behavioral deficit by suppressing normal behaviors, as is the case with attentiveness. It is much more difficult to fake a positive symptom as this entails production of new behaviors. Other faked behaviors can include fidgeting, forgetfulness, and poor concentration. Given the ease with which ADHD can be simulated among adults and that the possible motive may be to obtain disability status, Social Security and disability offices have memorandums of warning signs for potential malingerers (Quinn, 2003). Adolescents and adults are more likely to feign ADHD symptoms for ulterior motives. Adolescent students may be motivated to exaggerate symptoms causing impairment to obtain academic accommodations or prescriptions for stimulants which allow for enhanced performance or act as a study aid. Amphetamines are also used for recreational purposes as they are an inexpensive substitute to cocaine (Babcock and Byrne, 2000). Ritalin has been shown to possess similar effects to that of cocaine, including the addictive quality (Swanson and Volkow, 2003).

Self-report ADHD questionnaires are some of the easiest assessment tools for malingerers to use to simulate symptoms of ADHD. Quinn (2003) was one of the first to conduct an experiment in which college students were asked to feign ADHD symptoms on behavior checklists, and assessed their outcome in comparison to college students with diagnosed ADHD and a normal control group of college students without ADHD. Results indicated that the group asked to malinger performed similarly to the true ADHD group on the ADHD Behavior Checklist (Quinn, 2003). In another study by Fisher and Watkins (2008), it was established that 93% of college students with no diagnostic criteria for ADHD were successfully able to fake self-reported ADHD symptoms on the College ADHD Response Evaluation and 73% were successful on the ADHD Behavior Checklist. The results of the study effectively demonstrated that neither of these scales were of utility in ferreting out malingering from true ADHD (Fisher and Watkins, 2008). Multiple studies, thereafter, have used scales such as Conners' Adult ADHD Rating Scales (CAARS), Wender Utah Rating Scale, and ADHD Rating Scale (ARS) in assessing the ease with which the symptoms can be faked. All were found to be inadequate in detecting feigned ADHD symptoms.

A combination of CAARS and the Woodcock-Johnson Psychoeducational Battery test may be suitable in detecting malingered ADHD (Harrison, Edwards, and Parker, 2007). However, the combination was found only to be moderately accurate with a 25% error rate (Musso and Gouvier, 2014). The lack of effort on neuropsychological tests is indicative of malingering and thus, the use of these tests has been recently more encouraged to be a part of clinical assessments of ADHD. Promising results have been seen with Symptom Validity Tests (SVTs) and Continuous Performance Tests (CPTs), as they allow detection for simulated ADHD (Musso and Gouvier, 2014). Malingerers often search for signs within the environment and have done additional research in guiding their presentation of symptoms or performance on assessment checklists. Malingering tactics on CPTs or SVTs include random responses and intentionally wrong responses (Quinn, 2003). Leark et al. (2002) suggest that clinicians should consider response bias when patients obtain excessively elevated scores on the Test of Variables of Attention, a type of CPT (Leark, Dixon, Hoffman, and Huynh, 2003). Clinicians should also be suspicious of students or young adults who are presenting for a first-time diagnosis and are rating themselves as being significantly symptomatic, yet have been able to achieve good academic standings and achieve well in other aspects of life. Quinn (2003) also used the Integrated Visual and Auditory Continuous Performance Test to decipher between malingerers and true patients with ADHD. Results indicated that malingerers scored significantly worse than the subjects with diagnosed ADHD, indicating that simulators had difficulty faking ADHD on this test and that the test was useful in detecting malingering (Quinn, 2003). Both the Victoria Symptom Validity Test and the Test of Memory Malingering (TOMM) also demonstrate promise for diagnostic purposes (Tombaugh, 1996).

Additionally, neurological soft signs (NSS) may also be used in detection of true ADHD in children. NSS are abnormal signs which appear on neurological examinations of motor and sensory functioning in the absence of focal neurological lesions. Some positive symptoms of NSS include cerebellar dysfunction of speed or accuracy of limb movements, poor coordination, and dysrhythmias. Movement overflow (synkinesia) and mirrored movements, which have a higher incidence in younger children, can be used in ruling-in a diagnosis of ADHD (Barkley, 2006). Along with the comorbidity of specific learning disabilities, NSS indicate CNS dysfunction consistent with other disorders of the neural axis including attention and learning. Detection of such abnormalities implies the importance of performing a thorough history and psychological assessment, and as well a thorough neurological examination.

Heuristically, ADHD is not too different than other purely self-reported conditions such as chronic pain, fibromyalgia, hallucinations, and migraines. Symptoms are quite subjective, making many psychiatric conditions, as well as ADHD symptoms, easy to feign. With the recent considerable rise in the number of college and university students and adults presenting with characteristics of ADHD, malingering ADHD has sparked interest. Currently, there is a lack of objective tests allowing to decipher between a true ADHD diagnosis and one of malingering. Clinicians should use caution when diagnosing ADHD in adults and should not base their diagnosis solely on the results of symptom checklist data. Self-report assessments are vulnerable to symptom exaggeration, especially in assessments with no embedded validity scales, and high scores on such scales should not be seen as confirmation of the diagnosis.

Unlike the other self-reported conditions, ADHD has the possible motive of obtaining amphetamines. The motivation for acquiring amphetamines can be multifold. Amphetamines have commonly been known to be used for enhancing performance to be more focused and attentive during examinations. Amphetamines can also be used to enhance or counteract the use of other medications or drugs. Lastly, one of the most common uses for amphetamines is for its monetary value.

9.4.1 Pharmacotherapy

The heart of the matter is what drives malingering in ADHD and what are the possible incentives. In adults, the motive may be to obtain access to disability status. As with students, the incentive may be special accommodations during school testing and/or access to the stimulants for enhanced performance. Such stimulants can be abused, used in conjunction with other drugs, or sold. These risks warrant the importance of how to accurately evaluate ADHD and finding possible alternatives to amphetamines. Given the minimum ability to detect malingering, one approach to this problem may be to possibly change the incentive for malingering.

Traditionally, ADHD may be treated in children seven years of age and younger by observing the tactics used in older children and adolescents which have been proven both efficacious and safe. There is no cure for ADHD; however, pharmacotherapy may be used to manage symptoms. Whilst pharmacotherapy shows remarkable benefits in young children with ADHD, it is important to evaluate the variation in response and tolerability. Because of this, physicians and parents alike should closely monitor children taking pharmacotherapy and assess ongoing risks and benefits of continued use of medication. For young children and adolescents, a vast amount of pharmacotherapy has been proven beneficial in the management of ADHD, such as stimulants (methylphenidate, amphetamine compounds), noradrenergic agents (atomoxetine), antidepressants (tricyclic antidepressants), antihypertensives (clonidine, guanfacine), and arousal agents (modafinil). Across all ages, the stimulants used to treat ADHD are mutually agreed upon. Inattention and hyperactivity–impulsivity is primarily due to the dysregulation of dopamine and norepinephrine. Stimulants primarily act on these two neurotransmitters as they are CNS medications which block the reuptake of dopamine. The alpha agonists have been shown to markedly reduce hyperactivity and aggression in children while antidepressants, such as Bupropion, have been shown to moderately reduce ADHD symptoms. Aside from stimulants, all other drug classes do not provide the same rush or addictive effects. Substituting amphetamines with alternative drugs will help in deterring the urge for malingering.

As literature on adult ADHD has increased, today, many more adults are presenting for diagnosis and treatment, as mentioned earlier. Much of the same medications used in children can be used to treat adult ADHD. While for children we believe that cognitive behavior therapy should first be implemented in the treatment of ADHD, medication is the primary source for the treatment in adult ADHD. Noradrenergic agents like atomoxetine were one of the first medications to be approved by the U.S. FDA for specific use in adults. The benefit of atomoxetine is that it is not a controlled substance so risk of addiction is less likely. Atomoxetine specifically inhibits presynaptic norepinephrine reuptake which results in increased synaptic norepinephrine and dopamine. In addition to atomoxetine in the treatment of adult ADHD, the U.S. FDA has also approved of the extended-release formulations of amphetamine salts and dexmethylphenidate.

A practical approach to ensuring clinicians are not being taken advantage of with their diagnosis of ADHD is to obtain a thorough history of symptoms in childhood and obtaining external corroboration in the case of adults. It may also be beneficial to not to prescribe amphetamines as your first approach to treatment, and to instead, searching for alternatives. Along with behavioral modification, starting treatment with phosphatidylserine (PS) with mega-3 fatty acids with eicosapentaenoic acid, a nondrug clinical dietary therapy, may be a better initial alternative. If the need for stimulants persists, starting with the lowest possible dose may be a means to deter motives behind stimulant prescriptions. In the future, possible use of electrophysiological devices such as fMRI, PET scans, or computerized EEG may help to delineate the diagnosis.

REFERENCES

American Psychiatric Association. 1968. *Diagnostic and statistical manual of mental disorders*, second edition, 50. Washington, D.C.: American Psychiatric Association.

American Psychiatric Association. 1980. *Diagnostic and statistical manual of mental disorders*, third edition, 41. Washington, D.C.: American Psychiatric Association.

American Psychiatric Association. 1994. *Diagnostic and statistical manual of mental disorders*, fourth edition, 78–85. Washington, D.C.: American Psychiatric Association.

American Psychiatric Association. 2013. *Diagnostic and statistical manual of mental disorders*, fifth edition, 61. Washington, D.C.: American Psychiatric Association.

Bakcock, Q. and T. Byrne. 2000. Student perceptions of methylphenidate abuse at a public liberal arts college. *Journal of American College Health* 49:143–145.

Barkley, R.A. 2017. Fact sheet: Attention deficit hyperactivity disorder (ADHD) topics. http://www.russellbarkley.org/factsheets/adhd-facts.pdf. (Accessed October 7, 2017.)

Barkley, R.A. 2006. *Attention-deficit hyperactivity disorder: A handbook for diagnosis and treatment*, third edition. New York: Guilford Press.

Barkley, R.A. and H. Peters. 2012. The earliest reference to ADHD in the medical literature? Melchior Adam Weikard's description in 1775 of "Attention Deficit" (Mangel der aufmerksamkeit, attentio volubilis). *Journal of Attention Disorders* 16:8:623–630.

Danielson, M.L., S.N. Visser, M.M. Gleason, G. Peacock, A.H. Claussen, and S.J. Blumberg. 2017. A national profile of attention-deficit hyperactivity disorder diagnosis and treatment among US children aged 2 to 5 years. *Journal of Developmental and Behavioral Pediatrics* 38:7:455–464.

Epstein, J.N. and R.E.A. Loren. 2013. Changes in the definition of ADHD in DSM-5: Subtle but important. *Neuropsychiatry* 3:5:455–458.

Fisher, A.B. and M.W. Watkins. 2008. ADHD rating scales' susceptibility to faking in a college student sample. *Journal of Postsecondary Education and Disability* 2:81–92.

Harrison, A.G., M.J. Edwards, and K.C.H. Parker. 2007. Identifying students faking ADHD: Preliminary findings and strategies for detection. *Archives of Clinical Neuropsychology* 22:5:577–588.

Kessler, R.C., W.T. Chiu, W., O. Demler, and E.E. Walters. 2005. Prevalence, severity, and comorbidity of twelve-month DSM-IV disorders in the National Comorbidity Survey Replication (NCS-R). *Archives of General Psychiatry* 62:6:617–27.

Kessler, R.C., L. Adler, R. Barkley, J. Biederman et al. 2006. The prevalence and correlates of adult ADHD in the United States: Results from the National Comorbidity Survey Replication. *The American Journal of Psychiatry* 163:4:716–723.

Leark, R.A., D. Dixon, T. Hoffman, and D. Huynh. 2002. Fake bad test response bias effects on the Test of Variables of Attention. *Archives of Clinical Neuropsychology* 17:4:335–342.

Moncrieff, J. and S. Timimi. 2010. Is ADHD a valid diagnosis in adults? No. *The BMJ* 340:C547.

Musso, M.W. and W.D. Gouvier. 2014. "Why is this so hard?" A review of detection of malingered ADHD in college students. *Journal of Attention Disorders* 18:3:186–201.

Perugi, G. and G. Vannucchi. 2015. The use of stimulants and atomoxetine in adults with comorbid ADHD and bipolar disorder. *Expert Opinion on Pharmacotherapy* 16:14:2193–2204.

Quinn, C.A. 2003. Detection of malingering in assessment of adult ADHD. *Archives of Clinical Neuropsychology* 18:4:379–395.

Stergiakouli, E. and A. Thapar. 2010. Fitting the pieces together: Current research on the genetic basis of attention-deficit/hyperactivity disorder (ADHD). *Neuropsychiatric Disease and Treatment* 551.

Swanson, J.M. and N.D. Volkow. 2003. Serum and brain concentrations of methylphenidate: Implications for use and abuse. *Neuroscience and Biobehavioral Reviews* 27:615–621.

Tombaugh, T.N. 1996. *Test of Memory Malingering (TOMM)*. New York: Multi-Health Systems, Inc.

10 Detection and Management of Malingering to Obtain Narcotics

Anum Wani, HBSc, Mariam Agha, HBSc, and Alan R. Hirsch, MD

CONTENTS

Tell the truth and you won't have so much to remember.

Abraham Lincoln

10.1 WHAT IS MALINGERING?

Malingering, a nonmedical condition, is defined as the intentional feigning or exaggeration of symptoms for secondary gain. While usually for financial reward, it also may be seen in the acquisition of narcotics (Adetunji et al., 2006). It is a diagnosis of exclusion (McDermott and Feldman, 2007) and therefore requires the art of detection and the use of a stepwise approach involving direct observation, complete physical examination, extensive assessment of the patient's past medical records, psychometric evaluations (including scales and questionnaires), and laboratory assessments.

These are important to avoid making an incorrect diagnosis of malingering or overlooking the possibility of feigning. With the assignment of such a diagnosis, one should be cautious and use all available (nonconfrontational) techniques of management which would maintain the patient–physician dyadic relationship while also being beneficial to the patient, preserving their sense of self-esteem and agency.

Malingering has been a recognized condition for millennia (see Chapter 1). This diagnosis has become problematic in recent years due to open access of medical records to the patient, and subsequent fear by the physician of patient backlash. Although the incidence of malingering cases might not be known due to the difficulty of diagnosis, a myriad of studies in past decades have shown that it is a greater problem than expected. Not only is the prevalence of malingering for medicinal gain remarkable, what is even more remarkable is the fact that malingering has been documented in children as young as nine years old, making it difficult to diagnose and even harder to manage (Adetunji et al., 2006).

10.2 CHRONIC PAIN SETTING: HOW COMMON IS MALINGERING FOR NARCOTICS?

Although malingering is a more common occurrence in the military, prisons, and criminal prosecutions, the incidence of malingering in the emergency department is as high as 13% of all visits, of which the majority involves the acquisition of narcotics (Adetunji et al., 2006). Malingering in the emergency department can be for a plethora of gains including food, shelter, financial, and medicinal. The medicinal gains have been of particular interest of study due to the inability to differentiate between patients who are malingering for narcotics and those who actually suffer from chronic pain. Since pain is a vital sign which requires subjective quantification, it is difficult to objectively assess its presence or severity, and therefore easier for the patient to feign. Unlike diseases where abnormal findings are part of the diagnostic process, for example, optic neuropathy with pale discs, polyneuropathy with absent reflexes, or Parkinson's disease with substantia nigra degeneration associated with movement disorder, cogwheel rigidity and instability, chronic pain is wholly a subjective complaint. It is important for clinicians to look for signs of pain, like positive guarding, reduction in movement of one part of the body, or primary pathology, as in the presence of a herniated nucleus pulposus or osteoarthritis.

On the other hand, the presence of subjective complaints alone, without objective, organic physical findings, do not indicate the absence of disease. If that were the case, then it would not be possible to diagnose disorders where the diagnosis relies on subjective complaints in the patient's history. These disorders include, but are not limited to delusional disorder, migraine headaches, schizophrenia, tinnitus, phantosmia, phantaguesia, and visual entopia and obscuration.

The second most abused class of drugs, following marijuana, is opioid prescription drugs, where the proportion of abuse has increased over fourfold in the past two decades (Office of National Drug Control Policy, 2011).

Between 2004 to 2009, visits to the emergency department, with the intention of seeking narcotics, doubled in patients who were 12 years or older (Office of National Drug Control Policy, 2011). The nonmedicinal use of narcotics prescribed by physicians 2010 was observed in approximately two million adults age 50 and older.

10.3 DETECTION IN A CHRONIC PAIN SETTING

Before being able to clinically diagnose and manage malingering, it is important to be able to detect the behavioral patterns of patients feigning to acquire narcotics. The abstract nature of pain, its varying presentation and ubiquitous experience, makes it an easy commodity to malinger and difficult to detect. Since everyone has experienced physical pain at some point in time, its presentation to others, especially physicians, is known and thus would be easy to prevaricate (McDermott and Feldman, 2007). Malingering patients will present with pain in accordance to the amount of medical knowledge and awareness they have of their fabricated condition. Patients who lack knowledge will present with pain that is inconsistent with the medical illness or anatomy. However, the ease of access to medical information today may be sufficient to provide enough medical knowledge to malingerers to be able to convince physicians that they suffer from the diagnoses they are trying to feign (McDermott and Feldman, 2007). Therefore, in order to separate a malingerer from a chronic pain patient, physicians should execute a stepwise approach starting with direct observation and detailed physical examination, analyzing past medical records, utilizing scales and questionnaires, and performing laboratory assessments. This approach cannot only aid in detecting malingering but can also lead to a more honest and more constructive patient–physician relationship.

10.3.1 Direct Observation and History

The first steps toward the detection of malingering are obtaining a detailed history, watching for discrepancies in description. The examiner should be attentive to vagueness regarding past and present doctors, use of narcotic-seeking behavior, (specifically asking for narcotics by name and dose), reluctance to provide personal information including insurance information (wishing to pay cash for visit), and the presence of chronic pain syndrome in apparently young healthy individuals whose history are without activities of daily living limitations, and without appearance of severe pain. The second technique facilitating the detection of malingering is direct observation of the patient for an extended and uninterrupted period. Such protracted observation becomes challenging for the patient due to the energy required to maintain the fabricated symptoms over prolonged periods of time. Eventually, there will be a discrepancy in the claims presented throughout the interview since the malingering patient may lack extensive knowledge of the disease they are claiming to have and may demonstrate inconsistent behavior during the interview (American Medical Association, 2012).

The patient can also proclaim symptoms which are quite uncommon for their feigned condition (Lebourgeois III, 2007). For example, the patient claiming to have sciatica will describe pain in both buttocks radiating down their thighs, which is relieved when sitting. On the contrary, true sciatica usually presents unilaterally with the pain radiating down the leg, which worsens when sitting.

10.3.2 Physical Examination

There are several specific tests used in the physical examination which aid in the diagnosis of malingering. "Burns' Test" may be used to differentiate between true or false back pain or sciatica (Evanski, Carver, Nehemkis, and Waugh, 1979). During this test, the patient is asked to kneel on a chair and touch the floor. Thinking this should cause pain, malingerers will claim that they cannot do the test, hence giving a negative Burns' test. On the other hand, patients with true pain will easily be able to perform the aforementioned maneuver demonstrating organic pain.

Waddell's Signs test, a group of signs, can also be used to confirm the presence of true chronic lower back pain (McDermott and Feldman, 2007). The test is comprised of eight signs; patients with true pain may have one or two, however, malingering patients will demonstrate three or more signs. These are as follows (Greer, Chambliss, Mackler, and Huber, 2005): (i) Overreaction: Inconsistent and exaggerated response to stimuli. A malingering patient who reacts to a stimulus initially may not show reaction to the same stimulus later in the examination due to distraction. (ii) Superficial tenderness: Normally, in a patient with true organic back pain, the skin over the area of pain will not be tender upon light palpation because organic back pain does not cause tenderness of overlying skin, but instead, pain in periosteal and ligamentous structures. Symptoms of superficial tenderness, on the other hand, can indicate malingering. An exception to this would be pain due to complex regional pain syndrome, wherein superficial tenderness is a common complaint (Fields, 1987). (iii) Nonanatomic tenderness: Normally in a patient with back pain, mediated through the lateral pain pathway (lateral spinothalamic tract), tenderness upon palpation will be localized to a single area (Zasler, Martelli, and Nicholson, 2011a). However, nonanatomic tenderness, tenderness over multiple areas, may be present without a valid reason in a malingering patient. The exception to this rule would be organic involvement of the medial pain pathway (anterior spinothalamic tract) (Zasler, Martelli, and Nicholson, 2011a). (iv) Axial loading: The physician exerts downward pressure on the standing patient's head (performed only in those without cervical disease), a maneuver which does not exaggerate low back pain in an organic chronic low back pain patient. A malingering patient may complain of low back pain in this maneuver. (v) Simulated rotation: The physician rotates the patient while keeping the shoulders and hips in the same plane. Normally, this will not cause pain since the back is not stressed; however, indication of pain denotes malingering. (vi) Distracted straight legraise: In this maneuver, the physician distracts the patient by checking for pulses or reflexes, while asking them to raise their leg. At this point, a patient with true chronic back pain may not be able to raise their leg, whereas a malingerer may be distracted enough to raise their leg unconsciously without complaints. This response would be a positive test for malingering or nonorganic disease. (vii) Regional sensory change: Organic pain associated sensory change is limited to specific dermatomal distributions in chronic back pain patients. Malingering patients might report sensory changes in multiple independent dermatomal distributions or entire limb or side of body. Alternatively, it is possible for true organic disease to have poorly localized dermatomal distribution associated with dysfunction of the medial pain pathway (Zasler, Martelli, and Nicholson, 2011a), or hemibody pain or hemi-anesthesia with thalamic infarction, as is seen in Dejerine-Roussy Syndrome with dysesthesia (Ramachandran, McGeoch, and Williams, 2007). (viii) Regional weakness: Organic pain patients with physical weakness will depict muscle movement which is smooth in nature during a resisted range of motion maneuver. With organic weakness, weakness will persist throughout varying muscle lengths. In contrast, with malingering weakness there is breakaway weakness. This is intermittent weakness associated with gradual change in the length of the muscle. A malingering patient will fail to replicate such smooth movement. A caveat to this rule would be clasp knife rigidity, whereby tone changes with flexion of joint. Care should be taken in misinterpretation of malingering of clasp knife rigidity, as this can be a finding associated with upper motor neuron lesions.

Another test to detect malingering during physical examination is the McBride's test (Greer, Chambliss, Mackler, and Huber, 2005). The physician asks the patient to stand on the asymptomatic leg while flexing the opposite knee to the chest. This maneuver decreases the pressure from the spinal facets by flexing the spine and reducing the stretch of the sciatic nerve. A decrease in lower back pain is experienced in true chronic lower back pain patients, whereas malingering patients will report an increase in pain or refuse to perform the test altogether.

Malingering pain can also be detected by assessing the pulse rate using Mankopf's test. This test applies the concept of an increase in pulse rate after the administration of pressure to the site of pain or injury (Greer, Chambliss, Mackler, and Huber, 2005). During this test, an increase in pulse rate of 5% is observed as pressure is applied to the painful area. In patients who are feigning pain there will be no observable change in the pulse rate.

10.3.3 Past Medical Records

The evaluation of the malingering patient requires careful review of past medical records and assessment for inconsistencies between the records and the current claims (American Medical Association, 2012). Other warning signs in the medical records of the malingering patient may include, but are not limited to, a history of frequent visits to the emergency department (specifically for headaches), back pain or dental pain which has been treated with narcotics; numerous refill requests for a specific narcotic because of unbearable pain; lost or stolen narcotics; pain level of ten out of ten or greater on multiple visits, and requests for parenteral administration of narcotics (Grover, Elder, Close, and Curry, 2012). Furthermore, if the patient refuses disclosure of his or her past medical records, it may also be a red flag and might warrant further investigation as the patient may be trying to conceal information such as previous frequent emergency department visits, history of extensive narcotics use, or history of medically diagnosed drug abuse (American Medical Association, 2012).

10.3.4 Scales and Questionnaires

Psychometric evaluations are one of the most crucial steps in assessing possible malingering. These include a combination of scales and questionnaires which aid in identifying patient effort during the physical examination. Presence and intensity of pain and validity of symptoms and can help determine if the patient needs further psychological evaluation. Such scales and questionnaires include the following:

a. Pain Patient Profile (P3): Although this scale does not directly measure pain, it focuses on factors associated with chronic pain. This is a 44-item, self-report, multiple choice assessment which includes a set of three scales measuring anxiety, depression, and somatization. Patients who are feigning pain will have an abnormally high score on all three clinical scales (McGuire and Shores, 2001).
b. Hendler Chronic Pain Screening Test: This is a 15-question test designed to assess chronic pain. Scores of 21–31 indicate exaggeration of pain symptoms. A score of 31 or greater suggests psychological issues requiring further assessment, whereas a score of 21 or less indicates physical/somatic origin of pain (Zasler, Martelli, and Nicholson, 2011b).
c. Minnesota Multiphasic Personality Inventory-2: This is utilized in order to determine whether the patient is exaggerating their symptoms of pain as well as for the presence of underlying psychiatric disease. The Minnesota Multiphasic Personality Inventory-2 has nine validity scales which assess for lying, defensiveness, and the person's overall psychological state (Greve, Elder, Close, and Curry, 2009).
d. Barkemeyer-Callon-Jones Malingering Detection Scale: This is a clinical interview behavior questionnaire to help determine malingering in the setting of pain, loss of sensation, and other complaints. It is a formal method to assess malingering based on the presentation of the history (see Chapter 2). The scale is a list of findings which the physician elicits during the interview (Hall and Poirier, 2001). For example, "the patient describes an atypical or very unlikely response to treatment; the patient presents a constellation of complaints which are not consistent with a recognized abnormality of anatomical substrata; the patient describes the prestige of other people who allegedly found a pathological process, any physical effort resulted in enhancement of the patient's presentation of symptoms" (Hall and Poirier, 2001).
e. Portland Digit Recognition Test: This is used to determine the level of effort the patient is exerting during the evaluation in accordance with their symptoms. The Portland Digit Recognition Test consists of 72 trials in which a five-digit number is initially presented in each trial followed by distracting the patient. During this period, the patient is asked to count backwards. Then, two five-digit numbers are presented and the patient is asked to identify the number that was initially presented. In each trial, the distractor periods are lengthened, which increases the difficulty of the test (Allen, 2011). A malingering patient would not put in effort during such tests as they only want to reach their end goal, which is acquiring narcotics. However, there is a possibility that a patient with chronic pain may also show suboptimal effort due to ongoing pain. Furthermore, pain may act to inhibit cognition and memory, thus this test alone is not conclusive in diagnosing malingered pain (Zasler, Martelli, and Nicholson, 2011c).

f. The Symptom Checklist-90-Revised: This is a 90-item, self-report test which focuses on a variety of psychological issues and can also be used to identify true pain. A very high score on the checklist may indicate over-reporting of pain, a characteristic of malingered pain (McDermott and Feldman, 2009).
g. Modified Somatic Perception Questionnaire: This highly specific and sensitive assessment is a 13-symptom self-report scale of somatic perceptions, which is used to differentiate malingerers from chronic pain patients. Similar to the Symptom Checklist-90-Revised, a very high score on the questionnaire may indicate over-reporting of pain, a characteristic of malingered pain (McDermott and Feldman, 2009).

10.3.5 Laboratory Assessments

A future screening method of ongoing research is focusing on exploring definite objective evidence of chronic pain syndrome. For instance, IgM binding to a tri-sulfated heparin disaccharide is one such chronic pain syndrome marker (Strong and Kafaie, 2015). The absence of tri-sulfated heparin disaccharide could be crucial in the detection of malingering in patients who claim to have chronic pain syndrome. However, larger and more extensive studies are needed to confirm the diagnostic value of this marker.

10.3.6 Treatment Response Discrepancies

The last step in detecting malingering is checking for treatment response discrepancies and compliance with the prescribed treatment regimen. While checking for drug response discrepancies, a chronic pain patient is given an analgesic of the same magnitude as the requested narcotic, providing alleviation of pain. The malingering patient will claim no relief (Hall and Pritchard, 1996).

Transcutaneous electrical nerve stimulation TENS is an electric stimulus applied near the painful site which creates analgesia in chronic pain patients. TENS shows a lack of response in malingering patients (Hall and Pritchard, 1996).

Another factor to help detect malingering would be checking for patient compliance to the prescribed treatment (McDermott and Feldman, 2007). A patient with true chronic pain will be highly compliant as they want alleviation of pain compared to a malingerer who is interested in only acquiring the desired narcotic.

Since malingering is a heterogenous phenomenon, there is no one specific instrument that can be conclusively used to diagnose it. Therefore, it is important to incorporate multiple tools in the process of clinical diagnosis and differentiation between the real and the fabricated.

10.3.7 Physician's Response/Management

Considering the fact that malingering is a diagnosis of exclusion and not a primary medical condition, the patient must first be thoroughly evaluated for actual chronic pain or any overlapping or similarly presenting psychiatric illnesses. Both somatoform and factitious disorders can be mistaken for malingering, as they involve the feigning of exaggerated or absurd symptoms, which are either unconsciously produced or produced with the motive of appearing to be sick (Adetunji et al., 2006). Once malingering is diagnosed by exclusion, it is important to know that there is no specific treatment for it, but rather a set of tools which can be used for its management.

The initial response of the physician should be such that the patient should not feel accused of lying, but instead, the inconsistencies of the patient should be addressed in an empathic tone, which may lead to a confession from the patient highlighting any genuine underlying issues or coexisting psychosocial conditions (Adetunji et al., 2006). During this process, it is also important to make use of case appropriate tools, such as interpreters, referrals for drug counseling, or individual therapy.

Another, less preferred tool which may be added to the process of management is warning the patient of subsequent invasive testing or treatments according to their symptoms (American Medical Association, 2012). Here, for a malingering patient, it is important to emphasize the severity and degree of invasiveness of the tests and treatments which are needed to manage the symptoms presented. Such invasive tests or treatments, however, are not routinely performed as they can do more harm than good (American Medical Association, 2012).

Zasler (2011d) eloquently warned, "...clinicians would be wise to avoid dogmatic conclusions that any particular pain patient is malingering their pain, as there are few, if any, unambiguous indicators to state this conclusively (Nicholson and Martelli, 2007). The literature regarding assessment of nonorganic pain presentations remains highly debated, including the methods for determining the differential diagnosis of malingered pain, conscious symptom amplification of pain (whether or not for financial gain 'or acquiring narcotics'), factitious pain complaints, pain amplification due to poor coping, and somatoform and other psychogenic pain disorders" (Zasler, 2011d). Thus, the diagnosis and management of malingering of chronic pain remain a medical zugzwang requiring multipronged approaches, which often leads the physician to feel that no option is correct.

REFERENCES

Adetunji, B.A., B. Basil, M. Mathews et al. 2006. Detection and management of malingering in a clinical setting. *Primary Psychiatry* 13:1:61–69.

Allen, D.N. 2011. Portland digit recognition test. In *Encyclopedia of Clinical Neuropsychology*, eds. J. Kreutzer, J. DeLuca, and B. Caplan, 1966–1968. New York: Springer-Verlag.

American Medical Association. 2012. Detecting deception: How to handle malingering patient. *American Medical News*. Retrieved from: http://www.amednews.com/article/20120910/profession/309109942/4/

Evanski, P.M., D. Carver, A. Nehemkis, and T.R. Waugh. 1979. The Burns' test in low back pain: Correlation with the hysterical personality. *Clinical Orthopaedics and Related Research* 140:42–44.

Fields, H.L. 1987. *Pain*, 148. New York: McGraw-Hill.

Greer, S., L. Chambliss, L. Mackler, and T. Huber. 2005. Clinical inquiries. What physical exam techniques are useful to detect malingering? *Journal of Family Practice* 54:8:719–722.

Greve, K.W., J.S. Ord, K.J. Bianchini, and K.L. Curtis. 2009. Prevalence of malingering in patients with chronic pain referred for psychologic evaluation in a medico-legal context. *Archives of Physical Medicine and Rehabilitation* 90:7:1117–1126.

Grover, C.A., J.W. Elder, R.J. Close, and S.M. Curry. 2012. How frequently are "classic" drug-seeking behaviors used by drug-seeking patients in the emergency department? *Western Journal of Emergency Medicine* 13:5:416–421.

Hall, H.V., and J. Poirier. 2001. *Detecting Malingering and Deception: Forensic Distortion Analysis, Second Edition*, 165. Boca Raton: CRC Press.

Hall, H.V., and D.A. Pritchard. 1996. *Detecting Malingering and Deception: Forensic Distortion Analysis.* Del Ray Beach: St. Lucie Press.

Lebourgeois, III, H.W. 2007. Malingering: Key points in assessment. *Psychiatric Times* 24:5:21–21.

McDermott, B.E., and M.D. Feldman. 2007. Malingering in the medical setting. *Psychiatric Clinics of North America* 30:4:645–662.

McGuire, B.E., and E.A. Shores. 2001. Pain patient profile and the assessment of malingered pain. *Journal of Clinical Psychology* 57:3:40–49.

Nicholson, K., and M. Martelli. 2007. Malingering: Chronic pain. In *Causality of Psychological Injury: Presenting Evidence in Court*, eds. G. Young, A. Kane, and K. Nicholson. New York: Springer-Verlag.

Office of National Drug Control Policy (ONDCP). 2011. A response to the epidemic to prescription drug abuse. *Fact Sheet.* Retrieved from: https://www.ncjrs.gov/pdffiles1/ondcp/rx_epidemic.pdf.

Ramachandran, V.S., P.D. McGeoch, and L. Williams. 2007. Can vestibular caloric stimulation be used to treat Dejerine–Roussy Syndrome? *Medical Hypotheses* 69:3:486–488.

Strong, E., and J. Kafaie. 2015. A promising marker to detect chronic pain syndrome. *Neurology* 84:14:P5.055.

Zasler, M.D., M.F. Martelli, and K. Nicholson. 2011a. Chronic pain. In *Textbook of Traumatic Brain Injury, 2nd edition*, eds. J.M. Silver, T.W. McAllister, and S.C. Yudofsky, 376. Arlington, VA: American Psychiatric Publishing, Inc.

Zasler, M.D., M.F. Martelli, and K. Nicholson. 2011b. Chronic pain. In *Textbook of Traumatic Brain Injury, 2nd edition*, eds. J.M. Silver, T.W. McAllister, and S.C. Yudofsky, 381. Arlington, VA: American Psychiatric Publishing, Inc.

Zasler, M.D., M.F. Martelli, and K. Nicholson. 2011c. Chronic pain. In *Textbook of Traumatic Brain Injury, 2nd edition*, eds. J.M. Silver, T.W. McAllister, and S.C. Yudofsky, 377. Arlington, VA: American Psychiatric Publishing, Inc.

Zasler, M.D., M.F. Martelli, and K. Nicholson. 2011d. Chronic pain. In *Textbook of Traumatic Brain Injury, 2nd edition*, eds. J.M. Silver, T.W. McAllister, and S.C. Yudofsky, 382. Arlington, VA: American Psychiatric Publishing, Inc.

11 Chemosensory Malingering

Alan R. Hirsch, MD

CONTENTS

In the realm of neurologic deficits, the incidence of post-traumatic malingering has been estimated to be as low as 2% to as high as 50% (Henderson, 1986; Miller and Cartlidge, 1972), a disparity which indicates the true incidence is unknown.

Posttraumatic illnesses, the diagnoses of which sometimes rely upon the patient's self-reports, are often linked to financial incentives (Resnick, 1988). Such illnesses need close assessment to detect malingering. One type of self-reported posttraumatic illness known as chemosensory dysfunction occurs in as many as 24.5% of head trauma victims (Costanzo and Becker, 1986). Malingering is known to exist in this area (Hirsch and MacKenzie, Jr., 1993) but its incidence has not been estimated.

Ferreting out individuals pretending to have chemosensory dysfunction as part of litigation for economic gain is a clinical dilemma requiring a multimodal approach. This includes evaluation of historical context, complaints, physical examination findings, chemosensory testing, psychiatric evaluation, and ancillary testing.

The penultimate question, after trying to establish the presence of malingering, is why would one choose to malinger a chemosensory disorder? In our visual-oriented, ratiocinate, Cartesian world, vision is the more preeminent sense (Smith, 2007). For instance, the American Medical Association's *Guide to Permanent Disability* guideline for awarding compensation for functional losses provides compensations of 80–100% for vision, 80–100% for hearing, 100% for touch, but only 1–5% for both smell and taste (Cocchiarella and Anderson, 2001). On face value it would seem more profitable for a malingerer to choose visual or hearing loss as a focus for sensory attention. Logically, motoric or other functional deficits (i.e., behavioral, cognitive, psychological) would provide greater economic incentive for a malingerer than smell and taste dysfunction. However, possibly because the loss of other modalities causes greater functional deficits and thus is easier to objectively assess, the adept malingerer would retreat to the more obscure world of smell and taste. Complaining of such a deficit comforts the complainant that his or her pretended loss would have a marginal effect on everyday life and thus is likely to go undetected. However, the actual functional deficit due to true chemosensory abnormalities can manifest itself in the short and long-term and across multiple social and medical realms, ultimately having a markedly deleterious effect on the quality of everyday life (Keller and Malaspia, 2013).

Furthermore, the impact of true loss, on cursory inspection, is marginal. Thus, in the absence of testing malingering loss could be relatively easy to achieve compared to visual loss or hemiparesis, which an outside observer could easily detect.

11.1 OLFACTORY DYSFUNCTION

Olfactory dysfunction can present as hyposmia (reduced), anosmia (absent), hyperosmia (enhanced), dysosmia (distorted), phantosmia (hallucinated), palinosmia (persistent), cacosmia (bad, disgusting), or as a combination of these (Hirsch, 2009a; Wahlstrom, Hirsch, and Whitman, 2015). Hyposmia or anosmia may display itself through reduced retronasal smell which is perceived as impaired taste (Gruss and Hirsch, 2015). Since 90% of flavor is actually smell, olfactory deficit is usually perceived by the sufferer as impaired taste (Wahlstrom, Hirsch, and Whitman, 2015).

Normal olfactory ability is on a continuum in the general population, fluctuating with a myriad of demographic and physiologic factors. For instance, in the base state women have a better ability to smell than men, especially at ovulation (Mair, Bouffard, Engen, and Morton, 1978) when olfactory ability tends to be even greater (Doty, Applebaum, Zusho, and Settle, 1985; Mair, Bouffard, Engen, and Morton, 1978). Along with the other special senses, the vicissitudes of aging are also reflected in olfactory ability. From birth onwards, on an annual basis, abiotrophy of the olfactory bulb causes apoptosis in approximately 1% of olfactory neurons (Meisami, Mikhail, Baim, and Bhatnagar, 1998). By age 36, clinical testing demonstrates such a loss (Hawkes, Fogo, and Shah, 2005). By age 65, one-half of those tested will have a reduced ability to smell and by age 80 three-quarters will suffer such a loss (Doty et al., 1984). Moreover, the malingerer would also have to be cognizant of which nostril is being tested, since variability in olfactory threshold and identification ability depends on an individual's handedness. The dominant nostril correlates with the dominant hand. Left-handed individuals have greater sensitivity of left cranial nerve I and right-handed individuals have greater sensitivity of right cranial nerve I (Youngentob, Kurtz, Leopold, Mozell, and Hornumg, 1982).

Adding to this olfactory normative heterogeny, olfactory ability varies depending upon ethnicity. Korean Americans' olfactory ability surpasses that of Caucasians, which is greater than in Afro-Americans, followed by the Japanese whose baseline sense of smell is of the lowest acuity (J. Hirsch, 1992).

The potential malingerer who consider feigning hyposmia would need to be aware of these demographic variations. For instance, a hyposmic 20-year-old Korean female's olfactory ability would be considered normal in a 65-year-old Japanese male, even if she was feigning hyposmia.

Moreover, olfactory ability is readily malleable with normal physiological variation associated with change in horological parameters, hunger, consumption patterns, and focus of attention. Olfactory ability is keenest on awaking in the morning and progressively declines as the day progresses (Keller and Malaspia, 2013). Seasons also have an influence, with the greatest sense of smell in the spring/summer and worst in the winter (Keller and Malaspia, 2013). When fasting or with hunger, olfactory ability is the most intense, whereas when satiated olfactory ability plummets—except if the food consumed is milk—which has no or marginal impact on olfactory acuity (Hirsch, 1992a). Thus, when queried by the examiner the malingerer must factor into his or her olfactory dissimulation the time of day, season of year, time of last meal, and even what was consumed. Hence, in a winter office visit just after lunch the normal olfactory ability would be low enough as to render a low olfactory test score normal and convert malingering hyposmia to normosmia.

Even beyond this, the malingerer must not be on any medications. Both over-the-counter and prescription drugs are known to be etiologies of olfactory loss, just like over-the-counter zinc nasal spray (DeCook and Hirsch, 2000).

Drugs which interfere with the smell system:

CLASSIFICATION

1. Anesthetic, local (Zilstorff, 1995)
    a. Cocaine hydrochloride
    b. Tetracaine hydrochloride
2. Antihypertensive drugs (Berman, 1985; Levenson and Kennedy, 1985; Ackerman and Kasbekar, 1997)
    a. Diltiazem
    b. Nifedipine
    c. Amlodipine
    d. Enalapril
    e. Felodipine
    f. Beta blockers
3. Antimicrobial agents (Body, 1986; Zilstorff and Herbild, 1979; Seydell and McKnight, 1948; Ackerman and Kasbekar, 1997)
    a. Allicin
    b. Streptomycin
    c. Tyrothricin
    d. Ciprofloxacin
    e. Doxycycline
    f. Silver nitrates
    g. Terbinafine
4. Antithyroid agents (Erikssen, Seegaard, and Naess, 1975; Hallman and Hurst, 1953; Schneeberg, 1952; Grossman, 1953)
    a. Carbimazole
    b. Methimazole
    c. Methylthiouracil
    d. Propylthiouracil
5. Opiates (D. Macht and M. Macht, 1940)
    a. Codeine
    b. Hydromorphine hydrochloride
    c. Morphine

6. Psychopharmacologic drug (Farbman, Gonzales, and Chuah, 1988; Chuah and Hui, 1986)
    a. Amitriptyline
7. Radiation therapy (Carmichael, Jennings, and Doty, 1984)
    a. Radiation to head
8. Chemotherapy (Ackerman and Kasbekar, 1997)
    a. Cytosine arabinoside
    b. Methotrexate
9. Sympathomimetic drugs (Goetz and Stone, 1948; Schiffman, 1983b; Turner, 1965)
    a. Amphetamines
    b. Phenmetazine theoclate with fenbutazate hydrochloride
10. Other (Skouby and Zilstorff-Pedersen, 1954; Ackerman and Kasbekar, 1997)
    a. Acetylcholine-like substances
    b. Strychnine
    c. Alpha interferon
    d. Flusinolide
    e. Tobacco products and smoke

Furthermore, the malingerer must not suffer from disease states which are known to promote smell loss. These range from benign illness such as migraine and olfactotropic viruses to life-threatening disorders such as Parkinson's disease, amyotrophic lateral sclerosis, multiple sclerosis, and senile dementia of the Alzheimer's type (Hirsch 1992b; Hirsch and Skolnik, 1994; Hawkes, 2006; Keller and Malaspia, 2013; Doty, Reys, and Gregor, 1987).

Pathologic Conditions

Conduction defects:

Airway:

Nasal Polyposis (Scott, Cain, and Leonard, 1989)

Symptoms: hyposmia, olfactory windows, subjective hypogeusia.

Treatment: steroids (local/systemic), surgery, systemic steroids followed by nasal steroids, surgery followed by nasal steroids, surgery followed by systemic steroids (Scott, 1989a).

Mucus:

Allergic Rhinitis

Symptoms: hyposmia, olfactory windows, subjective hypogeusia.

Mechanisms: histamine release → change in mucus → decreased ability for the odorant molecule to dissolve in the mucus → blocked olfactory experience prior to reaching the olfactory nerve (Mott and Leopold, 1991).

Treatment: local or if ineffective, systemic steroids, (1) Flunesolide two puffs inhaled per nostril b.i.d. in head down position (Scott,Cain, and Clavet, 1988); (2) Prednisone 50 mg PO q day for five days (Apter, Mott, Cain, Spiro, and Barwick, 1992).

Cranial nerve disorder (1 neuron)

Olfactory Receptor Damage:

Post Viral Infection

Symptoms: hyposmia, dysosmia, no olfactory windows, subjective hypogeusia.

Treatment: none. Zinc, no effect in double blind placebo controlled study (Henkin, Schecter, Friedewald, Demets, and Raff, 1976).

Olfactory Nerve (receptor damage?)

Atmospheric pressure sensitive paroxysmal unilateral phantosmia (Hirsch, Lieberman, and Gay, 1991).

Symptoms: phantosmia, hyposmia, olfactory windows.

Mechanisms: virus causes receptor damage → partial denervation occurs → in response to denervation there are sprouting of new receptor sites which are sensitive to touch (trigeminal neuralgia model of synesthesia with perception of temperature or touch as pain).

Treatment: (1) mechanical obstruction, (2) valproic acid, (3) Tegretol, (4) Mysoline.

Olfactory Nerve Axon at the cribriform plate

Head Trauma (Hirsch and Wyse, 1993).

Symptoms: subjective hypogeusia, no olfactory windows, anosmia, hyposmia, phantosmia, dysosmia.

Mechanisms: "shearing of olfactory nerve" 40% of the time damage rostral to cranial nerve I "central hyposmia".

Treatment: for central hyposmia (1) Thiamine 100 mg PO q.d., (2) Phosphatidylcholine 9 gm q.d.

For peripheral anosmia: none.

Olfactory Nerve (at the axon hillock)

Toxins (Amoore, 1986; Doty, Gregor, and Monroe, 1986): trichloroethylene (Hirsch, 1995a), cigarettes (Frye, Schwartz, and Doty, 1990), nitrogen tetroxide (Hirsch, 1995b), pyrethoid insecticides (Hirsch, 1997a), hydrogen sulfide (Hirsch, 1996), lead, methyl ethyl ketone (Hirsch, 1997b), aluminosilicates (Roberts, 1986), mercury (Furuta, Nishimoto, Egawa, Ohyama, and Moriyama, 1994), solvents (Schwartz, Ford, Bolla, Agnew, Rothman, and Bleecker, 1990), chlorine (Hirsch, 1995c).

Symptoms: hyposmia, anosmia, subjective hypogeusia, no olfactory windows, phantosmia.

Mechanisms: with *no* blood–brain barrier, toxins overwhelm the nasal xenobiotic mechanism, inducing olfactory nerve cell death. Aluminosilicates, in addition, are transported transaxonally causing continued rostral destruction (a postulated mechanism for the pathogenesis of senile dementia of the Alzheimer's type).

Central Pathway Dysfunction:

Olfactory bulb and tract: Olfactory groove meningioma (Jafek and Hill, 1989).

Symptoms: phantosmia, hyposmia, subjective hypogeusia.

Treatment: surgical intervention.

Hippocampi: Wernicke–Korsakoff's Syndrome (Potter and Butters, 1980).
Symptoms: anosmia.
Treatment: Thiamine.

Temporal Lobe: complex partial seizures (Acharya, Acharya, and Luders, 1996)
Symptoms: anosmia ipsilateral to the seizure focus, hyposmia contralateral to the seizure focus, "uncinate fits," phantosmia, foul burning rubber, metallic phantageusia, not well localized.
Mechanism: spontaneous olfactory cortex discharge possibly ipsilaterally mediated.

Frontal Lobe: Pick's disease.

Anterior Olfactory Nucleus: Parkinson-dementia complex of Guam (Doty et al., 1991).
Symptoms: hyposmia.

Limbic Lobe: dysthymia, generalized anxiety disorder (Hirsch and Trannell, 1996), schizophrenia (Serby, Larson, and Kalkstein, 1990).
Symptoms: hyposmia, subjective hypogeusia, phantosmia.
Mechanism: neighborhood effect; reaction to narcissistic insult. the greater the duration of the schizophrenia, the greater the olfactory loss (Moberg et al., 1997).
Treatment: Amitriptyline, group therapy.

Schizophrenia (Rubert, Hollender, and Mehrof, 1961; Meats, 1988): olfactory hallucination—prevalence: acute schizophrenia 79%, chronic schizophrenia (hospitalized) 92%.

Olfactory dysmorphophobia (Hirsch, 1990b): Olfactory reference syndrome.
Symptoms: self-perception of cacosmia.
Treatment: haloperidol, MAOI.

Diffuse Brain Dysfunction

Senile dementia of the Alzheimer's Type.
Symptoms: anomic anosmia, subjective hypogeusia.
Mechanism: decreased choline acetyltransferase in the basal nucleus of Maeynart—questionable decreased acetylcholine in the olfactory bulb, tract, and cortex—pathology in the anterior olfactory nucleus, uncus, and medial amygdaloid nuclei olfactory vector hypothesis allows toxin or virus to penetrate transaxonally (Pearson, Esiri, Hiones, Wilcock, and Powell, 1985) deep into the brain where it causes selective damage based on susceptibility of specific neurons (Doty, 1997).
Treatment: Phosphatidylcholine 9 gm q.d.

Olfactory Dysfunction in Other Neurologic Diseases:

Movement Disorders:

Parkinson's disease (Markopoulou et al., 1977):
Symptoms: hyposmia, subjective hypogeusia.
Mechanism: due to depletion of dopamine in the olfactory bulb (not seen in MPTP-induced Parkinsonism) (Doty, Singh, Tetrude, and Langston, 1992).
Treatment: unresponsive to L-DOPA (Doty, Stern, Pfeiffer, Gollomp, and Hurtig, 1992).

Huntington's chorea:

Symptoms: hyposmia of threshold and identification.

Mechanism: not presymptomatic indicator of disease—appears coincident with motor findings (Moberg and Doty, 1997).

Progressive supranuclear palsy (Doty, 1995a): none.

Essential tremor (Busenbark, Huber, Greer, Pahwa, and Koller, 1992): none.

Multiple sclerosis:

Symptoms: hyposmia in 23% (Doty, Shaman, and Dann, 1984).

Mechanism: olfactory ability correlated with number of plaques in temporal lobes and frontal cortex (Doty, 1997).

Amyotrophic lateral sclerosis:

Symptoms: hyposmia in 64%, anosmia in 11% (Sajjadian, Doty, Gutnick, Chirurgi, Sivak, and Perl, 1994).

Headache:

Sinusitis (Apter, Mott, Cain, Spiro, and Barwick, 1992):

Symptoms: hyposmia, foul phantosmia, dysosmia, subjective hypogeusia, olfactory windows.

Mechanism: prevents odorant molecule from getting to, or dissolving in the mucus.

Treatment: antibiotics.

Migraine (Hirsch, 1992e):

Symptoms: subclinical hyposmia in 17%.

Mechanism:

1. Migraine may induce olfactory dysfunction:
   - Recurrent small vascular insults may induce a persistent neurologic deficit (as in complicated migraine) affecting the olfactory system.
   - Lacrimation and rhinorrhea may engorge the nasal passages to such a degree as to totally obstruct air flow to the olfactory epithelium.
   - A learned response to "tune out" environmental odorant triggers.
2. Olfactory loss may predispose to the development of migraines:
   - Decreased olfactory ability → increased likelihood of exposure to environmental chemical inducers of headache.
   - Olfactory sensory deprivation → compensatory psychological response → headache.
3. Unified limbic system theory:
   - A single pathogen induces both migraine and olfactory deficit concurrently (? neighborhood effect).
4. Genetics
5. Medication effect

Treatment: multipronged and may respond to specific anti-migraine agents.

Cluster headaches (Hirsch and Thakkar, 1995):

Symptoms: transient hyperosmia concurrent with, and ipsilateral to, the hemicephalgia.

Mechanism:

- Transient cortical deficiency (physiologic Addisonian state);
- Transient hypothalamic/pituitary axis dysregulation;
- Increased substance P: (? excitatory olfactory neurotransmitter);
- Change in 5HT (olfactory bulb neurotransmitter);
- Change in ACH (olfactory bulb neurotransmitter);
- Increased DA (olfactory bulb neurotransmitter);
- Increased NE (locus coeruleus projects to the olfactory bulb): NE → granule cell discharge → GABA → mitral cell discharge → increased olfaction);
- Increased gastrin (olfactory bulb neurotransmitter);
- Beta endorphin (olfactory bulb neurotransmitter);
- Decreased met-enkephalin (inhibitory olfactory bulb neurotransmitter);
- RAS activation;
- Generalized limbic/anterior hypothalamic discharge (neighborhood effect);
- Partial nasal congestion → eddy currents;
- Nasal engorgement → increase in air temperature;
- Nasal secretions → wet mucosal membrane → better dissolution of odorant;
- Change in estrogen/testosterone balances (estrogen changes mucosal composition → increased odorant absorption; testosterone changes mucosal composition → decreased odorant absorption);
- Cyclic limbic/hypothalamic instability → activation of the olfactory component of the limbic system → cyclic hyperosmia → detection of otherwise subthreshold ambient irritants → trigeminal nerve activation → substance P release → cluster headache;
- 1° hyperosmia (odor induced-limbic dysregulation; odor-induced changes in CNS electrical activity)

Columella variant of glossopharyngeal neuralgia (Bruyn, 1986):

Symptoms: unilateral or bilateral burning tongue, mouth grittiness, pain, dysesthesias, hyperpathia.

Mechanism: virus-induced denervation with reinnervation hypersensitivity, reinnervation synesthesia.

Treatment: Tegretol, Dilantin, valproic acid, Neurontin.

Features Common to Many Neurologic Diseases:

Medication effect (Scott, 1989b):

Symptoms: hyposmia, anosmia.

Mechanism: if inhibits olfactory nerve regeneration from stem cell.

Treatment: discontinue the medication, zinc sulfate.

Senescence (Venstrom and Amoore, 1968):

Symptom: subclinical hyposmia.

Mechanism: generalized reduction in neurotransmitters, cumulative effect of recurrent mild head trauma or recurrent viral infection-induced olfactory nerve destruction, medication effect, presence of other neurologic disease (i.e., senile dementia of the Alzheimer's type, multi-infarct dementia), cumulative effect of exposure to exogenous toxins (cigarette smoke), nutritional deficiency state.

Treatment: thiamine 100 mg q.d., phosphatidylcholine 9 gm q.d.; amantadine not effective; aminophylline not effective, amitriptyline not effective.

Malingering:

Symptoms: anosmia with loss of trigeminal preceptor as well; after head trauma or toxic exposure; no olfactory windows.

Mechanism: U.S. Armed Forces recognize anosmia as a 10% total body disability, awards in California exceeding $3,000,000 for smell loss.

Acute alcohol intoxication:

Symptom: subclinical hyposmia.

Mechanism: transiently anesthetizes olfactory nerve cells; inhibits the reticular activating system thus reducing attention to external stimuli.

Treatment: routine breathalyzer testing.

Individual variation:

Symptoms: subjective hyposmia (Hirsch, 1995d).

Subclinical hyposmia—4-star chefs (Hirsch, 1990c).

General Treatment Approaches:

Remove gas from house; gas detector, smoke detector. Food taster; date all food. Hygienic checker—smell buddy. Group therapy (Hirsch, Scott, and Koch, 1992).

Flavor enhancers (Schiffman and Warwick, 1988).

Modify foods: horseradish, black pepper, cayenne pepper, hot pepper, fresh mint texture, colorful visual displays (Duffy and Ferris, 1989), capsaicin, mustard, ginger, clove, cinnamon, peppermint, spearmint and pimento (Davidson, Jalowayski, Murphy, and Jacobs, 1987).

Stop smoking.

For idiopathic or not surgically correctable anosmia or hyposmia. From Z to A (Hirsch, Dougherty, Aranda, Vanderbilt, and Weclaw, 1996):

Zinc sulfate (Davidson, Jalowayski, Murphy, and Jacobs, 1987) (no better than placebo) (Henkin, Schecter, Friedewald, Demets, and Raff, 1976).

Vitamin B_1 (Goodspeed, Gent, and Catalanotto, 1987).

Vitamin A (Snow, Jr. and Martin, 1994) 100,000 IU IM q week for 6 weeks, followed by 50,000 I.U PO q.d. for 12 weeks (Duncan and Briggs, 1963).

Strychnine (CNS stimulant) (Estrem and Renner, 1987).

Prednisone 40 mg, taper by 5 mg/day (Knight, 1988).

Phosphatidylcholine (Hirsch, 1990d; Hirsch and Dougherty, 1992).

L-Cysteine ethylester hydrochloride (topical) +/– topical steroids (Takagi, 1984).

Alcohol.

Amantadine (Hirsch and Aranda, 1992).

Aminophylline 500 mg—1 gm q day (Henkin, Aamodt, Babcock, Agarwal, and Shatzman, 1981).

Amitriptyline (Hirsch and Vanderbilt, 1992).

Amphetamine (methylphenidate) (Doty and Ferguson-Segall, 1987).

For Smell Blindness:
  Sniff therapy—3 minutes t.i.d. for 6 weeks (Wysocki, Dorries, and Beauchamp, 1989).
Unusual Treatment Approaches of Questionable Validity:
  Chiropractic manipulation.
  Intranasal steroid injection.
  Acupuncture.
  Homeopathic.

Confounding agents may also be a stumbling block to the aspiring olfactory malingerer. Commonly abused substances acutely reduce olfactory ability including cigarettes, alcohol, and marijuana (Frye, Schwartz, and Doty, 1990; Hirsch and Bissell, 1998; Hummel, Sekinger, Wolf, Pauli, and Kobal, 1997). Olfactory dysfunction as a result of chronic exposure has also been seen with alcohol, cigarettes, both direct and passive, and marijuana (Hirsch and Bissell, 1998; Keller and Malaspia, 2013; Lötsch and Hummel, 2014; Hummel, Sekinger, Wolf, Pauli, and Kobal, 1997). Thus, the potential malingerer must have been presciently vigilant in his or her past life to have avoided popular social hedonic temptations. They also must have avoided the many olfactotoxins in the environment and workplace which are ubiquitous in American society. These include hydrogen sulfide, pyrethroid insecticides, chlordane/heptachlor termiticide, chlorine, lead, and trichloroethylene (Hirsch, 2002a; Hirsch, 2002b; Hirsch, 1998a; Hirsch, 1995a; Hirsch, 2003; Hirsch, 1995b). Hence, the successful malingerer must have been a virtual boy scout of virtue and virginal in olfactory pathology.

Thus, variability of olfactory ability is not binary but rather a continuum. Such a heterogeneous condition is highlighted in the concept of normal olfaction. An example in another sensory system can be observed in vision. Visual acuity is relatively homogenous in the general population and 20/20 is defined as the normal value. On the other hand, at two standard deviations from the population mean the definition of normal olfactory ability is so widespread that two individuals can still be considered in the normal range even though one individual's olfactory ability may be a thousand times better than the other's. Hence, identification tests of olfactory ability may be classified as normosmia, but which the previously nasute individual would perceive as severely reduced (Hirsch, 1995d). All this serves to demonstrate that as a malingerer's chimera hyposmia would be the wrong avenue to pursue. Furthermore, since it would be a partial loss only the potential monetary gain would be less substantial. The malingerer would have to know how much deficit should be present: if too little, it would be considered normal for his or her age and sex, and if too great, trigeminal loss may be demonstrated, which may be inconsistent with true olfactory loss (see later). The malingerer would have to be very bright and continuously aware of the degree of the deficit malingered or otherwise his deception will be revealed when challenged with olfactory tests, which will be positive at one time and negative at another either in identification, detection, or both. This complex feat is made so much more difficult due to the lack of pure odors (like only three colors), the presence of a virtual aromatic kaleidoscope continuously bombarding the proboscis—a literal universe of kippage at the tip of the nose. Moreover, odors blend and diffuse together, with a normosmic normal able to detect over one trillion unique odors (Keller, Cushdid, Magnasco et al., 2014). The olfactory malingerer must demonstrate superior cognitive functioning to remember all the odors he or she cannot smell to maintain consistency from test to test. He must first correctly detect and identify the odor and then correctly choose the wrong answer on the objective tests. This would be a gargantuan task (i.e., jasmine detected but not identified, lavender not detected, nor identified, violet identified, but not detected). Any absent-mindedness or distraction would reveal discrepancies between visits in history, examination, or testing which would place the hyposmic malingerer at great risk of being discovered.

All of the above might serve to encourage the malingerer, to present not with a partial loss but rather with a complete loss, or anosmia. However, even this approach is not without risk of detection. This is because almost all odors at a high enough intensity, are a combination of olfactory (cranial nerve I) and trigeminal (cranial nerve V) sensory input, which are integrated in the brain as a single synesthetic sensation—smell (Doty et al., 1978). Yet conditions states that affect cranial nerve I usually spare cranial nerve V and vice versa. For instance, amoebiasis (naegleria) destroys cranial nerve I while leaving cranial nerve V intact (Jacobson, 2014). Leprosy during the early stages affects cranial nerve V, only spreading to cranial nerve I very late in the disease (Kumar, Alexander, and Gnanamuthu, 2006). Head trauma is a special case—if mild and under the usual conditions it affects cranial nerve I without cranial nerve V involvement. However, if severe, it can also compromise cranial nerve V although the exact mechanism for this remains elusive (Hirsch, Sherman, Roussos et al., 2014). Hence, the malingerer of anosmia would be expected to be able to detect trigeminally prominent odors—mint, ammonia, Vicks® Vaporub,™ as well as almost all other odorants if their concentrations are high enough (Doty et al., 1978). Thus, the malingerer of anosmia would thus have to keep track of what he or she "can" detect and be consistent from visit to visit and within each visit from test to test. So, unlike a malingerer of total blindness with an all or none option, olfactory malingering does not possess such an easily dichotomous choice.

Assuming the malingerer has chosen to pretend olfactory loss, what are the implications of such a deficit? Over the long-term, such a deficiency can be significant on five different fronts: (1) Safety, with increased risk of food poisoning due to inability to "taste" the odiferous component of spoiled food (Gates and Kraemer, 2008). Moreover, there is also an impairment in the ability to detect ethyl mercaptan, which is added to natural gas, to provide the gas-like aroma and thus subjects the sufferer to an increased chance of being involved in a gas explosion (Croy, Nordin, and Hummel, 2014; Stevens, Cain, and Weinstein, 1987). (2) Loss of enjoyment of nature's diverse spectrum—a rainbow of aromas—with inability to appreciate the scent of a rose or the odor of a newly born baby. Along with this is the inability to access olfactory-evoked nostalgia, which is found in 84% of the population, leading to loss of memorable pleasures (Hirsch, 1992c). Nostalgia, or the bittersweet yearning for the past, has been eloquently analyzed in terms of society and consumerism, but what of its neuropsychiatric substrate and its implication (Havlena and Holak, 1991)? It is these I shall address.

Within the psychiatric framework, nostalgia may be considered a yearning to return home to the past. More than this, it is a yearning for an idealized past—a longing for a sanitized impression of the past, which in psychoanalysis is referred to as screen memory—not a true recreation of the past, but rather a combination of many different memories all integrated together; in this process, all negative emotions are filtered out. For a personal example of screen memory, think of your very first vivid memory. Although to you it seems a realistic recall of an early childhood event, in fact it is a compilation of memories all integrated into one. This can be demonstrated in psychoanalysis: during the analysis of the transference neurosis the patient's earliest memory undergoes changes and divides into multiple components which are separate definable childhood memories.

If one defines nostalgia as a yearning for an idealized past, its bittersweet nature becomes clearer. One can never return to this past, it never truly existed. And the present reality, no matter how good, can never be as good as an ideal—which nostalgia has created. Thus, the saying "you can't go home again."

Nostalgia, unlike screen memory, does not relate to a specific memory, but rather to an emotional state. This idealized emotional state is framed within a past era and the yearning for the idealized emotional state manifests itself in an attempt to recreate that past era by reproducing activities performed then and by using symbolic representations of the past.

Idealized past emotions become displaced onto inanimate objects, sounds, smells, and tastes which were experienced concurrently with the emotions. This same mechanism of displacement is utilized in medicine for its negative impact in the treatment of alcoholism. Disulfiram (Antabuse) is used as an aversive conditioning agent to inhibit recurrent use of alcohol in addicts (Kaplan and Sadock, 1988a).

The nostalgic urge to recreate the past within the present is, in many ways, a driving force for behavior. For instance, how frequently we marry spouses with characteristics reminiscent of those of our parents. Other examples might be how we may adopt the political affiliations and prejudices of our forebearers, become Democrats, Republicans, or even racists because our parents were.

Similarly, the nostalgic urge to recreate the past explains why so many abused children marry alcoholic spouses—not because their childhood was happy, but rather, because they seek to recreate their idealized, sanitized memories of their childhood by identifying with symbolic manifestations of the past, which they find in their alcoholic or abusive spouses.

This same paradigm governs the repetition of failures on the part of "neurotics" who behave as if oblivious to logical rationale. This is seen in persons with recurrent failing relationships (those marrying seven or eight times), those with recurrent failures at business, and even those with recurrent experiences of being victimized.

Through daily behavior, the nostalgic urges may also be partially gratified—food choices for example (hence the passing down from generation to generation of family recipes)—with an actual primitive incorporation into the self of the nostalgic object.

Observing holidays precipitates nostalgic desires, while it simultaneously recreates past experiences, hence fulfilling the nostalgic energies through the physical activity of the ritual while forging linkages with the past. Religious practices may be viewed as an immersion in institutionalized nostalgia—unchanged over the millennia, hence gratifying nostalgic wishes. This explains how the intertwining of religion with the major holidays (Christmas, Thanksgiving, Easter) achieves the greatest impact and relief of nostalgic drives.

Thus, nostalgia may be viewed, in psychiatric terms, as a driving force for actual behavior. By attempting to recreate an idealized past in the present. By attempting to recreate this idealized past one discharges psychic energies to fulfill nostalgic yearnings. Some results of these attempts throughout society may be seen in the production of sequels to movies, TV shows, and in the common practice of naming first born sons after their fathers.

Nostalgia exists in the pathological as well as the normal states. Some severely regressed schizophrenics actually live within the delusional system of their idealized memories (Hill, 1955). In pathological bereavement, obsession with loss of the idealized past causes depression (Kaplan and Sadock, 1988b). In senile dementia of the Alzheimer's type or Wernicke–Korsakoff syndrome, where recent memory is markedly hampered, nostalgic memories are still available substituting the past for the present (Lishman, 1978; Hales and Yudofsky, 1987).

On the other hand, in an antithetical state to nostalgia, those suffering from post-traumatic stress disorder do not yearn for the past, but rather, desire to eliminate memory for the past (American Psychiatric Association, 1987). However, in both nostalgia and in post-traumatic stress disorder immediate stimuli can precipitate emotionally laden memories. These stimuli are context specific. For instance, many Vietnam veterans with posttraumatic stress disorder describe odors of seafood or burning diesel fuel as triggers for the flashbacks phenomena (Kline and Rausch, 1985). Flashbacks of Korean war veterans with posttraumatic stress disorder are about odors of beaches and wet canvas Persian Gulf veterans describe recall from drinking ionized water (Coombs, 1991, personal communication).

Homesickness is not true nostalgia, but rather a geographic nostalgia—a yearning for a different space rather than different time—for return to idealized memories of a location and people left behind.

All the senses may be used to precipitate nostalgic experiences—hearing music (witness the popularity of "classics" of the '60s, '70s, '80s, etc.), seeing pictures (photo albums in fashion with their recurring trends), and possibly the most significant—smelling odors.

Even as early as 1908, Freud recognized a strong link between odors and emotions (Freud, 1908). Anatomically, the nose directly connects with the olfactory lobe in the limbic system—that area of the brain considered the seat of the emotions. The olfactory lobe is actually part and parcel of the limbic system (MacLean and Kral, 1973). Therefore, the most powerful impact upon the emotions is through the sense of smell. In a universal phenomenon called olfactory-evoked recall, an odor can bring back a memory from the past. Often a vivid visual image is evoked along with an associated positive mood state. A classic example was described by Marcel Proust in the first volume of his novel *A La Recherche Du Temps Perdu* (English translation: Remembrance of Things Past) (Proust, 1934). The aroma of a madeleine dipped in tea evoked in the author a flood of memories and feelings of nostalgia.

The understanding that odors evoke more powerful reactions than the other senses is not particularly new. It is well known that the aroma of freshly baked goods conjures up warm childhood memories. When an odor of baked bread is released in a U.S. supermarket, sales in the bakery section increased threefold. Movie theater managers infuse the air in their lobbies with the aroma of popcorn to entice patrons to buy. The smell of chocolate chip cookies released into the air in front of cookie stands induces people to salivate and buy cookies. The unique, leathery "new car scent" is an exciting enticement to most customers and a positive inducement to make a purchase. Victoria's Secret, a successful women's underclothing chain, uses a special floral potpourri scent throughout its stores. Many of the customers say that the aroma lifts their spirits.

Some odors, however, can have a negative impact. Among 1002 people queried in a 1989 Gallup poll throughout the United States, the most disliked odor was that of fish. We might well expect any store located next to a seafood market to have their sales negatively affected by the odor.

An ordinary person can smell 10,000 odors (Ackerman, 1990). But no two people react in exactly the same way.

In general, women are more sensitive to odors than men (Doty et al., 1984). Ethnicity and geographical background strongly affect odor sensitivity. Japanese perfume may not be a popular sales item in North America. Among sample populations taken across the U.S., Korean-Americans had a keener ability to identify odors than either Afro-Americans or white Americans. Native Japanese were least able to identify the odors used in this study.

As might be expected, our judgment as to the pleasantness or the unpleasantness of various odors depends also upon who we are and where we live. In one study, sample populations from 20 nations were asked to evaluate 22 different fragrances (Davis and Pangborn, 1985). The populations with similar odor preferences could be grouped geographically. One group with similar odor preferences included residents of California, Kansas, Japan, West Germany, Taiwan, Canada, Italians in Brazil, Philippines, and Taiwanese in California. A second group with similar preferences included residents of Australia, Sweden, France, Norway, East Germany, Finland, Mexico, Japanese in Brazil, and Africans in Brazil. This clustering of odor preferences implies a similar clustering of preferences with regard to foods and perfumes.

Among the 1002 people mentioned previously, the area of the United States from which they came had a decisive influence on their responses to odors (see Table 11.1). In general baked goods were the most common precipitant of an olfactory-evoked recall of their childhoods. Among persons from the south, the smell of fresh air prompted similar recalls. Among those from the Midwest it was the smell of farm animals and among those from the West Coast the smell of meat cooking or barbecuing. Evoked memories of childhood are usually associated with a positive emotional state which may then be transferred to the place where the evoked memories are experienced—the store and the items for sale. The makers of certain perfumes already take advantage of this effect by adding the smell of baby powder to their formulas; baby powder being associated in most persons' minds with a safe, clean environment.

In order to further investigate olfactory-evoked recall, in September of 1991, 989 English-speaking individuals selected at random in the Water Tower Place shopping

TABLE 11.1
Question: What Smells or Odors Remind You of Your Childhood? Childhood Smells and Odors (*n* – 1002) (Three Responses)

Response	Who Gave Total	Percent of Those Specific Response
Baking bread, cookies, cakes, etc.	18	23
Fresh air, rain, outdoors	5	7
Baby powder, powder	4	6
Chicken	4	5
Flowers	4	5
Farm smells	4	5
Meat cooking	4	5
Cut grass	3	5
Burning leaves, wood	3	4
Popcorn	2	3
Apples	2	3
Spaghetti	2	3
General food cooking	2	3
Apple pie	2	2
Cleaning products	2	2
Bacon	2	2
Soap	2	2
Fish, seafood	2	2
Other (1% or less)	50	65
Don't know	20	

mall in Chicago consented to be interviewed an Institutional Review Board-approved study. Respondents reported basic demographic data including the decade of their birth and where they predominantly lived geographic location during childhood. Psychological data revealed the existence of olfactory evoked recall, the particular smells that precipitated childhood memories, and the overall level of happiness with the individual's childhood.

The demographic profile of the study group was 478 male and 511 females. Decades of birth ranged from the 1900s to the 1970s as follows: 1900s—3, 1910s—16, 1920s—43, 1930s—70, 1940s—118, 1950s—204, 1960s—338, 1970s—197 (see Table 11.2). In order to achieve statistical significance data for people born in the 1900s, 1910s, and 1920s was combined into a single grouping. While most were reared in Chicago (325) or its suburbs (176), 45 states were represented, and 39 countries as well.

Statistics were analyzed using Chi-square test on contingency tables or Z-test for the difference between pairs of proportions.

TABLE 11.2
Demographic Profile

Decade of Birth (all decades)	Positive Smell Persons	No Smell Persons	Total
1970s	171	26	197
1960s	290	48	338
1950s	186	18	204
1940s	98	20	118
1930s	60	10	70
1920s	28	15	43
1910s	8	8	16
1900s	2	1	3
TOTALS	843	146	989

The results show that 85.2% displayed olfactory-evoked recall and a generational effect was demonstrated in this regard (see Table 11.3).

Of those born after 1930, 86.8% displayed olfactory-evoked recall whereas only 61.3% of those born before 1930 displayed it. This implies that the marketing of products through nostalgia with odors would be more efficacious in a target consumer group born after 1930. This is not surprising since olfactory ability decreases with age: one-half of those over 65 and three-quarters of those over 80 years of age have a reduced ability to smell (Doty et al., 1984). In addition, memory worsens with age, further explaining our findings in the elderly (Bartus, Dean, III, Beer, and Lippa, 1982).

As mentioned, women have better olfactory ability than men. Yet, in our study at Water Tower no statistically significant difference was shown between the genders in their self-reports of odor-evoked nostalgia (see Table 11.4). Hence, regardless of sex, aroma is an important nostalgia inducer. Based on the Z-test for the difference between two proportions, a statistically significant generational difference was found (see Table 11.5). Those born in the 1930s and afterwards were more likely to

TABLE 11.3
Results

Decade of Birth	Percent of Persons in Each Birth Decade Who Are "Positive Smell"
1970s	85.8% — 171/197
1960s	85.8% — 290/338
1950s	91.2% — 186/204
1940s	83.1% — 098/118
1930s	85.7% — 060/70
1920s	65.1% — 028/43
1910s	50.0% — 008/016
1900s	85.8% — 002/003

TABLE 11.4
Gender Difference of Self-Reported Odor-Induced Nostalgia (Combined Total 85.2%)

Male	Female
83.7%	86.7%

TABLE 11.5
Generational Difference of Self-Reported Odor-Induced Nostalgia

	Combined 1930s–1970s	Combined 1900s–1920s
Food or cooking smells	40.2%	26.3%
Nature-related smells	30.6%	44.7%

have nostalgia induced by food odors and were less likely to have nostalgia induced by nature odors than those born before the 1930s.

Those born before the 1930s cited smells of nature including pine, hay, horses, sea air, and meadows, whereas those born from 1930 to 1979 were reminded of their childhood by such smells as plastic, scented markers, airplane fuel, Vicks® Vaporub™, sweet tarts, and Play-Doh. This shift away from natural odors and toward artificial ones may portend future problems for society. If we are concerned about ecology partly out of nostalgia for natural odors, then 50 years from now how will environmental conservation be of much concern to the people who are nostalgic only for manmade chemical aromas?

Clearly, in targeting a younger consumer group, food smells would be more efficacious than the smell of nature, but the opposite would be true in targeting an older group. Odors were divided into foul and nonfoul smells. Foul smells (i.e., garbage, urine, manure) were defined by a panel of olfactory experts. Those who reported olfactory-induced nostalgia (8.8%) said that foul smells were the precipitant. One person in 12 reported an unhappy childhood. This was independent of birth decade or gender. Whether one had a happy childhood influenced which kind of smell evoked a childhood memory. The one person in 12 who reported having an unhappy childhood was more than twice as likely to describe such foul odors as mothballs, body odor, dog waste, sewer gas, bus fumes, and mother's menstrual cycle (see Table 11.6). This suggests that psychotherapists might do well to inquire which kind of odor induces childhood memories as a further method of gaining insight into personality.

TABLE 11.6
Precipitants of Childhood Happiness

	Unhappy Childhood	Happy Childhood
Foul smells evoked nostalgia	19.7%	7.8%

Interestingly, happiness in childhood did not correlate with ability for olfactory-evoked recall suggesting the universal nature of this phenomenon.

About equal numbers, 91% of men and 92% of women, reported a happy childhood.

Implications of our findings are that approximately 85% of both men and women report smell-induced nostalgia. While a wide range of smells could be utilized to induce nostalgic recall, food smells are a more effective stimulus for the younger while nature smells are more effective for the older.

Nostalgia may be induced with greatest ease through odors. One may speculate that nostalgic desires will increase in the coming decade since it seems likely that the more dissatisfied we are with the present the more we idealize the past (a temporal equivalent of "the grass is greener on the other side" or, as Richard Llewellyn wrote, "How green was my valley") (Llewellyn, 1939).

The olfactory malingerer may not realize the olfactory nostalgia connection and thus, not relate any recalled nostalgic response to odors. (3) Also associated with chemosensory dysfunction is psychiatric dysfunction, including a 96% incidence of DSM-IIIR Axis I or II diagnoses, with the most common Axis I diagnosis being generalized anxiety disorder and dysthymia (Hirsch and Trannel, 1996). This high incidence of comorbidity between chemosensory and psychiatric dysfunction is conceived given that the olfactory lobe is anatomically part of the limbic system or emotional brain (MacLean and Kral, 1973). In order to demonstrate this correlation, 46 consecutive patients (28 men and 18 women) who presented with chemosensory problems at the Smell and Taste Treatment and Research Foundation in Chicago during 1989 and 1990 were studied. Their ages ranged from 18 to 70 years with a mean age of 40 years. All underwent olfactory tests including the University of Pennsylvania Smell Inventory Test (UPSIT), a series of 40 scratch-and-sniff odor identification tests (Doty, Newhouse, and Azzaslina, 1985), and the Unilateral Threshold Odor Detection Tests of sensitivity for one nostril at a time exposed to various concentrations of the following standard odorants: phenylethyl methylethyl carbinol (PM carbinol), W-hydroxypentadecanoic acid lactone (PD lactone), cineole, -chloroace-tophenone (CA phenone), para-ethyl phenol (PE phenol), pyridine, and thiophane (Amoore and Ollman, 1983). Gustation was assessed according to the Accusens T Taste Test which measures threshold taste detection of salt (NaCL), sweet (sucrose), sour (HCl), and bitter (urea and propyl thiocarbinol (PTC) (Westport Pharmaceuticals, 1982). Written tests to delineate psychological function, included the Minnesota Multiphasic Personality Inventory-2 (MMPI-2) (Friedman, Webb, and Kewak, 1989; Hathaway and McKinley, 1989), the Millon Clinical Multiaxial Inventory II (MCMI-II) (Million, 1987), and the Beck Depression Inventory (Beck and Beamesderfer, 1974). Psychiatric histories were also obtained.

The longer the duration of the patients' chemosensory complaints, the more likely they were to have fulfilled criteria for DSMIII-R diagnoses based upon their MCMI-II and MMPI-2 scores and the more likely their reported mood states and subjective complaints were to be worse. Longer histories of chemosensory problems were associated with depression as indicated by increasing values on the Beck Depression Inventory ($p < 0.001$).

Long-standing chemosensory complaints seemingly produce or exacerbate psychiatric problems in various ways. As chemosensory problems persist over time, patients may become pessimistic about an eventual recovery and this may lead to depression. Prolonged sensory deprivation in auditory and visual spheres has been shown to produce depression (Berrios and Brook, 1984; Guensberger and Fleischer, 1974) and hearing loss has been postulated to play a role in the development of schizophrenia as well as depression (Cooper and Curry, 1976). Thus, chemosensory deprivation may play a similar role in the development of psychiatric problems. Moreover, the narcissistic insult, the lack of public understanding, physician apathy, and subsequent social isolation suffered because of chemosensory loss may combine to induce depression (Tennen, Affleck, and Mendola, 1991).

Conversely, psychiatric disturbances may predispose patients to complain and seek medical intervention for their chemosensory problems, real or imagined. Just as pain, dizziness, and headache are commonly seen in depressed patients (Diamond, 1965), chemosensory complaints may be somatic manifestations of emotional problems (Chen and Dalton, 2005).

The more severe the patients' subjective perception of olfactory problems are, the more likely they were to have a DSMIII-R Axis II diagnosis of obsessive compulsive personality disorder based on their MCMI-II test ($p < 0.018$). This association may not be surprising since it is in the nature of patients with this disorder to amplify somatic complaints. Fliess' model of the phallic nose adds credence to the theory of a primary psychiatric disorder (Freud, 1892); the displacement of attention from the genitals to the nose allows the "safe" manifestation of the sexual.

Cortical representation of chemosensation and of emotion are both localized in the frontal lobe/limbic systems (MacLean and Kral, 1973); thus, the common anatomic substrate of the emotional and olfactory systems must be considered. A single pathogen, whether a virus (Monath, Cropp, and Harrison, 1983), toxin (Roberts, 1986), degenerative disease (Serby, Corwin, Novatt, Conrad, and Rotrosen, 1985), or trauma (Levin, High, and Eisenberg, 1985), might involve both systems.

The common link may be biochemical degenerative diseases which deplete neurotransmitters and could cause dysfunctions in both the olfactory and emotional systems as in Parkinson's disease, which depletes dopamine or in senile dementia of the Alzheimer's type, which depletes acetylcholine (Ward, Hess, and Calne, 1983; Serby, Larson, and Kalkstein, 1991). Serotonin, known to mediate olfaction (Halasz and Shepherd, 1983; Haberly and Price, 1978; Macrides and Davis, 1983; Mair and Harrison, 1991), has been postulated also as a neurotransmitter which regulates affective states (Davis and Glassman, 1989). Similarly, legal and illegal drugs can adversely affect biochemical pathways in both systems (Schiffman, 1983a).

Autoimmune similarities in the olfactory and limbic lobes may produce dysfunction in both systems in a phenomenon analogous to basal ganglia dysfunction in response to anticardiac antibodies in Sydenham's chorea (Nausieda, 1980).

Disease may affect one system before the other. A pathogen may invade the blood–brain barrier and cross the olfactory lobe causing damage there; it could then secondarily spread through the limbic system. This sequence has been postulated in senile dementia of the Alzheimer's type seen in some infectious processes (Berrios and Brook, 1984; Guensberger and Fleischer, 1974).

Olfactory loss may more directly produce psychiatric disease by preventing exogenous anxiolytic agents which may be present in the environment from acting upon the limbic system via the olfactory lobe. Such natural external agents can regulate mood as evidenced by the action of pheromones (Mucignat-Caretta, 2014).

Inability to detect interpersonal olfactory cues and associated misperception and apprehension in social situations may lead to chronic maladaptive behavior and predispose to depression. Sixty-three percent of the patients studied admitted being functionally disabled by their chemosensory loss, that is were fearful of being unable to detect smoke, natural gas, spoiled food, or body odor. Older patients were less likely than younger ones to complain of functional disability ($p < 0.003$), but this may be due to their experience with deterioration in other sensory areas (hearing, vision, and peripheral neuropathy) and consequently have lower expectations.

On the other hand, psychiatric dysfunction may precede or induce chemosensory dysfunction. Hallucinations, misperceptions, and distortions of reality are inherent in many psychiatric diseases such as schizophrenia, bipolar disorder, and major depression with psychotic features (Hathaway and McKinley, 1989). Such distortions may extend to chemosensation as well. Often psychiatric illness involves withdrawal, apathy, and internalization of focus so that external stimuli including chemosensations, are reduced or excluded (Hurwitz, Kopala, Clark, and Jones, 1988). Affected individuals may ignore odors and flavors, then perceive a reduction or distortion in their sensations.

The medical treatment of psychiatric disorders also may cause secondary physiologic chemosensory dysfunction. Many psychiatric drugs affect chemosensation, for example, amitriptyline (Schiffman, 1991). (See list "Drugs which Interfere with the Smell System" in Section 11.1.)

Additional psychiatric dysfunction associated with olfactory loss includes the onset of claustrophobia. This was observed when patients in group therapy for olfactory problems reported developing claustrophobia coincident with their loss of ability to smell (Hirsch and Gruss, 1998a). (4) Relational discord with increased risk of sexual dysfunction is also observed coincident with chemosensory dysfunction. This connection may be ratiocinate given that, like chemosensation, sex drive is localized within the limbic system (Adams and Victor, 1989).

We also found that the complaint of hyperosmia is accompanied by a diminished sex drive. Perhaps detection of a competing pheromone may result in limbic system inhibition (Lee, 1976). Or, hyperosmia may lead to olfactory reference syndrome with a contrite reaction and anxiety regarding bodily odors, triggering social isolation as a paranoid avoidance reaction (Hirsch, 1990a).

Diminished sex drive has been associated with affective disorders (Both, Laan, and Schultz, 2010). We found phantosmic women manifest diminished sex drive and other signs of depression including energy loss and increased Beck Depression Inventory scores. Phantosmia may be a somatic manifestation of a psychiatric disorder, but it is also possible that the travails of living with persistent phantosmia may induce depression and other psychiatric disorders in a phenomenon analogous to that seen with other somatic disease states including chronic pain, cancer, and heart disease (Kaplan and Sadock, 1988c). Phantosmia and subjective hyposmia in patients with diminished sex drive may reflect underlying psychiatric dysfunction rather than chemosensory loss (Hirsch and Trannel, 1996). (5) Disruption of appetite and weight dysregulation also accompanies olfactory loss (Wahlstrom, Jr., Hirsch, and Whitman, 2015) (see Table 11.7). The competent olfactory malingerer would be

TABLE 11.7
Change In Nutrition With Chemosensory Disorders

Chemosensory Disorders	Food Complaints	Increased Appetite	Decreased Appetite	Decreased Enjoyment	Increased Use of Sugar, Salt and Spices	Mean Energy Intake Compared to Normosmics	Mean Micronutrient Intake Compared to Normosmics	Mean Body wt Compared to Normosmics	% Who Gained 10% or More of Body Weight Prior to Chemosensory Dysfunction	% Who Lost 10%or More Body wt Prior to Chemosensory Dysfunction
Anosmia (noncongenital)	50% to 60%	20%	31%	88%	20% to 40% 4% decreased	No change	No change	No change	14%	6.50%
Anosmia (congenital)	20%									
Hyposmia	31% to 80%	30%	10% to 20%	50%	20% to 50% 20% decreased				1.50%	10.60%
Dysosmia & Phantosmia	75% to 85%		24%	83%	50%			113%		
Ageusia	100%		100%							
Hypogeusia	75%		67%	33%					Reported	Reported
Dysgeusia & Phantageusia	72% to 85%	24%	30% to 67%	42% to 70%	40% to 60% 18% decreased	No change	No change		15% to 20%	15% to 20%

Source: Mattes, R.D. and B.J. Cowart, *J Am Dietet Assoc*, 94, 50–56,1994; Ferris, A.M., J.L. Schlitzer, M.J. Schierberl et al. *Nutr Res*, 5, 149–156, 1985; Ferris, A.M., J.L.Schlitzer, and M.J. Schierberl, *Clinical measurement of taste and smell*, 264–278, New York, MacMillan, 1986; Mattes-Kulig, D.A. and R.I. Henkin, *J Am Dietet Assoc*, 85, 822–826, 1985; Mattes, R.D., B.J. Coward, M.A. Schiavo et al. *Am J Clin Nutr*, 51, 233–224, 1990.

expected to malinger similar problems, the absence of which would raise red flags as to the mendacity of the chemosensory complaints.

Dysosmia, or smell distortions, usually presents itself concurrent with hyposmia and often manifests itself as unpleasant odors. This can occur either with some specific aromas, i.e., in response to fried foods or bathroom aromas, in response to any odor presented, or perceived as having the same unpleasant odor of variable intensity (such as that of dirt). The first type usually has better olfactory ability than the second and demonstrates a greater response to medication intervention.

While olfactory testing has been utilized in detection of malingering (Linschoten and Harvey, 2004), historical aspects indicating malingering have been relatively ignored. Kurtz noted that inconsistency in a patient's history may help to delineate chemosensory malingering (Kurtz, White, Hornung, and Belknap, 1999); however, specific descriptions are lacking. For other senses historical inconsistencies have been utilized in the differential diagnoses. For instance, in vision "Malingerers add strange details and odd characteristics" (Mason, Cardell, and Armstrong, 2013). Presentation of isolated malingering of dysosmia in the absence of hyposmia or anosmia has not been reported, and must be exceedingly rare and not worthy of questionable monetary value for a potential malingerer. Such historical distortion in the chemosensory realm is exemplified in a patient who is malingering, with odd and strangely detailed history of smell and taste functioning.

In this instance, a 47-year-old right-handed female housekeeper was examined after nine months of having been exposed at work to a cleaner made from the combination of peroxyacetic acid, hydrogen peroxide, acetic acid, and sulfuric acid. She found that the smell became overwhelming and felt like her throat was closing and she would had frequent nosebleeds. Soon thereafter she noted that the smell changed to the aroma of fish. This aroma was only present when exposed to the smell of the cleaner five hours per day while at work. She also noticed soreness in her mouth and changes in appetite. During this time, she observed her taste was reduced at work but normal at home. Other times, she described her taste as being reduced to 70% of normal and that she could not taste the difference between substitute and real sugar and dark or milk chocolate. "Sweet-N-Low" had tasted like diet soda her whole life, but after the exposure it now tasted like normal sugar. She described that dark chocolate all always tasted bitter, but now tasted like milk chocolate. She never liked diet cola because it always tasted chemical-like, but now she liked it because it tasted like sweetened soda. Pomegranate now tasted too tart, like cranberry, which she cannot tolerate. Other times, she affirmed she could taste everything. She feels her smell has decreased to 80% of normal and that vinegar smells like fish and cologne smells awful. Despite not having been exposed to the cleaner for four months, she felt as though she was still exposed because a coworker used it and this was contaminating her just by being in her presence.

Abnormalities on her physical examination included:

- General: diffuse thyromegaly.

Abnormalities on her neurological examination included:

- Mental status examination: memory: immediate recall: five digits forwards and three digits backwards. Recent recall: two of four objects in three minutes without reinforcement, and three of four with reinforcement.

- Motor exam: mild right pronator drift with bilateral abductor digiti minimi sign, right more than left, and right Holmes phenomenon. Reflexes: 3+ brachioradialis and biceps bilaterally, 0–1+ quadriceps femoris bilaterally. Zero ankle jerks bilaterally. Positive Hoffman bilaterally. Neuropsychiatric testing:
- Clock Drawing Test, four (normal).
- Center for Neurological Study Lability Scale: seven (normal).
- Minnesota Multi*phasic Personality Inventory-2* (*MMPI-2*): invalid, consistent with malingering.
- Millon Clinical Multiaxial Inventory-III (MCMI-III): no Diagnostic and Statistical Manual of Mental Disorders-V Axis I diagnosis.
- Validity Indicator Profile (VIP): inconsistent, suggesting malingering.
- Chemosensory testing:

    Olfaction: Brief Smell Identification Test (BSIT): seven (anosmia). Alcohol Sniff Test (AST): seven (anosmia). Pocket Smell Test (PST): three (normosmia). Olfactometer Identification Test: left 14, right 17 (hyposmia). Sniff Magnitude Test: Sniff Magnitude Ratio: 0.46 (normosmia). The Odor Discrimination/Memory Test: two at ten seconds, three at 30 seconds, and four at 60 seconds; 9/12 (normosmia). *Phenylethyl Alcoholl*Smell Threshold Test: left greater than –2.0, right greater than –2.0 (anosmia). Suprathreshold Amylacetate Odor Hedonic Testing: crossed pattern. Suprathreshold Amylacetate Odor Intensity Testing: parallel pattern (normal). Retronasal Smell Testing: Retronasal Smell Index: four (abnormal).

    Gustatory Testing: Propylthiouracil Disc Taste Test: ten (normogeusia). Taste Threshold and Suprathreshold Testing: normogeusia to sucrose and phenylthiocarbamide. Mild hypogeusia of 10–30% for sodium chloride and urea. Ageusia to hydrochloric acid. Other: Candida Culture: positive. Patient refused Taste Quadrant Testing, *Fungiform Papillae Count, and Electrogustometry Test.*

In this instance, a kaleidoscope of clues points to a malingering diagnosis. The result of psychological tests, inconsistency of olfactory chemosensory test (some totally normosmic, others anosmic), refusal to perform confirmatory chemosensory test, and formal involvement with litigation and disability assessment all strongly suggest this possibility. Moreover, the strange and bizarre history further supports this diagnosis. This is manifest with changing description of her taste problem from normal to reduced, to oddly different during the same interview. Even the time frame of the taste problem from normal at home with a reduction at work, to a reduction all the time is unusual. The apogee of her complaints, however, is that dark chocolate has converted from tasting bitter to tasting like milk chocolate. This is inconsistent since with true smell loss chocolate either tastes like nothing or tastes bitter. There is no known disease whereby dark chocolate suddenly tastes like milk chocolate. This is a particularly odd description since smell loss would cause milk chocolate to taste like bitter dark chocolate, not the reverse. Furthermore, her bizarre description of being contaminated by the mere presence of a coworker also seems to indicate the nonorganic nature of her symptoms. This case highlights the importance in those who present with chemosensory problems while in the process of litigation, the physician should obtain detailed chemosensory description to aid in facilitating the diagnoses.

Malingering of isolated phantosmia, or hallucinated smells, in the absence of loss, would be highly unusual and would most likely occur as part of another syndrome, which includes phantosmia as one of its components. Phantosmia occurs in a wide variety of conditions from temporal lobe epilepsy (Luciano, Alper, and Nadkarni, 2011), schizophrenia (Meats, 1988), LSD intoxication (Preston, O'Neal, and Talga, 2010), to sinusitis (Hirsch, 2004) and Parkinson's disease (Meats, 1988a; Hirsch, 2004; Hirsch, 2009b). Even weather changes are associated with phantosmia (Aiello and Hirsch, 2013). But, all these usually occur in association with reduced or absent ability to smell. Those who suffer from phantosmia often display psychological distress and depression (Hirsch and Trannel, 1996). Detection of malingering of phantosmia, as would detection of the malingering of any hallucination (whether it be visual entopias, or even formed visual scenes) would rely on inconsistency of presentation in history (changing from one visit to the next or even during the same visit) and absence of evidence of any other chemosensory, otorhinologic, or neurologic dysfunction.

Palinosmia is the persistence of an odor, even after leaving the physical vicinity where the odor was detected, or prolonged perception of an odor, after the true odor should have dissipated (Hirsch, 2009a). Although a common phenomenon associated with head trauma-induced olfactory impairment, malingering of palinosmia has never been reported (Hirsch and Gruss, 1998b).

Cacosmia, or the condition in which previously perceived pleasant odors are now unpleasant, is particularly bothersome to the sufferer and routinely is associated with dysosmia. Under usual circumstances, these two conditions are linked: cacosmia only occurs when dysosmia is also present. Frequently cacosmia is associated with a strong emotional reaction to the odor, often evoking drastic behavioral changes—moving out of the house, separating from marital partners, quitting one's work—all to avoid the aromas. Furthermore, the odor is often attached to a psychologically important item, such as a daughter's cosmetics or a wife's hairspray. The sufferers' disorder often leads to major changes in those around him or her to accommodate for the cacosmia—modifications in job to accommodate the patient in helping to avoid the derisive odors or removal of the carpeting at one's house. In many respects, cacosmia is reminiscent of multiple chemical sensitivity where odors may precipitate a wide variety of psychological and behavioral responses, forcing major changes in the environment of the sufferer. In both cacosmia and multiple chemical sensitivity it is difficult to differentiate between malingering for nonmonetary reward (job change, social change), psychological dysfunction, or true dysosmia paired with negative hedonics (with or without sympathetic nervous system dysfunction). The severe response to these odors appears to be extreme.

The massive nature of the behavioral, environmental, and workplace changes this engenders raises the specter of malingering or a volitional conscious basis for these complaints; however, severe psychiatric disorders may also be the origin—anywhere from an isolated delusional disorder to borderline personality disorder with the need to control others (Hirsch and Trannel, 1996).

Along parallel lines are odor-induced headaches and odor-induced migraines. Clearly, odor can be a precipitant for migraines, and osmophobia has been described in 25% as a precipitant of migraines (Kelman, 2004). The offending odors range from perfume and cosmetic smells to alliaceous miasma of garlic and onion (Roussos and Hirsch, 2014). How much of this is a form of conscious malingering to control the environment of the sufferer as opposed to obtaining financial reward is unclear. It may best be delineated through evaluation of other aspects of the patient's complaints, in particular the headaches (Carlson and Rosser-Hogan, 1994).

A homologous situation can also be considered with odor-induced panic attacks or odor-induced posttraumatic stress disorder flashbacks (Hirsch and Wyse, 1993). Furthermore, odor-induced or exacerbated burning mouth syndrome has also been observed (Yakov, Yakov, and Hirsch, 2010). We followed three patients, when exposed to odorants precipitated severe burning exacerbation:

- An 83-year-old woman:
  - Complaints:
    - Two years of burning,
    - Salty phantageusia,
    - Onset immediately following application of nitroglycerin,
    - Burning worsened with ingesting hot or spicy food, stress, and lidocaine application.
  - Olfactory testing:
    - Acute severe exacerbation of burning mouth syndrome precipitated with exposure to Carbinol in the Olfactory Test of Amore.
- A 57-year-old male:
  - Complaints:
    - One-year, sudden onset of idiopathic metallic phantageusia,
    - Burning mouth syndrome,
    - Burning worsened after consuming coffee, chocolate, and cola, and was reduced with chewing gum or eating salty food,
    - Upon exposure to aromas of shampoo or soap, the burning mouth syndrome and associated phantageusia were exacerbated.
- A 59-year-old woman:
  - Complaints:
    - One year, gradual onset of hypogeusia,
    - Metallic and spicy phantageusia,
    - Salty and spicy dysgeusia,
    - Burning mouth syndrome,
    - Burning worsened with eating spicy food,
    - Burning was reduced with sucking sweet candy and drinking Diet Coke,
    - With exposure to odors of gas or garage, severe burning mouth symptoms recurred.

Possible mechanisms of odorants: stimulate hunger, thus precipitate salivary flow, change chemical content of the mouth, which hypersensitive pain fibers interpret as pain; induce eating memories, stimulate gastroesophageal reflux change in mouth PH causing pain; induce cephalopancreatic reflex, causing decreased blood sugar allowing dysfunctional pain nerve fibers to fire; trigeminal component of odors may act on tongue to precipitate prolonged, intense burning; stressors which worsens burning mouth syndrome. Burning mouth syndrome may represent a form of synesthesia, seen in neurological conditions such as odor-sensitive migraine, or postamputation phantom limb—in which otherwise innocuous stimuli precipitate pain.

In a parallel fashion are those who complain of hyperosmia. While true hyperosmia has been described with adrenal insufficiency states and during the headache phase of those with cluster-like headaches, usually this complaint is not actual hyperosmia, but rather, a hedonic change towards specific odors—cacosmia (with or without the associated severe behavioral responses) (Henkin, 1971). It even can be seen in those with true hyposmia or anosmia (hyposmic hyperosmia) (Hirsch, 2009a). Malingering hyperosmia, unlike that of cacosmia alone, can be delineated by olfactory testing. Such testing almost never demonstrates true hyperosmia, but rather normosmia, or the actual reduction in olfactory ability—possibly representing a disinhibition phenomenon. Instead of detecting all of the notes in an odor chord, both stimulatory and inhibitory, the sufferer detects only a portion, losing more inhibitory than excitatory smells, thus allowing the remaining odors to be perceived as more intense than normal.

These conditions—cacosmia, odor-induced headaches, subjective hyperosmia, odor-induced panic attacks, odor-induced flashbacks in PTSD, and odor-induced burning mouth syndrome—are closest to classical malingering in terms of their often massive deleterious impact on the life of those associated with the sufferer. Management of these conditions requires intensive psychological and behavioral intervention, working with both the patient and the family.

Another component of the history which may help ferret out the malingerer, is to carefully screen for other nonchemosensory symptoms which often cooccur with olfactory dysfunction. Specifically, olfactory dysfunction has been demonstrated to be the most sensitive and specific indication of traumatic injury to the ventromedial prefrontal cortex (Fujiwara, Schwartz, Gao, Black, and Levine, 2008; Zald, 2006). For instance, due to the neighborhood effect, if head trauma induces olfactory loss then often other indications of frontal lobe dysfunction appear. These include behavioral changes such as a state of abulia, amotivation, inattention, executive dysfunction, anhedonia, and symptoms of pseudobulbar affect. These can manifest in changes in interaction and functioning at work and in social situations.

For instance, in trauma-induced partial or complete olfactory loss without other neurologic loss, Varney demonstrated (on long-term follow-up of two years or longer) that patients displayed substantial disability behaviors including 100% suffering of absentmindedness, 95% of poor planning, 93% of faulty decision-making or indecisiveness, 83% of confusion, 80% of impairment in quality of work, 74% of unreliability, 74% of having inability to learn from mistakes, and 60% of trouble getting along with others (Varney, 1988).

On the other hand symptoms consistent with dysfunction in areas of the body unrelated to olfaction, based on somatotopic CNS localization, may suggest malingering as the origin of the complaints. For instance, generalized pain and itching teeth are not symptoms neuroanatomically close on the homunculus to the nose or near the olfactory regions of the brain. Thus, the presence of these and similar complaints indicates the possibility of either an extraordinarily rare syndrome or malingering.

A challenge arises when there is a "Christmas tree lights" neurologic review of systems, which is positive for virtually everything indicating possible damage in the neighboring regions of the olfactory cortex, tract, or both. This could be a person malingering or someone with enhanced self-awareness, a somatization disorder (where the symptoms reflect an underlying psychological conflict), a diffuse central nervous system damage, or a combination of all of these. In such a situation one is often forced to rely on the neuropsychiatric examination and other objective tests to determine the diagnosis of malingering (see Chapter 3).

Historical clues indicating malingering also include complaints of trauma-induced absolute loss of chemosensory ability. No smell, no taste—ever. On the other hand, historical items suggestive of true olfactory loss include episodic olfactory windows, of a whiff in duration.

In the gustatory sphere, an indication of true taste loss is the occurrence of the first taste phenomena, where with the first few bites of a food have a true taste and then rapidly disappears.

This is not unique to the sense of taste. In a variety of sensory disorders or states of sensory deprivation, illusions or hallucinations in the deficient sensory sphere have been described to occur. For instance, those who are blind, describe intermittent photopsia and those with hemi-field deficits occasionally describe continuation of the visual scene from the normal side into the visually impaired field, as in Bonnet Syndrome (Santos-Bueso, Serrador-Garcia, Sanez-Frances, and Garcia-Sanchez, 2010). Individuals suffering from traumatic deafness habitually complain of episodes of unremitting tinnitus (Roberts, Eggermont, Caspary, Shore, Melcher, and Kaltenback, 2010). Intrusion of normal sensation into the realm of sensory lacunae is also seen with chemosensation. In particular, those suffering from olfactory deficit have olfactory brief windows of whiffs of smell in response to true odor and phantosmias, at times in contextually appropriate scenarios, is absent (Hummel, Landis, and Hutenbrink, 2011).

In the gustatory spectrum, those with ageusia or hypogeusia often note the first taste phenomenon. For instance, after radiotherapy for metastatic squamous cell carcinoma of the throat, despite having no ability to taste. The first bite of food has normal flavor with rapid deterioration (Williams, 2016).

Classic first taste syndrome is defined as episodes where the first bite of food has full or nearly full flavor followed by a rapid (less than one minute) decrement in flavor of the food to the baseline of reduced or absent flavor.

Six patients with classic first taste syndrome were evaluated having ages ranging from 44 to 63 years old. Four were male, and two were female. Orthonasal smell ability ranged from anosmic (four) to hyposmic (one) to normosmic (one), and taste testing ranged from ageusic (one) to normogeusic (Williams, 2016; Santos-Bueso, Serrador-Garcia, Sanez-Frances, and Garcia-Sanchez, 2010; Overbosch, Van den Eden, and Keur, 1986). All had absent retronasal smell on Retronasal Smell Index testing. Half of them noted olfactory windows (see Table 11.8).

All six patients demonstrated a consistent pattern with impaired olfactory ability and absent retronasal smell. This suggests that the origin for this phenomenon is a dysfunction in the olfactory system with misperception of loss of retronasal smell as loss of taste. The mechanism for this phenomenon may be a pathological olfactory system with hyper-rapid adaptation, as a rapid shift on the exponential curve (Overbosch, Van Den

TABLE 11.8
First Taste Syndrome: Patient Characteristics

Case No.	Age in Yrs	Sex	Chemosensory Diagnosis	Origin	Smell Test	Retronasal Smell Test	Olfactory Window	Taste Test
1	56	M	HYPOSMIA DYSOSMIA SUBJECTIVE HYPOGEUSIA DYSGEUSIA	VIRAL INFECTION	BSIT = 6 (Anosmic) PST = 0 (Anosmic)	RSI = 0 (Absent)	Absent	Prop Disc = 10 (Normogeusia)
2	63	M	HYPOSMIA HYPOGEUSIA DYSOSMIA	TRAUMATIC	AST = 5 (Anosmia) BSIT = 8 (Hyposmic) PSIT= 3 (Norml) QSIT= 2 Olfactometer identification R = 13; L = 15 (normal) Olfactometer Threshold R = 1.5; L = 1 (anosmic) Sniff'N' Stick Threshold R = 4; L = 4: B = 4 (anosmic) Discrimination R = 7; L = 8; B = 8 (abnormal) Identification R = 7; L = 8; B = 6 (abnormal1) Sniff Magnitude Test = 1.26 (Anosmia) Suprathreshold Amyl Acetate Odor Intensity Test = Paralell pattern Hedonic Test = Cross pattern	RSI = 0 (Absent)	Absent	Prop Disc = 5 (Normogeusia) Normal to NaCI, sucrose, urea PTC and Hypogeusic to HCI Taste quadrants with patchy and front to back reduction Taste weakness to NaCI, Alcohol and Prop Electogustometry = 34 at all sites Fungiform papillae R = 20; L= 18

(Continued)

TABLE 11.8 (CONTINUED)
First Taste Syndrome: Patient Characteristics

Case No.	Age in Yrs	Sex	Chemosensory Diagnosis	Origin	Smell Test	Retronasal Smell Test	Olfactory Window	Taste Test
3	43	F	ANOSMIA DYSOSMIA Phx of PHANTOSMIA SUBJECTIVE HYPOGEUSIA	IDIOPATHIC	BSIT = 3 (Anosmic)	RSI = 0 (Absent)	Present	Prop Disc = 6 (Normogeusia)
4	52	F	SUBJECTIVE ANOSMIA SUBJECTIVE HYPEROSMIA DYSOSMIA SUBJECTIVE HYPOGEUSIA CACOGEUSIA PHANTOSMIA, PALLINOGEUSIA	URI INDUCED	AST = 2 (Anosmia) BSIT = 9 (Normosmia) QSIT = 3 (Nornmal) PSIT = 2 (Hyposmic) UPSIT = 24 (Hyposmia) Olfactometer Butanol Threshold R = 0.0; L-1 (anosmia)	RSI = –3 (Abnormal)	Present	Prop Disc = 7 (Normogeusia}
5	44	M	ANOSMIA SUBJECTIVE HYPOGEUSIA	IDIOPATHIC	BSIT = 9 (Normosmic)	RSI = 1 (Absent)	Absent	Prop Disc = 6 (Normogeusia)
6	67	M	HYPOSMIA DYSOSMIA PHANTOSMIA HYPOGEUSIA DYSGEUSIA		AST = 8 BSIT = 7 (Hyposmia)	RSI = 1 (Absent)	Present	Prop Disc = 1 (Ageusia)

Note: AST-Alcohol Sniff Test; BSIT-Brief Smell Identification Test; F-Female; M-Male; Prop-Propylthiouracil; PSIT-Pocket Smell Identification Test; PST-Pocket Smell Test; QSIT-Quick Smell Identification Test; RSI-Retronasal Smell Index; UPSIT-University of Pennsylvania Smell Identification Test; URI-Upper Respiratory Infection.

Eden, and Keur 1986). As such, one may anticipate that olfactory ability would not be totally absent, but rather severely reduced, as seen in these described cases. Only half demonstrated the parallel phenomenon of hyper-rapid adaptation in orthonasal smell, as manifested by olfactory windows. Despite the findings of normogeusia in five of six of these patients, pathology of other nontested aspects of the gustatory system may be present and thus, this may represent pathological hyper-acceleration of gustatory adaptation or synergistic or additive hyper-acceleration of both olfactory and gustatory systems (Gent and McBurney, 1978). Alternatively, first taste syndrome might represent an expectation with an associated projection with transient illusion of taste due to the perceived flavor based on visual cues (Van der Laan, de Ridder, Viergever, and Smeets, 2011). Such a transient hallucinatory phenomenon is seen in those suffering from cortical blindness as well as with haptic hallucinations with spinal cord injury and proprioceptive/kinesthetic hallucinations after amputation (Bors, 1951). In further characterizing this, six other specific variants of classic first taste syndrome are delineated.

One variant of first taste syndrome is that of delayed return of first taste and prolonged flavor loss. This type of first taste syndrome is manifested with delayed return of first taste or prolonged flavor loss; after the initial taste of the food, there is a prolonged period as long as three weeks until the first taste would resurface. Such is demonstrated in the case of a 67-year-old male who suffered from an upper respiratory infection seven months prior to presentation, followed by complete loss of smell and taste. He described burning leaves and coffee having a distorted, chemical-like smell. He also suffered from phantosmia of an indescribable smell, occurring predominantly at night. He affirmed being able to taste seasoned croutons, Triscuit's, and whole grain Tostito's. He experienced first taste syndrome describing that he tastes 90% of food's flavor, and within a minute it decreases, while the ability to taste the food remains poor for up to three weeks. Upon reexposure to the same food after three weeks, the first bite again produces 90% of the flavor followed by another period of rapid and prolonged flavor loss (see Table 11.9).

Abnormalities on physical examination included:

- General physical examination:
  - Bilateral 1+ pedal edema.
- Neurological examination:
  - Mental Status Examination:
    - Immediate recall: six digits forwards and five digits backwards,
    - Recent recall: four of four objects in three minutes without reinforcement.
  - Cranial nerves IX, X:
    - Gag absent bilaterally.

TABLE 11.9
First Taste with Prolonged Flavor Loss

Food	First Taste	One Week Later	Three Weeks Later
Strawberries	90%	10%	10%
Watermelon	90%	50%	50%
Chocolate	90%	0%	40%

- Chemosensory testing:
  - Olfactory testing:
    - Brief Smell Identification Test: seven (hyposmia),
    - Quick Smell Identification Test: two (hyposmia).
  - Gustatory testing:
    - Retronasal Smell Index: one (abnormal),
    - 6-n-Propythiouracil Disc Taste Test: one (ageusia).
- Neuropsychiatric testing:
  - Clock drawing test: four (normal),
  - Semantic Fluency Test: 48 (normal).

Potential mechanisms for the above include olfactory and gustatory pathological persistent adaptation due to viral-induced nerve dysfunction. Alternatively, the first taste could be a false one due to the expectation effect, which rapidly dissipates and thus remaines minimal. The mechanism for the quicker recovery of chocolate taste remains unknown. Even the usual duration of taste loss after the first bite is unknown and requires further exploration.

Another variant of first taste syndrome is that of prolonged duration of first taste. Unlike those patients with classic first taste syndrome or delayed return of first taste syndrome, where the first taste is brief (approximately 0.5–1 min), prolonged duration of first taste syndrome variant demonstrates the ability to taste after the first bite for a relatively long time period, followed by a loss of taste. This is illustrated in the case of a 60-year-old right-handed female who fell and struck her head with loss of consciousness, precipitating a loss of taste and which persisted for over a year. She frequently would note that the first bite of food had normal flavor which then rapidly disappeared. Most food had either minimal taste, no taste, or distorted a taste (metallic or salty) and she perceived her taste as 20% of normal. For some foods, the taste of the first bite persisted for more than just the first bite. For example, she could eat one-half of a cantaloupe and then the taste would fade away. This would also occur after the first half of a chicken sandwich with lettuce, cheese, bacon, and mayonnaise. Similarly, she could taste two to three bites of egg rolls, shrimps, hot dogs, tomato soup, and fortune cookie until the taste disappeared. Moreover, she was able to taste an entire bowl of chicken tortilla soup two days in a row at lunch at 100% normal. On day three, it had zero taste even after adding salt and pepper, which could last up to a month.

Abnormalities on physical examination included:

- General physical examination:
  - Scalloped tongue.
- Neurological examination:
  - Mental status examination:
    - Immediate recall: four digits forwards and backwards,
    - Recent recall: two of four objects in three minutes without improvement with reinforcement.
  - Cranial nerve VIII:
    - Hearing intact to CALFRAST AD 35 strong, and AS 15 strong,
    - Absent AU to Ambassador Hear Pen.

- Motor:
  - Drift testing:
    - Mild left pronator drift,
    - Left cerebellar spooning,
    - Left abductor digiti minimi sign.
  - Gait:
    - Heel walking with decreased right arm swing.
  - Sensory:
    - Decreased vibration in both lower extremities, distally,
    - Reflexes: 2+ throughout except absent right ankle jerk.
- Chemosensory testing:
  - Olfactory Testing:
    - Brief Smell Identification Test: 11 (normosmia),
    - Quick Smell Identification Test: two (hyposmia),
    - Pocket Smell Identification Test: two (hyposmia),
    - Alcohol Sniff Test: 19 (normosmia),
    - Retronasal Smell Index: two (reduced)
  - Gustatory Testing:
    - Propylthiouricil Disk Taste Test: nine (normogeusia),
    - Taste Threshold Testing: Normogeusia to sucrose, hydrochloric acid, and urea and phenylthiocarbamol. Mild hypogeusia to salt.
- Neuropsychiatric Testing:
  - Animal Fluency Test: 14 (normal),
  - Center for Neurologic Studies Lability Scale: 17 (abnormal) (Moore, Gresham, Bromberg, Kasarkis, and Smith, 1997),
  - Clock Drawing Test: four (normal).
- CT scan of brain: moderate white matter ischemic changes.
- Sjogren's Antibody: SSA and SSB: negative.

The exact mechanism for prolonged ability to taste until loss is unclear. Possibly, she had a greater residual taste ability and therefore was more resistant to taste adaptation than in the case of classic first taste syndrome. However, with multiple bites, adaptation occurred and she lost taste. Possibly, prolonged adaptation was exhibited as a result of the food being so different from her traditional diet. Maybe, she was so invested in the idea that her taste would return that she had a prolonged denial of loss of taste and replaced it with taste memory. Perhaps the high spice and sodium content of this food allowed her to overcome the gustatory and trigeminal thresholds, which allowed her to continue to taste the soup (Bartoshuk, 1978). Alternatively, due to a primary defect these taste and smell receptors may have remained saturated and did not return to normal. Such prolonged loss is consistent with delayed return of first taste syndrome.

Whereas in first taste syndrome there is temporal desensitization to olfactory retronasal stimuli, another variant of first taste syndrome is that of temporal summation-induced sensitization and perceived flavor. In this manifestation of first taste syndrome, prolonged exposure to flavor (of up to half an hour) induces the flavor to appear. This is demonstrated in a 50-year-old male following an upper respiratory illness. He noted over nine months a gradual reduction in his ability to smell and taste, to the point of total loss of smell and taste upon initial consumption. He also noticed dysosmia wherein water smells different and chemical-like. He experiences dysgeusia wherein olives taste fecal, pickles taste like vinegar, cottage cheese tastes unpleasant, Oreos taste like flowers, and sour cream is no longer sour. He affirms having gustatory rhinitis which has worsened since his illness. Most noteworthy is that the patient has a heightened sensitivity to the taste of food after having eaten it for 30 minutes. He discovered that a temporal relationship exists such that after 20 to 30 minutes of leisurely consumption, the food gradually became imbued with flavor. For instance, initially he had no taste when eating popcorn, but after 20 minutes of relaxed mastication he was able to taste the popcorn and the flavor persisted until he finished eating. While the flavor was subjectively only 1% of the usual strength, its presence was noteworthy. Additionally, after eating three chocolate chip cookies he was able to taste the chocolate chips, again at 1% of full capacity.

Abnormalities on physical examination included:

- General physical examination:
  - Bilateral palmar erythema,
  - Bilateral pedal edema.
- Neurological examination:
  - Cranial nerve examination: visual acuity: 20/60 OD, 20/30 OS, right Marcus Gunn pupil.
  - Motor examination:
    - Drift testing:
      - Left cerebellar spooning.
    - Reflexes:
      - 1+ both upper extremities,
      - 2+ knee jerks,
      - 3+ ankle jerks,
      - Positive right Hoffman's reflex.
- Neuropsychiatric testing:
  - Clock Drawing Test: four (normal),
  - Semantic Fluency Test: 44 (normal),
  - Center for Neurologic Studies Lability Scale: seven (normal).
- Chemosensory testing:
  - Olfactory Testing:
    - Brief Smell Identification Test: six (anosmia),
    - Olfactometer Identification: left nine, right nine (anosmia),
    - Pocket Smell Test: one (anosmia),
    - Alcohol Sniff Test: zero (anosmia),
    - Retronasal Smell Index: zero (abnormal).
  - Gustatory Testing:
    - Propylthiouracil Disc Taste Test: ten (normosmia).
- Mental Status Examination:
  - Short term memory: remember zero of four objects in three minutes, and two of four objects with reinforcement.
  - Similarities: poor.

- MRI of the head: moderate pansinusitis.
- MRA of the head: negative.
- CT scan of the sinuses: mucosal retention cyst in the left maxillary sinus.
- ENT evaluation: normal.

The mechanism for prolonged exposure induction of flavor in the subject is unclear. Possibly this is due to a temporal summation in the olfactory, gustatory, trigeminal, or retronasal smell spheres or a combination of these (Hummel, Landis, and Hutenbrink, 2011; Bagla, Klasky, and Doty, 1997; Migaud, Durieux, Viereck, Soroca-Lucas, Fournie-Zaluski, and Roques, 1996; Mialon and Ebeler, 1997; Veldhuizen, Shepard, Wang, and Marks, 2010). Alternatively, this could represent a somesthetic/tactile illusion combined with an expectation effect.

A more pathological subtype of first taste syndrome is that of dysgeusic first taste syndrome. Dysgeusia, or distorted taste, is associated with a myriad of conditions including head trauma, upper respiratory infections, and toxins (Hummel, Landis, and Huttenbrink, 2011). In these states, the duration of dysgeusia is either not described or categorized as constant. In classic first taste syndrome in those complaining of taste deficit, the first taste of normal flavor dissipates within a few bites. Alternatively, in first taste syndrome distorted by dysgeusia, dysgeusia instead of true taste occurs in the first bite, which rapidly fades away, followed by no taste.

This is exemplified in a 52-year-old right-handed female. Six years prior to presentation, she noted a new onset of loss of taste and smell. She underwent sinus surgery for nasal polyps as well as treatment with antibiotics and prednisone. These treatments caused her sense of smell to return for five months, until it gradually faded away to total absence where it remains today. She feels her smell and taste are totally absent and denies dysosmia, phantosmia, palinosmia, cacosmia, phantogeusia, cacogeusia, palinageusia, and flavorful eructation. She did admit to olfactory windows for a few months. She describes dysgeusia whereby she did not taste vanilla coffee when drinking it, but it had a distorted sweet taste. This would occur only for the first sip and the flavor would disappear for at least two hours. Such a dysgeusic taste on first taste occurred almost daily.

Abnormalities on physical examination included:

- General physical examination:
  - 1 + bilateral pedal edema.
- Neurologic examination:
  - Reflexes: bilateral quadriceps femoris 3+ and pendular.
- Chemosensory testing:
  - Olfactory testing:
    - Brief Smell Identification Test: six (anosmia),
    - Alcohol Sniff Test: zero (anosmia),
    - Pocket Smell Test: one (anosmia),
    - Olfactometer Identification Test: left, six, right, six (anosmia).
    - Snap Phenyethyl Alcohol Threshold Test: left less than –2.0, right less than –2.0 (anosmia),
    - Retronasal Smell Index: zero (abnormal).

- Gustatory testing:
    - Propylthiouracil Disc Taste Test: five (normogeusia).
- Mental Status Examination:
    - Immediate recall: six digits forwards and three digits backwards.

Possibly, this represents pathological olfactory or gustatory pathways which are rapidly adapting. This demonstrated a more severe dysfunction than persistent dysgeusia, whereby even the dysgeusic pathological pathway is not stable enough to sustain the discharge, leading to hyperadaptation and dysgeusic disappearance.

An additional variation of first taste syndrome is that of cooccurrence of flavor temporal summation and classic first taste syndrome. In those with classic first taste syndrome with absent or reduced taste the first bite of the food is flavorful but rapidly dissipates over a few bites. Temporal summation of taste is the condition whereby initially food has no taste, but over time (typically 20 to 30 minutes) the flavor of food appears. In the new subtype of first taste syndrome described below both classic first taste and temporal summation are present simultaneously. The cooccurrence of symptoms in this variant is illustrated in one individual.

Two months prior to presentation this 57-year-old right-handed male developed an upper respiratory tract infection associated with the loss of his sense of smell and taste. This had happened to him in the past with upper respiratory tract infections, but unlike in the past, after resolution the smell did not return. He feels his ability to smell is 40% of normal and he can smell strong odors including tar, gasoline, and exhaust. He affirms one period of phantosmia of dirty dishwater for one second. He denies olfactory windows, dysosmia, cacosmia, palinosmia, and flavorful eructations. He describes his taste as 30% of normal and can taste only salt, spice, and tomatoes. He denies dysgeusia, cacogeusia, phantageusia, and palinageusia.

For most foods, he can taste 65% of the flavor with the first bite, but with rapid decrement, so that by the fifth bite he has no flavor, which remains absent for the remainder of the meal. On the other hand, he noticed that once a week with certain foods, for instance strawberries, he has no ability to taste at all initially and then, after four to five bites, the taste appears at 60% of normal flavor and which persists for the entire meal.

Abnormalities on physical examination included:

- General physical examination:
    - Decreased blink frequency.
- Neurological examination:
    - Cranial nerve VIII: hearing absent to Ambassador Hear Pen AU.
    - Motor examination:
        - Drift testing: bilateral cerebellar spooning.
        - Reflexes:
            - 1+ bilateral brachioradialis,
            - Biceps 3+
            - Bilateral quadriceps femoris,
            - Bilateral ankle jerks.
- Chemosensory testing:
    - Olfactory testing:
        - Brief Smell Identification Test: seven (hyposmia),

    - Quick Smell Identification Test: three (normosmia),
    - Pocket Smell Identification Test: two (hyposmia),
    - Alcohol Sniff Test: four (anosmia),
    - Olfactometer Identification Test: right 17 (normosmia), left 16 (hyposmia).
    - Snap Phenylethyl Alcohol Threshold Test: left –3.5 (hyposmia), right less than –2.0 (anosmia),
    - Retronasal Smell Index: three (abnormal).
  - Gustatory testing:
    - Propylthiouracil Disc Taste Test: one (ageusia),
    - Taste Threshold Test: normogeusic to hydrochloric acid; mildly hypogeusic, 10–30%, to sucrose; ageusia to sodium chloride, urea, and phenylthiocarbamide,
    - Saxon Test: eight grams (normal).
- Neuropsychiatric testing:
  - Animal Fluency Test: 23 (normal),
  - Center for Neurologic Study Lability Scale: seven (normal),
  - Clock Drawing Test: four (normal).
- CT of brain and sinuses: normal,
- MRI scan of brain and sinuses: normal,
- Fiber optic endoscopy: normal.

The mechanism for such cooccurrence is not readily apparent. Possibly, this represents an abnormality in retronasal smell, gustatory response, or both. In classic first taste phenomena there may be rapid saturation whereas in temporal summation impairment of chemosensation may require a greater duration and intensity of sensory stimuli for taste to be perceived. Perhaps, dysfunctional sensory receptors involving strawberries require a greater or longer stimulation whereas receptors for other foods rapidly saturate. Conceivably, temporal summation is not due to the actual taste or smell of the food but rather due to memory filling the sensory lacunae. The tactile and masticatory experience of the food may provide a sensory illusion. This then complements the memory and creates an expectation effect with his past experience eating strawberries, and thus, is perceived as flavor. Consistent with his physical findings, both first taste and temporal summation indicate problems within the chemosensory system.

Another form of first taste syndrome is first taste syndrome followed by dysgeusia. In this condition, instead of rapid conversion from normal taste to nothing, there is rapid normal taste followed by dysgeusic taste. First taste syndrome rapidly adapting to dysgeusia is exhibited in a 60-year-old, right-handed female with Hashimoto's thyroiditis, peripheral neuropathy, and restless leg syndrome. She was nasute until six months prior to presentation, after falling and striking the back of her head on concrete, with loss of consciousness for approximately one minute. Within the next few days after the fall, she noted a reduced taste to 20% of normal. She could taste pickles and sweets without problem, but very little else. She also described dysgeusia wherein food tasted salty or like nothing. The salty taste was temporally related to ingestion of food such that lemonade initially tastes like lemon and within a few seconds transformed into the taste of salt. Similarly, Oreo and chocolate chip cookies, lemon pancakes, meatloaf, and spaghetti, tasted as they for the first and second bites but after the third bite rapidly acquired a salty taste. Once the food had acquired the salty taste eating other foods between exposures did not change the perception of the original food's salty taste on reexposure.

Abnormalities on physical examination included:

- General physical examination:
  - Scalloped tongue.
- Neurologic examination:
  - Cranial nerve examination:
    - Cranial nerve VIII: CALFRAST AS 35 strong, AD 10 strong. Absent Ambassador Hear Pen AU.
    - Motor examination:
      - Drift testing: left pronator drift: left cerebellar spooning: left abductor digiti minimi sign.
      - Gait examination: heel walking with decreased right arm swing:
      - Sensory examination:
        - Rydel-Seiffer Vibratory Sense Evaluation: bilateral upper extremity: seven; right lower extremity: four, left lower extremity: one.
    - Reflexes: absent right ankle jerk.
- Chemosensory testing:
  - Olfactory testing:
    - Brief Smell Identification Test: 11 (normosmia),
    - Alcohol Sniff Test: 19 (normosmia),
    - Pocket Smell Test: two (hyposmia),
    - Quick Smell Identification Test: two (hyposmia),
    - Retronasal Smell Index: two (abnormal).
  - Gustatory Testing:
    - Propylthiouracil Disk Taste Test: nine (normogeusia),
    - Taste Threshold: Normogeusia to sucrose, hydrochloric acid, urea and phenylthiocarbamide. Mild hypogeusia to sodium chloride.
    - Taste Quadrant Test: impaired posteriorly to citric acid. Whole mouth taste weakness to sodium chloride, and sucrose.
- Neuropsychiatric Testing:
  - Clock Drawing Test: four (normal),
  - Animal Fluency Test 14 (normal),
  - Center for Neurological Studies Lability Scale Test: seven (normal),
  - Mental Status Examination:
    - Memory testing:
      - Immediate recall: four digits forwards and four digits backwards,
      - Recent recall: two of four objects in three minutes, without improvement with reinforcement

Myriad mechanisms can be postulated for this phenomenon. Primary olfactory loss might cause rapid olfactory adaptation. This then leads to a decrease in olfactory input with an associated reduction in retronasal smell (loss of physiologic synesthesia) combined with food, whereby food texture induces a salty taste (pathologic gustatory synesthesia in which texture was perceived as taste). In this model, the physiologic synesthesia of retronasal smell was initially predominant and inhibited the pathological synesthesia. As smell adapted the salty dysgeusia prevailed. Another way of viewing this is that as the first taste phenomenon diminishes the pathologic taste manifests. This may thus represent a dual diagnosis of (1) olfactory dysfunction with rapid adaptation, and (2) primary taste distortion. Thus, delayed dysgeusias could be understood as the chemosensory analogue to the double crush phenomenon in peripheral nerve itself disease where two lesions are needed for symptoms to occur (Wood and Biondi, 1990). If the subject did not have the olfactory deficits the taste distortion would not manifest itself.

Change in food preferences towards salty, spicy, and more textured foods, or cacogeusia towards some foods as a result of dysgeusia, texture, or absent flavor both suggest true chemosensory dysfunction (Hirsch 1992, Hirsch and Trannel, 1996).

11.2 THE NEUROLOGIC EXAMINATION

A wide variety of neurologic signs suggest the possibility of malingering (see Chapter 3) from extremely slow responses to volitional attempts at avoiding instructions (i.e., not volitionally following finger with eye movements on command). Also, positive malingering signs on examination (such as the Hoover sign or Waddell's sign) point towards this diagnosis.

Negativism and lack of cooperation also suggest malingering. Alternatively, these behaviors may indicate nonmalingering uncooperative attitudes manifest with confusion, belligerence, anger, irritability of mania, conduct disorder. This could be a learned response on the part of the patient who has a negative view of the examiner as a result of the adversarial nature of criminal justice or civil litigation systems. The neurologist's negative countertransference in response to this and the realization that he or she has been fooled, is often so strong as to cause the examiner to ignore the other diagnostic possibilities and prematurely and punitively label the patient as a malinger.

Physical signs consistent with central forms of olfactory and gustatory dysfunction include unilateral or bilateral upper motor neuron findings, frontal lobe damage, or lower cranial nerve dysfunction with pontomedullary damage associated with central taste dysfunction. These are due to pathology of neighboring anatomic structures close to the damaged chemosensory apparatus. To appreciate this more fully, let's review the anatomy and physiology of chemosensation and pathological states which can impair these, as delineated by Wahlstrom (Wahlstrom, Jr., Hirsch, and Whitman, 2015).

Dirhinous inhalation occurs asymmetrically and is mostly unilateral due to the olfactory cycle, which alternately opens one nostril and closes the other nostril every 40 minutes to four hours (Eccles, 1978). Ipsilateral to the restricted nostril, olfaction demonstrates the greatest sensitivity as a result of eddy currents created by the smaller aperture. Such vortiginous gusts of odorants, like tornadoes of the proboscis in an anfractuous kippage, distribute the odorants with greater concentration reaching the olfactory epithelium at the top of the nose, as opposed to bypassing this area in favor of the bronchi and lungs (Frye, 2003).

For an aroma to be processed, it needs to be solubilized in mucous.

After passing through the olfactory epithelium, the odorants must stimulate the olfactory nerve composed of unmyelinated olfactory fila, which have the slowest conduction rate of any nerve in the body (Wolfe, 2006). The olfactory fila conduct the odorant represented through electrical depolarization or hyperpolarization, through the cribriform plate of the ethmoid bone into the olfactory bulb. Different odors are localized in specific areas of the olfactory bulb (Kratskin and Belluzzi, 2003). With trauma, damage is often manifest in this region, resulting in greater impact on identification than threshold (Hirsch and Wyse, 1993). See Figure 11.1.

Inside the olfactory bulb is an organized system of neuropil, the glomeruli. There exist 2000 glomeruli inside the olfactory bulb. The four different cell types which the glomeruli are comprised of includes: processes of receptor cell axons, mitral cells, tufted cells, and second-order neurons which give off collaterals to the granule cells and to cells in the periglomerular and external plexiform layers. Projections from the mitral and tufted cells form the lateral olfactory tract, establishing a reverberating circuit with the granule cells. The mitral cells stimulate firing of the granule cells, which in turn inhibit firing of the mitral cells and create a negative feedback loop (Brodal, 1969).

Reciprocal inhibition between the mitral and tufted cells results in a sharpening of olfactory acuity. The olfactory bulb receives several afferent projections, which include the primary olfactory fibers, the contralateral olfactory bulb, the anterior nucleus, the inhibitory prepiriform cortex, the diagonal band of Broca (with the neurotransmitters acetylcholine and gamma-aminobutryric acid), the locus coeruleus, the dorsal raphe, and the tuberomammillary nucleus of the hypothalamus.

The olfactory bulb's efferent fibers project into the olfactory tract, which divides at the olfactory trigona into the medial and lateral olfactory striae. The striae project to the anterior olfactory nucleus, the olfactory tubercle, the amygdaloid nucleus (which

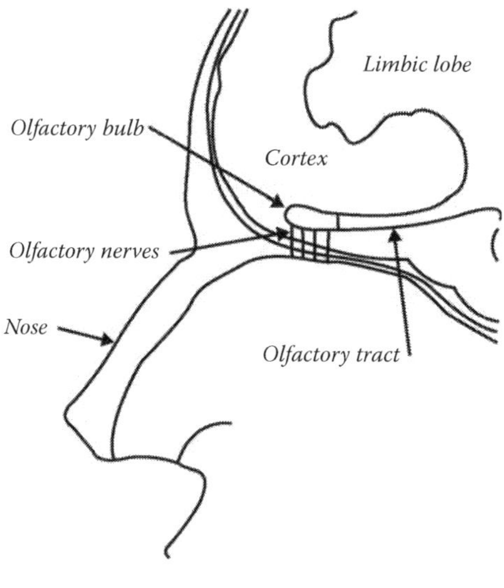

FIGURE 11.1 Distal olfactory pathway.

in turn projects to the ventral medial nucleus of the hypothalamus, a feeding center), the cortex of the piriform lobe, the septal nuclei, and the hypothalamus, especially the anterolateral regions of the hypothalamus, which may partially explain the mechanisms of olfactory effects in reproduction processes (Hirsch, 1998b; Hirsch, 1998c).

The anterior olfactory nucleus receives afferent fibers from the olfactory tract and projects efferent fibers, decussating in the anterior commissure, and synapsing in the contralateral olfactory bulb. Efferent projections from the anterior olfactory nucleus, nondecussating, synapse on internal granular cells of the ipsilateral olfactory bulb.

The olfactory tubercle receives afferent fibers from the anterior olfactory nucleus and the olfactory bulb. Efferent fibers from the olfactory tubercle project to the nucleus accumbens and the striatum. Neurotransmitters of the olfactory tubercle include both acetylcholine and dopamine (Kratskin and Belluzzi, 2003).

The primary olfactory cortex includes the prepiriform area, the periamygdaloid area, and the entorhinal area. The piriform cortex and the amygdala are the primary olfactory cortex, while the insula and orbitofrontal cortex are secondary olfactory cortex association areas (Doty et al., 1997). Afferent projections to the primary olfactory cortex include the mitral cells, which enter the lateral olfactory tract and synapse in the prepiriform cortex (lateral olfactory gyrus) and the corticomedial part of the amygdala. Efferent projections from the primary olfactory cortex extend to the entorhinal cortex, the basal and lateral amygdaloid nuclei, the lateral preoptic area of the hypothalamus, the nucleus of the diagonal band of Broca, the medial forebrain bundle, the dorsal medial nucleus and submedial nucleus of the thalamus, and the nucleus accumbens.

The entorhinal cortex is both a primary and a secondary olfactory cortical area. Efferent fibers project via the uncinate fasciculus to the hippocampus, the anterior insular cortex next to the gustatory cortical area, and the frontal cortex. This may explain why temporal lobe epilepsy which involves the uncinate frequently produces phantosmia of burning rubber, as a feature of "uncinate fits" (V. Acharya, J. Acharya, and Luders, 1998).

Some of the efferent projections of the mitral and tufted cells decussate in the anterior commissure and form the medial olfactory tract. They then synapse in the contralateral parolfactory area and the contralateral subcallosal gyrus.

The accessory olfactory bulb receives afferent fibers from the bed nucleus of the accessory olfactory tract and the medial and posterior corticoamygdaloid nuclei. Efferent fibers from the accessory olfactory bulb project through the accessory olfactory tract to these same afferent areas. The medial and posterior corticoamygdaloid nuclei project secondary fibers to the anterior and medial hypothalamus, the areas associated with reproduction. Therefore, the accessory olfactory bulb in humans may be a mediator for human pheromones (Hirsch, 1998a).

11.3 NEUROTRANSMITTERS THAT MEDIATE SMELL

A panopoly of neurotransmitters function in the olfactory cortex including, but not limited to, glutamate, aspartate, cholecystokinin, lutenizing hormone-releasing hormone, and somatostatin. Odor perception causes modulation of olfactory neurotransmitters within the olfactory bulb and the limbic system. Since almost all known neurotransmitters exist in the olfactory bulb, odorant modulation of neurotransmitter levels in the olfactory bulb, tract, and limbic system intended for transmission of sensory information may have unintended secondary effects on a variety of behaviors and disease states which are regulated by the same neurotransmitters. For instance, it is possible that odorant modulation of dopamine in the olfactory bulb/limbic system may affect manifestations of Parkinson's disease contributing to limbic system override of Parkinson's disease motoric manifestations (Javoy-Agid and Algid, 1980; Thierry, Dassin, Blanc et al., 1976).

11.4 THE PHYSIOLOGY OF TASTE

Taste receptors on taste buds located primarily in the fungiform and circumvallate papillae (Witt, Reutter, and Miller, Jr., 2003) mediate true tastes—salt, sweet, sour, bitter, unami, and possibly lipids. The circumvallate papillae are more sensitive to sweet stimuli (Jeppson, 1969; Smith, 1986) whereas the fungiform papillae have the lower thresholds to salt and sweet. Cranial nerves VII, IX, and X mediate the gustatory stimuli and enter the pons at the pontomedullary junction ascending and descending through the tractus solitarius, finally terminating topographically on the ipsilateral nucleus of the tractus solitarius. Cranial nerve VII chorda tympani fibers synapse rostrally whereas glossopharyngeal fibers synapse caudally. Second order taste neurons progress through the parabrachial pontine nuclei where they diverge. Some of these synapse in the thalamus with tertiary order neurons which progress to the primary gustatory cortex in the insula. The remainder bypass the thalamus and project diffusely to the ventral forebrain with widespread limbic system connections.

Thus, the presence of findings suggesting dysfunction of adjacent structures to the olfactory or gustatory pathways would be suggestive of the absence of malingering. These include indicators of orbital frontal damage with unilateral or bilateral hyperreflexia or atavistic reflexes (Hoffman's, Grasp, Snout, Suck, Myerson's, Palmomental, Jaw Jerk, and Babinski), perseveration or inattention as demonstrated on the distractibility of the history (Jones et al., 2016), and on the formal mental status examination with tests of attention, including digit span forwards and backwards and Continuous Performance Testing. In this testing paradigm, the patient claps whenever the letter "A" is stated while the examiner in a monotone voice reads off a list of letters at one per second with letter "A" randomly embedded in the list (Strub and Black, 1993). Errors of omission could indicate inattention whereas errors of commission point to perseveration. Disinhibited limbic system functioning can be revealed with pseudobulbar affect or emotional disinhibition (posttraumatically, most usually manifest by irritability, anger, and aggression) (Silver, Yudofsky, and Anderson, 2011). In a parallel fashion, objective dysfunction of anatomic structures adjacent to the taste pathway would cast doubt of malingering as the origin of the taste complaints. Objective dysfunction of anatomic structures may include evidence of damage of other peripheral structures involved in the chordae tympani from cranial nerve VII or the brain stem itself involving other components of cranial nerves VII, IX, and X, beyond those mediated through the nucleus and tractus solitarius. Thus, other pontine or medullary cranial nerves or brain stem dysfunction or nontasting components of cranial nerves VII, IX, and X, all would point to true disease. This may include unilateral or bilateral absent gag reflex or facial weakness. If the etiology is from head trauma more widespread damage may be seen throughout the neuroaxis and of wide diverse damage involving other sensory systems and can range from auditory impairment or intractable tinnitus to blindness or a limbic system dysfunction as manifest by depression or psychosis (Wolkin et al., 2011). Likewise, when the chemosensory disorder is due to another primary disease, other neurologic or nonneurologic manifestations may be evident. For instance, in B12 deficiency along with smell loss there may appear signs of posterior column dysfunction with absence of vibration or proprioception (Healton, Savage, Brust, Garrett, and Lindebaum, 1991). Similarly, in the case of Parkinson's disease, decreased eye blinking, limited upward gaze, saccadization of horizontal eye movements, masked face, cogwheel rigidity, akinesia, tremor, gait instability, as well as other signs may follow or co-occur with olfactory loss (Doty, 2012). In terms of smell loss due to demyelinating disorders, such as MS, evidence of white matter dysfunction is a reflection of where the demyelinating plaques are located and thus, dysfunction may appear anywhere subsuming the olfactory pathway within the central nervous system. Neurotoxicity-induced chemosensory dysfunction, depending upon the specific neurotoxin, may manifest not only in the central nervous system but also in peripheral nervous system pathways and even may reveal specific markers of the toxin extraneuronally, as in conjunctival hemorrhage in hydrogen sulphide poisoning or Mees' lines due to lead exposure (Fawcett, Linford, and Stulberg, 2004; Beauchamp, Jr., Bus, Popp, Boreiko, and Andjelkovich, 1984). Chemosensory dysfunction in the absence of these neighborhood or associated signs—when claimed to be due to a specific cause (trauma, toxins, etc.)—further advances the consideration of the diagnosis of malingering within the differential diagnosis. What makes this particularly challenging is that oftentimes the malingering occurs when litigation associated with the head injury is involved. Those with head injury also have a higher incidence of sociopathy and antisocial personality disorders, a perfect storm of sorts, where there is both a strong financial incentive to malingering combined with moral lacunae for mendacity. Because those who have had one head trauma are also more likely to have a second head trauma, it is distinctly possible that multiple objective neurologic signs of dysfunction in the nervous system exist in widespread regions due to past traumas, which makes use of such neighborhood signs more difficult as an indicator of true disease (Langlois-Orman, 2011). In particular, if the patient has had past trauma without loss of smell and now has loss of smell from trauma, the past traumas may have caused neurologic damage which is apparent on the physical examination. Thus, in the absence of a past neurologic examination prior to the trauma-induced smell loss the patient's abnormalities may be misattributed to the current—as opposed to the past—trauma. Under these circumstances, malingering may be falsely excluded as a diagnosis.

Theoretically, any combination of the above olfactory complaints can present a myriad of permutations in the malingerer. However, there are no documented cases of malingering smell loss and dysosmia combined, or the combination of hyposmia and phantosmia. Such conditions are not uncommon in the smell and taste clinic (Deems et al., 1991) and their presence may be evidence for the veracity of the patient's complaints.

What occasionally happens are groups who share similar chemosensory complaints. Olfactory impairment or phantosmia due to a shared olfactotropic virus among family members, a connubial olfactotropic virus, or an olfactotoxic exposure in those who share contaminated ground water or soil (for instance, due to trichloroethylene) can produce similar chemosensory complaints amongst groups. When presented with such collective chemosensory symptoms the presence of malingering rarely is diagnosed (Hirsch 1995a; Hirsch 1995b; Hirsch and Skolnik, 1994). However, in other group symptom situations, malingering is frequently considered—that of hysterical or mass illness. In these circumstances, often involving school children in a common classroom or workers in a shared office space, those affected will frequently report the same irritating odor and developing a wide range of symptoms including shortness of breath, dizziness, paresthesias, headaches, and occasional palinosmia (with presentation of the initial precipitating odor). In these events, the nidus for the symptoms is often not a primary neurotoxin, but rather a benign ambient aroma which is a nontoxic bystander. However, the origin of the symptoms has often a primary situational or psychological basis and is transmitted due to group effect of conformity. Once a key member admits smelling an odor all others follow suit.

The phenomena of psychologically-induced spread or transmission of a perception of an odor has been demonstrated in a classroom. When the professor opened a container and advised the students in a lecture hall that a noisome odor was being released the students reacted as if a true miasma was engulfing them. This reaction progressed sequentially from the nearest to the furthest rows. These students perceived both an odor and complained about the odor's mephitic nature (Demaitre, 2004).

A similar group effect was described during a radio station broadcast where supposedly an aroma was being released by the listeners' home radios. After the station was inundated with phone calls complaining of the aroma, they had to discontinue the charade (O'Mahony, 1978).

A benign odor can induce medical symptoms in psychiatrically normal individuals, as was demonstrated by Knasko. In this paradigm, normal subjects were instructed that an aroma released into the environment could cause a variety of medical symptoms. Upon exposure to this otherwise benign odor subjects manifested these symptoms and more (Knasko, 1992).

Such mass hysteria is not really malingering, since the motivations are unconscious, but prolonged persistence of symptoms may generate secondary gain, which eventually could lead to malingering.

In ferreting out malingering of olfactory symptoms, it is essential to rule out probable organic origins which would account for the patient's complaints. There are a wide range of illnesses which precipitate chemosensory complaints. These range from AIDS and leprosy to Parkinson's disease and senile dementia of the Alzheimer's type as well as everything in between (Wahlstrom, Hirsch, and Whitman, 2015). Because the diagnosis of malingering is so emotionally laden and a missed diagnosis of malingering can have major economic, social, and legal ramifications, the diagnosis should not be made lightly. Hence, the diagnosis of malingering should be reserved for clear-cut malingering. Given the negative effects of such a diagnosis it is better to err on the side of true pathology or nonmalingering psychiatric dysfunction (hysteria) rather than misdiagnose malingering.

One of the pitfalls of such a diagnosis is in the attribution of conscious intent—was the patient consciously trying to pretend to have chemosensory symptoms or were they unconscious manifestations of an underlying conflict, like hysterical paralysis, blindness, or mutism.

The conundrum remains, in the presence of history, symptoms, and findings of chemosensory malingering. How to ferret out if this is of conscious intent or on an unconscious hysterical basis? Approaches to differentiate these two are onerous for both complaints of smell and taste as well as all neurologic and psychiatric conditions. This will be addressed at the end of this chapter.

If one identifies and labels these individuals as malingerers, a negative countertransference is often established causing the doctor to unintentionally (and occasionally intentionally) reject the patient and induce the patient to seek treatment elsewhere. Alternatively, not labeling these personalities as malingerers, but rather, seeing them within the spectrum of the patient's life in a Rogerian, nonjudgmental manner with unconditional acceptance, may allow a therapeutic alliance to be achieved and promote a stable treatment atmosphere between the doctor and the individual (O'Flaherty, 2013). In this manner, such a therapeutic approach provides both a way of dealing directly with the symptoms and also the underlying psychological conflicts which may be the nidus for the symptoms.

Given the diagnosis of olfactory malingering, beyond psychological intervention, should the diagnosis be withheld and pharmacologic treatment in the form of placebo be offered? Such an approach clearly does not comport with the philosophy of equality and patient–physician partnership but rather harkens back to the era of physician authoritative dominance of the physician–patient dyadic relationship. However, in the management of malingering such an approach anecdotally seems to be effective. Providing a placebo (with some theoretical mechanism) would allow the malingerer a sense of self-esteem, avoiding confrontation, and prevent him from seeking care elsewhere, at which time he or she may receive treatments with more dangerous side effects. This would serve to prevent harm far greater than any risk form the placebo. Furthermore, there is scientific justification for doing so in that placebos have been shown to affect a variety of neurotransmitters and neural system involved in the transmission of olfaction (Benedetti, Mayberg, Waer, Stoller, and Zubieta, 2005). Addressing the diagnosis is also riddled with potential ethical, legal, and relationship land mines. Direct confrontation, while the most intellectually honest, destroys the therapeutic relationship and does not benefit the patient. Diagnosis based on subjective complaints (i.e., subjective anosmia, dysosmia, phantosmia) is mendacious without assigning blame. If origin is queried, a fallback position may be idiopathic until a more matured dyadic relationship can be developed. During the development of this relationship, the underlying psychological and social distress motivating the malingerer may be openly shared and addressed. It is essential to prevent developing an adversarial position with the malingerer—for without compassionate understanding it will just serve to magnify the malingered symptoms.

11.5 TASTE

The malingered disorders of taste are homologous to smell disorders. These may occur independently or combined with complaints of disorders of smell. Beyond the complaint of taste loss—because of misperception of smell as flavor due to retronasal smell—taste dysfunction can be categorized into hypogeusia (reduced taste), ageusia (absent taste), dysgeusia (distorted taste), phantageusia (hallucinated taste), palinageusia (persistent taste), and cacogeusia (severe transformation of hedonically positive tastes to hedonically negative tastes with associated behavioral response of avoidance and change in diet) (Leopold, 2002).

Isolated gustatory malingering with absence of olfactory complaints is exceedingly rare but has been occasionally seen in head trauma cases, or related to isolated intraoral trauma (i.e., dental procedures) and ingestion of caustic or toxic agents. It is also seen in those less sophisticated malingerers who believe taste is flavor and unrelated to smell. When a patient presents with isolated total ageusia without loss of orthonasal or retronasal smell, foods usually retain their normal flavor, especially if the taste loss is gradually progressive. Thus, a malingerer of such a condition should be without complaints. Furthermore, approximately 15% of the population has a gustatory dysfunction and is unaware of such loss, demonstrating a relative lack of subjective complaints resulting from such dysfunction (Leopold, 2002).

More frequent are those who complain of isolated taste loss—all sweet. While such a phenomenon has been seen in autoimmune disease (Bartoshuk, personal communication, 2015), isolated sweet ageusia is rarely seen with other conditions including diabetes mellitus (Gondivkar, Indurkar, Degwekar, and Bhowate, 2009), myasthenia gravis with thymoma (Chabwine, Tschirren, Zekeridou, Landis, Kuntzer, 2014), and Guillain-Barré Syndrome (Combarros, Pascual, de Pablos, Ortega, and Berciano, 1996). In these situations, foods tastes too bitter and often is unpalatable, often causing associated anorexia and weight loss.

Ageusia and hypogeusia can be of three types: (1) global, that is, to all areas involving the entire tongue and palate—in which case all tastes and all areas are affected—a condition which occurs with some toxic exposures; (2) localized or a patchy loss, that is, involving discrete regions of the tongue and palate—as often occurs with head trauma and upper respiratory infections; and (3) unilateral, that is, usually associated with chorda tympani damage from otitis media. These losses can affect all taste modalities, just a specific taste, or combination of tastes.

Despite these geographical differences, malingered taste loss does not seem to match any of these organic clinical patterns. While not entirely addressed in the literature, clinical experience suggests that malingering taste loss—whether from head trauma or toxic exposure—involves the whole mouth. Such global ageusia almost always is concurrent with complaints of anosmia. While this could represent a misunderstanding since complaints of taste loss usually mean smell dysfunction, on closer questioning the malingering ageusic will usually complain of not only retronasal olfactory components lost but also true taste: salt, sweet, bitter, and sour. In such circumstances, they frequently also complain of a trigeminal component of flavor loss as well.

The widespread neuroanatomic distribution of deficit required to present both smell and taste loss makes an organic etiology unlikely. This should be tempered by the possibility that the patient may have unknowingly suffered true ageusia prior to the event (head trauma, etc.), which was masked by normal olfactory ability. Upon destruction of olfactory function, the ageusia then presents itself.

It is important to reiterate that the complaint of absent taste in the presence of true taste, but the absence of retronasal smell is not malingering taste loss—it just represents the confusion of physiologic synesthesia, whereby retronasal smell is interpreted as taste (Gruss and Hirsch, 2015).

Isolated dysgeusia in the absence of other chemosensory complaints as a manifestation of malingering must be exceedingly rare and thus, has not been reported in the medical literature.

Cacogeusia, where otherwise enjoyed foods have acquired a horrible taste, forcing the sufferer to avoid such foods, is seen in those with severe psychological traumatic events such as PTSD and to a lesser degree as a normal part of a gustatory conditioned hedonic response. Evolutionarily, taste of food is used to protect the organism to enhance survival. If food "tastes" bad it is avoided. Such hedonics for food are developed in utero—the expectant mother who eats more garlic bears a child who also has greater hedonics for garlic-flavored food (Lipchock, Reed, and Mennella, 2011). The offspring of nursing mothers who drink carrot juice are also more likely to feel positive hedonics for the taste of carrots (Lipchock, Reed, and Mennella, 2011). For humans, food neophobia promotes survival through eating foods which are familiar and thus safe and avoidance of toxicity from ingestion of strange or novel foods. Thus, if food tastes unfamiliar, bad, or spoiled it induces disgust and rejection (Herz, 2012). A rat that gets sick but doesn't die after eating poison avoids eating poison with this flavor again. Similarly, after becoming disgusted or sick with ingestion of a food, humans avoid this food, often vehemently—such cacogeusia doesn't represent malingering, but rather a normal response to a past experience whether consciously recalled or not. However, the response often becomes so overwhelming as to cause change in the behavior of the sufferer and family alike—the family forced to make different intensively restrictive meals for the cacogeusic individual—leading to a type of intrafamilial social dominance and control by the sufferer, not unlike what is seen in families with a member suffering from life-threatening asthma, food allergies, or food sensitivity (gluten, etc.). Thus, while not strictly malingering it has a secondary effect on those around them and serves as a focus of control over family and friends.

Because of the potential for dissimulation there is a need for a means of distinguishing true olfactory loss from malingering. At present, physicians often fail to test olfactory ability or test it only in an informal manner with devices and odorants at hand, such as cloves or coffee (Hummel, Sekinger, Wolf, Pauli, and Kobal, 1997).

Standard medical (Bates, 1974) and neurological texts (Haerer, 1992; Parsons, 1983; Fuller, 1993) indicate that assessment of the olfactory nerve, cranial nerve I (CNI), is an essential part of a complete neurological examination. Also, to rule out malingering given the likelihood of olfactory dysfunction among hospitalized patients, particularly those with neurological disorders, olfactory testing should be routine.

Lack of olfactory data may impair diagnostic accuracy. For example, Post's pseudodementia, which does not involve olfactory impairment, is often misdiagnosed as Alzheimer's disease (Post, 1975), which does involve olfactory impairment. In recent experiments, Solomon et al. demonstrated that olfactory testing can aid in distinguishing these disorders (Solomon, Petrie, Hart, Jr., and Brackin, Jr., 1999). Similarly, olfactory deficits are seen in idiopathic Parkinson's disease but not 1-Methyl-4-Phenyl-1,2,3,6-Tetrahydropyridine (MPTP)-induced Parkinson's disease (Doty, Singh, Tetrude, and Langston, 1992), progressive supranuclear palsy (Sajjadian, Doty, Gutnick, Chirurgi, Sivak, and Perl, 1994), or essential tremor (Busenbark, Huber,

Greer, Pahwa, and Koller, 1992). Olfactory deficits are seen in a substantial proportion of those with sinusitis or migraines, but not in those with cluster headaches (Hirsch, 1992b; Loury and Kennedy, 1991; Hirsch and Thakkar, 1995).

Olfactory deficits may be the first manifestation of an underlying disease state. Without olfactory data, B12 deficiency (Estrem and Renner, 1987; Hirsch, 1995a), and olfactory groove meningiomas (Jafek and Hill, 1989), which display olfactory dysfunction early on, may remain undetected until more serious neurological deficits occur. Psychiatric disorders including general anxiety disorder (Hirsch and Trannel, 1996) and sexual dysfunction (Hirsch, 1998d) often present associated with hyposmia or anosmia. Treatment of the chemosensory dysfunction frequently alleviates the psychiatric complaints. Patients may then receive medications, vitamins, food supplements (Hirsch, Dougherty, Aranda, Vanderbilt, and Weclaw, 1996; Davidson, Jalowayski, Murphy, and Jacobs, 1987) or special treatment to correct the underlying pathology, that is polypectomy for nasal polyps (Scott, Cain, and Leonard, 1988) and steroids for allergic rhinitis (Scott, Cain, and Clavet, 1988). Appropriate counseling emphasizes risks to personal safety such as spoiled or over-salted food, gas leaks, and smoke (Chalke and Dewhurst, Jr., 1957; Costanzo and Zasler, 1991).

Simple and easy ways to assess olfaction include the presentation of readily available fragrant substances such as coffee, almond, lemon, tobacco, anise, oil of clove, toothpaste, eucalyptus, vanilla, peppermint, camphor, rosewater, and soap (Bates, 1974; Haerer, 1992; Parsons, 1983; Fuller, 1993). In addition, formalized tests of olfaction are widely available, including the Chicago Smell Test (Hirsch and Gotway, 1993; Hirsch, Gotway, and Harris, 1993), the University of Pennsylvania Smell Identification Test (UPSIT) (Doty, 1995b), the olfactory threshold test of Amoore (Amoore and Ollman, 1983), and the Alcohol Sniff Test (Davidson and Murphy, 1997; Schlotfeld, Geisler, Davidson, and Murphy, 1998; Middleton, Geisler, Davidson, and Murphy, 1998; Freed, Dalve-Endres, Davidson, and Murphy, 1998).

Yet anecdotal evidence and the medical literature suggest that in clinical practice CNI is rarely tested (Fuller, 1993). To determine whether this is true, we reviewed histories and physical examinations of patients at a Chicago teaching hospital.

Charts were inspected of all adult patients admitted between April and September 1988 who met the following criteria: a neurologic diagnosis upon discharge, ability to follow directions and respond verbally, and not intubated, comatose, or admitted to an intensive care unit.

A total of 90 charts were inspected. Internal medicine attending physicians performed 77 histories and physicals, while neurology attending physicians or consultants performed 17 histories, for a total of 94 histories and physical examinations.

Patients' ages averaged 69 years, ranging 24–100 years. They were given a total of 97 neurologic diagnoses, including 30 different neurological conditions with the most frequent being cerebral vascular accident (n=21), Alzheimer's disease (n=14), seizures and convulsions (n=10), and syncope (n=6).

None of the 94 records show that CNI was tested. Four charts (4.2%), however, note "cranial nerves intact" or "neuro exam grossly normal," thereby implying that olfactory testing may have been performed.

Whether any of the 90 patients complained of olfactory dysfunction is unknown. Had they voiced such complaints they possibly would have been tested.

Self-recognition of olfactory deficits, however, is poor. Geriatric patients and those with neurogenitive disorders such as Alzheimer's often are unaware of their olfactory losses (Nordin, Monsch, and Murphy, 1995). Of those with Parkinson's disease, fewer than 15% recognize their olfactory deficits (Doty, Deems, and Stellar, 1988). Younger people also lack insight into such problems. Half of anosmic workers exposed to cadmium (Adams and Crabtree, 1961) and 100% of hyposmic chefs (Hirsch, 1990c) were unaware of any deficits. And, according to an unpublished study by the authors 87.5% of hyposmic or anosmic firefighters were unaware of their deficits. Thus, to limit testing to those who complain of problems would leave many cases of smell loss undetected.

For several reasons the patients whose charts we studied were particularly predisposed to olfactory deficits. First, olfactory ability declines with age (Venstrom and Amoore, 1968; Stevens, Cain, and Weinstein, 1987)—half of persons over 65 years old experience some losses (Doty et al., 1984)—and the average age of our patients in the present study was 69. Second, since they were ill enough to be in a hospital, these patients were probably on medications and many of those most commonly used, including beta-blockers and calcium channel blockers, impair olfactory ability (Ackerman and Kasbekar, 1997; Vital, 1985; Levinsons and Kennedy, 1985). Third, aside from the medications used to treat them, neurologic disorders are often associated with olfactory impairment. The charts in our study indicated diagnoses of stroke (Smith and Seiden, 1991), senile dementia of the Alzheimer's type (Solomon, 1994; Hirsch, 1992d), epilepsy (Eskenazi, Cain, Novelly, and Mattson, 1986), spinal cord injury (Hirsch and Cleveland, 1998), head injury (VanDamme and Freihofer, 1992; Duncan and Seiden 1995), Parkinson's disease (Hawkes, 1995; Pearce, Hawkes, and Daniel, 1995), migraines (Hirsch, 1992e), and multiple sclerosis (Doty, Li, Mannon, and Yousem, 1997), all of which have been described to manifest olfactory deficits.

This study involved only a single teaching hospital where more comprehensive histories and physicals might be performed than ordinarily would be the case at a community hospital, particularly since here one of the authors (ARH) gives every few years Grand Rounds on olfactory dysfunction to the Department of Internal Medicine, calling attention to the problem and the need for olfactory tests.

The statement in examination records noting that "cranial nerves were intact" may simply be an over-generalization based on the other cranial nerves being intact and CNI was not actually tested.

Given the prevalence of olfactory disorders and the ease of testing it (and the substantial evidence that identifying such impairment can enhance accuracy of diagnoses) it seems well worth physicians' time and efforts to test olfaction. Moreover, patients suffering from hyposmia and anosmia can be treated and advised to take precautions to reduce risks related to spoiled food and leaking gas.

Yet, several formal olfactory tests are available for clinical use.

Objectifying chemosensory dysfunction is only possible for reduced or absent smell and taste. Phantoms, unless due to electrical discharge as in insular or uncal seizures, are diagnosed based on history without objective tests to support the diagnosis. If it due to electrical discharges electroencephalogram or electrocortical testing is helpful. Similarly, dysosmia, dysgeusia, palinosmia, palinageusia, cacosmia, and cacogeusia are all historical diagnoses. Fortunately for diagnostic accuracy, most of the time the suspected malingerer will complain of loss of chemosensory function rather than, or coexistent with, these other chemosensory abnormalities. Testing has four goals: (1) to objectify the presence of true abnormality, (2) to characterize the abnormality, (3) to quantify the abnormality, and (4) to identify probable malingering. The latter is diagnosed based on individual test results as well as incongruities between test results. The advantage of performing multiple chemosensory tests is that it allows for detection of discrepancies between tests which are highly unusual and may suggest a nonphysiologic basis for the patient's problems. In particular, if tests of threshold such as the SNAP Phenylethyl Alcohol Threshold Test, the Butanol Sniffin' Sticks Threshold Test, or the Olfactometer OLFACT-RL™ Olfactory Threshold to n-Butanol suggest anosmia, but the identification tests such as the University of Pennsylvania Smell Identification Test (UPSIT), the Olfactometer OLFACT-RL™ Olfactory Identification Test, or the Sniffin' Sticks Identification Test indicate normal identification. It is hard to understand how threshold can be totally absent but yet identification is normal since in order to identify the smell one must first detect the smell. Within tests, criteria for diagnosing malingering is based on probability of correct responses with a forced-choice paradigm. When an odor is presented, one of four answers must be chosen. In such a forced-choice condition random responses would generate 25% correct answers and to obtain 0% correct answers it, would require an effort to correctly miss all the responses. In a parallel fashion, if three choices are presented as with the Sniffin' Sticks discrimination tests, an anosmic random response would produce 33% correct answers. For the malingerer to miss all responses would require correctly determining the pen with the odor and then intentionally selecting the wrong aroma. An anosmic would randomly guess correctly 33% of the time. The odds for a true anosmic to miss all the responses would be 1:1296. In a two-choice study, as with SNAP Phyenylethyl Alcohol Threshold test, an anosmic response will generate 50% correct answers. In the absence of malingering, the probability of all incorrect on guess alone (as would occur with a true anosmic) would be 1/1032. Such results would be highly improbable unless based on intentionally choosing the incorrect response at each trial. Such statistical indications of malingering are seen with the Olfactometer OLFACT-RL™ Olfactory Threshold and Identification, the Sniffin' Sticks, the SNAP Phenylethyl Alcohol Threshold Test, and the University of Pennsylvania Smell Identification Test.

The Chicago Smell Test consists of three forced-choice questions pertaining to odor detection and three open-ended questions pertaining to identification of the three odorants. This test was standardized for a normal population of the University of Illinois undergraduate students (Hirsch and Cain, 1992) and for neurology patients with no chemosensory disorders (Hirsch and Gotway, 1993); no guidelines were established for detecting malingering in this test.

Amoore's olfactory threshold tests (Amoore, 1988) were standardized among normal populations, but again, no guidelines have been established with regard to malingering. Amoore describes two criteria, however, for identifying malingerers. First, they consistently misidentify odors compared to blanks on all the forced-choice tests rather than randomly responding correctly as individuals with real deficits would do. Second, they show failure to detect odorants both at the olfactory threshold and at the trigeminal threshold. A drawback of this second criterion is that some hyposmics and anosmics may also have trigeminal impairment (Hummel et al., 1996).

Kobal and Hummel's (Kobal and Hummel, 1991) olfactory evoked responses assess olfactory dysfunction but their technique does not address malingering either.

A common method of formally measuring olfactory ability is the University of Pennsylvania Smell Identification Test (UPSIT) (Doty, 1995b), a series of 40 scratch-and-sniff forced-choice odor identification questions. This is the only test of olfaction that provides specific guidelines with published scores purporting to delineate the categories of true deficits and malingering.

Some authors have suggested that malingerers are typically desperate or transient individuals (Cunnien, 1988; Hall and Pritchard, 1996) but other research shows that overachievers and better-educated people are both more frequent and more successful liars (Grinder, 1961; Mischel and Gilligan, 1964). One recent study indicates that 95% of college students are "willing to lie" (Rowatt, Cunningham, and Druen, 1998).

It seems possible that the present UPSIT guidelines detected only the least competent malingerers. Hirsch and Gruss conducted an experiment to determine whether highly educated subjects could successfully dissimulate olfactory dysfunction in the UPSIT (Hirsch and Gruss, 1998b). The subject were highly educated, and could lie with little moral upheaval, were future lawyers—law students.

To determine whether such highly educated volunteers could successfully dissimulate smell loss, the UPSIT was administered twice to 62 second and third year law students while instructing them to feign smell loss to the best of their ability during the first test while to perform honestly in the second. The tests were then scored according to the published UPSIT guidelines, which purport to discriminate between scores of malingerers and those of true hyposmics. Seventeen (50%) of the 34 normosmic students feigning smell loss successfully malingered and scored as having true deficits. Seventeen (61%) of the 28 hyposmic students feigning greater deficits successfully exaggerated their losses and scored within the category of true smell loss rather than as probable malingerers. For various reasons, highly educated persons may be better able to dissimulate than those with less formal schooling. Where malingering seems a possibility clinicians need such strategies as repeat procedures, parallel tests, and psychological evaluation to differentiate olfactory malingering from true olfactory deficits.

When feigning olfactory loss, 34 normosmic law students had a mean score of 8.3 with a range from 0 to 32. This mean score is not classified as malingering under current guidelines. On the basis of the published guidelines, out of 40 possible correct, scores of five and below indicate malingering. Seventeen (50%) of the 34 normosmic subjects feigning loss fell into this category and 17 (50%) had scores falling into the category of true smell loss.

Thus, to accurately identify 95% of these normosmic malingerers the UPSIT guidelines would have to be raised from the present level of five correct to 24 correct.

To accurately identify 95% of these malingering but truly hyposmic law students who exaggerated their true olfactory losses the UPSIT guidelines for malingering would have to be reset from the present level of five or less to 22 or less.

Based on this, malingerers with some true olfactory loss are more apt to escape detection than malingerers with normal olfaction (61% successful compared to 50%). This extends Trimble's assertion that the more common form of malingering is to exaggerate a loss rather than to invent one (Trimble, 1986) and to exaggerate a loss is more likely to indicate a successful malingerer.

Law students may not be representative of individuals seeking medical advice for a complaint of smell loss. They are familiar with multiple-choice testing and consequently could devise cheating strategies on such tests. Also, they undoubtedly have grasped the concept of randomness and understand that randomly correct and incorrect answers make more successful malingering than wholly incorrect ones do. We might speculate that law students could defeat most existing tests.

Since no surefire technique presently exists for detecting all who malinger in cognitive or sensory tests, we suggest that clinicians diagnosing chemosensory disorders of a suspect nature follow certain strategies to help ensure accurate diagnosis of true illness and of malingering even among the well-educated: (1) use a battery of investigative modalities, (2) repeat tests, (3) perform parallel tests, and (4) perform careful psychological tests in difficult cases.

An intelligent or well-coached malingerer may be able to overcome such internal scales of the UPSIT which emphasizes the importance of other tests to validate the diagnosis.

A further objective test in helping to diagnose malingering is the Sniff Magnitude Test. In a normosmic individual, under normal conditions, odor-induced apnea occurs, wherein when presented with an odor there is a reflex which inhibits inhalation to a greater degree when the odor is strong. The Sniff Magnitude Test is conducted whereby the sniff magnitude is determined by the area of the sniff (duration times amplitude) when the patient is presented with odors of different intensities or a blank, no-odor condition. This can be performed while the patient is awake, unattended, or even asleep. Under normal conditions, strong odors inhibit sniffing. Under pathologic states where the odors are not being processed there is no or partial inhibition of sniff magnitude. The advantage of this study is it can be performed when the subject is awake or asleep and is particularly hard to malinger since odors are presented at different levels of intensity. This makes difficult if not impossible for a malingerer to adjust their sniff threshold accordingly. This test is particularly helpful in detection of malingering since it does not even require a subjective response from the potential malingerer.

However, in the realm of taste such tests for malingering are not nearly as well-developed as for those assessing smell, and reliance on objective characterization of different levels of taste still requires subjective responses. The only test that does not is the Electrogustometer; however, this still requires the subject to identify if they taste a metallic taste or feel electrical shock as different levels of electricity are applied to the tongue. While this has been described for use in the detection of taste malingering (Hirsch and Mackenzie, Jr., 1993), the tests for olfactory malingering are far better developed in this regard.

However, in those with concurrent cognitive and chemosensory complaints standard cognitive malingering tests may be helpful. These include the Test of Memory Malingering (TOMM) (Tombaugh, 1996), the Validity Indicator Profile (VIP) (Frederick, 2003), the Paulhus Deception Scale (PDS) (Paulhus, 1998), the Minnesota Multiphasic Personality Inventory-2 (MMPI-2) (Butcher, Dahlstrom, Graham, Tellegen, and Kreammer, 1989), and the Millon Clinical Multiaxial Inventory-III (MCMI-III) (Millon, 1987). By inference, if the patient shows malingering on these tests, it may be assumed that the patient is malingering in their chemosensory complaints as well. However, this assumption may not be true as it is distinctly possible that the malingerer may have malingered in one area (for instance, in cognitive problems) yet is truthful in chemosensory problems, or vice versa. Further investigation into the pervasiveness of cross-modal malingering is warranted.

Another technique in helping to determine malingering is through having a myriad of different testing methods performed repeatedly by different physicians, all of which should show patterns consistent across time suggesting a normal, pathological, or a malingering pattern. Disparate response patterns may indicate malingering or other factors including level of cooperation, changes in condition, or even attitude of the examiner.

Furthermore, testing the patient before and after settlement occurs or compensation is provided may indicate change in the test patterns, which may be definitive for the diagnosis of malingering. The clinical practicality of this latter method at this time would render such an approach somewhat limited.

Another mechanism of testing for olfactory malingering would be through testing of trigeminal sensation. Traditionally the trigeminal nerve, which mediates irritation, was considered to be independent of olfaction. However, a physiologic synesthesia occurs on inhalation of irritating substances, with olfaction and irritation acting additionally or synergistically, combining into the perception of an aroma. Such combinations include the aroma of mint or citrus. However, virtually any odor, if in a high enough concentration, will induce trigeminal stimulation; since the trigeminal nerve is anatomically separate from cranial nerve I, it has long been thought that trigeminal loss would not occur when olfactory loss is present. Thus, it has been suggested that a telltale differentiating feature for malingering was the complaint of inability to detect trigeminally stimulating chemicals (i.e., ammonia, Vicks, menthol), which would demonstrate the subject's denial of detection of these irritating items despite showing a behavioral response to the trigeminal irritant—apnea, wrinkling up one's nose, closing the eyes, etc. However, with severe olfactory loss from tricholorethylene exposure or head trauma, trigeminal loss is sometimes seen possibly due to more diffuse damage in the brain itself (Sumner, 1964; Parma et al., 2012). Thus, a complaint of trigeminal loss concurrent with olfactory loss as an indicator of malingering cannot be relied upon.

Another aspect to consider within the framework of malingering is that of the effect of an individual's personal experience with chemosensory problems. If a patient in the past did have smell loss for whatever reason, whether it be head trauma or upper respiratory infection, the malingerer is already knowledgeable of what experiences such a loss entails, and thus, is more likely to believably malinger this problem. Furthermore, if there is someone in their family who has experienced this loss the malingerer may have learned the manner in which such a loss is displayed.

What is particularly difficult to delineate is the exaggerating malingerer who actively possesses true pathology. If he or she has some pathology the malingerer can exaggerate this and making it very difficult to detect especially if the deficit is severe and they are malingering an even more severe deficit.

Also, the potential of an individual having an eggshell skull must be considered. In this situation an individual already has a mild deficit, for instance due to smoking, alcohol, being an older male, diabetic, or taking a plethora of medications which can cause smell loss (Doty and Hastings, 2001) (see list "Drugs which Interfere with the Smell System" and "Pathologic Conditions" in Section 11.1). All of these conditions reduce olfactory reserve causing a clinical loss, which through a double crush phenomenon upon additional trauma, toxin, virus, or other insult becomes manifest. In these situations even mild trauma may be enough to cause a severe smell or taste loss. In this case, because the preexisting underlying disease may be known to induce smell loss, the presence of smell loss attributable to the new traumatic or toxic event would be hard to delineate as the causative agent. In the absence of baseline pre-event chemosensory testing one is forced to rely on the history combined with tests of malingering.

Another area of consideration regarding chemosensory malingering is the lack of sympathy for smell loss. The vast majority will describe that they would rather lose their sense of smell and taste than their hearing or vision; therefore, a jury would be inclined to provide less monetary reward than could be derived for the loss of other senses. Thus, on face value, taste and smell are less logical realms for the malingerer to choose—again suggesting that chemosensory malingering would be relatively rare.

Malingering chemosensory dysfunction other than loss, such as odor-induced headaches or olfactory hallucinations, are subjective experiences based on a history, as is true with headaches or pain in general, and hallucinations. Thus, history is necessary for this diagnosis and in the absence of complaints of smell loss and taste deficiency chemosensory tests will often be unrevealing.

Concurrent pathological conditions often occur with malingering (such as traumatic brain injury) and may also cause smell and taste loss. In these cases it is best to defer to the history since testing may demonstrate abnormalities but their origin may be very hard to define indeed.

Given the above, there exists some clinical pearls which may be helpful in differentiating malingering from true chemosensory problems. Indication of potential malingering: (1) Is the source for secondary gain obvious (i.e., ongoing litigation)? (2) Is the history inconsistent from examiner to examiner? (3) Are there complaints of total loss of smell and taste without olfactory windows (occasional, brief whiff of smell) or without first taste phenomena (first bite of food as flavorful, then fades away)? And (4), is there absence of compensating changes in eating pattern (lack of flavor in foods which is compensated by an increased salt and increased spices)?

Thus, a detailed history, physical examination, and chemosensory testing are worthwhile to help detect and treat the chemosensory malingerer.

LIST OF ABBREVIATIONS

AD Auris Dextra/right ear
AST Alcohol Sniff Test
AU Auris Utraque/both ears
BSIT Brief Smell Identification Test
CN Cranial nerve
CT Computed Tomography
ENT Ear, Nose, Throat
F Female
L Left
M Male

MRA	Magnetic Resonance Angiogram
MRI	Magnetic Resonance Imaging
OD	Oculus Dexter/right eye
OS	Oculus Sinister/left eye
Prop	Propylthiouracil
PSIT	Pocket Smell Identification Test
PST	Pocket Smell Test
QSIT	Quick Smell Identification Test
R	Right
RSI	Retronasal Smell Index
UPSIT	University of Pennsylvania Smell Identification Test
URI	upper respiratory infection

REFERENCES

Acharya, V., J. Acharya, and H. Luders. 1996. Olfactory epileptic auras. *Neurology* 46:A446.

Ackerman, B.H., and N. Kasbekar. 1997. Disturbances of taste and smell induced by drugs. *Pharmacotherapy* 17:482–496.

Ackerman, D. 1990. *A Natural History of the Senses*, 5. New York: Random House.

Adams, R.D., and M. Victor. 1989. *Principles of Neurology*, 441. New York: McGraw-Hill, Inc.

Adams, R.G., and N. Crabtree. 1961. Anosmia in alkaline battery workers. *British Journal of Industrial Medicine* 18:216–221.

Aiello, S.R., and A.R. Hirsch. 2013. Phantosmia as a meteorological forecaster. *International Journal of Biometeorology* doi: 10.1007/x00484-013-0639-x.

American Psychiatric Association. 1987. *Diagnostic and Statistical Manual of Mental Disorders III-R*, 427–251. Washington, DC: American Psychiatric Association.

Amoore, J., and B. Ollman. 1983. Practical test kits for quantitatively evaluating the sense of smell. *Rhinology* 21:49–54.

Amoore, J.E. 1986. Effects of chemical exposure on olfaction in humans. In *Toxicology of the Nasal Passages*, ed. C.S. Barrow, 155–190. Washington, DC: Hemisphere Publishing.

Amoore, J.E. 1988. Proposal for a unifying scale to express olfactory thresholds and odor levels: The decismel scale. *Proceeding of the APCA 81st Annual Meeting*.

Apter, A.J., A.E. Mott, W.S. Cain, J.D. Spiro, and M.C. Barwick. 1992. Olfactory loss and allergic rhinitis. *Journal of Allergy and Clinical Immunology* 90:670–680.

Bagla, R., B. Klasky, and R.L. Doty. 1997. Influence of stimulus duration on a regional measure of NaCl taste sensitivity. *Chemical Senses* 22:171–175.

Bartoshuk, L.M. 1978. The psychophysics of taste. *Journal of Clinical Nutrition* 31:1068–1077.

Bartus, R.T., R.L. Dean, III, B. Beer, and A.S. Lippa. 1982. The cholinergic hypothesis of geriatric memory dysfunction. *Science* 217:408–417.

Bates, B. 1974. *Guide to Physical Examination*, 272. Philadelphia: JB Lippincott.

Beauchamp, Jr., R.O., J.S. Bus, J.A. Popp, C.J. Boreiko, and D.A. Andjelkovich. 1984. A critical review of the literature on hydrogen sulfide toxicity. *Critical Reviews in Toxicology* 13:1:25–97.

Beck, A.T., and A. Beamesderfer. 1974. Assessment of depression: The depression inventory. In *Psychological Measurements in Psychopharmacology: Modern Problems in Psychopharmacology*, ed. P. Pinchot, 151–169. Basel, Switzerland: Karger.

Benedetti, F., H.S. Mayberg, T.D. Waer, C.S. Stoller, and J.K. Zubieta. 2005. Neurobiological mechanisms of the placebo effect. *Journal of Neuroscience* 25:10390–10402.

Berman, J.L. 1985. Dysosmia, dysgeusia, and diltiazem. *Annals of Internal Medicine* 102:717.

Berrios, G.E., and P. Brook. 1984. Visual hallucinations and sensory delusions in the elderly. *British Journal of Psychiatry* 144:662–664.

Body, S.C. 1986. A taste of allicin? *Anaesthesia and Intensive Care* 14:94.

Bors, E. 1951. Phantom limbs of patients with spinal cord injury. *AMA Archives of NeurPsych* 66:5:610–631.

Both, S., E. Laan, and W.W. Schultz. 2010. Disorders in sexual desire and sexual arousal in women, a 2010 state of the art. *Journal of Psychosomatic Obstetrics & Gynecology*, 31:4:207–218.

Brodal, A. 1969. *Neurological Anatomy in Relation to Clinical Medicine, Ed. 3, Vol. 10*, 53. New York: Oxford University Press.

Bruyn, G.W. 1986. Glossopharyngeal neuralgia. In *Handbook of Clinical Neurology. Headache*, ed. R.F. Clifford, 4:48:459–473. New York: Elsevier.

Busenbark, K.L., S.I. Huber, G. Greer, R. Pahwa, and W.C. Koller. 1992. Olfactory function in essential tremor. *Neurology* 42:1631–1632.

Butcher, J.N., W.G. Dahlstrom, J.R. Graham, A.M. Tellegen, and B. Kreammer. 1989. *The Minnesota Multiphasic Personality Inventory-2 (MMPI-2) Manual for Administration and Scoring*. Minneapolis: University of Minneapolis Press.

Carlson, E.B., and R. Rosser-Hogan. 1994. Cross-cultural response to trauma: A study of traumatic experiences and posttraumatic symptoms in Cambodian refugees. *Journal of Trauma and Stress* 7:1:43–58.

Carmichael, K.A., A.S. Jennings, and R.L. Doty. 1984. Reversible anosmia after pituitary irradiation. *Annals of Internal Medicine* 100:532–533.

Chabwine, J.N., M.V. Tschirren, A. Zekeridou, B.N. Landis, and T. Kuntzer. 2014. Sweet taste loss in myasthenia gravis: More than a coincidence? *Orphanet Journal of Rare Diseases* 9:50.

Chalke, H.D., and J.R. Dewhurst. 1957. Accidental coal-gas poisoning. *British Medical Journal* 2:915–917.

Chen, D., and P. Dolton. 2005. The effect of emotion and personality on olfactory perception. *Chemical Senses* 30:345–351.

Chuah, M.I., and B.S. Hui. 1986. Effect of amitriptyline on laminar differentiation of neonatal rat olfactory bulb. *Neuroscience Letter* 70:28–33.

Cocchiarella, L., and G.B.J. Anderson. 2001. *Guides to the Evaluation of Permanent Impairment, 5th ed.* Chicago: American Medical Association.

Combarros, O., J. Pascual, C. de Pablos, F. Ortega, and J. Berciano. 1996. Taste loss as an initial symptom of Guillain-Barré syndrome. *Neurology* 47:1640–1645.

Cooper, A.F., and A.R. Curry. 1976. Pathology of deafness in the paranoid and affective psychoses of later life. *Journal of Psychosometric Research* 20:97–105.

Costanzo, R.M., and D.P. Becker. 1986. Smell and taste disorders in head injury and neurosurgery patients. In *Clinical Measurements of Taste and Smell*, 565–578, eds. H.L. Meiselman and R.S. Rivlin. New York: MacMilan Co.

Costanzo, R.M., and N.D. Zasler. 1991 Head trauma. In *Smell and Taste in Health and Disease*, ed. T.V. Getchell, 711–730. New York: Raven.

Croy, I., S. Nordin, and T. Hummel. 2014. Olfactory disorders and quality of life: An updated review. *Chemical Senses* 39:185–194.

Cunnien, A.J. 1988. Psychiatric and medical syndromes associated with deception. In *Clinical Assessment of Malingering and Deception*, ed. R. Rogers, 13–33. New York: Guilford Press.

Davidson, T.M., A. Jalowayski, C. Murphy, and R.J. Jacobs. 1987. Evaluation and treatment of smell dysfunction. *Western Journal of Medicine* 146:434–438.

Davidson, T.M., and C. Murphy. 1997. Rapid clinical evaluation of anosmia: The alcohol sniff test. *Archives of Otolaryngology Head and Neck Surgery* 123:591–594.

Davis, J.M. and A.H. Glassman. 1989. Antidepressant drugs. In *Comprehensive Textbook of Psychiatry, Vol. 2, 5th Edition*, eds. H.I. Kaplan and B.J. Sadock, 1643–1644. Baltimore: Williams & Wilkins.

Davis, R.G., and R.M. Pangborn. 1985. Odor pleasantness judgments compared among samples from 20 nations using microfragrances. *Chemical Senses* 10:413.

DeCook, C.A., and A.R. Hirsch. 2000. Anosmia due to inhalational zinc: A case report. *Chemical Senses* 25:5:659.

Deems, D.A., R.L. Doty, G. Settle et al. 1991. Smell and taste disorders: A study of 750 patients from the University of Pennsylvania Smell and Taste Center. *Archives of Otolaryngology—Head and Neck Surgery* 117:519–528.

Demaitre, L. 2004. Air, miasma and contagion – epidemics in antiquity and the Middle Ages. *Bulletin of the History of Medicine* 782/2:466–468.

Diamond, S. 1965. Mask of depression. *Clinical Medicine* 72:1620.

Doty, R., P. Reyes, and T. Gregor. 1987. Presence of both odor identification and detection deficits in Alzheimer's disease. *Brain Research Bulletin* 18:598.

Doty, R., and M. Ferguson-Segall. 1987. Odor detection performance of rats following d-amphetamine treatment: A signal detection analysis. *Psychopharmacology* 93:87–93.

Doty, R.L. 1995a. Clinical studies of olfaction. Olfactory Bioresponses in Man [Abstract] *Chemical Senses* 481.

Doty, R.L. 1995b. *Smell Identification Test Administration Manual.* Haddon Heights: Sensonics.

Doty, R.L. 1997. Studies of human olfaction from the University of Pennsylvania Smell and Taste Center. *Chemical Senses* 22:565–586.

Doty, R.L. W.E. Brugger, P.C. Jurs et al. 1978. Intranasal trigeminal stimulation from odorous volatiles: Psychometric responses from anosmic and normal humans. *Physiologic Behavior* 20:2:175–185.

Doty, R.L., P. Shaman, and M. Dann. 1984. Development of the University of Pennsylvania Smell Identification Test: A standardized microencapsulated test of olfactory function. *Physiology & Behavior* 32:489–502.

Doty, R.L., T. Gregor, and C. Monroe. 1986. Quantitative assessment of olfactory function in an industrial setting. *Journal of Occupational Medicine* 28:6:457–460.

Doty, R.L., D.P. Perl, J.C. Steele et al. 1991. Odor identification deficit of the Parkinsonism-dementia complete of Guam: Equivalence to that of Alzheimer's and idiopathic Parkinson's disease. *Neurology* 41:1:77–80.

Doty, R.L., A. Singh, J. Tetrude, and J.W. Langston. 1992a. Lack of olfactory dysfunction in MPTP-induced parkinsonism. *Annals of Neurology* 32:97–100.

Doty, R.L., M.B. Stern, C. Pfeiffer, S.M. Gollomp, and H.I. Hurtig. 1992b. Bilateral olfactory dysfunction in early stage treated and untreated idiopathic Parkinson's disease. *Journal of Neurology, Neurosurgery, and Psychiatry* 55:138–142.

Doty, R.L., and L. Hastings. 2001. Neurotoxic exposure and olfactory impairment. *Clinical Occupational and Environmental Medicine* 1:547–575.

Doty, R.L., C. Li, L. Mannon, and D.G. Yousem. 1997. Olfactory dysfunction in multiple sclerosis. *New England Journal of Medicine* 336:1918–1919.

Doty, R.L., D.A. Deems, and S. Stellar. 1988. Olfactory dysfunction in Parkinsonism: A general deficit unrelated to neurologic signs, disease stage, or disease duration. *Neurology* 38:1237–1244.

Doty, R.L., M.G. Newhouse, and J.D. Azzaslina. 1985. Internal consistency and short-term test-retest reliability of the University of Pennsylvania Smell Identification Test. *Chemical Senses* 10:297–300.

Doty, R.L., P. Shaman, S.L. Applebaum et al. 1984. Smell identification ability: Changes with age. *Science* 226:1441–1443.

Doty, R.L., S. Applebaum, H. Zusho, and R.G. Settle. 1985. Sex differences in odor identification ability: A cross-cultural analysis. *Neuropsychologia* 23:5:667–672.

Doty, R.L., S.M. Bromley, P.J. Moberg, and T. Hummel. 1997. Laterality in human nasal chemoreception. In *Cerebral in Sensory and Perceptual Processing*, ed. S. Christman, 492–542. Amsterdam (the Netherlands): Elsiever.

Drayton, M. 2009. The Minnesota multiphasic personality inventory-2 (MMPI-2). *Occupational Medicine* 59:135–136.

Duffy, V.B., and A.M. Ferris. 1989. Nutritional management of patients with chemosensory disturbances. *Ear, Nose and Throat Journal* 68:395–397.

Duncan, R.B., and M. Briggs. 1963. Treatment of uncomplicated anosmia by vitamin A. *Archives of Otolaryngology* 75:36–43.

Duncan, H.J., and A.M. Seiden. 1995 Long-term follow-up of olfactory loss secondary to head trauma and upper respiratory tract infection. *Archives of Otolaryngology Head Neck Surgery* 121:1183–1187.

Eccles, R. 1978. The central rhythm of the nasal cycle. *Acta Otolaryngol* 86:464–468.

Erikssen, J., E. Seegaard, and K. Naess. 1975. Side-effect of thiocarbamides. *Lancet* 1:231–232.

Eskenazi, B., W.S. Cain, R.A. Novelly, and R. Mattson. 1986. Odor perception in temporal lobe epilepsy patients with and without temporal lobectomy. *Neuropsychology* 24:553–562.

Estrem, S.A., and G. Renner. 1987. Disorders of smell and taste. *Otolaryngologic Clinics of North America* 20:1:133–147.

Farbman, A.I., F. Gonzales, and M.I. Chuah. 1988. The effect of amitriptyline on growth of olfactory and cerebral neurons in vitro. *Brain Research* 457:281–286.

Fawcett, R.S., S. Linford, and D.L. Stulberg. 2004. Nail abnormalities: Clues to systemic disease. *American Family Physician* 69:6:1417–1424.

Frederick, R.I. 1997. *Validity Indicator Profile manual*. Minnetonka: NCS Assessments.

Freed, C.L., A.M. Dalve-Endres, T.M. Davidson, and C. Murphy. 1998. Rapid screening of olfactory function in Down's syndrome. *Chemical Senses* 23:610.

Freud, S. 1886. *Report* on *my studies* in *Paris* and *Berlin*. *Extracts* from the *Fliess Papers. Standard Edition 1892–99*:1:173–280. London: Hogarth.

Freud, S. 1908. Bemerkungen uber einen fall von zangs neurosis. *Ges. Schr.* VIII:350.

Friedman, A.F., J.T. Webb, and R. Kewak. 1989. *Psychological assessment with MMPI.* Hillsdale: Lawrence Earlbaum Associates.

Frye, R.E. 2003. Nasal patency and the aerodynamics of nasal airflow: Measurement by rhinomanometry and acoustic rhinometry, and the influence of pharmacological agents. In *Handbook of olfaction and gustation, second ed., revised and expanded*, ed. R.L. Doty, 439–459. New York: Marcel Dekker, Inc.

Frye, R.E., B.S. Schwartz, and R.L. Doty. 1990. Dose-related effects of cigarette smoking on olfactory function. *JAMA* 263:9:1233–1236.

Fujiwara, E., M.L. Schwartz, F. Gao, S.E. Black, and B. Levine. 2008. Ventral frontal cortex functions and quantified MRI in traumatic brain injury. *Neuropsychologia* 46:2:461–474.

Fuller, G. 1993. *Neurological Examination Made Easy*, 47. Edinburgh: Churchill Livingstone.

Furuta, S., K. Nishimoto, M. Egawa, M. Ohyama, and H. Moriyama. 1994. Olfactory dysfunction in patients with Minamata disease. *American Journal of Rhinology* 8:259–263. 1–18.

Gates, P., and T. Kraemer. 2008. In *Textbook of Clinical Neurology, 3rd ed.*, ed. C. Goetz. Milton, Australia: Blackwell Publishing Asia.

Gent, J.F., and D.H. McBurney. 1978. Time course of gustatory adaptation. *Perception & Psychophysics* 23:2:171–175.

Goetzl, F.R., and F. Stone. 1948. The influence of amphetamine sulfate upon olfactory acuity and appetite. *Gastroenterology* 10:708–713.

Gondivkar, S.M., A. Indurkar, S. Degwekar, and R. Bhowate. 2009. Evaluation of gustatory function in patients with diabetes mellitus type 2. *Oral Surgery, Oral Medicine, Oral Pathology, Oral Radiology, and Endodontics* 108:6:876–880.

Goodspeed, R.B., J.F. Gent, and F.A. Catalanotto. 1987. Chemosensory dysfunction. Clinical evaluation results of a taste and smell clinic. *Postgraduate Medicine* 81:251–257, 260.

Grinder, R. 1961. New techniques for research in children's temptation behavior. *Child Development* 32:679–688.

Grossman, S. 1953. Loss of taste and smell due to propylthiouracil therapy. *New York State Journal of Medicine* 53:1236.

Gruss, J.J., and A.R. Hirsch. 2015. Retronasal olfaction. In *Nutrition and Sensation*, ed. A.R. Hirsch, 65–79. Boca Raton: CRC Press.

Guensberger, E., and J. Fleischer. 1974. Depresia a poruchy vnimania. Klinicke sdeleni. *Ceskoslovenska Psychiatrie* 70:369.

Haberly, L.B., and J.L. Price. 1978. Association and commissural fiber systems of the olfactory cortex of the rat. *Journal of Comparative Neurology* 178:4:711–740.

Haerer, A.F. 1992. *DeJong's the neurologic examination, 5th ed.*, 89. Philadelphia: J.B. Lippincott.

Halasz, N., and G.M. Shepherd. 1983. Neurochemistry of the vertebrate olfactory bulb. *Neuroscience* 10:579–619.

Hales, R., and S. Yudofsky. 1987. *Textbook of Neuropsychiatry*, 128. Washington, DC; American Psychiatric Press, Inc.

Hall, J.V., and D.A. Pritchard. 1996. *Detecting Malingering and Deception: Forensic Distortion Analysis*, 83. Delray Beach: St. Lucie Press.

Hallman, B.I., and J.W. Hurts. 1953. Loss of taste as toxic effect of methimazole (Tapazole) therapy: Report of three cases. *Journal of the American Medical Association* 152:322.

Hathaway, S.R., and J.C. McKinley. 1989. *Minnesota Multiphasic Personality Inventory-2*. St. Paul: Regents of the University of Minnesota.

Hawkes, C. 2006. Olfaction in neurodegenerative disorder. In *Taste and Smell: An Update*, eds. T. Hummel and A. Welge-Lussen, 133–151. Basel: S. Karger AG.

Hawkes, C.H., A. Fogo, and M. Shah. 2005. Smell identification declines from age 36 years and mainly affects pleasant odours. *Mov. Disorders* 20:10:160.

Hawkes, C.M. 1995. Diagnosis and treatment of Parkinson's disease: Anosmia is a common finding. *British Medical Journal* 310:447–452.

Healton, E.B., D.G. Savage, J.C. Brust, T.J. Garrett, and J. Lindebaum. 1991. Neurologic aspects of cobalamin deficiency. *Medicine* 70:4:229–245.

Henderson, J. 1986. Psychic trauma claims in civil and administrative law. (Panel presentation). Philadelphia: American Academy of Psychiatry and the Law.

Henkin, R.I. 1971. Disorders of taste and smell. *JAMA* 218:13:1946.

Henkin, R.I., P.J. Schecter, W.T. Friedewald, D.L. Demets, and M. Raff. 1976. A double-blind study of the effects of zinc sulfate on taste and smell dysfunction. *American Journal of Medical Science* 272:285–299.

Henkin, R.I., R.L. Aamodt, A.K. Babcock, R.P. Agarwal, and A.R. Shatzman. 1981. Treatment of abnormal chemoreception in human taste and smell. In *Perceptions of Behavioral Chemicals*, 229–253, ed. D.M. Norris. New York: Elsevier.

Herz, R. 2012. *That's Disgusting: Unraveling the Mysteries of Repulsion*, 6–8. New York: W.W. Norton & Company.

Hill, L. 1995. *Psychotherapeutic Intervention in Schizophrenia*. Chicago: The University of Chicago Press.

Hirsch, A.R. 1990a. The nose knows. *Chicago Medicine* 9:17–31.

Hirsch, A.R. 1990b. Smell and taste: How the culinary experts compare to the rest of us. *Food Technology* 44:96–102.
Hirsch, A.R. 1990c. Open label of phosphatidylcholine for olfactory and gustatory problems. *Chemical Senses* 15:5:591–592.
Hirsch, A.R. 1990d. Open label trial of phosphatidylcholine for olfactory and gustatory problems. *Chemical Senses* 15:5:591–592.
Hirsch, A.R. 1992a. Scentsation, olfactory demographic and abnormalities. *International Journal of Aromatherapy* 4:1:16–17.
Hirsch, A.R. 1992b. Demography of olfaction. *The Proceedings of the Institute of Medicine of Chicago Journal* 45:6.
Hirsch, A.R. 1992c. Nostalgia: Neuropsychiatric understanding. *Advances in Consumer Research* 19:390–395.
Hirsch, A.R. 1992d. Olfactory dysfunction as a symptom in various conditions. *Journal of Neurologic Orthopaedic Medicine and Surgery* 13:298–302.
Hirsch, A.R. 1992e. Olfaction in migraineurs. *Headache* 32:5:233–236.
Hirsch, A.R. 1995a. Denham Springs, Louisiana: Neurotoxicity as a result of ambient chemicals: Denham Springs, LA. *International Congress on Hazardous Waste: Impact on Human and Ecological Health.* [Abstract Book] U.S. Department of Health and Human Services. Atlanta, GA: Public Health Agency for Toxic Substances and Disease Registry, 229.
Hirsch, A.R. 1995b. Chronic neurotoxicity as a result of landfill exposure in Port Orchard, Washington. [Abstract]. *International Congress on Hazardous Waste: Impact on Human and Ecological Health.* U.S. Department of Health and Human Services. Atlanta, GA: Public Health Agency for Toxic Substances and Disease Registry, p. 126.
Hirsch, A.R. 1995c. Chronic neurotoxicity of acute chlorine gas exposure. [Abstract] The 13th International Neurotoxicology Conference, Developmental and Neurotoxicity of Endocrine Disrupters Proceedings, 13.
Hirsch, A.R. 1995d. Subjective hyposmia. *Journal of Neurology, Orthopaedics and Medicine and Surgery* 16:157–161.
Hirsch, A.R. 1996. Chronic neurotoxicity of acute hydrogen sulfide exposure without loss of consciousness. [Abstract]. *American College of Occupational and Environmental Medicine*, 4.
Hirsch, A.R. 1997a. Pyrethoid induced neurologic dysfunction in flight attendants. [Abstract]. Fifteenth International Neurotoxicology Conference, Little Rock, AR, 74, 75. 1–14
Hirsch, A.R. 1997b. Neurotoxicity in dialysis tubing assembly line workers. [Abstract]. Fifteenth International Neurotoxicology Conference, Little Rock, AR. Abstract Book, 73:74.
Hirsch, A.R. 1998a. Neurotoxic effects of chlordane/heptachlor termiticide sprayed in an apartment complex. [Abstract Book] *Sixteenth International Neurotoxicology* 64.
Hirsch, A.R. 1998b. Scent and sexual arousal. *Medical Aspects of Human Sexuality* 1:3:9–12.
Hirsch, A.R. 1998c. *Scentsational Sex.* Boston: Element Books.
Hirsch, A.R. 1998d. Concurrence of chemosensory and sexual dysfunction. *Biologic Psychiatry* 43:52S.
Hirsch, A.R. 2002a. Hydrogen sulfide exposure without loss of consciousness: Chronic effects in four cases. *Toxicology and Industrial Health* 18:2:51–61.
Hirsch, A.R. 2002b. Neuropsychiatric effects of exposure to pyrethroid insecticides: A review. *Journal of Neurological and Orthopaedic Medicine and Surgery* 22:2:22–26.
Hirsch, A.R. 2003. Neurological effects of TCE in groundwater and soil in Lisle, Illinois. [Abstract Book] *Soils, Sediments and Water*, 86.
Hirsch, A.R. 2004. *What your Doctor May Not Tell You about Sinusitis: Release Your Symptoms and Identify the Real Source of your Pain.* NY: Warner Books.
Hirsch, A.R. 2009a. Palinosmia: Olfactory preservation. *Chemical Senses* 34:A35–A36.

Hirsch, A.R. 2009b. Parkinsonism: The hyposmia and phantosmia connection. *Archives of Neurology* 66:4:538–539.

Hirsch, A.R. and D.R. Cain. 1992. Evaluation of the Chicago Smell Test in a normal population. *Chemical Senses* 17:642–643.

Hirsch, A.R., and D.D. Dougherty. 1992. Phosphatidyl choline for olfactory problems. *Chemical Senses* 17:5:643.

Hirsch, A.R., and J.G. Aranda. 1992. Treatment of olfactory loss with amantadine—An open label trial. *Chemical Senses* 17:5:642.

Hirsch, A.R., and J.G. Vanderbilt. 1992. Treatment of olfactory loss with amitriptyline. *Chemical Senses* 17:5:643–644.

Hirsch, A.R. and M.B. Gotway. 1993. Validation of the Chicago Smell Test (CST) in subjective normosmic neurologic patients. *Chemical Senses* 18:570–571.

Hirsch, A.R., and B.M. MacKenzie, Jr. 1993. Gustatory loss—A taste of malingering? *Chemical Senses* 18:5:71.

Hirsch, A.R., and J.P. Wyse. 1993. Post-traumatic dysosmia: Central vs. peripheral. *Journal of Neurological Orthopaedic Medicine and Surgery* 14:152–155.

Hirsch, A.R., and D. Skolnik. 1994. Olfactory loss in a brother and sister following their simultaneously contracted upper respiratory viral infections: A case report. *Journal of Neurological and Orthopaedic Medicine and Surgery* 15:130–132.

Hirsch, A.R., and N. Thakkar. 1995. Olfaction in a patient with unclassifiable cluster headache-like disorder. *Headache Quarterly, Current Treatment and Research* 6:2:113–122.

Hirsch, A.R., and T.J. Trannell. 1996. Chemosensory disorders and psychiatric diagnoses. *Journal of Neurologic and Orthopaedic Medicine and Surgery* 17:25–30.

Hirsch, A.R. and G. Bissell. 1998. Effects of acute alcohol inebriation and human olfaction. A preliminary report. *Journal of Neurology and Orthopaedic Medicine and Surgery* 18:114–121.

Hirsch, A.R., and J.J. Gruss. 1998a. Ambient odors in the treatment of claustrophobia: A pilot study. *Journal of Neurological and Orthopaedic Medicine and Surgery* 18:98–103.

Hirsch, A.R., and J.J. Gruss. 1998b. How successful are malingerers? Dissimulating olfactory dysfunction. *Journal of Neurology and Orthopaedic Medicine and Surgery* 18:154–160.

Hirsch, A.R., and J.P. Wyse. 1993. Posttraumatic dysosmia: Central vs peripheral. *Journal of Neurological and Orthopaedic Medicine and Surgery* 14:152–155.

Hirsch, A.R., and L.B. Cleveland. 1998. Olfaction and chronic spinal cord injury. *Journal of Neurological Rehabilitation* 12:101–104.

Hirsch, A.R., and N. Thakkar. 1995. Olfaction in a patient with unclassifiable cluster headache-like disorder. *Headache Quarterly* 6:113–122.

Hirsch, A.R., and T.J. Trannel. 1996. Chemosensory disorders and psychiatric diagnoses. *Journal of Neurological and Orthopaedic Medicine and Surgery* 17:25–30.

Hirsch, A.R., S. Lieberman, and S. Gay. 1991. The syndrome of atmospheric pressure sensitive paroxysmal unilateral phantosmia. *Chemical Senses* 16:5:535–536.

Hirsch, A.R., J.M. Scott, and S.H. Koch. 1992. Efficacy of group therapy in the treatment approach to chemosensory disorders. *Chemical Senses* 17:5:643.

Hirsch, A.R., D.D. Dougherty, J.G. Aranda, J.G. Vanderbilt, and G.C. Weclaw. 1996. Medications for olfactory loss: Pilot studies. *Journal of Neurological Orthopaedic Medicine and Surgery* 17:109–114.

Hirsch, A.R., M.B. Gotway, and A.T. Harris. 1993. Validation of the Chicago Smell Test (CST) in patients with subjective olfactory loss. *Chemical Senses* 18:571.

Hirsch, M., S. Sherman, A. Roussos, and A.R. Hirsch. 2014. Anosmia with absent alliaceous lacrimation. [Abstract Book] *AChemS XXXVI, The Association for Chemoreception Sciences 36th Annual Meeting* 257:127.

Holak, S.L., and W.J. Havlena. 1992. Nostalgia: An exploratory study of themes and emotions in the nostalgic experience. In *Advances in Consumer Research, volume 19* eds. J.F. Sherry, Jr. and B. Sternthal. Provo: Association for Consumer Research, pp. 380–387.

Hummel, T., B. Sekinger, S.R. Wolf, E. Pauli, and G. Kobal. 1997. Sniffin'sticks': Olfactory performance assessed by the combined testing of odor identification, odor discrimination and olfactory threshold. *Chemical Senses* 22:39–52.

Hummel, T., B.N. Landis, and K.B. Huttenbrink. 2011. Smell and taste disorders. *GMS Current Topics in Otorhinolaryngology, Head and Neck Surgery* 10:18–32.

Hummel, T., S. Barz, J. Lotsch et al. 1996. Loss of olfactory function leads to a decrease of trigeminal sensitivity. *Chemical Senses* 21:75–79.

Hurwitz, T., L. Kopala, C. Clark, and B. Jones. 1988. Olfactory deficits in schizophrenia. *Biologic Psychiatry* 23:123–128.

Jacobson, R. 2014. What happens when an amoeba "eats" your brain? *Scientific American.* http://www.scientificamerican.com/article/what-happens-when-an-amoeba-eats-your-brain/. (accessed 10/16/2016).

Jafek, B.W., and D.P. Hill. 1989. Surgical management of chemosensory disorders. *ENTJournal* 68:398–404.

Jeppson, P. 1969. Studies on the structure and innervation of taste buds. *Acta Otolaryngologica* 259:1–95.

Jones, D., P. Drew, C. Elsey et al. 2016. Conversational assessment in memory clinic encounters: Interactional profiling for differentiating dementia from functional memory disorders. *Aging & Mental Health* 20:5:500–509.

Jütte, R. 2005. *A History of the Senses. From Antiquity to Cyberspace*, 54–71. Cambridge: Polity Press.

Kaplan, H.I., and B.J. Sadock. 1988a. *Synopsis of Psychiatry, Behavioral Sciences and Clinical Psychiatry*, 227. Baltimore: Williams & Wilkins.

Kaplan, H.I., and B.J. Sadock. 1988b. *Synopsis of Psychiatry, Behavioral Sciences and Clinical Psychiatry*, 299. Baltimore: Williams & Wilkins.

Kaplan, H.I., and B.J. Sadock. 1988c. *Synopsis of Psychiatry, Behavioral Sciences and Clinical Psychiatry*, 299–301. Baltimore: Williams & Wilkins.

Keller, A., and D. Malasina. 2013. Hidden consequences of olfactory dysfunction: A patient report series. *BMC Ear, Nose and Throat Disorders* 1313:8.

Keller, A., C. Dushdid, M.O. Magnasco, and L.B. Vosshall. 2014. Humans can discriminate more than one trillion olfactory stimuli. [Abstract Book] *AChemS XXXVI, The Association for Chemoreception Sciences 36th Annual Meeting*, Bonita Springs, FL 120:77–78.

Kelman, L. 2004. Osmophobia and taste abnormality in migraineurs: A tertiary care study. *Headache* 44:1019–1023.

Kline, N., and J. Rausch. 1985. Olfactory precipitants of flashbacks in post traumatic disorder. *Journal of Clinical Psychiatry* 46:383–384.

Knasko, S. 1992. Ambient odor's effect on creativity, mood, and perceived health. *Chemical Senses* 17:1:27–35.

Knight, A. 1988. Anosmia. *The Lancet* 332:8609:512.

Kobal, G., and T. Hummel. 1991. Olfactory evoked potentials in humans. In *Smell and Taste in Health and Disease*, eds. T.V. Getchell, R.L. Doty, L.M. Bartoshuk, and J.B. Snow, 255–275. New York: Raven Press.

Kratskin, I.L., and O. Belluzzi. 2003. Anatomy and neurochemistry of the olfactory bulb. In *Handbook of Olfaction and Gustation. Second Edition. Revised and Expanded*, ed. R.L. Doty, 139–164. New York: Marcel Dekker, Inc.

Kumar, S., M. Alexander, and C. Gnanamuthu. 2006. Cranial nerve involvement in patients with leprous neuropathy. *Neurology India* 54:283–285.

Kurtz, D.B., T.L. White, D.E. Hornung, and E. Belknap. 1999. What a tangled web we weave: Discriminating between malingering and anosmia. *Chemical Senses* 24:697–700.

Langlois-Orman, M.A., J.F. Kraus, E. Zaloshnja, and T. Miller. 2011. Epidemiology. In *The American Psychiatric Publishing Textbook of Traumatic Brain Injury, 2nd ed.*, eds. J.M. Silver, T.A. McAllister, and S.C. Yudofsky, 3–22. Washington, DC: American Psychiatric Publishing.

Lee, C.T. 1976. Agonistic behavior, sexual attraction, and olfaction in mice. In *Mammalian Olfaction, Reproductive Processes, and Behavior*, ed. R.L. Doty, 161–180. New York: Academic Press.

Leopold, D. 2002. Distortion of olfactory perception: Diagnosis and treatment. *Chemical Senses* 27:611–615.

Levin, H.S., W.M. High, and H.M. Eisenberg. 1985. Impairment of olfactory recognition after closed head injury. *Brain* 108:579–591.

Levenson, J.L., and K. Kennedy. 1985. Dysosmia, dysgeusia, and nifedipine. *Annals of Internal Medicine* 102:135–136.

Linschoten, M.R. and L.O Harvey. 2004. Detecting malingerers by means of response-sequence analysis. *Perception & Psychophysics* 66:7:1190–1201.

Lipchock, S.V., D.R. Reed, and J.A. Mennella. 2011. The gustatory and olfactory systems during infancy: Implications for development of feeding behaviors in the high-risk neonate. *Clinics in Perinatology* 38:4:627–641

Lishman, W. 1978. *Organic Psychiatry*, 530. London: Blackwell Scientific publications.

Llewellyn, R. 1939. *How Green Was My Valley*. London: M. Joseph, Ltd.

Lotsch, J. and T. Hummel. 2014. Cannabinoid-related olfactory neuroscience in mice and humans. *Chemical Senses* doi: 10.1093/chemse/bju05

Loury, M.C., and D.W. Kennedy. 1991. Chronic sinusitis and nasal polyposis. In *Smell and Taste in Health and Disease,* eds. T.V. Getchell, R.L. Doty, L.M. Bartoshuk, and J.B. Snow, 517–528. New York: Raven, 1991.

Luciano, D.J., K. Alper, and S. Nadkarni. Posttraumatic epilepsy. In *The American Psychiatric Publishing Textbook of Traumatic Brain Injury, 2nd ed.*, eds. J.M. Silver, T.A. McAllister, and S.C. Yudofsky, 267. Washington, DC: American Psychiatric Publishing.

Macht, D.I., and M.B. Macht. 1940. Comparison of effect of cobra venom and opiates on olfactory sense. *American Journal of Physiology* 129:P411–P412.

MacLean, P.D., and A. Kral. 1973. *A Triune Concept of the Brain and Behaviour.* Toronto: University of Toronto Press.

Macrides, F. and B.J. Davis. 1983. Olfactory bulb. In *Chemical Neuroanatomy*, ed. P.C. Emson, 391. New York: Raven Press.

Mair, R.G., and L.M. Harrison. 1991. Influence of drugs on smell function. In *Human Sense of Smell*, eds. D.G. Laing, R.L. Doty, and W. Breiphol, 336–355. Berlin: Springer-Verlag.

Mair, R.G., J.A. Bouffard, T. Engen, and T.H. Morton. 1978. Olfactory sensitivity during the menstrual cycle. *Sensory Processes* 2:90–98.

Markopoulou, K., K.W. Larsen, E.K. Wszolek, M.A. Denson, A.E. Lang, R.F. Pfeiffer et al. 1977. Olfactory dysfunction in familial Parkinsonism. *Neurology* 49:1262–1267.

Mason, A.M., R. Cardell, and M. Armstrong. 2013. Malingering psychosis: Guidelines for assessment and management. *Perspective Psychiatric Care* 50:51–57.

Meats, P. 1988. Olfactory hallucinations. *British Medical Journal* 296:645.

Meisami, E., L. Miklhail, D. Baim, and K.P. Bhatnagar. 1998. Human olfactory bulb: Aging of glomeruli and mitral cells and a search for the accessory olfactory bulb. *Annals of the New York Academy of Sciences* 855:708–715.

Mialon V.S., and S.E. Ebeler. 1997. Time-intensity measurement of matric effects of retronasal aroma perception. *Journal of Sensory Studies* 12:303–316.

Middleton, C.B., M.W. Geisler, T.M. Davidson, and C. Murphy. 1998. Relationship between the alcohol sniff test and sensory olfactory event-related potentials: Validation of a psychophysical test. *Chemical Senses* 23:610.

Migaud, M., C. Durieux, J. Viereck, E. Soroca-Lucas, M.C. Fournie-Zaluski, and B.P. Roques. 1996. The in vivo metabolism of cholecystokinin (CCK-8) is essentially ensured by aminopeptidase A. *Peptides* 17:4:601–607.

Miller, H., and N. Cartlidge. 1972. Simulation and malingering in relation to injuries of the brain and spinal cord. *Lancet* 1:580–586.

Millon, T. 1987. *Manual for the MCMI-II, 2nd ed.* Minneapolis: National Computer Systems.

Mischel, W., and C. Giligan. 1964. Delay of gratification, motivation for the prohibited gratification, and response to temptation. *Journal of Abnormal Sociology & Psychology* 4:411–427.

Monath, T., B. Cropp, and A. Harrison. 1983. Mode of entry of a neurotrophic arbovirus into the central nervous system. *Laboratory Investigation* 48:399.

Moberg, P.J., and R.L. Doty. 1997. Olfactory function in Huntington's disease patients and at-risk offspring. *International Journal of Neuroscience* 89:133–139.

Moberg, P.J., R.L. Doty, B.I. Turetsky, S.T.E. Arnold, R.N. Mahr, R.C. Gur et al. 1997. Olfactory identification deficits in schizophrenia: Correlation with duration of illness. *American Journal of Psychiatry* 154:1016–1018.

Moore, S.R., L.S. Gresham, M.B. Bromberg, E.J. Kasarkis, and R.A. Smith. 1997. A self-report measure of affective lability. *Journal of Neurology, Neurosurgery & Psychiatry* 63:1:89–93.

Mott, A.E., and D.A. Leopold. 1991. Disorders in taste and smell. *Medical Clinics of North America* 75:1321–1353.

Mucignat-Caretta, C. 2014. Human pheromones: Do they exist? In *Neurobiology of Chemical Communication*, ed. R.L. Doty, 535–559. Boca Raton: CRC Press.

Nausieda, P.A. 1980. Sydenham's chorea: Update. *Neurology* 30:331–334.

Nordin, S., A.U. Monsch, and C. Murphy. 1995. Unawareness of smell loss in normal aging and Alzheimer's disease: Discrepancy between self-reporting and diagnosed smell sensitivity. *Journal of Gerontology* 50:187–192.

O'Flaherty, L. 2013. Psychological and social perspectives on malingering and symptom exaggeration: Conceptualization and interventions using acceptance and commitment therapy. PhD diss., University of Denver. http://digitalcommons.du.edu/capstone_masters/76/ (accessed 12/16/2016).

O'Mahony, M. 1978. Smell illusions and suggestion: Reports of smells contingent on tones played on television and radio. *Chemical Senses* 3:2:183–189.

Overbosch, P., J.C. Van Den Eden, and B.M. Keur. 1986. An improved method for measuring perceived intensity/time relationships in human taste and smell. *Chemical Senses* 111:331–338.

Parma, V., E. Straulino, D. Zanatto et al. 2012. Implicit olfactory abilities in traumatic brain injured patients. *Journal of Clinical and Experimental Neuropsychology* 34:9:977–988.

Parsons, M. 1983. *Color Atlas of Clinical Neurology*, 18. Chicago: Year Book Medical.

Paulhus, D.L. 1998. *Paulhus deception scales.* Toronto: Multi-Health Systems.

Pearce, R.K., C.H. Hawkes, and S.E. Daniel. 1995. Anterior olfactory nucleus in Parkinson's disease. *Movement Disorders* 10:283–287.

Pearson, R.C.A., M.M. Esiri, R.W. Hiones, G.K. Wilcock, and T.P.S. Powell. 1985. Anatomical correlates of the distribution of the pathological changes in the neocortex in Alzheimer's disease. *Proceedings of the National Academy of Science, USA* 82:4531–4534.

Post, F. 1975. Dementia, depression, and pseudodementia. In *Psychiatric Aspects of Neurologic Disease*, 99–120, eds. D.V. Benson, D. Blumer, eds. New York: Grune and Stratton.

Potter, H., and N. Butters. 1980. An assessment of olfactory deficits in patients with damage to prefrontal cortex. *Neuropsycholgia* 18:621–628.

Preston, J.D., J.H. O'Neal, and M.C. Talaga. 2010. *Child and Adolescent Clinical Psychoparmacology Made Simple*, 102. Oakland: New Harbinger Publications, Inc.

Proust, M. 1934. Swann's Way. *Remembrance of things past*, Vol. 1, Ch. 3, 36. Translated by C.K. Scott Moncrieff. New York: Random House.

Resnick, P.J. 1988. Malingering of posttraumatic disorders. In *Clinical Assessment of Malingering and Deception*, ed. R. Rogers, 84–103. New York: Guilford Press.

Roberts L.E., J.J. Eggermont, D.M. Caspary, S.E. Shore, J.R. Melcher, and J.A. Kaltenback. 2010. Ringing Ears: The neuroscience of tinnitus. *Journal of Neuroscience* 30:45:14972–14979.

Roberts, A. 1986. Alzheimer's disease may begin in the nose and may be caused by aluminosilicates. *Neurobiology of Aging* 7:561–567.

Roussos, A.P., and A.R. Hirsch. 2014. Alliaceous migraines. *Headache* 54:2:378–382.

Rowatt, W.C., M.R. Cunningham, and P.B. Druen. 1998. Lying to a potential date or potential employer: Social uses of deception. (Poster) presented at the *Meeting of the International Network on Personal Relationships*, University of Washington, Seattle.

Rubert, S.L., M. H. Hollender, and E.G. Mehrof. 1961. Olfactory hallucinations. *Archives of General Psychiatry* 5:121–126.

Sajjadian, A., R. L. Doty, D.N. Gutnick, R.J. Chirurgi, M. Sivak, and D. Perl. 1994. Olfactory dysfunction in amyotrophic lateral sclerosis. *Neurodegenerative Diseases* 3:153–157.

Santos-Bueso, E., M. Serrador-Garcia, F. Saenz-Frances, and J. Garcia-Sanchez. 2010. Charles Bonnet syndrome in patient with impaired visual field and good visual acuity. *Neurología* 31:3:208–209.

Schiffman, S.S. 1983a. Taste and smell in disease. *New England Journal of Medicine* 308:1275–1279.

Schiffman, S.S. 1983b. Taste and smell in disease. *New England Journal of Medicine* 308:1337–1343.

Schiffman, S.S. 1991. Drugs influencing taste and smell perception. In *Smell and Taste in Health and Disease,* eds. T.V. Getchell, R.L. Doty, L.M. Bartoshuk, and J.B. Snow, 847, table 2. New York: Raven Press.

Schiffman, S.S., and Z.S. Warwick. 1988. Flavor enhancement of foods for the elderly can reverse anorexia. *Neurophysiology of Aging* 9:24–26.

Schlotfeld, C.R., M.W. Geisler, T.M. Davidson, and C. Murphy. 1998. Clinical application of the alcohol sniff test on HIV positive and HIV negative patients with nasal sinus disease. *Chemical Senses* 23:610.

Schneeberg, N.G. 1952. Loss of sense of taste due to methylthiouracil therapy. *Journal of the American Medical Association* 149:1091–1093.

Schwartz, B.S., P. Ford, K.I. Bolla, J. Agnew, N. Rothman, and M.L. Bleecker. 1990. Solvent-associated decrements in olfactory function in paint manufacturing workers. *American Journal of Industrial Medicine* 18:697–706.

Scott, A.E. 1989a. Caution urged in treating steroid-dependent anosmia. *Archives of Otolaryngology Head and Neck Surgery* 115:109–110.

Scott, A.E. 1989b. Clinical characteristics of taste and smell disorders. *Ear, Nose and Throat Journal* 68:297–298.

Scott, A.E., W.S. Cain, and G. Clavet. 1988. Topical corticosteroids can alleviate olfactory dysfunction. *Chemical Senses* 13:735.

Scott, A.E., W.S. Cain, and G. Leonard. 1989. Nasal/sinus disease and olfactory loss at the Connecticut Chemosensory Clinical Research Center. *Chemical Senses* 14:745.

Serby, M., J. Corwin, A. Novatt, P. Conrad, and J. Rotrosen. 1985. Olfaction in dementia. *Journal of Neurology, Neurosurgery, and Psychiatry* 48:849.

Serby, M., P. Larson, and D. Kalkstein. 1990. Olfactory sense in psychoses. *Biologic Psychiatry* 28:829–830.

Serby, M., P. Larson, and D. Kalkstein. 1991. Nature and course of olfactory deficits in Alzheimer's disease. *American Journal of Psychiatry* 148:357.

Seydell, E.M., and W.P. McKnight. 1948. Disturbances of olfaction resulting from intranasal use of tyrothricin: A clinical report of seven cases. *Archives of Otolaryngology* 47:465–470.

Silver, J.M., S.C. Yudofsky, and K. Anderson. 2011. Aggressive disorders. In *The American Psychiatric Publishing Textbook of Traumatic Brain Injury, 2nd ed.*, eds. J.M. Silver, T.A. McAllister, and S.C. Yudofsky, 225–238. Washington, DC: American Psychiatric Publishing.

Smith, D.V. 1986. Taste, smell and psychophysical measurement. In *Clinical Measurement of Taste and Smell*, eds. H.L. Meiselman and R.S. Rivlin, 1–18. New York: Macmillan Co.

Smith, D.V., and A.M. Seiden. 1991. Olfactory dysfunction. In *Human Sense of Smell*, eds. D.G. Laing, R.L. Doty, and W. Breiphol, 291. Berlin: Springer-Verlag.

Smith, M.M. 2007. *Sensing the Past. Seeing, Hearing, Smelling, Tasting, and Touching in History*, 31. Berkeley: University of California Press.

Snow, Jr. J., and J. Martin. 1994. Disturbances of smell, taste and hearing. In *Harrison's Principles of Internal Medicine, 13th Ed.*, 109–115, ed. K.J. Isselbacher, E. Braunwald, J.D. Wilson, J.B. Martin, and A.S. Fauci. New York: McGraw Hill.

Solomon, G.S., W.M. Petrie, J.R. Hart, and H.B. Brackin, Jr. 1999. Olfactory dysfunction discriminates Alzheimer's dementia from major depression. *Journal of Neuropsychiatry and Clinical Neurosciences* 10:1:64–67.

Stevens, J.C., W.C. Cain, and D.E. Weinstein. 1987. Aging impairs the ability to detect gas odor. *Fire Technology* 23:3:198–204.

Strub, R.L., and F.W. Black. 1993. *The Mental Status Examination in Neurology, Revised*, 43. Philadelphia: F.A. Davis Company.

Sumner, D. 1964. Post-traumatic anosmia. *Brain* 87:107–120.

Takagi, S.F. 1984. A standardized olfactometer in Japan. A review over ten years. Preliminary studies for manufacture of a standardized olfactometer. *Annals of New York Academy of Sciences* 510:113–118.

Tennen, H., G. Affleck, and R. Mendola. 1991. Coping with smell and taste disorders. In *Smell and Taste in Health and Disease*, eds. T. Getchell, R. Doty, L. Bartoshuk, and J. Snow, 787–804. New York: Raven Press.

Tombaugh, T.N. 1997. The test of memory malingering (TOMM): Normative data from cognitively intact and cognitively impaired individuals. *Psychological Assessment* 9:3:260–268

Trimble, M.R. 1986. *Posttraumatic Neurosis from Railway Spine to the Whiplash*. New York: John Wiley.

Turner, P. 1965. Some observations on centrally-acting drugs in man. *Proceedings of the Royal Society of Medicine* 58:913–914.

Van Der Laan, L.N., D.T. deRidder, M.A. Viergever, and P.A. Smeets. 2011. The first taste is always with the eyes: A meta-analysis on the neural correlates of processing visual food cues. *NeuroImage* 55:1:296–303.

VanDamme, P.A., and H.P. Freihofer. 1992. Disturbances of smell and taste after high central midface fractures. *Journal of Craniomaxillofacial Surgery* 20:248–250.

Varney, N.R. 1988. Prognostic significance of anosmia in patients with closed-head trauma. *Journal of Clinical and Experimental Neuropsychology* 10:2:250–254.

Veldhuizen, M.G., T.G. Shepard, M.F. Wang, and L.E. Marks. 2010. Coactivation of gustatory and olfactory signals in flavor perception. *Chemical Senses* 35:2:121–133.

Venstrom, D., and J.E. Amoore. 1968. Olfactory threshold in relation to age, sex or smoking. *Journal of Food Science* 33:264–265.

Vital Durand, M. 1985. Recurrent anosmia under beta-blockers. *Presse Medicale* 14:2064.

Wahlstrom, Jr., C.M., A.R. Hirsch, and B.W. Whitman. 2015. Chemosensory disorders: Emerging roles in food selection, nutrient inadequacies, and digestive dysfunction. In *Nutrition and Sensation*, ed. A.R. Hirsch, 25–63. Boca Raton: CRC Press.

Ward, C.D., W.A. Hess, and D.B. Calne. 1983. Olfaction impairment in Parkinson's disease. *Neurology* 33:943–946.

Westport Pharmaceuticals. 1982. *Accusen T Taste Function Kit Instruction Manual*. Westport: Westport Pharmaceuticals.

Williams, D.B. 2016. Tasteless insights. *JAMA* 315:17:1835–1836.

Witt, M., K. Reutter, and I.J. Miller, Jr. 2003. Morphology of the peripheral taste system. In *Handbook of Olfaction and Gustation, Second Edition, Revised and Expanded*, ed. R.L. Doty, 651–677. New York: Marcel Dekker, Inc.

Wolfe, J.M. 2006. *Sensation & Perception*, 32. Sunderland, MA: Sinauer Associates, Inc.

Wolkin, A., D. Malaspina, M. Perrin, T.W. McAllister, and C. Corcoran. 2011. Psychotic disorders. In *The American Psychiatric Publishing Textbook of Traumatic Brain Injury, 2nd Ed.*, eds. J.M. Silver, T.A. McAllister, and S.C. Yudofsky, 189–197. Washington, DC: American Psychiatric Publishing.

Wood, V.E., and J. Biondi, J. 1990. Double-crush nerve compression in thoracic-outlet syndrome. *Journal of Bone & Joint Surgery-American* 72:1:85–87.

Wysocki, C.J., K.M. Dorries, and G.K. Beauchamp. 1989. Ability to perceive androstenone can be acquired by ostensibly anosmic people. *Proceedings of the National Academy of Sciences* 86:7976–7978.

Yakov, Y.L., S. Yakov, S., and A.R. Hirsch. 2010. Olfaction in burning mouth syndrome. *Chemical Senses* 31:A114–A115.

Youngentob, S.L., D.B. Kurtz, D.A. Leopold, M.M. Mozell, and D.E. Hornung. 1982. Olfactory sensitivity: Is there laterality? *Chemical Senses* 7:1:11–21.

Zald, D.H. Neuropsychological assessment of orbitofrontal cortex. 2006. In *The Orbitofrontal Cortex*, eds. D.H. Zald and S.L. Rauch, 449–480. Oxford UK: Oxford University Press.

Zilstorff, K. 1965. Sense of smell alterations by cocaine and tetracaine. *Archives of Otolaryngology* 82:53–55.

Zilstorff, K., and O. Herbild. 1979. Parosmia. *Acta Otorlaryngol* 47:465–470.

12 Malingering in Geriatrics

Jason J. Gruss, MD

CONTENTS

The field of geriatrics is sometimes a subtle field, where the differences between a typical adult and an aging adult are slight. However, in other circumstances these differences can be stark. The study of aging adults needs to be approached as a spectrum which transcends the patient's age and considers their emotional circumstance and living environment as well as their medical and social history and preferences. When considering malingering in older adults, many of the aspects of typical adult malingering apply. However, this chapter will deal with circumstances less likely to be encountered in general adulthood, and more often encountered with aging patients.

12.1 DISTINCTIONS BETWEEN GENERAL ADULTS AND OLDER ADULTS

In general, the ability of older adults to safely cope with acute illness is diminished. For example, the physical reserve of strength can be rapidly depleted by a cold or flu. Something that might cause a 40-year-old to merely miss a day of work may trigger a prolonged hospitalization in an 80-year-old. A week later, the recently ill 40-year-old might be back to exercise and full activity. Conversely, the 80-year-old patient may struggle to walk and perform basic activities of daily living. This discrepancy is a function of increased physiological demand of the recovery process as well as a decreased tolerance to activity. In fact, aging alone is predictive of a longer length of hospital stay, regardless of the precipitating medical issues (Weingardten, 1988). Other mild illnesses, such as gastroenteritis, would cause a few unpleasant days in a typical, healthy adult (Polage, 2012). The same circumstances in an older adult may lead to significant dehydration.

Renal function declines with age (Weinstein and Anderson, 2010). Compounding the worsening of renal function is the increased likelihood of taking more medications as chronic medical issues accumulate. Polypharmacy is a well-recognized problem in geriatrics (Ferreira, Martins, and Fernandes, 2016). As chronic illnesses accumulate with age, the need for pharmacological intervention increases. Medications beneficial for one condition may lead to injury in another. For example, taking a nonsteroidal anti-inflammatory for osteoarthritis is helpful, until gastritis prevents its safe use. Alternatively, a diuretic is commonly used in heart failure, exacerbates renal dysfunction. While these interactions can happen at any age, they are more common and more dangerous with older patients.

Functionally, there are additional differences. Reflexes and strength diminish with age (Keller and Engelhardt, 2014). The ability to recover from a small stumble is decreased, therefore falling increases with age (Rubenstein, 2006). Due to osteoporosis and degenerative joint disease fractures are more likely to occur from falls in the elderly than from falls in typical adults (Ensrud, 2013). Additionally, sacropenia is more common in the elderly. Sarcopenia is defined as the loss of muscle mass in an older person, which is two standard deviations less than the mean for young persons (Morley, 2008). Sarcopenia has a prevalence of 5% in persons aged 65, and as high as 50% in persons over the age of 80 (Janssen, 2010). This process leads to gradual and persistent weakening. Additionally, patients with sarcopenia have increased difficulty regaining their strength after injury or illness.

While physical slowing occurs, neurological slowing also occurs as a function of normal aging (Eckert, 2011). The process of recalling information may be less complete and take longer in older adults than in typical adults. The effort required to retain and recall information increases in normal aging (Danckert and Craik, 2013). Acquiring new information requires increased time.

The above-mentioned issues are not disease processes. These issues are all part of the vicissitudes of normal aging. However, as time progresses, chronic medical problems accumulate and acute medical issues become more likely. Hypertension, type 2 diabetes, cancer, heart disease, and gout are a few of the many other conditions which have an increased risk of occurence with increased age (Davis, Chung, and Juarez, 2011). The treatment of these medical issues can be complicated by aging. It should be no wonder that there are many neurological and psychiatric conditions which also increase in occurrence with aging. Thus, many forms of neurologic diseases, including dementia and depression increase with aging (Plassman et al., 2007; Fiske, Wetherell, and Gatz, 2009).

Just as the medical background of elderly patients can become more complex, the social background of aging patients can become more complex. Older adults are less likely to be able to live independently. They are more likely to require assistance at home. Additionally, many older adults live in long-term care facilities when they can no longer care for themselves. There are also a large number of older adults who are in-between, and have transitioned out of fully independent living, into "senior housing," or assisted living communities. Understanding the patient's social background is necessary to understand their motivations for seeking out medical care (or avoiding medical care).

The need for social and emotional support does not change significantly with age, but the ability to fulfill those needs may change (Charles and Carstensen, 2014). Beyond housing and personal care as people age it is common for their social circle to shrink. There are strong cultural differences in how society interacts with the aged and how it approaches the aging process. However, a lack of social support is more common across cultures for the elderly than for younger adults (Matthews, 1984). For all patients social relationships can affect how they approach medical care (Umberson and Montez, 2011).

All of these physical, neurological, psychiatric, and social issues must be taken into account when interacting with aging patients. Certainly, when presenting symptoms are unusual, irregular, or otherwise concerning, determining the patient's motivation for accepting or denying medical care is a major concern.

12.2 MALINGERING IN GERIATRIC POPULATIONS

Malingering, in the geriatric population can sometimes be seen as one of two requests: "come here" or "go away." "Come here" forms of malingering can be thought of as asking for assistance. "Go away" forms of malingering are forms where the patient is denying problems in order to be left alone. There are multiple etiologies for these behaviors and determining the underlying cause of the patient's malingering is essential for successful care.

The patient's environment is an important component in determining whether malingering is an issue. The first step of providing health care is to determine whether a patient's safety is at risk. The risk of harm varies depending upon the patient's environment. When a patient is living alone, is he or she competent to provide himself or herself with food? Is a patient able to go to the pharmacy to obtain medications? Is he or she driving safely? For many patients who live independently, identifying areas of functional need can be helpful in identifying dangerous issues.

As we age our ability to perform more vigorous tasks changes. For homeowners, mowing the lawn or cleaning the gutters may be too difficult. Sometimes, ascending and descending stairs becomes too burdensome due to osteoarthritis in knees. Taking out the garbage might be a challenge in older adults. Getting to and from the grocery store may be difficult. Malingering in a "come here" mode for these patients might be to gain assistance with household tasks. A complaint of knee pain or other ailment might actually be a call for additional help around the house. Alternatively, the patients may request assistance with a specific task in an effort to obtain help for another condition. It may be emotionally easier to ask a family member for help with driving to the pharmacy than with help setting up a pillbox. It may be easier to ask for assistance with laundry than to admit that one can no longer ascend or descend stairs without assistance. For the patient, they may or may not recognize that the need for assistance is a sign of a permanent change in condition, not a temporary malady.

An elder might ask a family member, or personal aide, to "stop at the store and pick up my medication," but also asks for groceries. There may be two areas of gain in this scenario. The gain from this level of malingering might be for an assistant to perform a functional task which the malingerer can no longer perform, or the gain might simply be financial. As adults age and leave the workplace many are not able to meet their growing need to spend money on unplanned medical expenses or physical assistance. Medicare does not pay for people to mow the lawn. Retired adults often do not have the financial resources to meet all of their physical and environmental needs. Asking for assistance to go to the doctor's office because the patient feels too unwell to go alone may be malingering because they cannot afford to call for a cab or keep their automobile.

Another avenue of gain for older adults is companionship. As we age our ability to be independently mobile declines. This reduces access to recreational activities. For older adults social circles shrink as friends move, or pass away, or as their ability to remain mobile similarly declines. A call for help—with household tasks, with medical needs—may be masking the true gain of companionship. These forms of malingering may present as an exaggeration of existing symptoms or problems, instead of the creation of problems which do not exist at all.

The incidence of depression and anxiety increases with age (Mirowsky and Ross, 1992). Patients who did not previously have depressive symptoms may find changes in their mood as they get older. These patients and their families might not recognize the existence of mood disorders, as the patient "never suffered from this before." The patient's fear of these symptoms may lead them to look for support in other ways. Because of the stigma of mental illness it may be difficult for patients to either identify the issue or ask for help directly. An aging patient who is dealing with depression may attribute the depression to outside sources such as bereavement or loneliness. In order to satisfy the need for companionship, without the stigma of mental illness, minor conditions or problems might be invented or exaggerated.

In general, the "come here" mode of malingering in older adults changes when patients live in a more supportive environment. When patients move to senior housing, assisted living, or long-term care, many of the environmental issues no longer require the patients' management; there is no longer a need to mow the lawn. However, in these environments, the patients have decreased control over their environment. While living independently in their own home, patients may keep the thermostat low to save money on the heating bill or because they prefer a cooler room. In a long-term care setting the patient may not be able to control the temperature of their room at all. Handing over control is often stressful. Transitions from independent living into more supportive environments are challenging. Changes in environment are particularly stressful for elderly populations.

Patients may call family members and report problems with the staff or environment because it is no longer under their control. The patients are seeking a gain of greater control so they may report other issues to staff or family. The patient may complain to staff that the room is too warm, but environmentally there may be nothing that the staff can do. When change in the room's temperature does not occur the patient may report to family that "nobody is listening to me." Great caution needs to be exerted here. It is easy to dismiss older adults' complaints as "attention seeking" or "acting out of frustration." Clinicians, administrators, and the family involved in the care of older adults needs to be mindful that malingering needs to be a diagnosis of exclusion. Patients are vulnerable. As we remove their control of their environment they become more vulnerable. Thorough investigation of their complaints is required. Malingering, the presentation of a complaint in order to achieve another gain does not mean the patient does not require the gain which they are seeking. In patients who live in more supportive settings, "come here" malingering may actually be an opportunity to provide improved care.

12.3 NEGATIVE MALINGERING

The loss of control is a great fear for many older adults. Declining health, limited physical ability, a fixed income, and a shrinking social circle all present new limitations. As we age, these limitations gradually reduce our independence. There is a strong desire among older adults to cling to all the independence they can. The desire for independence may be stronger than the patient's ability to live safely. Patients may overestimate their ability to perform tasks as they internally deny and minimize the effects aging has on their ability to function. In situations like this, it is difficult to determine whether patients are denying the presence of problems to themselves as well as to others.

Some adults deny the presence of problems in order to maintain their independence. I refer to this as "negative malingering." They deny complaints which actually exist in order to achieve a gain. A patient may have severe knee arthritis. Functionally, they would have an increasingly difficult time ascending and descending the stairs inside their home. The patient wants to stay independent and live in their home without assistance or modification to the house. They want to maintain control of the environment even as they lose control of their function. Instead of going upstairs to their bedroom they may begin sleeping on the couch. Instead of using the bathroom upstairs they take sponge baths downstairs. When asked about their health they may deny the existence of limitations, or minimize the severity of their pain and loss of function. They do not want to admit to their physicians, their families, or sometimes even themselves, that they need a modification in their environment. They ignore or deny the existence of symptoms for the gain of maintaining control.

Patients in this scenario are at risk for self-neglect and injury. Falls may not be reported. Injuries which could be repaired or rehabilitated may be ignored. Easy interventions which would improve outcome are not pursued. Simple environmental changes, like grab bars in the bathroom, are not installed. The inability to take out the garbage can lead to unsafe living conditions. The inability to bathe appropriately can lead to hygiene issues, infections, or skin breakdown. Home maintenance may be neglected. Similarly, for patients who drive automobile maintenance may be ignored. Patients may fail to renew their driver's licenses out of a sense of fear of failing the exam.

Ignoring environmental problems may come from the same emotional state as ignoring clinical symptoms. In order to maintain their home situation, patients may ignore symptoms as they progressively get worse. When such patients arrive at the hospital, they present with a "one-day history" of coughing but turn out to be critically ill. These patients may be found to be too weak to feed themselves or get out of bed. Medical staff familiar with older adults often recognize that the symptoms are more than "one-day old." Patients may also report that they were "doing everything fine at home." Close assessment of their functional ability may show many chronic issues. Family who visit the home in the absence of the patients may be surprised with the poor condition of the home. In many ways, negative malingering can easily lead to self-neglect in dangerous conditions.

12.4 CONDITIONS AFFECTING MALINGERING IN GERIATRICS

Malingering requires an external motivation. There is a deliberate, intentional goal. This goal is clear to the patient. Often the goal is not to act maliciously to others but to obtain a benefit for the patient. The benefit to the patient is sometimes obvious: exaggerating an injury to obtain greater rewards from a lawsuit or exaggerating pain to obtain narcotics. However, many times the benefit for the patient is less obvious. The complex medical, financial, and social conditions which affect our elderly patients further complicate our ability to identify malingering. There are several medical, neurological, and psychiatric conditions that should be specifically addressed.

12.4.1 Pain

Malingering in the treatment of pain is familiar to many physicians. Narcotics are easily abused, and physicians are increasingly cognizant of their risks. In older adults, there is greater likelihood of clearly identified and obviously present musculoskeletal problems (such as gout, degenerative disc disease, and osteoarthritis). When a patient presents with pain, and imaging shows a severely degenerative joint, physicians may be more likely to provide narcotics. The presence of clinically apparent or radiologically established tissue destruction is more likely to decrease a physician's suspicions. When a patient presents with a clear injury, obtaining opiates will be less complicated than with a patient with symptoms that lack anatomical correlation. Additionally, aging patients may be less likely to tolerate nonopiate medications such as nonsteroidal anti-inflammatory drugs, leaving the prescribing physician with fewer options. Physicians may be less concerned with the effects of addiction in older patients. Physicians also may be more willing to allow for increased opiate loads for patients closer to the end of their life (Chau, Walker, Pai et al., 2008).

In older adults, it is important to be equally mindful of patients minimizing their symptoms of pain. Older patients may be fearful of additional testing. They may be anxious with a change in routine. They may be fearful of a change in their living situation, or the need for additional care. These fears may cause them to deny that a fall happened. The desire to continue living in their house, even with a flight of stairs they can no longer climb because of knee pain, may induce them to negatively malinger about this pain. This pattern of malingering by omission, denying the presence of symptoms or denying problems within the environment, or just not mentioning these, is more likely to occur when a patient wants to protect their freedom.

12.4.2 Chronic Disease

For many chronic diseases, such as diabetes or hypertension, lifestyle modification is a cornerstone of treatment. Low salt diets, increased exercise, weight loss, consistent carbohydrate diets, are very commonly recommended by physicians. Many adults, especially older adults, may not want to make these changes. In these circumstances an elderly patient may "like their routine." They have "always" enjoyed a few glasses of wine at night, or dessert after dinner. They may have smoked tobacco their entire lives and feel they are "too old to quit." This may not seem like malingering. However, establishing the incidence of elderly patients who lie to their physicians about how much they drink or how much desert they eat is not easily done. Patients may lie about their sugar consumption so their physician will be more likely to increase their medication, therefore they can continue to eat more sugar. Another consideration is access to opportunity to make changes. Patients who have their meals prepared or provided by others may not be able to select what they eat. Patients who have difficulty leaving the house may not be able to maintain the higher levels of activity needed to see a physiological change. For these patients, the lack of control may lead to malingering in order to prevent further loss of control.

Similarly, patients may lie about taking their medications regularly. They may be malingering in this instance to save money or to maintain their independence. A patient who admits to forgetting to take medication may have family intervene and force care upon them, or compel them to move out of their house. But if they malinger they may be able to continue to live at home, albeit dangerously.

12.4.3 Fear of Diagnosis

People are afraid of dying. They fear diseases which lead to death such as heart disease, pulmonary disease, and cancer. Older patients are more likely to have many of these diseases. Often a family member will bring a patient to the hospital after a fall, or after recognizing that their loved one is particularly weak. The patient will admit that they have had problems "for a few days" or "for a little while." Workup may then reveal extensive heart disease or extensively metastatic cancer. In other words, patients and families are discovering acute disease processes which take far more than "a few days" to establish a clinical symptom. While some of this can be explained by naiveté, some can be explained by ignorance; it is important to consider the patient who is deliberately misleading their family and their physicians to avoid the inevitable diagnosis. The patients may wish to avoid surgery, to avoid treatment, or to avoid upsetting loved ones. To gain this benefit, they mislead their physician.

12.5 CLINICAL APPROACH TO SUSPECTED MALINGERING

There is a Russian proverb, "*Doveryai, no proveryai*," which was used, once translated, by President Ronald Reagan. It means to "Trust, but verify." There are a number of ways to accomplish such verification in an office setting.

12.5.1 Functional Verification

If malingering is suspected which may relate to a patient's mobility and functional performance, the physician may order a physical therapy or occupational therapy evaluation. If the patient is reluctant to see a physical therapist or occupational therapist, office testing can be done. The American College of Rheumatology has recommended the "Timed Up and Go" test as a rapid assessment of mobility. The patient is asked while seated, to stand, walk three meters, turn around and return to the chair and sit back down. A time of less than ten seconds is normal. Eleven to 20 seconds indicates some level of disability, and 21 to 30 seconds indicates that the patient requires assistance on uneven surfaces and outside, and requires additional testing. A score of more than 30 seconds suggests that the patient is at increased risk of falling (Panel on Prevention of Falls in Older Persons, American Geriatrics Society, and British Geriatrics Society, 2011).

12.5.2 Verification of Medications

If malingering is suspected, prior to the patient's appointment staff can ask the patient to bring all medications to the office. Counting the remaining pills is a simple way to assess if medications are being taken. Asking the patient to explain their medication routine can provide additional information. Many patients, regardless of age, have difficulty remembering medication regimens. Discussing a pillbox or a checklist would be appropriate for any patient on multiple medications, but is especially important in the elderly. Additionally, the physician or staff may call the patient's pharmacy to see if refills are being filled in a timely fashion. If a patient has only obtained 30 tablets over the past three months, it is unlikely that they are taking them daily.

12.5.3 Verification in Chronic Illness

Routine health screening is essential to effective treatment. Patients may be reluctant to pursue routine monitoring tests. Patients with either positive or negative malingering may be reluctant to pursue testing. In these situations, a strong relationship with the patient is helpful. Reducing the patient's barriers to testing is also effective. Testing that can be done in the office, without an additional visit, or with little additional cost is more likely to be completed than testing which requires a return trip and a significant investment from the patient. Advanced imaging centers may offer pick up and drop off services. Many labs may be drawn in the office or in the same building. Physicians may find themselves having to convince a reluctant patient of a simple course of action. The better the understanding of the patient's reluctance, the more likely the physician will be able to break through the reluctance for the patient. Ultimately, if the physician is able to understand the patient's goals for health care then they are able to provide better care.

If the patient wishes to remain home at all costs, the physician may discuss more aggressive symptom control and access to home-based services. If the patient in a more supportive environment wants to have more control, discussions with social workers and facility volunteers may be helpful. Identifying helpful resources is part of the job of a good practitioner. Often the routine of clinical practice leads practitioners to think first of medications, imaging, and diagnostic studies. It is important to remember to access other resources which may allow the patient to accomplish their goals in a safer way. Social services, therapy services, and recreational services may be available. Religious services and chaplain services may fill this role for some patients. Malingering is the pursuit of a gain through deceit. Identifying the gain (pain reduction, social support, independence) and meeting it to the greatest degree possible will provide the patient with their goal and then allow for the possibility of appropriate care in any setting.

REFERENCES

Charles, S., and L.L. Carstensen. 2010. Social and emotional aging. *Annual Review of Psychology* 61:383–409.

Chau, D.L., V. Walker, L. Pai, and L.M. Cho. 2008. Opiates and elderly: Use and side effects. *Clinical Interventions in Aging* 3:2:273–278.

Danckert, S.L., and F.I. Craik. 2013. Does aging affect recall more than recognition memory? *Psychology & Aging* 28:4:902–909.

Davis, J.W., R. Chung, and D.T. Juarez. 2011. Prevalence of comorbid conditions with aging among patients with diabetes and cardiovascular disease. *Hawai'i Medical Journal* 70:10:209–213.

Eckert, M.A. 2011. Slowing down: Age-related neurobiological predictors of processing speed. *Frontiers in Neuroscience* 5:25.

Ensrud, K.E. 2013. Epidemiology of fracture risk with advancing age. *The Journal of Gerontology, Series A, Biological Sciences and Medical Sciences* 68:10:1236–1242.

Ferreira, A.R., S. Martins, and L. Fernandes. 2016. Comorbidity and polypharmacy in elderly living in nursing homes. *European Psychiatry* 33:S585.

Fiske, A., J.L. Wetherell, and M. Gatz. 2009. Depression in older adults. *Annual Review of Clinical Psychology* 5:363–389.

Jassen, I. 2010. Evolution of sarcopenia research. *Applied Physiology and Metabolism* 35:5:707–712.

Keller, K., and M. Engelhardt. 2014. Strength and muscle mass loss with aging process. Age and strength loss. *Muscles, Ligaments, Tendons Journal* 3:4:346–350.

Matthews, A.M. 1984. Social support in normal aging. *Canadian Family Physician* 30:676–680.

Mirowsky, J., and C.E. Ross. 1992. Age and depression. *Journal of Health and Social Behavior* 33:3:187–205.

Morley, J.E. 2008. Sarcopenia: Diagnosis and treatment. *Journal of Nutrition, Health and Aging* 12:7:452–456.

Plassman, B.L., K.M. Langa, G.G. Fisher et al. 2007. Prevalence of dementia in the United States. The Aging, Demographics, and Memory study. *Neuroepidemiology* 29:1–2:125–132.

Rubenstein, L.Z. 2006. Falls in older people: Epidemiology, risk factors and strategies for prevention. *Age and Ageing* 35:2:ii37–ii41.

Umberson, D., and J.K. Montez. 2011. Social relationships and health: A flashpoint for health policy. *Journal of Health and Social Behavior* 51:S54–S66.

Weingarten, M.S., S.T. Wainwright, and A.D. Sacchetti. 1988. Trauma and aging effects of hospital costs and length of stay. *Annals of Emergency Medicine* 17:10–14.

Weinstein, J.R., and S. Anderson. 2010. The aging kidney: Physiological changes. *Advances in Chronic Kidney Diseases* 17:4:302–307.

13 Forensic Psychiatric Approach to the Detection of Malingered Neuropsychiatric Symptoms

Carl M. Wahlstrom, Jr., MD

CONTENTS

> The malingerer "sees less than the blind, he hears less than the deaf, and he is more lame than the paralyzed..."
>
> **Jones 1917**

Having a strong foundation in the underlying relevant disciplines such as psychiatry, psychology, and neurology is essential in order to sufficiently address medicolegal questions involving the likelihood of malingering, defined here as the conscious fabrication or amplification of mental or physical disorders for secondary gain.

In approaching any forensic medical evaluation—regardless of which side has retained me—I always consider whether it's the defendant in a criminal case or the plaintiff in a civil case, which could be presenting manufactured or exaggerated symptoms of an illness, injury, or impairment for the purposes of secondary gain. I then set out, through careful case analysis, to rule in or rule out the hypothesis that malingered symptoms exist for secondary gain. The secondary gain in a criminal case, for example, could be a reduced sentence or being found not guilty by reason of insanity. In a civil case, it's about the nature and extent of injury and damages, attributions of causality, and being ultimately compensated financially. In fitness for duty cases it's about fitness to return to work after an intervening incident or injury.

Malingering itself is not considered to be a medical illness and, at times, pursuing an identifiable secondary gain, can even be considered adaptive behavior such as to avoid a dangerous situation. An example given in the Psychiatric Diagnostic and Statistical Manuel of Mental Disorders Fifth Edition (DSM-V) mentions feigning illness while a captive of the enemy during wartime (American Psychiatric Association, 2013). In my clinical experience, it is not uncommon for incarcerated individuals, whether awaiting trial in jail or postconviction in prison, to malinger illness to get various secondary gain needs met. One extreme example could be malingering on death row to avoid or delay execution in states having the death penalty.

Malingered symptoms are typically infrequent in our general clinical work, where we meet with and evaluate our patients who are seeking relief and present to us with genuine medical concerns. We most often trust that our patients are telling the truth, are suffering, and are genuinely seeking our help and therefore, we do not engage in a more detailed forensic analysis to be used for medicolegal purposes. Malingering in the clinical setting is distinguished from false attributions as to the cause of a patient's clinical circumstances or distress in which they may naively make secondary to their lack of clinical knowledge or experience (Rogers, 2012). Drug seeking is a more common exception to this general observation in clinical practice. Malingering one's clinical condition is more common in a patient who has been referred by an attorney or one who has self-referred with litigation pending secondary to injury at work, complications from accidents, mental trauma, head trauma, and other physical injuries, claims of various discriminations, fitness for duty, and so on (Rogers, 2012). Malingering should be considered in incarcerated individuals who have issues related to pending trials such as fitness to intelligently and knowingly appreciate and wave Miranda rights and make a voluntary statement, fitness to stand trial, insanity, or mitigation in sentencing.

The presentation of functional neurological or psychiatric symptoms without clear evidence of voluntary production or secondary gain, as in Conversion Disorder is also known as Functional Neurological Symptom Disorder, 2017 ICD-10-CM F44.4-44.7 (e.g., nonepileptic seizures, sensory loss, weakness, or paralysis) (Rosner and Scott, 2017). Although these conditions are incompatible with recognized psychiatric, neurologic, or medical conditions, careful clinical examinations help to distinguish them from malingering.

Somewhat more confusing diagnostically are conditions in which psychological or physical symptoms are lacking in clear secondary external incentives, and yet the patient is intentionally producing false physical or psychological signs or symptoms or an induction of injury for the purpose of assuming the sick role. These are called Factitious Disorders, formerly known as Munchausen syndrome.

The 2017 ICD-10-CM, F68.10-13 Diagnostic Codes distinguish whether Factitious Disorder is predominately physical, psychological, or with combined presentations. Though voluntarily produced, the lack of external incentives distinguishes Factitious Disorder from malingering. The codes for Factitious Disorder under ICD 10 are grouped under acute adjustment reactions and psychosocial dysfunction, and disorders of personality and impulse control (Rosner and Scott, 2017).

After careful clinical ruling out of any of the circumstances listed above, determination of malingering by presenting exaggerated or false symptoms for secondary gain should be part of a complete clinical exam. Being able to rule in or rule out malingering could influence a patient's clinical and/or medicolegal presentation and course. The DSM-V advises that "malingering should be strongly suspected if any combination of the following is noted (American Psychiatric Association, 2013):

1. Medicolegal context of presentation (e.g., the individual is referred by an attorney to the clinician for examination, or the individual self-refers while litigation or criminal charges are pending).
2. Marked discrepancy between the individual's claimed stress or disability and the objective findings and observations.
3. Lack of cooperation during the diagnostic evaluation and in complying with the prescribed treatment regimen.
4. The presence of antisocial personality disorder.

13.1 COMMON MALINGERED MENTAL ILLNESS

- Hallucinations
- Delusions
- Mutism
- Dementia/intellectual disability
- Memory or other cognitive impairments
- Posttraumatic stress disorder
- Major depressive disorder

It is helpful to think of malingerers as actors who portray their mental illness as they know it. This often creates a confusing, crowded collage of symptoms where the malingerer imagines that more is better.

It is more difficult to malinger certain disorders than others. For example, it is much harder to feign an ongoing manic episode versus complaints of manic symptoms. It is easier to imitate the content of psychosis by reporting delusions, auditory, or visual hallucinations than it is to imitate the actual psychotic thought process or to present the negative or residual schizophrenic symptoms. It is easier to present with symptoms as opposed to the signs of mental illness. It is essential to keep the phenomenology of the illness in mind when attempting to assess the likelihood of real versus malingered illness (Sadock, Sadock, and Ruiz, 2009).

The following are guidelines to approaching likely or defined medicolegal cases. These include approaches to thinking about deciding and presenting findings whether written in a report, or verbally in deposition or court.

- It is important to perform a sufficient examination for medicolegal purposes to credibly support a clinical opinion to a reasonable degree of various medical specialty certainties such as psychiatric, neurological, psychological, or other. This level of certainty is defined as more likely than not, and consistent with generally accepted approaches and standards within one's specialty.
- While there is always more that can be done in evaluating a case even despite painstaking efforts in complex cases, what is essential is doing enough to

be able to establish a sufficient foundation to support your opinions. In our legal system, the foundation of your opinion is part of the report, if one is made, and will be further examined in a deposition or testimony in court by direct or cross-examination.

- Be thorough in your clinical and forensic analysis, performing an examination where possible or explaining why not by understanding the relevant legal issue or standards, obtaining original records and reports where available, conducting studies, utilizing other collateral sources of information such as interviews or witnesses, and utilizing other disciplines as needed, to establish the foundation to formulate and support your opinions (Scott, 2015).
- While admittedly it's more fun to "win" (i.e., feel like your analysis and testimony etc. carried the day and was correct and successful) than to lose and feel that your work didn't matter, don't get hung up on "winning" a case. That's someone else's job (occasionally maddening). While our examinations, analysis, reports and testimony may be brilliant (at least by our own standards) we don't decide—it's someone else (like a judge or a jury, a principal or school board, business executive or police chief, an insurance company, or a federal or state agency). Our role is to assist in that process.

An over emphasis on winning and pleasing whoever hired you is different than strongly yet rationally advocating for your opinion. This can result in over-advocating and putting forward unsupported or ridiculous statements, or even worse, being dishonest. Over-advocating can result in a scenario which can damage or even destroy your credibility as an expert witness as well as affect the judge or jury's impression of your testimony. Insufficiently supported advocators will likely be exposed by the other side's expert and legal team. Remember your opinions, reports, and testimony lives on beyond a case and you will carry them with you now more than ever due to technology.

13.2 EXAMPLES OF OVER ADVOCACY

Case 1

State's Attorney: "Doctor, could knowing that the crime scene itself differs from the account given to you by the defendant affect your opinion in this case?"

Defense Expert: "No, the crime scene doesn't matter."

State's Attorney: Re-counts the above to me prior to my testimony adding "I thought this was forensics."

Case 2

Defense Attorney: "Wasn't the defendant in fact delusional in his belief that he could create Zombies in his apartment?"

State's Expert: "It wasn't a delusion, because despite evidence of the defendant performing crude brain "surgeries" resulting in severe brain damage and death to his victims he could have actually done that (made zombies in his apartment)."

Case 3

Judicial Opinion 1: What you don't want is to be referenced in the judge's written opinion commenting about you and your testimony as "this is the kind of expert if you pay him enough, he will say anything."

Case 4

Judicial Opinion 2: After your careful clinical examination report and testimony in open court what you hope not to hear either in the judge's opinion is: "Well, two experts say this, and one says that so it's 2 to 1." To address this kind of reasoning my advice in hindsight is to retain more experts and do more so it's 3 to 2. Principle: always try to do more.

When evaluating a malingerer as someone simulating a condition, there will be "bad actors" as seen with situations which are easy to analyze and "good actors" as seen with situations that require complex analysis across multiple disciplines to detect malingering (Rogers, 2012). Some examples of feigned or exaggerated presentations are various neurological symptoms such as memory or cognitive impairments, dementia, seizures, gait problems, or other neurological deficits seen in closed head injuries, or other physical injuries resulting in disability. Attempts can be made to feign or exaggerate various mental illnesses for secondary gain such as psychosis, depression, anxiety problems or post traumatic stress disorder leading to claims in civil or criminal cases.

In evaluating cases for malingering by utilizing various clinical areas of expertise and experience as indicated below, allows us to bring together the right tools to synthesize information in ruling in or ruling out the likelihood of malingered pathology. For secondary gain, these tools are specialized areas of expertise and familiarity, with the typical clinical presentations and expected course of recovery in injury, as well as the specialized testing available in various areas of expertise.

The following are areas of clinical expertise which, while not exhaustive, depending on the case, can be useful or central in the analysis or synthesis of malingered pathology in medicolegal cases. Examples from cases below have utilized specialists in psychiatry, neurology, general and neuropsychology, neuroradiology and internal medicine.

Four vignettes are given to illustrate the clinical presentation and analysis of a case.

NEUROCOGNITIVE DYSFUNCTION

Vignette 1. Claims of a car accident with closed head injury resulting in ongoing complaints of cognitive slowing, confusion, and memory loss.

Neuropsychological examination: Clinical interview—improbable and exaggerated cognitive and memory complaints. Testing including

- Test of Memory Malingering (TOMM): Scoring well below chance.
- Structured Interview of Reported Symptoms (SIRS): Scores consistent with feigned mental illness on numerous scales.

- Minnesota Multiphasic Personality Inventory-2 (MMPI-2): Identified endorsements of rare and infrequent symptoms consistent with faking badly.

Impression: Malingering of neurocognitive dysfunction.

Psychiatric examination: records reviewed—auto accident—six months ago, questionable brief loss of consciousness, and CT negative. He was receiving no psychiatric or other current treatment, and had complaints of confusion, and memory problems causing distress and impairment in daily activities.

This is a good example of the "floor effect" where obviously overlearned material is presented as extremely challenging, bewildering, or impossible to comprehend.

At the outset of the evaluation he was asked to sign his name—one letter was omitted out of his first and last name.

During the interview he mentions that he was able to get a new driver's license a month ago. I examined it—intact signature. He asks for a bathroom break—right around corner in the hall—he returns 60 minutes later and said, "I couldn't find the bus stop you sent me to." I asked him to sign in again—this time he omitted a different letter in both his first and last name. I asked him to spell the word "it." After a 60 second delay where he simulated strong effort, he responded "T" (followed by a 15-second delay) "I." I said, "Okay, now spell it backwards," and, after another long delay in which he appeared puzzled, responded "I–T."

Opinion: The nature and extent of any true mental disorder could not be determined secondary to malingering.

Outcome: Plaintiffs' lawyer dropped the case after receiving the report.

Vignette 2. Examination of a plaintiff with claims of brain damage, severe physical trauma, confusion, cognitive slowing, gait and balance disturbance, chronic back pain, severe memory problems, speech deficits, and seizures, three years ago following an unwitnessed industrial accident. The plaintiff claimed to have fallen off a forklift and being hit with its contents. At the time of the accident, there was no known loss of consciousness, although he claimed to have hit his head, and had back, leg, and side pain. In the emergency room, the patient was oriented, able to give the history of the accident, his current medications, but left out a prohibited medication, and his medical history. Findings were a left lower leg and flank contusion. A CT of the brain was negative and a neurological examination was negative. There were no other physical or psychiatric findings. After several weeks, he was cleared to return to work, but never did. He continued to complain that his symptoms were worsening. This continued for a three-year period, leading to a claim of 100% disability. A claim had been filed in civil court for damages.

An extensive series of examinations were performed including psychiatric, neurological, and neuropsychiatric along with neuroradiological reviews of the original and subsequent brain images studies. A 48-hour ambulatory EEG was also done which was read as, "normal EEG."

Opinion: Plaintiff malingering neurocognitive, psychiatric, physical, and neurologic symptoms.

There was no evidence of brain injury after the neuroradiologist's review of multiple imaging studies. In addition, there was no evidence of seizure disorder. All clinical examinations, including psychiatrist's psychological and neurological examinations, opined a malingered presentation.

Outcome: Case dismissed with prejudice.

Vignette 3. Claims of physical and psychological trauma, and a request for political asylum in the United States.

Medicolegal issue: Determining competence to stand trial, and the creditability of the patient as to his accounts of being tortured. He had claims of severe physical and emotional trauma following arrests in Singapore while being held as a political prisoner.

Examinations:

- Psychiatric examination and treatment,
- Psychological treatment for trauma consisting of Eye Movement Desensitization and Reprocessing (EMDR),
- Psychological testing,
- Orthopedic opinion regarding fractures,
- Medical examination by an internist familiar with evaluating torture victims.

Opinion:

- Diagnosis: Posttraumatic Stress Disorder—severe.
- Patient cooperative and responsive to psychological and psychiatric treatment.
- No evidence of malingering clinically or on psychological testing (MMPI and Rorschach).
- Physical findings and history consistent with torture.
- Competent to stand trial.

Outcome: I testified in his case as to his condition and the above findings and opinions. He was able to testify in his case. He was granted political asylum.

Vignette 4. Claims of loss of fitness for an execution while awaiting execution on death row.

> *"There is a strange, entirely unfounded superstition even among psychiatrists that if a man simulates insanity there must be something mentally wrong with him in the first place. As if a sane man would not grasp at any straw if his life were endangered by the electric chair."* (Wertham, 1949)

In 1998, I was retained by the state's attorney's office to examine a defendant for competency to be executed.

The test for competence to be executed elucidated in *Ford v. Wainwright* (U.S. Supreme Court, 1986) is whether the prisoner is aware of his impending execution and the reason for it.

Examinations: psychiatric examination, psychological examination, and neurological examination.

The defendant was a 43-year-old male who had been convicted and sentenced to death for murder. He was convicted and placed on death row where he resided for 15 years. He started to display extreme communication difficulties with his attorneys and family members for a period of about 2 weeks prior to his execution date. Hours away from being executed, an evaluation for competency to be executed was ordered by the court. His school records indicated his IQ tests were in the borderline range of the intellectual functioning range (IQ 72–76). Recent psychological testing had found him to be in the mental retardation range with an IQ of 51. However, the results of IQ testing can be falsely lowered by any situation which results in less than a full effort being expended by the test taker whether voluntarily, by deliberate distortion (malingering), or involuntarily by physical or mental illness. While in prison, he had received a nonspecific personality disorder diagnosis and had engaged in some antisocial conduct. He had no documented communication difficulties and had been noted to be able to play chess by calling out moves to neighboring cells. He also was reported to engage in other appropriate social interactions. Mental retardation (now Intellectual Disability, DSM-V) had never been diagnosed in the past. I performed a psychiatric examination of this individual and gave a report which included incorporating psychological and neurological examinations was performed by other experts. This individual's current presentation was not consistent with his history. Along with a lack of cooperation, he presented with a constellation of exaggerated and unusual symptoms.

On psychological testing, an attempt was made to administer a battery of psychological tests. The psychologist reported "This individual did not directly refuse to be tested, but either used distraction techniques or acted as if he could not comprehend the requested task." She also reported that on the Wide Range Achievement tests he denied he could read any words, even the ones as simple as "in" or "cat." The Rorschach Test produced a protocol that was not valid for scoring due to his unwillingness to complete the instrument. The psychologist stated, "He did not directly refuse, but did not stay on task…jumping back from a card and telling me it scared him, as well as smelling the cards or scratching at them." The psychologist noted that similar problems occurred on attempting the Wechsler Adult Intelligence Scale. The psychologist also reported giving this individual two tasks which detect malingering. On the first, he was presented with five sets of three characters. This includes simple numbers and letters in order. On the first, she noted that, "All but the most severely brain damaged individuals can recall at least three of the five-character sets." She said that allowing him to study the paper on three occasions and even upon giving him extended time to complete the sets he failed to reproduce any symbol or letter. This lack of response was indicative of malingering. On an additional task, the Hiscock and Hiscock, he produced over a 90% error rate "indicative of malingering." She reported that an individual should get 50% right, even by chance. Such a low score indicated that this individual "Had to put in considerable effort to get so many wrong." At one point during the testing, she reported that he got up and began to chase around the room for "a friend" he called "little Peter," which escaped from his pocket. He appeared to scoop him up and put him back in his pocket and asked if she could see him. The psychologist indicated that, within a reasonable degree of psychological certainty, it was her opinion that, "He is not mentally retarded and is malingering mental retardation and mental illness. His presentation of these symptoms is clearly feigned and inconsistent with any diagnosable mental illness."

I performed a psychiatric examination which lasted over one hour. During the examination, the inmate generally mumbled unintelligibly with occasional audible words and grunts, but generally with nonresponsive answers to my questions. I introduced myself and showed him the court order allowing for his examination. He took it, turned it upside down and stared at it as if attempting to read it. Often times he stared at me, made faces at me, bared his teeth and later began eating toilet paper. He watched the jail personnel walking by the interview room commenting on their behavior at times. Examples of understandable utterances included "huh… I want to eat… they over there… hey doc… he go over there… [and] mama come." At one point after I recounted some details I knew about his case and past functioning while in prison he shrugged his shoulders, jerked his head to the side a few times, turned away from me to look out the window and stated, "lady out there," and continued to mumble incoherently, grunting, groaning, and yawning. When I asked him if he was taking the option to refuse to talk to me and not cooperate with the exam, he mumbled "yeah" then paused and continued to groan and mumble. I indicated to him that his psychological test results from the other day had indicated that he was not being completely honest with the testing. At that point, I was unable to illicit any further cooperation and he remained essentially mute thereafter. He sat looking out the window, watching the guards, and ignoring me. At the point when I terminated the interview and asked the guard to come in, he did follow the guard's command to get up and he walked back cooperatively and slowly to his cell. On mental status examination, he was an alert, uncooperative male who was moderately disheveled with braided hair and no body odor. He related poorly to the interviewer throughout the examination. His intellect was intact for selective ability to follow commands and answer questions. He was able to selectively attend to stimuli and expressed a realization that I was a doctor. He was uncooperative overall, refusing to answer most questions or to speak distinctly when asked. His affect was restricted and he appeared agitated at times. Moderate psychomotor agitation was observed, staring at me while pulling at his cuffs and scraping them against the table as well as baring his teeth at times. He did not discuss any bizarre or psychotic phenomena as he had during the psychological testing. No involuntary motor movements were seen.

The neurological examination revealed inconsistent cooperation throughout the examination with some angry affect although "no evidence of gross abnormalities were found which would suggest organic brain dysfunction."

The neurologist reported, "As the technician was attempting to do the EEG, the inmate was told that this would measure brain waves, and could determine if he truly had brain disease or whether his brain was functioning normally. When told he could not voluntarily control how this test would come out (that he could not voluntarily control his brain wave pattern), he ripped the leads off his head and scalp, and he refused to have this test done." His lack of cooperation for this test is consistent with the diagnosis of malingering.

The neurologist reported, "Evidence of functional impairment on neurological examination which, in his current state, is most consistent with a diagnosis of malingering. In summary, this individual appears to be malingering his impaired neurologic status."

The experts' findings: Malingering.

State examiners' findings: Not cooperating with the examination, and therefore, no opinion on Fitness for Execution—malingering.

Court examiners' findings: Fit for execution; not malingering.

Defense Examiners' findings: Confusing neurological signs and symptoms—not fit for execution.

Outcome: Due to new evidence uncovered in the case, he was never executed.

REFERENCES

American Psychiatric Association. 2013. *Diagnostic and Statistical Manual of Mental Disorders, 5th edition.* Arlington: American Psychiatric Publishing.

Rogers, R. 2012. *Clinical Assessment of Malingering and Deception, 3rd edition.* New York: The Guilford Press.

Rosner, R., and C.L. Scott. 2017. *Principles and Practice of Forensic Psychiatry, 3rd edition.* New York: CRC Press.

Sadock, B.J., V.A. Sadock, and P. Ruiz. 2009. *Kaplan & Sadock's Comprehensive Textbook of Psychiatry, 9th edition.* New York: Lippincott Williams & Wilkins.

Scott, C. 2015. *DSM-5 and the Law: Changes and Challenges.* New York: Oxford.

Wertham, F. 1949. *The Show of Violence.* New York: Doubleday & Company.

14 Feigning ≠ Malingering
A Case Study

Gregory DeClue, PhD, ABPP

CONTENTS

In the fourth edition of *The Clinician's Handbook*, Meyer and Deitsch (1996a) assert that in the practice of assessing for malingering the Structured Interview of Reported Symptoms (SIRS) (Rogers, Bagby, and Dickens, 1992) "is of questionable usefulness since even its author has been consistently disinclined to offer cutoff point decision rules" (Meyer and Deitsch, 1996b). In fact, Rogers et al. (1992) present clear-cut scores for feigning but insist, "Feigning should be established first, and motivation for feigning second." And, in sharp contrast to the "questionable usefulness" characterization, Rogers et al. (1998) considers the SIRS to be a gold standard for malingering research.* This case study compares the usefulness of Meyer and Deitsch's versus Rogers' assessment-of-malingering models for practicing forensic psychologists and illustrates that malingering should never be diagnosed by test score(s) alone. This case study also offers some guidance for how practicing forensic clinicians should present assessment-of-malingering data in reports and testimony.

* Rogers et al. (1998) write, "The use of the SIRS as a gold standard requires a brief explanation. Extensive research (see Rogers et al., 1992; Rogers, 1997b) with both simulation designs and known-groups comparisons has established stable and accurate cutoff scores for establishing feigners and genuine patients. Use of the combined rules (see Rogers et al., 1992) has a high degree of accuracy in classifying both feigners (.98) and genuine patients (.95)."

14.1 MALINGERING

Both Meyer and Deitsch (1996a) and Rogers (1997a) consider the recommendations of the *Diagnostic and Statistical Manual* (American Psychiatric Association, 1994), which advises that

> Malingering should be strongly suspected if any combination of the following is noted:
> 1. Medico-legal context of presentation (e.g., the person is referred by an attorney to the clinician for examination).
> 2. Marked discrepancy between the person's claimed stress or disability and the objective findings.
> 3. Lack of cooperation during the diagnostic evaluation and in complying with the prescribed treatment regimen.
> 4. The presence of Antisocial Personality Disorder.

Meyer and Deitsch (1996c) assert, "This is good advice" and advise that "it is often appropriate to broaden the concept of malingering to any type of response that distorts the production of an accurate record."

In contrast, Rogers (1997a) is critical of DSM-IV's approach and summarizes data from a study (Rogers, 1990), which showed that using the DSM-IV's guidelines, "for every malingerer correctly identified, nearly four times as many *bona fide* patients were miscategorized as malingerers" (Rogers, 1997a). Because of the serious consequences generated by a classification of malingering such a false positive rate is clearly unacceptable.

14.2 DEFINITIONS

In contrast to Meyer and Deitsch's suggestion to broaden the use of the concept of malingering, Rogers (1997a) presents more narrow definitions. Rogers' definitions, presented next, are used throughout the remainder of this chapter. *Dissimulation* is a general term to describe an individual who is deliberately distorting or misrepresenting psychological problems. *Dissimulation* can incorporate any, or a combination of the following: malingering, defensiveness, irrelevant responding, or random responding. *Malingering* and *defensiveness* are reserved for cases in which there is unequivocal evidence of deliberate dissimulation. In *defensive* responding, the person minimizes or denies psychological problems or symptoms. A person who is *malingering* is intentionally exaggerating or fabricating psychological problems or symptoms; this is a conscious choice, motivated for external gain. Finally, *feigning* refers to exaggerating or fabricating psychological problems or symptoms, regardless of what the intent—if any—may be.

14.3 MODELS FOR ASSESSING MALINGERING

Meyer and Deitsch (1996) endeavor to integrate "common behavior features, … test data, and … treatment recommendations" into a practical guidebook for clinicians, including those doing forensic work. Although they make some reference to research, many—perhaps most—of their recommendations do not show a clear scientific basis. This may limit the admissibility of testimony guided by their handbook, particularly in federal cases and in states guided by *Daubert v. Merrell Dow Pharmaceuticals*, 509 U.S. 579 (1993); *General Electric v. Joiner*, 522 U.S. 136 (1997); and *Kumho Tire Co. v. Carmichael*, 526 U.S. 137 (1999); see e.g., O'Connor and Krauss (2001).

Meyer and Deitsch's chapter 16 presents separate 16 to 28 item checklists for hypochondriasis, factitious disorder, and malingering. These lists provide some guidance for clinical decision-making, but there is no empirical support to provide a basis for testimony. Additional drawbacks of this approach are the absence of a theory to guide interpretation of data and the aforementioned overbroad conceptualization of malingering to include "any type of response that distorts the production of an accurate record" (p. 412).

According to Rogers' *adaptational model* of malingering (Rogers, 1990, 1997a; Rogers, Bagby, and Dickens, 1992), would-be malingerers engage in a cost–benefit analysis involving estimation of their likelihood of success in an assessment. A person would be more likely to malinger when the context of the evaluation is perceived to be adversarial and the stakes are high. The cost–benefit analysis would involve estimation of the likelihood of success if one were honest versus the likelihood of success if one attempts to malinger. In some forensic contexts, people (e.g., some criminal defendants) may estimate that they are unlikely to succeed (be found not guilty) if they are honest, have a fair chance of succeeding (be found not guilty by reason of insanity) if they successfully malinger, have a fair likelihood of pulling it off (fooling the examiner and the judge or jury), and risk little by trying (no additional penalty if caught).

Whereas DSM-IV describes when malingering should be "strongly suspected," Rogers (1997a) presents (a) a *threshold model* for when clinicians should thoroughly evaluate suspected dissimulation and (b) a *clinical decision model* involving "accurate classification of 90% or more of individual persons based on extensive, cross-validated research" (Rogers, 1997a). This provides a clear framework for a forensic clinician to report findings.

Rogers' adaptational model of dissimulation is more useful for practicing forensic clinicians than that provided by Meyer and Deitsch and the guidelines in DSM-IV because Rogers' model (a) provides a coherent theory to guide investigation and report, (b) provides a clear framework (with the threshold and clinical decision models) for describing the degree of certainty about whether a subject is dissimulating, and (c) facilitates distinct discussion of the likelihood of, type of, and motivation for malingering.

14.4 MODELS FOR CLINICAL DECISION-MAKING

In a more recent publication, Rogers and Shuman (2000) present two models of clinical decision-making: A *hypothesis-testing model* and a *linear best-fit* model. Forensic examiners who use a hypothesis-testing model formulate a hypothesis about the person's behavior and diagnosis near the beginning of the evaluation, and then gather data to confirm or disconfirm the hypothesis. If the hypothesis is disconfirmed, a new hypothesis is formed and tested. Borum et al. (1993) address potential problems with this approach and recommend that experts always test alternative hypotheses.

Although they believe that the hypothesis-testing model is the one most used by forensic experts,* Rogers and Shuman (2000) advocate the use of a linear best-fit model, in which the examiner conducts the assessment in two phases. First, in the data-collection phase, the examiner amasses comprehensive and relevant data, undistorted by bias and preconceptions. Second, in the decision phase, the examiner considers the relative merits of competing hypotheses, and, where possible, forms opinions and conclusions. The linear best-fit model has the advantage of avoiding such biases as primacy bias, confirmatory bias, over-reliance on unique data, and premature closure. The disadvantage is that by seeking to comprehensively collect all relevant data, the linear best-fit model will typically take longer than the hypothesis-testing model.†

14.5 CUT SCORES WITH THE SIRS

As the SIRS was initially presented, its developers noted there was no "gold standard" or "ground truth" against which to validate a new measure of response style (Rogers, Bagby, and Dickens, 1992). Five years later, Rogers (1997b) wrote, "The SIRS appear to be established as a standard method for the assessment of malingering. The SIRS has a high level of reliability and well-established validity (Berry, Wetter, and Baer, 1995). In addition, the SIRS appear unparalleled in its ability to distinguish between feigned and genuine disorders" (Rogers, 1995). Melton et al. (1997) report "Research on the SIRS has...consistently reported respectable indices of *sensitivity*‡ and *specificity*.§ ... Thus, the SIRS is worthy of serious consideration by forensic clinicians investigating the malingering of symptoms of psychopathology." I concur.

In contrast to Meyer and Deitsch's (1996) criticism about the lack of cutoff point decision rules for the SIRS, Melton et al. (1997) applaud that "the interpretation of the SIRS scales is geared to minimize the risk that a respondent will be inappropriately identified as malingering."

In the SIRS manual, Rogers et al. (1992) present cut scores for classifying responders as *Honest*, *Indeterminate*, *Probable Feigning*, and *Definite Feigning* for each of the eight primary scales of the SIRS. A respondent is to be classified as definitely feigning if he or she (a) scores in the definite range on any of the eight primary scales—99% likelihood of feigning, (b) scores in the probable range on three or more of the primary scales—97% probability of feigning, or (c) above 76 on

* At least for insanity evaluations, the context of Rogers and Shuman's book.

† The time difference is likely to be less for clinicians who follow Rogers and Shuman's (2000) guidance regarding incremental validity and psychological testing. Rather than using a test battery of multiple measures of the same construct, clinicians would use the single, best-validated instrument for measuring the relevant issue (e.g., symptom or diagnosis) and only use additional instruments for which there is evidence of incremental validity (improved accuracy by adding the less-validated instrument).

‡ Sensitivity reflects a test's capacity to select many or most of the individuals who possess the trait or exhibit the behavior which the test is designed to measure.

§ Specificity is an index of the degree to which the test selects only those individuals possessing the trait or expressing the behavior which the test is designed to detect.

the total SIRS score—100% likelihood of feigning (Rogers, 1997b). Rogers (1997b) also presents a threshold model for suspecting malingering based on (a) four or fewer SIRS scales in the honest range, (b) two SIRS scales in the probable range, or (c) a total SIRS score of greater than 66.

It is abundantly clear that Rogers and his colleagues offer cutoff point decision rules for *feigning*. Why do they not do so for *malingering?*

The determination of malingering is a multimethod assessment which incorporates and integrates data from unstructured interviews, psychological tests, and collateral sources. Despite the unmatched accuracy of SIRS for the classification of feigned psychopathology, such an important determination should not rely solely on a single measure. Therefore, the clinical decision model requires confirmatory data in addition to the SIRS (Rogers, 1997b).

The SIRS provides the single most accurate indication of whether a person is feigning (exaggerating or fabricating) psychopathology (particularly psychotic symptoms), and allows the clinician to quantify the likelihood that the subject is dissimulating. Additional data, from interview and observation, other tests, records review, and collaterals, help to confirm or disconfirm the presence of feigning. *The SIRS does not identify the person's motivation for feigning—nor does any psychological test.* The person's motivation for feigning may be inferred from additional information, including the context of the evaluation and collateral sources, if enough information is available and if the evaluator considers enough hypotheses.

14.6 CASE DATA

14.6.1 SIRS Scores

This case involves a 20-year-old male referred for a forensic psychological assessment.* On the SIRS, no scores were in the Definite range; four scores, Rare Symptoms (RS), Blatant Symptoms (BL), Severity of Symptoms (SEV), and Reported vs. Observed Symptoms (RO), were in the Probable range; three scores, Symptom Combination (SC), Subtle Symptoms (SU), and Selectivity of Symptoms (SEL), were in the Indeterminate range; and one score, Improbable and Absurd Symptoms (IA) was in the Honest range.† According to the SIRS manual (Rogers, Bagby, and Dickens, 1992), among research samples with a 51% base rate of feigning, subjects with four or more primary SIRS scales in the Probable range have a 100% likelihood of feigning. The basic interpretation recommended by the SIRS manual would be:

> *The client has moderately elevated scores on the Rare Symptoms scale, which consists of symptoms that occur very infrequently in bona fide patients; the Blatant Symptoms scale, which consists of symptoms that untrained individuals are likely to identify as*

---

* The SIRS scores are purposely presented before setting, referral question, and additional information, which are provided below.

† The score on Inconsistency of Symptoms (INC) was 6; scores greater than 6 are considered high (Rogers et al., 1992; see Tables 8–12). Only one of the five criteria for suspecting malingering rather than factitious disorder was met: IA > 5. See Table 19, p. 26, in Rogers et al. (1992).

obvious signs of a major mental illness; the Subtle Symptoms scale, which consists of symptoms that an untrained individual is likely to associate with everyday problems or minor maladjustment; and the Selectivity of Symptoms scale, which indicates the nonselective or indiscriminate endorsement of psychiatric problems. This combination of elevated scores is characteristic of individuals who are feigning a mental disorder, and is rarely seen in clients responding truthfully.

The pattern of scores on the SIRS meets Rogers' criteria for a clinical decision that the subject is not responding in a reliable manner. It is very likely that the subject is feigning a mental disorder, but additional information is required for consideration of whether or not the subject is malingering.

14.7 ADDITIONAL INFORMATION

Intelligence testing yielded a Verbal IQ score of 75, a Performance IQ score of 70, and a Full Scale IQ score of 70.* Could the person's performance on the SIRS somehow be due to low intelligence? A study of 39 mentally retarded male patients in a forensic mental hospital suggests otherwise. In this study, in which the base rate of malingering was 23%, Hayes et al. (1998) found that the SIRS led to 95% overall classification accuracy. This supports using standard interpretation of SIRS scores in cases where the person's IQ is low.

On the Personality Assessment Inventory (PAI) (Morey, 1991, 1996), T-scores on the validity scales were as follows: Inconsistency 70, Infrequency 51, Negative Impression 66, Positive Impression 15; with a Malingering Index of 1. These scores do not meet PAI criteria for suspecting malingering (Rogers, Sewell, Cruise, Wang, and Ustad, 1998); they show (a) nonrandom responding, (b) some inconsistency in responding but not enough to invalidate the profile, and (c) more of a tendency to describe problems than virtues. This *pattern* is generally consistent with results from the SIRS, but the *degree* of overreporting is not as high.†

This 20-year-old male had been in the same prison for over a year. He was not prescribed any psychotropic medication and was not receiving any psychiatric treatment at the time of the assessment, but had recently started participating in group treatment for sex offenders. School records show that at various times he had been placed in special classes for children with specific learning disabilities, emotional handicaps, and severe emotional disturbances. Symptoms of Attention Deficit-Hyperactivity Disorder and one or more personality disorders had been noted in the psychiatric records. Socially, he was described as having "impaired ability to appropriately interact with others," he "saw the world in a very self-centered way," he "suffered from poor peer relationships," he "was easily upset, socially immature, and unpredictable," and he was "often telling elaborate lies."

Recalling that DSM-IV recommends malingering should be strongly suspected when any combination of four factors is present, it is noteworthy that three of those

* The average IQ score is 100. The cutoff between the Borderline and Mentally Deficient ranges is 70.

† Multiple clinical scale elevations led to multiple diagnostic possibilities, including psychotic disorders, mood disorders, and personality disorders.

four factors are present in this case. There was a medico-legal context to the evaluation, there was a marked discrepancy between the person's claimed stress or disability and the objective findings,* and the person meets criteria for a diagnosis of antisocial personality disorder.† The person's performance on the SIRS (the single best-validated instrument for assessing response style) leads to classification as feigning; people in malingering studies with comparable scores are classified as feigning, with 100% accuracy. Is there any doubt that this person is malingering? Yes, there is.

This young man was referred for evaluation under the state's civil commitment of sexually violent predators law, in anticipation of a hearing to determine whether he has a mental abnormality and/or personality disorder which makes him likely to engage in future acts of sexual violence. In this context, the presence of a psychiatric disorder would enhance the likelihood that he would be involuntarily, and indefinitely, committed to a secure treatment facility. This provided no external motivation to try to malinger psychiatric symptoms. Various possible motivations for malingering were considered,‡ but not supported by collateral information or other data. Unstructured and semistructured interviews yielded some highly improbable accounts of past and present experiences.§

Although his self-report was unreliable, the subject did not meet DSM-IV criteria for a diagnosis of malingering because there was no discernable external motivation for feigning symptoms. He did not meet criteria for a diagnosis of Factitious Disorder because his feigning did not appear to be motivated by a desire to "assume the sick role." A comprehensive view of his records and current symptom presentation clearly showed the presence of a psychiatric disturbance. He met criteria for a diagnosis of Schizoaffective Disorder, Bipolar Type, in that he had experienced both major depressive episodes with delusions and hallucinations, and a manic episode with delusions and hallucinations; both the mood episodes and the psychotic symptoms were prominent and the disturbance was not due to direct physiological effects of a substance or a general medical condition.

14.8 CONTRASTING MODELS

If a clinician approached the forensic psychological evaluation of this subject by testing alternative hypotheses with Meyer and Deitsch's (1996) handbook as a guide, it appears likely that potential diagnoses of Malingering or Factitious Disorder would be briefly considered and rejected, if considered at all. In one sense that would be correct, because the subject does not meet criteria for either of those diagnoses.

* Notable on the Reported vs. Observed Symptoms scale of the SIRS.

† Met criteria for Conduct Disorder prior to age 15, repeatedly violated the law, impulsive, irritable and aggressive, and lack of remorse.

‡ Schizophrenia is negatively weighted in some actuarial prediction instruments. An institutionalized inmate may fear freedom.

§ He described having six children by six different mothers in six different states. He described killing several people, though he has never been charged with a crime involving death of a victim. He described personal involvements in violent deaths on three different continents.

But this approach would likely lead to overlooking or underemphasizing the fact that the subject's self-report was unreliable.

If, instead, Rogers' adaptational model of malingering (Rogers, 1990; Rogers, 1997a; Rogers, Bagby, and Dickens, 1992) was utilized,* the evaluator would establish that the subject's self-report was unreliable *and* that the unreliability was not due to malingering or an attempt to assume the sick role. An evaluator's "responsibility goes beyond the mere identification of dissimulators and extends to his or her understanding of their motivations for these deliberate distortions" (Rogers 1997c), which requires consideration of information beyond the test data.

In the present case, the examiner's opinion was that the person's self-report was unreliable, but not malingered. His report could not be taken at face value, and it was clear that he was over-reporting unusual experiences. Yet it did not appear that he was exaggerating or feigning symptoms in order to be considered more severely mentally ill than he really was. He enjoys telling stories, he enjoys getting attention, and he does not appreciate the consequences of his actions.†

14.9 PRESENTING ASSESSMENT-OF-MALINGERING DATA IN REPORTS AND TESTIMONY

This study illustrates that cutoff point decision rules are possible for *feigning* but not for *malingering*. No test score or combination of test scores can determine whether or not a person is malingering. Even when test scores lead to virtual certainty that a person's self-report is unreliable, that alone tells nothing about a person's motivation for giving an unreliable account. "An important guideline is that *feigning should be established first, and motivation for feigning second*. Most individuals, including clients, are motivated by external incentives" (Rogers, Bagby, and Dickens, 1992). Psychological tests, even ones with excellent sensitivity and specificity, cannot replace careful investigation by the forensic examiner.

In preparing forensic reports or testimony regarding response styles, evaluators should communicate findings about unreliability of self-report, direction of unreliability (e.g., overreporting, underreporting, or random reporting), and motivation for that unreliability, separately. In the present case, there was a high level of certainty about the fact that the subject's self-report was unreliable, clear indication that the subject's self-report involved overreporting psychopathology, but less certainty about the subject's reasons for overreporting symptoms.

When an expert says that test scores show a 97% or 100% likelihood of *feigning*, the judge or jury may "hear" this as a 97% or 100% likelihood of *malingering*. Forensic examiners have an affirmative obligation to take steps to ensure that their data and opinions are not misconstrued (Committee on Ethical Guidelines for Forensic Psychologists, 1991). Whenever an examiner presents data showing a near-certainty that a person's self-report is unreliable, the examiner must

* With either clinical decision model: either the hypothesis-testing model or the linear best-fit model.

† It is likely that if he were facing criminal charges he would be found incompetent to proceed. If he were to be interrogated by police detectives, he might confess to crimes he did not commit.

clearly communicate that this does not equate to a near-certainty that the person is malingering.

This last point should be kept in mind as we consider how the same clinical data from this case might be considered in different assessment contexts. This same individual was previously arrested for a serious sex offense, was interrogated, and subsequently entered a plea and was sentenced. He could very well have been referred for forensic evaluations relevant to competency to waive Miranda or other rights, competency to proceed, criminal responsibility, sentencing, or other issues. In many of those contexts, there would be clear external motivation to malinger. Imagine the same subject presenting the same symptoms in a different forensic context. With clear motivation to malinger; inconsistent, extreme, and highly improbable symptom presentation; and test scores associated with a 100% likelihood of feigning, how could a forensic examiner not conclude that the person was malingering? There are two ways that we know of, both mentioned earlier in this chapter.

Borum et al. (1993) emphasize the importance of testing alternative hypotheses. Rogers and Shuman (2000) recommend comprehensive data collection prior to hypothesis testing. In the present case, either of these approaches would require the examiner to gather and consider additional information, which would show that the person had been giving exaggerated and improbable descriptions of events and symptoms for years. A competent evaluation of the same person in a different forensic context would necessarily entail extensive data collection and consideration of alternatives, even though the examiner's initial hypothesis would likely be that the person was malingering.

Evaluators must also clearly communicate that the fact that a person's self-report is unreliable does not answer the referral question. For example, if someone pleading insanity is found to be feigning symptoms of psychopathology, that finding does not answer questions about what his mental state was at the time of the offense. The evaluator should communicate that the person's presentation cannot be taken at face value, and it will be important for the evaluator and ultimately the factfinder to utilize other data sources to construct or reconstruct the person's mental state.

In the context of civil commitment, the U.S. Supreme Court noted that factual issues represent only the beginning of the inquiry, and the ultimate issue "turns on the *meaning* of the facts which must be interpreted by expert psychiatrists and psychologists. Given the lack of certainty and the fallibility of psychiatric diagnosis, there is serious question as to whether a state could ever prove beyond a reasonable doubt that an individual is both mentally ill and likely to be dangerous" (*Addington v. Texas*, 99 S.Ct. 1804 at 1811, 1979). The parallel here is that, using the best assessment techniques, there is potential for evaluators to say with a specifiable level of certainty that a person is feigning (exaggerating or fabricating) psychopathology, but whether or not the person is malingering (deliberately distorting responses for external gain) requires interpretation of the *meaning* of the facts. Evaluators may be able to provide a scientific basis to support an opinion that a person is feigning psychopathology, but rely on a less certain clinical interpretation as to whether the person is malingering. Evaluators must acknowledge the decrease in the level of certainty when going from reporting about feigning to reporting about malingering, and will need to adhere to their jurisdictions' rules for admissibility.

14.10 RECOMMENDATIONS FOR FORENSIC CLINICIANS

The following recommendations are made for clinicians assessing for malingering in forensic cases:

1. Use Rogers' adaptational model of malingering (Rogers, 1990; Rogers, 1997a; Rogers, Bagby, and Dickens, 1992) for theoretical and practical guidance.
2. Using either a hypothesis-testing model or a linear best-fit model, gather sufficient information to test multiple hypotheses.
3. Apply a multimethod assessment approach, using the best forensic assessment instruments (e.g., SIRS), clinical interview, records review, and collateral interviews.
4. Clearly explicate logical links between data and opinions (Borum, Otto, and Golding, 1993; Skeem and Golding, 1998).
5. Carefully distinguish opinions about whether the subject's responses are reliable, the quantitative nature of the unreliability (e.g., overreporting, underreporting, random responding), and the likely motivation for the unreliability.
6. Clearly present information about the basis for the expert's opinion about unreliability, acknowledging that error rates for detecting feigning do not equate to error rates for detecting malingering.

Researchers and academicians are making excellent progress in developing tools and techniques for assessing response style, including malingering (Rogers, 1997d). As forensic clinicians apply these tools and techniques, we must take care that our work is not the weak link in the process. It is hoped that the comments and recommendations presented here will assist forensic clinicians to conduct assessments useful to courts.

REFERENCES

American Psychiatric Association. 1994. *Diagnostic and Statistical Manual of Mental Disorders, 4th Edition*, 683. Washington, DC: American Psychiatric Association.

Berry, D.T.R., M.W. Wetter, R.A. Baer. 1995. Assessment of malingering. In *Clinical Personality Assessment: Practical Approaches*, ed. J.N. Butcher, 236–248. New York: Oxford University Press.

Borum R., R. Otto, and S. Golding. 1993. Improving clinical judgment and decision making in forensic evaluation. *Journal of Psychiatry and Law* 21:35–76.

Committee on Ethical Guidelines for Forensic Psychologists. 1991. Specialty guidelines for forensic psychologists. *Law and Human Behavior* 15:6:1991.

Hayes, J.S., D.B. Hale, W.D. Gouvier. 1998. Malingering detection in a mentally retarded forensic population. *Applied Neuropsychology* 5:1:33–36.

Melton, G.B., J. Petrila, N.G. Poythress, and C. Slobogin. 1997. *Psychological Evaluations for the Courts, 2nd Edition*. New York: Guilford Press.

Meyer, R.G., and S.E. Deitsch. 1996c. *The Clinician's Handbook: Integrated Diagnostics, Assessment, and Intervention in Adult and Adolescent Psychopathology, 4th Edition*, 412. Needham Heights, MA: Allyn & Bacon.

Meyer, R.G., and S.E. Deitsch. 1996b. *The Clinician's Handbook: Integrated Diagnostics, Assessment, and Intervention in Adult and Adolescent Psychopathology, 4th Edition*, 422. Needham Heights, MA: Allyn & Bacon.

Meyer, R.G., and S.E. Deitsch. 1996a. *The Clinician's Handbook: Integrated Diagnostics, Assessment, and Intervention in Adult and Adolescent Psychopathology, 4th Edition*. Needham Heights, MA: Allyn & Bacon.

Morey, L.C. 1991. *Personality Assessment Inventory: Professional Manual*. Odessa, FL: Psychological Assessment Resources.

Morey, L.C. 1996. *An Interpretive Guide to the Personality Assessment Inventory (PAI)*. Odessa, FL: Psychological Assessment Resources.

O'Connor, M., and D. Krauss. 2001. Legal update: New developments in rule 702. *American Psychology-Law Society News* 21:1–4:18.

Rogers, R. 1990. Development of a new classificatory model of malingering. *Bulletin of the American Academy of Psychiatry and Law* 18:323–333.

Rogers, R. 1995. *Diagnostic and Structured Interviewing: A Handbook for Psychologists*. Odessa, FL: Psychological Assessment Resources.

Rogers, R. 1997a. Introduction. In *Clinical Assessment of Malingering and Deception, 2nd Edition*, ed. R. Rogers, 1–19. New York: Guilford Press.

Rogers, R. 1997b. Structured interviews and dissimulation. In *Clinical Assessment of Malingering and Deception, 2nd Edition*, ed. R. Rogers, 301–327. New York: Guilford Press.

Rogers, R. 1997d. *Clinical Assessment of Malingering and Deception, 2nd Edition*. New York: Guilford Press.

Rogers, R. 1997c. Current status of clinical methods. In *Clinical Assessment of Malingering and Deception, 2nd Edition*, ed. R. Rogers, 373–397. New York: Guilford Press.

Rogers, R., and D. Shuman. 2000. *Conducting Insanity Evaluations*. New York: Guilford Press.

Rogers, R., K.W. Sewell, K.R. Cruise, E.W. Wang, and K.L. Ustad. 1998. The PAI and feigning: A cautionary note on its use in forensic-correctional settings. *Assessment* 5:4:399–405.

Rogers, R., R.M. Bagby, and S.E. Dickens. 1992. *Structured Interview of Reported Symptoms (SIRS): Professional Manual*. Odessa, FL: Psychological Assessment Resources.

Skeem, J.L., and S.L. Golding. 1998. Community examiners' evaluations of competence to stand trial: Common problems and suggestions for improvement. *Professional Psychology: Research and Practice* 294:357–367.

15 Malingering, Noncompliance, and Secondary Gain

Henry Phillip Gruss, JD and
Valerie Gruss, PhD, APN, CNP-BC

CONTENTS

Malingering can be defined as pretending to be ill or otherwise incapacitated. Malingering is deliberately exaggerating symptoms for personal gain. When the definition is limited to "feigning of illness for material gain," the data suggests a prevalence of 10–15% of civil suits or disability claims (Young, 2014). When the definition includes exaggeration, noncompliance, poor effort, and suboptimal performance, the numbers increase to 40% (Young, 2014). However, most definitions do not include exaggeration in its definition of malingering.

Secondary gain, though similar, is defined as an external motivation for behavior. If exaggerating the patient's disease allows him/her to miss work, avoid military duty or obtain financial compensation, that would be an example of secondary gain. Included in the concept of secondary gain is the fact that occasionally patients can subconsciously be focusing on secondary gain. For example, if the patient's primary motivation is to avoid work or the military, their avoidance behavior can also elicit sympathy from friends or family. That sympathy is actually secondary gain. The patient may not have intended or desired sympathy. His feigning illness or injury to avoid work could also result in sympathy from friends and family.

Noncompliance, on the other hand is much different. It can be defined as a failure to comply or a refusal to comply. An examination of hundreds of medical charts will reveal some form of noncompliance in a vast majority of cases. Patients frequently do not follow doctor's orders 100% of the time. Noncompliance is not malingering.

Compliance is the consistency and accuracy with which someone follows a regimen prescribed by a physician or other health care professional. Noncompliance is the deviation or violation of that prescribed regimen.

Malingering is primarily a legal term; however, *Tabor's Cyclopedic Medical Dictionary* (Venes and Taber, 2013) states, "One who pretends to be ill or to be suffering from a nonexistent disorder to arouse sympathy." This medical definition is similar to the legal context. Occasionally, defense attorneys will suggest malingering as an attack against the credibility of the person filing the complaint. The term malingering is rarely used in medical records; however, the term noncompliance is frequently found in medical records. It is important, therefore, to distinguish noncompliance from malingering.

First, malingering is almost always used in context of a lawsuit and it is almost always associated with secondary gain. The malingering party is attempting to obtain sympathy or compensation in some form from friends, family, employers, or parties to a lawsuit.

If malingering relates to *subjective* symptoms it can be difficult to prove absent sophisticated neurological, psychological, or psychiatric evaluations. If malingering relates to *objective* symptoms it can be demonstrated with diagnostic testing, such as X-rays, MRI, ultrasound; in addition to neurologic and psychiatric evaluation (see Chapter 3). This evaluation consists of a battery of tests administered by a professional designed to elicit multiple neurologic and psychiatric conditions including, but not limited to, malingering. Of course, the neuropsychological evaluation should never make a judgment of malingering in isolation. The neuropsychological evaluation in connection with other medical evaluations and the legal system may detect malingering (Gutiérrez and Ruben, 2012).

This raises questions about the appropriateness and ability of a physician to testify accurately on a person's suspected malingering. There are concerns that physicians and psychologists falsely attribute client behavior to malingering when this judgment is based on poor nonvalidated assessment tools and no consideration is given to the influence of culture or psychosocial factors.

Case in point is *State v. Cooey*, 46 Ohio St. 3d 20 (1989) and *State v. Harris*, 2013-Ohio-349. On September 26, 2010, Shane Gulleman was shot to death while attempting to buy drugs in Cincinnati, Ohio. He was found slumped in the driver's seat of his vehicle with eight gunshot wounds on his right side. His own gun—a realistic-looking pellet gun—and $210 in cash were also in the car. Although there were no witnesses to the shooting, two people saw Joseph Harris and another man running from the scene after the shots were fired. Ultimately, Harris was charged with Gulleman's murder.

Harris entered a plea of not guilty by reason of insanity and argued that he was not competent to stand trial. Under Ohio law, this authorized the court to order Harris to undergo competency and insanity examinations by a court-appointed psychologist. Based on the psychologist's report, the court concluded that Harris was competent to stand trial and the case proceeded to trial before a jury.

Before Harris submitted any evidence in his own defense, the psychologist testified that Harris "was malingering both cognitive and psychiatric difficulties" and "basically making up or exaggerating already existing symptoms to seem worse than they are" during the competence and insanity assessments. The prosecution also presented testimony from inmate informants who claimed that Harris admitted he was going to fake a mental illness.

In his defense, Harris testified that he did enter Gulleman's car to sell him drugs, but when he believed he saw Gulleman reaching for a gun, he shot Gulleman and fled the scene. He did not claim that he was legally insane at the time of the shooting.

The jury found Harris guilty and he was sentenced to life without the possibility of parole. Ohio's First District Court of Appeals concluded, however, that Harris' due process rights were violated when the trial court allowed the jury to consider the psychologist's testimony about malingering. In support of this conclusion, the Court of Appeals cited Ohio Revised Code 2945.37(J), which prevents statements made by the defendant during this type of court-ordered evaluation from being used "on the issue of guilt in any criminal action or proceeding." The Supreme Court of Ohio is considering the case at the time of this writing.

Harris' case raises legal questions about the fairness of allowing a psychologist to testify that a defendant malingered during a court-ordered evaluation. Although it is permissible to present such testimony to refute an insanity defense (*State v. Cooey*, 1989), here that defense was never offered. Thus, the Court of Appeals concluded that the psychologist's testimony necessarily related to Harris' knowledge of his guilt and his credibility, and therefore, it should not have been allowed (*State v. Harris*, 2013-Ohio-349). According to the prosecution, however, the purpose of the rule excluding these statements is to protect the rights of people who legitimately raise an insanity defense, not people who try to mislead authorities by malingering.

The case also raises questions about psychologists' ability to comment reliably on the truthfulness of a particular client. A number of well-documented problems—such as the shortcomings of certain assessment tools, cultural variables, the presence of pathology which influences responses and biases—can contribute to false attributions of malingering in forensic evaluations (Drob, Meehan, and Waxman, 2009). A finding of malingering is arguably based on judgments about motives, intentions, and the influence of context on behavior rather than the type of assessments that are more common in clinical practice.

Though the result may seem odd, the Ohio Supreme Court may conclude that the jury should not have heard evidence that Harris tried to mislead the psychologist who assessed his competence and sanity (Pearce, 2014).

15.1 PAIN

The symptom most often exaggerated, is pain. A slight discomfort in walking may become excruciating pain leading to inability to walk or to limping while walking. This may be either because the person involved simply wants attention and sympathy or because he seeks monetary gain.

Everyone appears to have been guilty at one time or another of sympathy-producing exaggeration of pain; but, few people have malingered in order to receive compensation. When an attorney speaks of malingering, therefore, he or she usually speaks of the latter type.

Medical experts can detect objective signs of pain. Typically, redness, swelling, bleeding, bruising is proof of pain. The absence of such signs, on the other hand, suggests that the pain is not genuine.

"Pain feigning" (Young, 2014) is giving a false appearance or impression, purporting that it is true. Pain feigning is symptom exaggeration or minimization, not the absence or presence of pain. Because of the subjectivity of the pain experience and its relationship to other facets of the pain experience (individual pain sensitivity, stress, anxiety, fear, etc.), the accuracy of malingering related to pain is questionable.

The assertion of malingering is typically raised by the defense. To prove malingering pointed questions must be asked to elicit evidence of malingering. The conscious malingerer must have acting talent. Not only must he or she know what symptoms to simulate, but he or she must also be able to display such symptoms. Simulation of back pain may often be detected by observing the patient's response to certain movements. For example, if a patient does not complain of pain upon being asked to lower his thigh against examiners' resistance this could be evidence of malingering with regard to back pain since such movement does require use of lumbar muscles. With focused and sophisticated medical testing malingering may be detected under certain circumstances, but this remains most challenging in relation to the experience of pain.

15.2 DIZZINESS

Dizziness or vertigo is a symptom commonly feigned by those who attempt to malinger. The tendency to "overact" is the first clue the examiner should note. Unless there is a tumor in the brain, the person who suffers from actual dizziness will seldom have great inability when he stands or walks. It is "some" proof of malingering if the patient, when made to stand with his feet close together and his eyes closed sways violently or falls. The possibility of "overacting" is what the examiner will look for to determine whether the patient actually suffers from dizziness or is malingering. Thus, the determination of malingering related to dizziness may be more evidence based.

15.3 COMPARATIVE ANALYSIS

Noncompliance is a straightforward, relatively easy thing to prove. Noncompliance is almost always documented. The patient could be noncompliant with diet or smoking. These issues are always charted or documented by a clinician. The patient typically admits to the noncompliance. If the noncompliance involves medication or the failure to take medication that fact can be determined by blood work or lab analysis. Noncompliance is a word more frequently used in a medical context rather than malingering. It is frequently used by physicians, nurses or health professionals to describe behavior of their patient. However, if that patient somehow becomes involved in litigation their deviation or failure to follow the prescribed regimen could be used against them in a legal context.

Nonadherence is a more modern term of art for noncompliance. It is said to be more politically correct. In and of itself, it does not nullify a claim. It sometimes can be explained, and even excused. The patient will be given an opportunity to explain the behavior.

There may be factors that are affecting the client's ability to be compliant. Contributing factors include poor health, illiteracy, memory deficits, functional deficits, financial concerns (saving money by taking less medication), or disorganization related to a complex medical regime that is too difficult to follow.

I have had cancer patients continue to smoke. It was their only pleasure left in life. I have had noncompliant clients prevail. When comparing the conduct of the parties, the negligence is frequently far more damaging than the noncompliant behavior.

Neurologists and psychiatrists frequently encounter the concept of secondary gain. It can be seen in cases of malingering. However, occasionally patients can subconsciously be focused on secondary gains. For example, if the patient's primary motivation is to avoid work or the military then their avoidance behavior can also elicit sympathy from friends/family. That sympathy is actually secondary gain. The patient may not have intended or desired sympathy. His feigning illness or injury to avoid work could also result in sympathy from friends/family. That is secondary gain.

Secondary gain rarely manifests itself in litigation issues. It may be present in the behavior of a patient; however, it might not ever result in evidence at trial.

Malingering is never a straightforward thing to prove. Malingering is always disputed by the person accused of being a malingerer. Not doing something that should be done because of malingering, if proven, will almost always defeat a claim. Because it is never easy to prove, it is rarely alleged, unless there is ample evidence. Simply to accuse a party of malingering without proof will not work and can have a direct backlash effect.

Evidence such as photos, video, or surveillance can be used to establish malingering. Social media can also be used to prove malingering. Facebook can be a claimant's worst enemy. Posting photos or videos on Facebook has been used in litigation. Photos on Facebook can destroy a claim. If a claimant is accused of malingering and evidence of malingering is proven the claim is easily defeated. No explanation or justification by the claimant will overcome evidence of malingering.

Each of these examples can be proven with different forms of evidence.

Examples:

- Sleeping on the job
- Not showing up for work
- Taking too long to perform a task
- Not exerting effort
- Feigning an illness/injury

Sleeping on the job can be proven with photographs or testimony. If proven by a photograph no excuse or explanation will suffice.

Not showing up for work when otherwise healthy can be proven, and if it is proven, no excuse will suffice. Going to a baseball game instead of work is an example of such behavior.

Taking too long to perform a task is classic malingering. Doing a 4-hour job in 8 hours, if proven, is unacceptable. However, an excuse or explanation will be forthcoming.

Not exerting effort is very subjective; however, it can be a form of malingering.

The most typical form of malingering is feigning an injury/illness. While this can be subjective, objective diagnostic testing can be used to prove the claimant is a malingerer.

15.4 SECONDARY GAIN

Feigning symptoms for secondary gain means playing the "sick role" usually for the purpose of filing a lawsuit for financial gain. Secondary gain is the conscious or unconscious desire to benefit from a lawsuit in some way, such as obtaining the attention of others, being able to avoid responsibility (i.e., working), or getting something for nothing in the form of financial gain.

Secondary gain is not always related to litigation. Subconsciously, a patient may play the "sick role" to get sympathy, support from family/friends, or just to skip work or school.

If the claimant is a malingerer, the fact that there is a component of secondary gain is not as important. Once the malingering is established secondary gain becomes irrelevant. However, for the purposes of this analysis it is important to know about the concept of secondary gain. Once I began my analysis of malingering, the concept of noncompliance and secondary gain seemed to flow naturally from one to the other.

15.5 CONCLUSION

Malingering is almost always a legal concept used by the defense to defeat a claim. The defense must come forward with affirmative evidence or conduct on the part of the claimant.

Noncompliance is a term which is used both in legal and medical contexts. It can frequently be raised by the defense. It does not always defeat a claim.

Secondary gain is a term rarely used in a legal or medical context. It frequently can exist in conjunction with malingering. It is rarely used to defeat or defend against a claim. However, its existence is real and cannot or should not be ignored to explain behavior.

REFERENCES

Drob, S.L., K.B. Meehan, and S.E. Waxman. Clinical and conceptual problems in the attribution of malingering in forensic evaluations. *Journal of the American Academy of Psychiatry and the Law* 37:1:98–106.

Gutiérrez, J.M., and R.C. Gur. 2012. Detection of malingering using forced-choice techniques. In *Detection of Malingering During Head Injury Litigation*, eds. C.R. Reynolds and A. MacNeil-Horton, Jr., 151–167. New York: Springer.

Pearce, M.W. 2014. Can evidence for court-ordered psychological exam be used at trial? *American Psychological Association* 45:9:24.

Venes, D., and C.W. Taber. 2013. *Taber's Cyclopedic Medical Dictionary*. Phildelphia: F.A. Davis.

Young, G. 2014. *Malingering, Feigning, and Response Bias in Psychiatric/Psychological Injury: Implications for Practice and Court*. Dordrecht: Springer.

16 Physician Response to Neurological Malingering

Kamran Hanif, MD and Alan R. Hirsch, MD

CONTENTS

"The pride of a doctor who has caught a malingerer is akin to that of a fisherman who has landed an enormous fish" (Asher, 1972). Physicians take extreme measures to avoid being fooled by patients, because they feel betrayed and angry when confronted with malingerers. They feel personally insulted—an affront to the idealized self as a competent and caring doctor who knows the difference between pathology and normality. To be fooled by the "layperson" is too much for the ego to bear. Too often, the doctor strikes back in anger at the potential malingerer. The physician validates their diagnostic abilities while obtaining a subtle, if vengeful, conclusion—branding the patient with the stigma of a diagnosis of malingering. The *Diagnostic and Statistical Manual of Mental Disorders* (DSM-V) defines malingering as "intentional production of false or grossly exaggerated physical or psychological problems. Motivation for malingering is usually external (e.g., avoiding military duty or work, obtaining financial compensation, evading criminal prosecution, or obtaining drugs)" (American Psychiatric Association, 2013).

Malingering can present in seemingly kaleidoscopic variations. A criminal may pretend to be ill to avoid standing for trial, or plead insanity in the act of the crime and malinger the corresponding symptoms in order to escape the death penalty. It can be seen in the military where soldiers malinger to avoid duty or during times of war. While malingering is most common among those trying to achieve financial gain is context-dependent. For instance, prisoners malinger to get drugs, a psychiatric hospital admission, to avoid jail, or due to homelessness.

Malingering can be found along with disorders such as conversion disorder, Munchausen syndrome, and various personality disorders (Gorman, 1982). When it comes to psychiatric disorders, these can be easily malingered—whether it's antisocial personality disorder, amnesia, depression, mental retardation, posttraumatic stress disorder, or schizophrenia. Spotting a patient malingering is not an easy task. An in-depth examination of a patient's current and past history is required before any diagnosis can be made.

Once the diagnosis of malingering is established there often is the initial urge to dismiss the malingerer from one's care. However, when it comes to removal or firing a malingerer from a physician's practice, it is never an easy step to take and it should be the last option. The physician tries to maintain good communication and carefully evaluates the physician–patient relationship. The physician even considers having the patient transferred to another doctor before firing the patient. It is generally a good idea for a physician to notify the patient ahead of time about the difficulties they're facing in their relationship try to understand how the patient feels and figure out a way to resolve the situation without severing the relationship. This could prevent the patient from misbehaving in the future and will allow the doctor to keep a good reputation in the community. A patient who gets fired is usually either someone who is hard to deal with due to their personality, a malingerer, or otherwise abusive. The removal of a patient is usually the last option a doctor has because it goes against what a physician went into medicine to do—help patients. Thus, firing a patient is a narcissistic insult to the physician and also produces a real risk of retribution from an unhappy patient who can negatively impact the physician in a plethora of ways ranging from internet grades to complaints to regulatory commissions. A patient who shows signs of aggression or goes as far as threatening the physician may fall in this list.

Studies show that patient removal is a rare event and around 40% of general practices fire one patient in a period of six months (Macleod and Hopton, 1998). The group of patients in which there is a higher frequency of removal are usually young adults who come from a lower socioeconomic status and have poor health. There are myriads of ways patients can cause unhappiness in their physician–patient relationships. Patients make a doctor unhappy by misbehaving and being abusive, threatening, or violent. This includes verbal abuse and unreasonable requests. Misbehavior, which puts the physician under stress or makes him or her feel threatened, doesn't allow for the best possible care to be provided (Macleod and Hopton, 1998). Patient firing can be avoided if there is good communication between the office staff and the patient and the staff makes the patients' needs a priority.

There are several categories of patients which may get a cold shoulder or even be refused care by the physician. These include "the self-abusers" (Mizrahi, 1986): individuals with diseases that are self-induced from the abuse of alcohol, cigarettes, drug usage, overeating, and anorexia nervosa. In regards to these diseases, most physicians hold the same moral beliefs as society—patients are responsible for their own disease. In the second category are "system abusers" (Mizrahi, 1986): these are the malingering, manipulators, psychosomatic complainers, and demanders. The third category includes "house/staff abusers" (Mizrahi, 1986): these are difficult, demanding, suspicious, disrespectful, hostile, or ungrateful.

"Bosses dismiss employees. Spouses divorce each other. Patients leave their doctors. But can doctors ever fire their patients?" (Friedman, 2005). There has been a point in time in almost every physician's life where their waters of cool, calm, and collectedness have been tested by a patient. The American Psychiatric Association does not have any guidelines for firing a patient, but the American Medical Association advises doctors to continue providing medical care according to ethical guidelines until the patient is transferred to another physician's care. At the same time, if a patient demands a treatment which is against the physician's "personal, religious, or moral beliefs" (Friedman, 2005) or "scientifically invalid," such requests can be denied.

If a patient is noncompliant with his medications it does not warrant that he be fired. Dr. Richard C. Hughes has similar views. "Patients often didn't do what I told them, but I never thought it made much sense to refer them to a colleague, because they would probably do the same thing with a different doctor" (quoted in Friedman, 2005). He believed that the fact that he knew them would make it easier for him to try something else which may help.

Certain patients show lack of patience and become anxious and irritable when they are sick. They end up transferring those emotions of anger onto their doctors, but physicians universally reflect long and hard before embarking on the steps of firing a patient. Dr. Robert Michels, from Weill Medical College of Cornell University, says that, "Any physician who is thinking of firing a patient should first speak to a colleague" (Friedman, 2005). He believes that, "This is an enormous decision and, while it might even be right at times, the physician is probably having a countertransference reaction to his patient and should really understand that before taking action" (Friedman, 2005).

"Much of what we do and how we do it is influenced by emotions and the conditions that generate them" (Lazarus, 1991). In this world of increased violence it is pertinent to understand the origin of anger and how to regulate it so that it does not accumulate and produce pathological effects. When it comes to anger, "the crucial factor is the individual—both in terms of his own inner needs and his reaction to his environment" (Madow, 1972a).

Anger can be subdivided into three categories. The first category being "modified expression of anger" (Madow, 1972b), the second being "indirect expression of anger" (Madow, 1972c), and the third is referred to as "variation of depression" (Madow, 1972d).

Individuals in the first category directly express their feelings such as "I am annoyed" (Madow, 1972b), or "I am irritated" (Madow, 1972b), or you may even hear someone say "You make me laugh" (Madow, 1972b) but they are angry. A person may say "I was annoyed by my wife but not angry" (Madow, 1972b). In reality, he is angry at his wife but must deny it. As Shakespeare observed, "The lady doth protest too much, methinks" (Shakespeare and Bevington, 1994a), and this denial is revealing his feelings. An individual may tell you that they are not feeling a certain way, but they are. These expressions are used as a way to hold back or discard anger.

Those who fall in the second category of anger put on a greater false front and this leads to anger being masked by the speaker and listener. When a child brings home a report card from school with all D's, the mother buries her anger and believes she's being more understanding by saying "I'm not angry. I'm just disappointed in you" (Madow, 1972c). The mother may have feelings of guilt first, and then unrecognized anger because she's not getting any relief. When individuals who use "indirect expressions of anger" (Madow, 1972c) is asked about his or her feelings of anger he or she will deny it and this self-denial can cause pathological symptoms.

The third category of individuals are distant from anger and have "variations of depression" (Madow, 1972d) which are harder to be observed. They often use remarks like "feeling blue" (Madow, 1972d) or "down in the dumps" (Madow, 1972d). An individual may claim that he or she is not angry but his or her feelings of anger are being transferred into depression. As these feelings of depression become severe, he or she can develop feelings of hopelessness and the individual may feel life is not worth living. This person may start using phrases like, "I feel like killing myself" (Madow, 1972d), or "I wish I were dead" (Madow, 1972d). These patients instead, need to see if there is something they are angry about.

There is no quick fix to the problem of anger, but there are four steps which can be followed to manage it better. The first step starts with "recognizing that you're angry" (Madow, 1972e). Apparent anger is much less hurtful than the anger which is unknown. "It is essential that we uncover the feelings first" (Madow, 1972e). The second step is the most challenging, which is to "recognize the source of the anger" (Madow, 1972f). Then, to be able to manage anger, one must identify the origin of the anger. The third step is to "understand why you are angry" (Madow, 1972g) and the most significant thing to ask here is if the anger is realistic or not. If you get angry at someone's careless driving you may say, "How can he or she do that?" (Madow, 1972h), which is realistic. On the other hand, if you say, "How can he or she do that to me?" (Madow, 1972h) this would be unrealistic. Anger due to unrealistic reasons like "hidden feelings, wishes, or expectations" (Madow, 1972h) is harder to manage. The fourth step is to "deal with the anger realistically," which is the least challenging. Once you know that you are angry, where the origin is from and that it is valid then you can start to manage it realistically. "If someone pushes ahead of you in line it is reasonable to ask him or her to go back to the end of the line, it is not realistic to just swallow the anger" (Madow, 1972h).

Physicians are intrinsically trusting people and would rather have the patient undergo all sorts of extreme testing to make sure of the diagnosis of malingering rather than falsely accusing him or her. A neuroimaging study to detect malingering found that subjects who were the pretending memory impairment had a broader activation of the medial and superior frontal gyrus compared to those who were not. This study suggests that a detection of malingering can be made by a much broader activation of the prefrontal cortex (Kosheleva, Spadoni, Strigo, Buchsbaum, and Simmons, 2016).

There are patients who lie to doctors for personal gain and are referred to as "crocks" (Stimson, 1976) by Kansas medical students. They do not present with any symptoms of disease and hence, medical students avoid seeing them as they cannot learn much from these patients. They would rather see a patient who presents with pathological symptoms of a disease which would allow them to learn something new and expand their clinical knowledge. Medical students "rate patients in order of preference from the actually ill, chronically ill, the emotionally ill, down to the crocks" (Stimson, 1976).

Lies are ubiquitous. Everyone lies and we see lies everywhere from private to public areas. "Lord, Lord, how this world is given to lying" (Shakespeare and Bevington, 1994b). There aren't many people who can claim that they have never lied or have never been lied to by another. Mark Twain had a similar view—"None of us could live with a habitual truth teller, but, thank goodness, none of us has to." A lie is defined as intended deception which is told in the form of a statement that is untruthful or a statement which is false to deceive people.

One would be surprised at the discovery of how much lying takes place around us. Just looking at the government and the problems of the United States, which aspires to be a nation where truth and justice prevail, gives an indication of lies' ubiquitous nature. Instead, the nature of lying has infiltrated to the apex of government—witness Bill Clinton's sex scandal or Richard Nixon's Oval Office Watergate, which led to his resignation from the presidency. The fact that people lie is not what we should be concerned about, but rather, why they lie, how much, why we believe them, and why some lies are harmless and others harmful. We also need to explore what role lying plays in a variety of domains from politics, the media, advertising, courts, warfare, bureaucracies, business world, and digital communication.

Lies are seen everywhere in the political arena as they are tolerable and commonly expected. Politicians who spend their lives in this profession become extremely skilled at it and are always considered suspect by the public. This is highlighted by a Russian joke: Q. How can you tell when a politician is lying? A. When he moves his lips.

Lies manufactured by the media or "fake news" are not far behind. During the opening ceremony of the Beijing summer Olympics in 2008, one billion people tuned in to watch and were deceived by a girl lip synching a Chinese patriotic ballad. She was lip synching to a recorded voice of another girl who was not allowed to perform due to her imperfect teeth. People in the United States and China were not happy and were outraged with this act of deception. "The people were so emotionally involved. If you asked them what's the most moving episode, I think the majority would tell you that moment, with the little girl in red clothes. The Chinese people felt they were fooled. The psychological hurt was enormous" (Collins, 2008). This was extremely embarrassing for the population in China as they expressed anger. Significantly, a high rate of lies is also present in the advertising industry as the consumer has virtually no way of verifying fraudulent claims put forth.

The idea of telling "the truth, the whole truth, and nothing but the truth" is a fictional practice in the courtroom. Witnesses and adversaries will go to different lengths to make false claims for maximizing gains. The accused have strong inclinations to lie to for their cause, and the lawyers are experts in the art of lying for strategic reasons.

Dr. House, an antisocial physician, does whatever it takes to diagnose and solve unique cases he encounters on the TV series *House, MD*. There are good and bad days in his life. On a good day you can see him sing and on a bad day you see the countertransference of his rude behavior in the form of anger and insults towards patients and onto his team of doctors. He comes across showing a lack of empathy; "It's a good thing that you failed to become a mother, because you suck at it," he said in the episode "Finding Judas."

When physicians see patients malingering, they become angry and intentionally or inadvertently sabotage the relationship because they feel deceived. The doctor feels betrayed and angry at the patient who is trying to fool and manipulate them. Thus, a physician may choose different paths in dealing with these sorts of situations. One can directly confront the situation, lose one's temper and rudely dismiss the patient, in which case they won't return. Alternatively, a physician's approach may be subtler. Physicians may consciously or unconsciously choose to take any of the following actions: schedule their appointments on a day that's inconvenient for the patient, be late for their appointments, express anger by not greeting them, or conveniently choose not to give them the correct number of medications. One could express anger by passively being late for appointments, not smiling when greeting them, and subtly discourage them from coming to see you by making appointments further and further apart. On the other hand, one could empathically try to understand the underlying motivation for malingering. Are they malingering in order to get money due to homelessness or to send money to a starving relative in a third world country, or for some other altruistic reason? How a physician handles a malingering patient can directly affect the lives of both the physician and the patient. There is no right way. But trying to understand the motivations may give the treating physician insight into the patients' reasons and how to best manage their complaints.

REFERENCES

American Psychiatric Association. 2013. *Diagnostic and Statistical Manual of Mental Disorders, Fifth Edition, DSM-5*, 726. Washington. DC: American Psychiatric Press Inc.

Asher, R. 1972. *Richard Asher talking sense*, 145. London: University Park Press.

Collins, G. 2008. I'm Singin' in Beijing. *The New York Times*, http://www.nytimes.com/2008/08/14/opinion/14collins.html (accessed December 19, 2016).

Friedman, R.A. 2005. Should a doctor fire a patient? Sometimes it is good medicine. *New York Times*. http://www.nytimes.com/2005/09/27/health/should-a-doctor-fire-a-patient-sometimes-it-is-good-medicine.html (accessed December 19, 2016).

Gorman, W.F. 1982. Defining malingering. *Journal of Forensic Science* 27:2:401–407.

Jones, F.A. 1972. *Richard Asher talking sense*. London: Pitman Medical.

Kosheleva, E., A.D. Spadoni, I.A. Strigo, M.S. Buchsbaum, and A.N. Simmons. 2016. Faking bad: The neural correlates of feigning memory impairment. *Neuropsychology* 30:3:377.

Lazarus, R.S. 1991. *Emotions and adaptation*. New York: Oxford University Press.

Macleod, L., and J. Hopton. 1998. *A study of the process of removing patients from general practitioners lists*. [Report] Edinburgh: Department of General Practice, University of Edinburgh.

Madow, L. 1972a. *Anger. How to Recognize and Cope with It*, ix. New York: Charles Scribner's Sons.

Madow, L. 1972b. *Anger. How to Recognize and Cope with It*, 5. New York: Charles Scribner's Sons.

Madow, L. 1972c. *Anger. How to Recognize and Cope with It*, 6. New York: Charles Scribner's Sons.

Madow, L. 1972d. *Anger. How to Recognize and Cope with It*, 8. New York: Charles Scribner's Sons.

Madow, L. 1972e. *Anger. How to Recognize and Cope with It*, 107. New York: Charles Scribner's Sons.

Madow, L. 1972f. *Anger. How to Recognize and Cope with It*, 111. New York: Charles Scribner's Sons.

Madow, L. 1972g. *Anger. How to Recognize and Cope with It*, 112. New York: Charles Scribner's Sons.

Madow, L. 1972h. *Anger. How to Recognize and Cope with It*, 115. New York: Charles Scribner's Sons.

Mizrahi, T. 1986. *Getting Rid of Patients: Contradictions in the Socialization of Physicians*, p. 77. New Brunswick: Rutgers University Press.

Shakespeare, W., and Bevington, D.M. 1994a. *Henry IV, Part 1*, 3.2.10. Oxford: Oxford University Press.

Shakespeare, W., and Bevington, D.M. 1994b. *Henry IV, Part 1*, 5.4.7. Oxford: Oxford University Press.

Stimson, G.V. 1976. General practitioners, 'trouble' and types of patients. *Sociological Review Monograph* 22:1:43–60.

Index

Page numbers followed by f, t, and n denotes figures, tables, and notes, respectively.

N

O

T

U

V

W

X

Z

Made in the USA
Las Vegas, NV
19 September 2026

0f108341-df65-4c57-b1d2-fb4c414613b9R01